BEGINNING STRUCTURED COBOL

Other titles in the Boyd & Fraser Computer Science Series

STANDARD BASIC PROGRAMMING: For Business and Management Applications
PASCAL PROGRAMMING: A Spiral Approach
STRUCTURED FORTRAN 77 PROGRAMMING
STRUCTURED FORTRAN 77 PROGRAMMING for Hewlett-Packard Computers
A STRUCTURED APPROACH TO GENERAL BASIC
A STRUCTURED APPROACH TO ESSENTIAL BASIC
INTRODUCTION TO COMPUTERS AND COMPUTER SCIENCE, Third Edition
AN INTRODUCTION TO ARTIFICIAL INTELLIGENCE: Can Computers Think?

Cover photo: A silicon wafer is oxide coated in a defusion furnace at The Foxboro Company/ ITC Facility in San Jose, California. Courtesy The Foxboro Company and Larry Long, Weymouth Design.

BEGINNING STRUCTURED COBOL

L. WAYNE HORN
GARY M. GLEASON

Pensacola Junior College

BOYD & FRASER PUBLISHING COMPANY

San Francisco

Credits:

Editor: Tom Walker
Production supervision: Dixie Clark
Copy editor: Lydia Walshin
Design/cover: Dixie Clark
Artwork: Marilyn Entwistle/Michelle Snyder
Typesetting: Information Sciences Corporation/Neil W. Kelley Graphic Services

Boyd & Fraser Publishing Company and the authors express their appreciation to The Foxboro Company and Larry Long, Weymouth Design for providing the cover photograph.

Material in the Appendix reprinted from *American National Standard Programming Language COBOL* ANSI X3, 23-1974.

COBOL is an industry language and is not the property of any company or group of companies, or of any organization or group of organizations.

No warranty, expressed or implied, is made by any contributor or by the CODASYL Programming Language Committee as to the accuracy and functioning of the programming system and language. Moreover, no responsibility is assumed by any contributor, or by the committee, in connection therewith.

The authors and copyright holders of the copyrighted material used herein

FLOW-MATIC (trademark of Sperry Rand Corporation), Programming for the UNIVAC® I and II, Data Automation Systems copyrighted 1958, 1959, by Sperry Rand Corporation; IBM Commercial Translator Form No. F 28-8013, copyrighted 1959 by IBM; FACT, DSI 27A5260-2760, copyrighted 1960 by Minneapolis-Honeywell

have specifically authorized the use of this material in whole or in part, in the COBOL specifications. Such authorization extends to the reproduction and use of COBOL specifications in programming manuals or similar publications.

Library of Congress Cataloging in Publication Data

Horn, Lister Wayne.
    Beginning structured COBOL.

    Includes index.
    1. COBOL (Computer program language)
2. Structured programming.   I. Gleason, Gary M.
II. Title.
QA76.73.C25H67 1983   001.64'24   82–74437
ISBN 0–87835–133–7

1234/6543

CONTENTS

PREFACE

This text is based on *Structured COBOL* by the same authors and on the combined experience of the authors and numerous consultants in the practical problems of teaching structured programming and COBOL. The primary emphasis in the book is on writing logically correct, well structured programs. The reading and conceptual levels are closely matched with the abilities of average college students. There are numerous programming examples and exercises based on realistic business applications. The text and teacher's manual have been carefully designed and include many pedagogical features to facilitate the teaching/learning task.

To a large extent beginning programmers learn by imitation. Each chapter (except Chapters 1 and 11) contains one or more completely coded COBOL programs and numerous coding segments which students can use as models for their own programs.

Students learn more and are more highly motivated if they begin programming early with realistic problems. Suitable programming exercises are included beginning in Chapter 2. In each chapter there are wide variety of exercises at several levels of difficulty to enable the instructor to choose appropriate assignments to meet the needs of individuals or groups with different ability levels and/or interests. Many programming assignments include sample data to ease the instructor's task of checking student programs.

Immediate feedback enhances learning. Each chapter contains extensive "Self Test Exercises" (short answer questions emphasizing vocabulary and programming techniques) with answers.

Debugging is a difficult problem for many beginning programmers. Each chapter (except Chapters 1 and 11) contain a section called "Debug Clinic" which covers debugging techniques and/or alerts students to potential problems and suggests solutions.

Vocabulary development is often a problem for students with no previous computer related background. A very complete glossary is contained in an appendix to aid the reader's comprehension of technical terms.

Students often have trouble remembering exact COBOL syntax and hence make unnecessary coding errors. Appendices with complete ANSI-74

COBOL language formats and COBOL reserved words are included. These appendices are invaluable aids for students as they code COBOL programs.

Programming logic is a problem for many beginning students. The text stresses the logic of structured programs at both the program and paragraph levels. At the program level there is early and continuing emphasis on top down program design, structure diagrams, and recognition of "good" program structure. At the paragraph level there is extensive use of program flowcharts to help the reader visualize flow of control. The text includes a flowchart template to further encourage the student to use flowcharts as a design tool.

Poor design of printed reports often causes students unnecessary hours of programming/debugging effort. The text includes professionally sized printer spacing charts for student use. These charts encourage students to design reports correctly from the start and will help ease the tedious job of ensuring that columns are aligned and headings are centered.

Students often have poor handwriting and/or poor habits in preparing written work. The text includes a set of professionally sized COBOL coding forms to encourage neatness and completeness in the preparation of COBOL code.

A major problem with many texts is their orientation to a specific computing system or mode of program preparation/data entry. This text describes ANSI-74 COBOL with any system specific features clearly noted. It is equally suited for traditional batch oriented systems or interactive/conversational systems such as those found on some time sharing and most microcomputing systems. An extensive appendix covers ACCEPT and DISPLAY verbs and techniques for interactive COBOL.

This text is equally suitable for a one or two semester COBOL course and most topics required in a second course (including sequential and indexed file processing, SORT, INSPECT, STRING, and UNSTRING, Report Writer, one, two and three dimensional tables, USAGE, and SEARCH).

The teaching process will be greatly facilitated by the available teacher's manual which contains a wealth of teaching suggestions, a test bank and numerous transparency masters.

BEGINNING STRUCTURED COBOL has been designed as a complete teaching/learning system. The system has been classroom tested with great success by the authors; we trust that others will be equally successful in using these materials. We would appreciate hearing from any user who has comments or suggestions.

L.W.H.
G.M.G.

ACKNOWLEDGMENTS

Upon completion of a major work of this kind, we find ourselves indebted to a number of individuals whose comments and suggestions were invaluable. Among them are: Dr. George C. Fowler, Business Analysis and Research Department, Texas A & M University; Dr. James C. Hershauer, Quantitative Systems Department, Arizona State University; Professor Marjorie Leeson, Data Processing, Delta College; Professor Kenneth W. Veatch, Data Processing Department, San Antonio College; Gary L. Cutler, Computer Science Department, SUNY at Albany; Helene P. Kearns, McDonnell-Douglas Corporation, and Robert R. Schadt, Burroughs Corporation.

In addition, we would like to thank Tom Walker, our editor at Boyd & Fraser, for his creative suggestions with regard to this book's organization, content, and design.

Finally, we express our appreciation to Dixie Clark for diligently guiding this book through production.

NOTES

The following conventions are used to describe the general form of COBOL elements.

1. All capitalized words are COBOL reserved words.

2. All underlined capitalized words are required. Capitalized words which are not underlined may be included at the discretion of the programmer. They generally have the purpose of improving readability.

3. Words written in small letters indicate elements that are to be supplied by the programmer.

4. Ellipses (. . .) are used when more than one element of the preceding type may be included.

5. Brackets ([ ]) indicate elements which are optional.

6. Braces ({ }) indicate that one of the enclosed elements, which are placed on separate lines, must be chosen.

COMPUTERS AND PROGRAMMING

1

1.1 WHAT IS A COMPUTER?

From astronomy to zoology, from business to medicine, from art to engineering, computers have become very important tools in almost all areas of human endeavor. Since the first primitive automatic computing machines were devised in the 1940s, computers have undergone steady improvement. Each substantial improvement yielded more computing power and greater reliability available at less cost, resulting in a greater number of applications for which the computer could be cost effective. Presently, computers are available in sizes ranging from the microcomputer, contained in an electronic chip smaller than a fingernail, to super computers which fill a large room. Computer prices range from one hundred dollars for a microcomputer, to several million dollars for a super computer, and in between, computers in a wide range of sizes, shapes, and prices (with an equally wide variety of capabilities) are available. Today it is possible to choose a computer for most any application at a reasonable cost.

What do such diverse devices have in common to enable us to classify them all as computer? All computers execute sequences of instructions called *programs*. Programs are written to solve specific problems; they are placed in the computer memory, which recalls the programs when they are needed. Thus, the same computer can solve different problems simply by changing the program it executes.

All computers share a basic logical organization composed of five logical components or units (Fig. 1.1):

1) Input Unit
2) Output Unit
3) Memory Unit
4) Control Unit
5) Arithmetic/logical Unit

The *input* unit transfers data from some external medium, such as a keyboard or magnetic tape, into the computing system. The *output* unit transfers

1

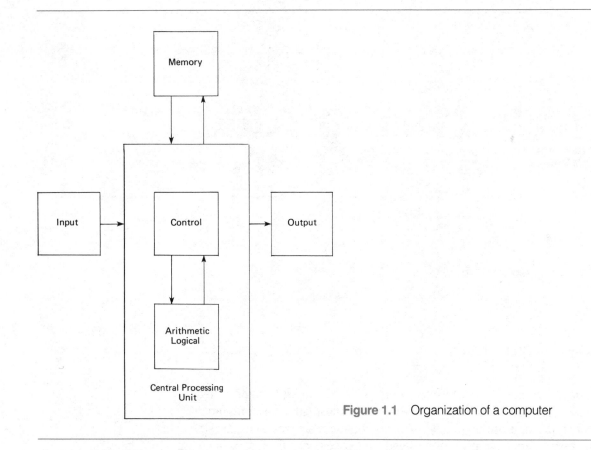

Figure 1.1 Organization of a computer

data from the system onto some external medium, such as paper or magnetic tape. Data is stored in the *memory* unit. The memory unit also stores the sequence of instructions (the program) required to manipulate the data to produce the desired results.

Memory is composed of storage locations, each of which has an *address*. The content of any location is made available to other units of the computing system by specifying to the memory unit the address of the desired data. Data is stored in a location by specifying to the memory unit the content and the address of the location into which the data is to be placed. The commands which order data to be placed, moved or used in various ways are given to the computer in *programs*, discussed at length in later chapters.

The *control* unit executes each program one instruction at a time. When the program requires data, the control unit activates the input unit. When a program instruction requires that data be written out, the control unit activates the output unit. When a program instruction requires that computations be performed, the control unit activates the *arithmetic/logical* unit, which performs all the arithmetic and logical operations. The control and arithmetic/logical units are often referred to collectively as the *central processing unit*, or *CPU*.

The hardware for these components varies greatly among computing systems; the central processing unit ranges from an electronic chip in a microprocessor (Fig. 1.2), to a small box in a microcomputer system (Fig. 1.3), to a larger unit in other computers (Fig. 1.4).

Input and output devices are available for a great variety of input and output mediums. A commonly used input/output device is the computer terminal,

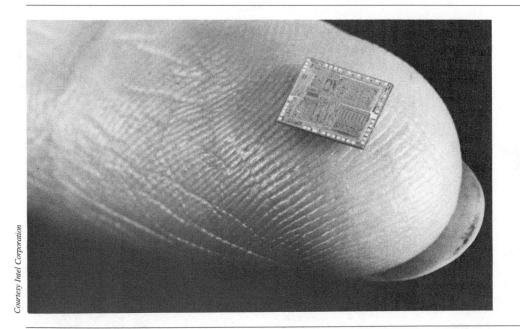

Courtesy Intel Corporation

Figure 1.2 CPU for a microcomputer

Courtesy Radio Shack, A Division of TANDY Corp.

Figure 1.3 The TRS-80™ Model II microcomputer system

Courtesy IBM

Figure 1.4   A medium-scale computing system

Courtesy IBM

Figure 1.5   A CRT terminal

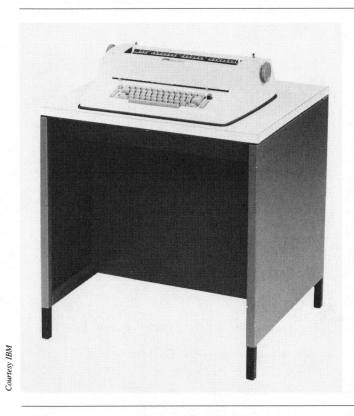

Courtesy IBM

Figure 1.6 A printing terminal

which contains a typewriter-like keyboard by which data is entered into the computing system. Some terminals have a video screen (also called a *cathode ray tube* or CRT) on which information is displayed to the operator (Fig. 1.5). Other terminals have the capability of printing data on paper in much the same fashion as a typewriter (Fig. 1.6). Since terminals allow the user to enter data and receive information, they serve as both input and output devices.

Courtesy IBM

Figure 1.7 A diskette

Courtesy IBM

Figure 1.8 A high-speed printer

Courtesy IBM

Figure 1.9 Magnetic tape drives

Courtesy IBM

Figure 1.10   Magnetic disk drives

Another common input device is the diskette data station. Data is recorded on a *diskette* (also called a *floppy disk*) as shown in Figure 1.7. A diskette data station similar to a terminal is used for this purpose. When the user has completed recording data on the diskette, the data station is used to transmit the data to the computer for processing. Since diskettes are inexpensive, easily portable and highly reliable, they often are used in academic computing systems.

Most computer systems have one or more high speed line printers used for applications which require a high volume of output. Printers such as the one shown in Figure 1.8 can produce printed output at rates varying from 300 to 1600 lines per minute.

Most computing systems have mass storage devices capable of storing many millions of characters in a form which can be readily accessed by the CPU. The two most common types of mass storage devices are magnetic tape drives (Fig. 1.9) and magnetic disk drives (Fig. 1.10). Both devices have the capability of writing data onto a magnetic medium (tape or disk) and reading data from the medium at a later time; hence, they function as both output and input units. Magnetic tapes most often are used for long term storage of large volumes of data. Magnetic disks usually are used for program libraries and short term low volume data storage. At one time the punched card was used for communicating with computing systems, and it still may be found in some installations.

1.2   COMPUTER PROGRAMMING LANGUAGES

The term *hardware* refers to the physical devices which make up a computing system. The devices pictured in Figures 1.9 and 1.10 are examples of computer hardware. The programs and their supporting documents required to make the hardware function are referred to as *software*. Computer hardware is completely useless without software.

Computer programs must be expressed in a *language* the computer hardware can read and use. Each central processing unit "understands" programs in machine language. Machine language is numerical (binary); the operation to be performed and the data to be operated on are expressed numerically. Machine languages tend to be very different from one computer to another, depending on the design of the CPU, and programs written in machine language for one particular computer usually cannot be executed by a computer built by a different manufacturer. It is very hard to write programs in machine language because every detail—every mark and letter of every message—must be turned into a coded expression built out of numbers.

Since there are a great many disadvantages to machine language, other languages (generally called *high level languages*) have been devised for constructing programs. Programs written in high level languages use words and other symbols to represent both the operations to be performed and the addresses of data items to be operated on. COBOL, an acronym for

*CO*mmon
*B*usiness
*O*riented
*L*anguage

is one example of a high level language. Other commonly available programming languages include:

BASIC (*B*eginners' *A*ll-purpose *S*ymbolic *I*nstruction *C*ode)
FORTRAN (*FOR*mula *TRAN*slation)
PL/I (*P*rogramming *L*anguage *I*)
ALGOL (*ALGO*rithmic *L*anguage)
RPG (*R*eport *P*rogram *G*enerator)
PASCAL (named for French mathematician Blaise Pascal)
WATBOL (*WAT*erloo *CO*BOL)

A program written in a high level language must be translated into machine language before it can be executed. Programs called *compilers* perform this task. A COBOL program, called a *source program*, is submitted to the COBOL compiler, which automatically translates the program into an equivalent machine language program, called the *object program*. The object program then can be executed by the computing system. In addition to translating the program into machine language, the compiler also produces a listing of the source program and checks its content for correctness.

There are many advantages to writing programs in high level languages. The languages are symbolic rather than numeric in nature, thereby enabling the programmer to formulate a problem solution in somewhat familiar terms. The more a language resembles ordinary speech, the faster the programmer can work. The details of the exact form of machine language are handled by the compiler; the programmer can be concerned only with the logic of his program. Furthermore, programs written in a high level language tend to be transportable (i.e., they can be used on machines of many different designs and manufacturers), whereas machine language programs are specific to individual types of machines.

1.3   COMMUNICATING WITH THE COMPUTER

The computer user must communicate his program and data to be processed to the computing system. As noted earlier, no two computing installations are completely the same in all particulars, so it is impossible to provide the reader with complete details of all that he or she will need to know in order to enter a program and data for processing at his or her installation. All installations have manuals or handouts which explain procedures to be followed at that installation; the reader must secure these instructions before attempting his or her first program. In the following paragraphs we offer a brief survey of common types of systems encountered in academic computing centers.

On Line/Off Line

The term *on line* means that a device is in direct communication with a computing system; *off line* means that a device is acting on its own without direct communication with a computing system. Most computer terminals are on line; all data and instructions entered by the user are communicated directly to the system. Diskette data stations may be on line or off line. In most installations utilizing these devices, the station is off line during the time that the user is recording programs and data on the diskette. The station is then turned on line (or the user takes his or her diskette to a station which is on line) to transmit the program and data to the computer. A key punch is another example of an off line device; a program prepared in punched card form must be read by an on line punched card reader to be processed by the computer system.

Batch/Interactive Computing

The term *batch computing* implies that data is collected for some period of time before being submitted for processing; *interactive computing* implies that the computer and user engage in a dialogue in which the user enters commands and/or data for immediate processing by the system. Punched card and diskette systems are batch systems. The user must completely prepare the program and data files to be processed utilizing off line devices. (A *file* is a collection of records. Each record contains a collection of data items pertaining to one entity, e.g., person, inventory item, bank transaction, or program statement.) Only when the program and data are completed can the system accept the program for compilation and execution.

Systems utilizing terminals usually offer interactive computing. A program called an *editor* enables the user to build a file containing the program to be executed. Once the user is satisfied with the program, he or she can give commands to execute the compiler and, if there are no errors, execute the program itself. The program can process data from a data file (which has been created utilizing the editor) or from the user who enters data at the terminal in response to messages from the program. If errors are encountered by the compiler or during execution, the user can use the editor to modify the program file and/or data file and repeat the compilation-execution process.

In an interactive computing system the entire program development process typically is carried out by the computer and user while the user is sitting at a terminal. In a batch system the user typically prepares his program and data at one station, submits the task to the computer at a second, and then waits for the output to be produced at a third. Some systems combine interactive and batch processing. Such systems generally use an interactive terminal for the user to enter a program and data; however, once program and data are entered, the tasks of compiling and executing the program are treated as in batch computing (i.e., the user must wait until the system can perform the tasks and produce the desired output).

Single User/Multiuser Systems

Some computing systems, particularly smaller systems, are single user systems because they can communicate with only one user at a time. Other systems are classified as multiuser systems because they can engage in simultaneous communications with several users. Multiuser systems behave as though each person is the sole user of the system; however, in most systems the computer is actually engaged in *timesharing* (i.e., allocating a small slice of time to each of many users, usually on a rotating basis).

Most multiuser systems require that any user be assigned an account number and a password before the user can utilize the system. The purpose of the account number is to enable the computing system to keep track of who uses what resources and in what quantity; the password protects one user's files from others, so it must be kept secret. Both the account number and the password must be entered using a *sign on* (or *log on*) procedure, when a user initiates communication with the computer. There are also *sign off* (or *log off*) procedures required when the user terminates communication. Details of these procedures are quite specific to individual computing systems.

1.4   PROGRAM FLOWCHARTS[1]

A program is a sequence of instructions describing actions to be taken by the computer. A *program flowchart* is a visual representation of these steps. Each type of instruction is represented in a flowchart by a different type of symbol, called a *block*. Inside each block, the programmer writes a description of the instruction to be executed. Figure 1.11 illustrates types of instructions and the corresponding blocks,

An oval-shaped symbol is used to describe the beginning and ending points in a flowchart. The instruction START typically denotes the beginning, while the instruction STOP or END denotes the ending point.

Flowlines such as → describe the direction of flow, that is, which instruction is to be executed next. All blocks in a flowchart are connected to others by flowlines.

A parallelogram-shaped symbol is used to describe input and output operations. The instruction READ is used to denote an input operation; the instruction WRITE is used for output. The name of the file may also be used in the block to define the file to which the instruction pertains. For example, a complete

---

[1]Using the flowchart template included with this text will enable the reader to draw neat and easy-to-read program flowcharts.

flowchart for a program to read a record from the file IN-FIL would be:

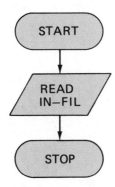

The rectangle is used to describe processing such as movement of an input record, as in the flowchart which follows:

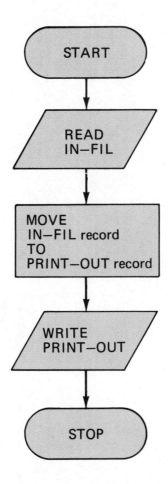

Block   Purpose

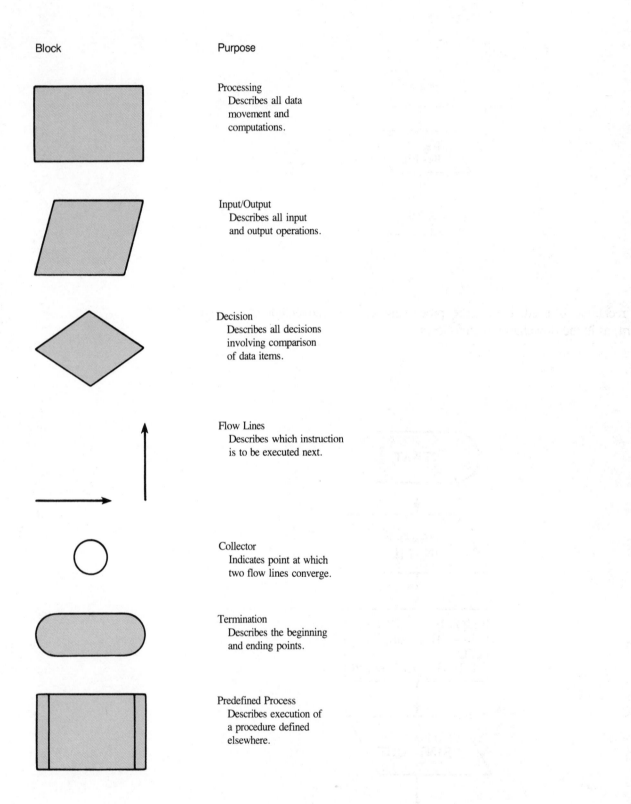

Processing
  Describes all data
  movement and
  computations.

Input/Output
  Describes all input
  and output operations.

Decision
  Describes all decisions
  involving comparison
  of data items.

Flow Lines
  Describes which instruction
  is to be executed next.

Collector
  Indicates point at which
  two flow lines converge.

Termination
  Describes the beginning
  and ending points.

Predefined Process
  Describes execution of
  a procedure defined
  elsewhere.

Figure 1.11   A summary of program flowchart symbols

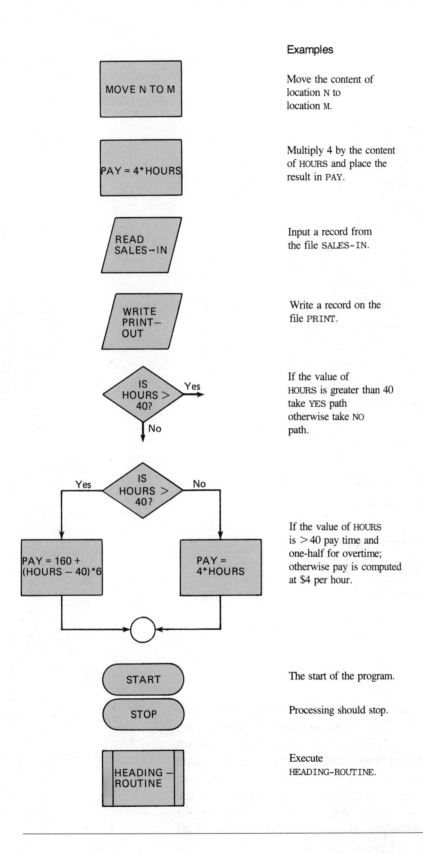

Examples

Move the content of
location N to
location M.

Multiply 4 by the content
of HOURS and place the
result in PAY.

Input a record from
the file SALES-IN.

Write a record on the
file PRINT.

If the value of
HOURS is greater than 40
take YES path
otherwise take NO
path.

If the value of HOURS
is >40 pay time and
one-half for overtime;
otherwise pay is computed
at $4 per hour.

The start of the program.

Processing should stop.

Execute
HEADING-ROUTINE.

A program flowchart to compute pay at $4 per hour for an employee is shown below:

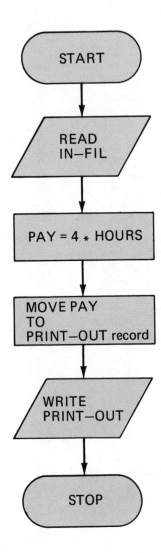

The diamond shaped symbol is used to denote decisions. Decisions involve relations such as greater than (>), less than (<), and equal to (=) between data items. If the relation is true, the "yes" path from the decision block is followed to determine the next instruction. If the relation is false, the "no" path from the decision block is followed. For example, suppose we wish to pay time and one-half for overtime hours worked by an employee. If the value of HOURS is less than 40, we shall pay him at $4 per hour. If the value of HOURS is more than 40, we shall pay him $4 times 40 equals $160 plus $6 for all hours in excess of 40. This program could be described by the following flowchart:

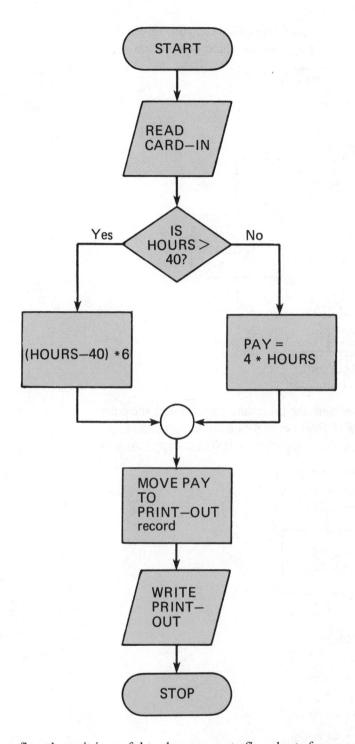

In some flowcharts it is useful to draw separate flowcharts for some complicated procedures and indicate that the procedures are to be executed by using the
predefined process block.

For example, let's construct a separate procedure called COMPUTE-PAY to take care of the details of determining the appropriate value of *PAY* based on HOURS.

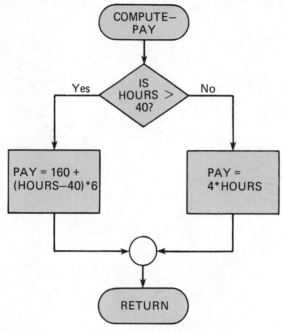

Note that the termination block is used with the procedure name to note the entry to the procedure and the statement RETURN to note the end of the procedure.

Using this procedure, the program to compute an employee's pay can now be written as:

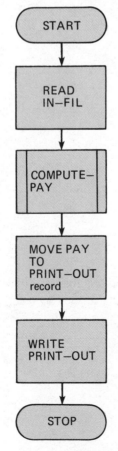

Program flowcharts are a useful means of describing a program in a rough form prior to writing the program in a programming language. They are also used as a form of documentation to enable a person unfamiliar with a program to understand how it works.

1.5   SELF TEST EXERCISES

1. Matching

1. program	a. computer and user engage in a dialog
2. input unit	b. communicates directly with a computing system
3. output unit	c. program which enables user to build and modify files
4. memory unit	d. procedure used to identify a user to a computing system
5. control unit	e. device used to communicate with computing system in an interactive mode
6. arithmetic/logical unit	f. carries out arithmetic and logical instructions
7. CPU	g. program written in machine language
8. microcomputer	h. Central Processing Unit
9. CRT	i. general term for computing machinery
10. terminal	j. collection of records
11. diskette	k. program written in a high level language
12. line printer	l. computer based on an electronic chip
13. hardware	m. carries out instructions which transfer data from outside into memory
14. software	n. video terminal
15. high level language	o. data is accumulated over a period of time before processing
16. source program	p. high speed printed output device
17. object program	q. stores currently active programs and data
18. compiler	r. computer engages in communication with more than one user
19. on line	s. carries out instructions which transfer data from memory to the outside world
20. batch computing	t. symbolic language such as COBOL
21. interactive computing	u. set of instructions for a computer
22. file	v. executes each program instruction
23. editor	w. general term for computer programs
24. time sharing	x. small disk often used in academic computing systems
25. sign on	y. program which translates a source program into an object program
26. mass storage	z. magnetic tape and disk

2. Matching

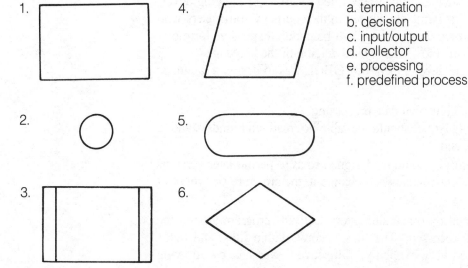

a. termination
b. decision
c. input/output
d. collector
e. processing
f. predefined process

INTRODUCTION TO COBOL 2

2.1 ORIGIN AND DEVELOPMENT OF COBOL

The origin of COBOL lies in the development in the late 1950s of programming systems which were better suited to commercial applications than the algebraic languages then in use. Much of the early work was carried out by Dr. Grace Hopper, at that time a commander in the Navy. Beginning in 1959 a series of meetings among concerned individuals of the Department of Defense, academic institutions, and computer manufacturers resulted in the organization of CODASYL (*CO*nference on *DA*ta *SY*stems *L*anguages). The avowed purpose of this group was the development and standardization of a commercial programming language.

CODASYL has developed several versions of the COBOL language. The earliest version was known as COBOL-60. This was superceded by COBOL-68 and then by COBOL-74, in 1968 and 1974 respectively. The American National Standards Institute formally adopts standards for the language; hence, these versions of the language are often referred to as ANSI-68 and ANSI-74 respectively. At the present time, a new standard tentatively titled COBOL-81 is being developed; however, CODASYL is being challenged in the courts by some users who object to certain changes which they contend will be unduly expensive to implement. COBOL-74 remains the most widely used version of the language.

The original intent in the development of COBOL was to design a language which was

1) naturally suited to commercial data processing,
2) self documenting (anyone should be able to read and understand a COBOL program), and
3) extensible (the language should be designed so as to permit later versions to add features without fundamental change in the structure or syntax of the language).

Objective 1 was attained by organizing every COBOL program around the data files which are to be processed. The files, records within files, and fields within records are described very explicitly. Objective 2 was met by allowing very long data-names which can completely describe a data item, by allowing operations (such as ADD, SUBTRACT, and so on) to be specified verbally rather than in symbolic form, and by insisting on a paragraph/sentence structure for each program segment. Objective 3 also was met by the original designers because COBOL has been redesigned and extended to include a multitude of features never envisaged by the original group, yet the fundamental organization and structure of COBOL programs remains the same now as in the beginning.

2.2   DIVISIONS OF A COBOL PROGRAM

Programs 2.1 and 2.2 illustrate sample COBOL programs. Program 2.1 creates a data file on disk containing records from an input file. Program 2.2 processes the data from that disk file and produces a report. Examination of these two programs will indicate some differences but many similarities.

All COBOL programs are organized into segments called *divisions*. The four divisions required in a COBOL program are:

1) IDENTIFICATION DIVISION
2) ENVIRONMENT DIVISION
3) DATA DIVISION
4) PROCEDURE DIVISION

Each division begins with a division header consisting of the division name, the word DIVISION and a period. Locate the division headers in each of the sample programs.

The purpose of the IDENTIFICATION DIVISION is to identify the program, its author and other related information. Examine the IDENTIFICATION DIVISIONS of Program 2.1 (lines 1 through 4) and Program 2.2 (lines 1 through 4). Note that the general type of information contained in each example is the same.

Sample Output

OLD BALANCE	CHECK AMOUNT	NEW BALANCE
0010.00	020.00	0030.00
0022.00	033.00	0055.00
0100.00	444.00	0544.00

The purpose of the ENVIRONMENT DIVISION is to describe the computing "environment" in which the program will function. Examine the ENVIRONMENT DIVISIONS of Programs 2.1 and 2.2 (lines 5 through 9 in each program). In each case the files to be processed are named and ASSIGNed to specific components of the computing system.

The purpose of the DATA DIVISION is to describe the data records and other data items to be processed by the program. Find the DATA DIVISIONS in Programs 2.1 (lines 10 through 19) and 2.2 (lines 10 through 37). In each case data items contained in data records are given names, and many items are described (via the PIC clause) and given an initial value (via the VALUE clause).

The PROCEDURE DIVISION describes the steps required to process the data files to accomplish the desired goal of the program. Find the PROCEDURE DIVISIONS of Programs 2.1 (lines 20 through 34) and 2.2 (lines 38 through 53). Note that in each case instructions are written in sentences which resemble standard usage.

Program 2.1   Sample COBOL program

```
 1        IDENTIFICATION DIVISION.
 2       PROGRAM-ID.  FILE-CREATION.
 3       AUTHOR.   WAYNE.
 4      *REMARKS.   PROGRAM 2-1.
 5       ENVIRONMENT DIVISION.
 6       INPUT-OUTPUT SECTION.
 7       FILE-CONTROL.
 8           SELECT INPUT-FILE   ASSIGN TO READER.
 9           SELECT OUTPUT-FILE ASSIGN TO DISK.
10       DATA DIVISION.
11       FILE SECTION.
12       FD   INPUT-FILE.
13           DATA RECORD IS INPUT-REC.
14       01   INPUT-REC   PIC X(30).
15       FD   OUTPUT-FILE
16           DATA RECORD IS OUTPUT-REC.
17       01   OUTPUT-REC   PIC X(80).
18       WORKING-STORAGE SECTION.
19       01   END-OF-FILE   PIC XXX VALUE "NO".
20       PROCEDURE DIVISION.
21       100-MAJOR-PROCESSING.
22          OPEN INPUT INPUT-FILE
23              OUTPUT OUTPUT-FILE.
24          READ INPUT-FILE
25             AT END MOVE "YES" TO END-OF-FILE.
26          PERFORM 200-BUILD-FILE
27             UNTIL END-OF-FILE = "YES".
28          CLOSE INPUT-FILE OUTPUT-FILE.
29          STOP RUN.
30       200-BUILD-FILE.
31          MOVE INPUT-REC TO OUTPUT-REC.
32          WRITE OUTPUT-REC.
33          READ INPUT-FILE
34              AT END MOVE "YES" TO END-OF-FILE.
```

Program 2.2   Sample report

```
 1        IDENTIFICATION DIVISION.
 2       PROGRAM-ID. CHAPTER 2 EXAMPLE 2.
 3       AUTHOR. PAULA.
 4      *REMARKS. PROGRAM 2-2.
 5       ENVIRONMENT DIVISION.
 6       INPUT-OUTPUT SECTION.
 7       FILE-CONTROL.
 8           SELECT IN-FD ASSIGN TO DISK.
 9           SELECT PRINT ASSIGN TO PRINTER.
10       DATA DIVISION.
11       FILE SECTION.
```

(continued)

Program 2.2 (continued)

```
12      FD   IN-FD
13           DATA RECORD IS INPUT-RECORD.
14      01   INPUT RECORD.
15           02   OLD BALANCE-IR    PIC 9999.
16           02   FILLER            PIC XX.
17           02   CHECK-AMOUNT-IR   PIC 999.
18           02   FILLER            PIC X(71).
19      FD   PRINT
20           DATA RECORD IS OUTPUT-RECORD.
21      01   OUTPUT-RECORD          PIC X(132).
22      WORKING-STORAGE SECTION.
23      01   EOF-FLAG               PIC 9    VALUE 0.
24      01   HEAD-LINE.
25           02   FILLER            PIC X(3)     VALUE SPACES.
26           02   FILLER            PIC X(11)    VALUE "OLD BALANCE".
27           02   FILLER            PIC X(3)     VALUE SPACES.
28           02   FILLER            PIC X(12)    VALUE "CHECK AMOUNT".
29           02   FILLER            PIC X(3)     VALUE SPACES.
30           02   FILLER            PIC X(11)    VALUE "NEW BALANCE".
31      01   DETAIL-LINE.
32           02   FILLER            PIC X(5)     VALUE SPACES.
33           02   OLD-BALANCE-DL    PIC 9999.99.
34           02   FILLER            PIC X(9)     VALUE SPACES.
35           02   CHECK-AMOUNT-DL   PIC 9(3).99.
36           02   FILLER            PIC X(7)     VALUE SPACES.
37           02   NEW-BALANCE-DL    PIC 9(4).99.
38      PROCEDURE DIVISION.
39      100-MAIN-LOGIC.
40          OPEN INPUT IN-FD, OUTPUT PRINT.
41          MOVE HEAD-LINE TO OUTPUT-RECORD.
42          WRITE OUTPUT-RECORD AFTER ADVANCING PAGE.
43          READ IN-FD AT END MOVE 1 TO EOF-FLAG.
44          PERFORM 200-SUB-LOGIC UNTIL EOF-FLAG = 1.
45          CLOSE IN-FD, PRINT.
46          STOP RUN.
47      200-SUB-LOGIC.
48          MOVE OLD-BALANCE-IR TO OLD-BALANCE-DL.
49          MOVE CHECK-AMOUNT-IR TO CHECK-AMOUNT-DL.
50          ADD OLD-BALANCE-IR, CHECK-AMOUNT-IR GIVING NEW-BALANCE-DL.
51          MOVE DETAIL-LINE TO OUTPUT-RECORD.
52          WRITE OUTPUT-RECORD AFTER ADVANCING 1 LINES.
53          READ IN-FD AT END MOVE 1 TO EOF-FLAG.
```

2.3 ORGANIZATION OF A COBOL PROGRAM

As noted above, the basic unit of organization of a COBOL program is the DIVI-
SION, which is broken down further into SECTIONS. In Programs 2.1 and 2.2,
the ENVIRONMENT and DATA DIVISIONS are subdivided into SECTIONS. A

SECTION is preceded by a SECTION header which contains the section name, the word "SECTION" and a period. Locate, for example, the INPUT-OUTPUT SECTIONs of the ENVIRONMENT DIVISION of Programs 2.1 (lines 6 through 9) and 2.2 (lines 6 through 9). In each example, the DATA DIVISIONs are organized into a FILE SECTION (lines 11 through 17 of Prog. 2.1, and lines 11 through 21 of Prog. 2.2) and a WORKING-STORAGE SECTION (lines 18 through 19 of Prog. 2.1, lines 22 through 37 of Prog. 2.2).

Another basic unit of organization of COBOL programs is the *paragraph*. A paragraph consists of a sequence of sentences preceded by a paragraph header. A paragraph header consists of a paragraph name followed by a period. Locate, for example, the two paragraphs of the IDENTIFICATION DIVISION (lines 2 and 3 of either Prog. 2.1 or Prog. 2.2). The paragraph names are "PROGRAM-ID" and "AUTHOR". Locate also the paragraphs of the PROCEDURE DIVISION in each example. In Program 2.1 the two paragraphs are named "100-MAJOR-PROCESSING" (line 21) and 200-BUILD-FILE (line 30). Although the PROCEDURE DIVISION of both of these examples contains two paragraphs, in general a PROCEDURE DIVISION may contain as many paragraphs as desired.

Entries within a section or paragraph are called *sentences*. A sentence is always terminated by a period. A section or paragraph may contain one or more sentences. A sentence may be contained on one line or may extend over many lines of code. A sentence will contain *data-names*, *constants* and *reserved words*. For example, the sentence (line 52 of Prog. 2.2):

WRITE OUTPUT-RECORD AFTER ADVANCING 1 LINES.

contains a data-name "OUTPUT-RECORD", a constant "1", and the reserved words "WRITE", "AFTER", ADVANCING and "LINES". In general, the following hierarchy of organization is observed in a COBOL program:

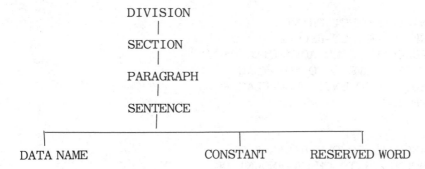

2.4   EXECUTION OF THE SAMPLE PROGRAMS

Figure 2.1 presents a program flowchart of Program 2.1. Compare the flowchart to the PROCEDURE DIVISION of the program. In the first statement to be executed (lines 22 and 23) the file to be read (INPUT-FILE) and the file to be created (OUTPUT-FILE) are opened. Any file to be processed in a COBOL program must be open before any records for that file can be read or written. Note that this statement is summarized in the program flowchart equivalent; summarizing a statement is quite common in flowcharting and serves to keep the flowchart from becoming too long and involved.

The second statement (lines 24 and 25) causes the first record from the file INPUT-FILE to be read. If there were no records in the file, the AT END clause

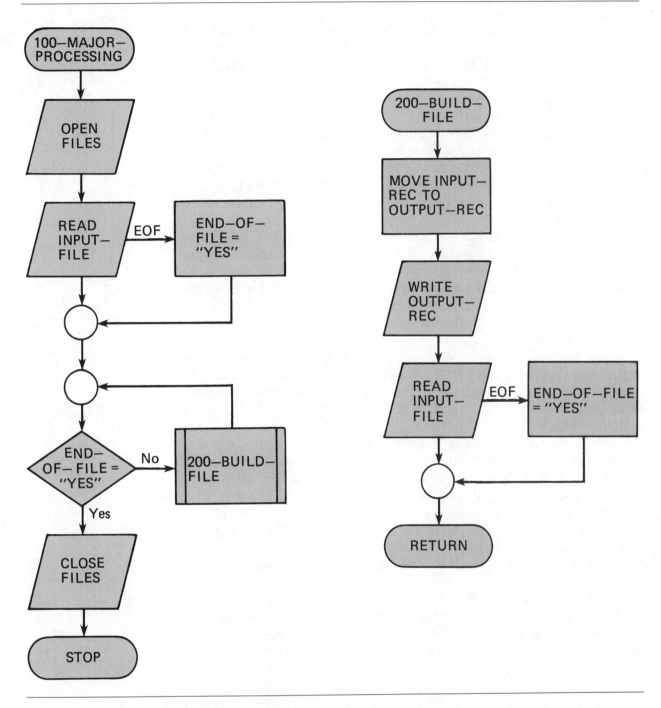

Figure 2.1   Program flowchart for file creation-program (Program 2.1)

(line 25) would be executed. In this case the characters "YES" would be moved
to the memory location END-OF-FILE. If there are records in the file (which is
the usual case), processing continues with the next sentence. Note the flowchart
version of the READ statement. The line labeled "EOF" leading to the right of
the input block is the flowchart equivalent of the AT END clause of the COBOL
program. Note also the use of the collector block to join the two flowpaths following the input block; this is a strict requirement for structured program
flowcharting.

The next statement to be executed is the PERFORM statement. This statement causes the program to enter a loop which will be terminated only when the content of memory location END-OF-FILE becomes "YES." Compare the program statement to the flowchart representation. The condition specified in the UNTIL clause (Fig. 2.1, line 27) is first tested. If it is not met, the named paragraph (200-BUILD-FILE in this case) is executed. After execution of this paragraph, control returns to the PERFORM statement and the test is made again. When ultimately the condition is met (END-OF-FILE="YES" in this example) the statement following the PERFORM statement is executed.

After termination of the loop the CLOSE statement signifies to the operating system that the program is finished processing records for the specified files. Finally the statement STOP RUN (Prog. 2.1, line 29) causes termination of the execution of the program.

The paragraph 200-BUILD-FILE (lines 30 through 34 of Prog. 2.1) is executed repeatedly by the program. The first statement (line 31) causes data from the INPUT-REC (the data record specified for INPUT-FILE) to be moved to the OUTPUT-REC (the data record specified for OUTPUT-FILE). When this paragraph is executed initially a data record will have been read from INPUT-FILE (lines 24 and 25) immediately prior to the PERFORM statement which causes execution of the paragraph.

After data is moved to the output record for OUTPUT-FILE, the record is written onto the file via the WRITE statement (line 32). Note that the WRITE statement addresses the record for the file (OUTPUT-REC in this example) while a READ statement address a file. The maxim "read a file, write a record" is useful in remembering this basic rule of COBOL.

After a data record has been written onto OUTPUT-FILE, the next data record is read from INPUT-FILE (Prog. 2.1, lines 33 and 34). Note again the use of the AT END clause (line 34) to take special action when there are no more records in the file. This paragraph (as should all paragraphs executed via a PERFORM/UNTIL) signifies that the condition which will cause termination of the loop has been met. Note that if the content of END-OF-FILE were not changed inside the paragraph 200-BUILD-FILE, the paragraph would be executed endlessly because the test END-OF-FILE equals "YES" would never be satisfied.

Program 2.2 utilizes the same basic structure for processing data from its input data file as used in the file creation program. A basic difference between the two programs is that fields within the input data-record are defined and processed. The purpose of the program is to create a report showing the current status of each account for a bank.

The data to be processed is contained on the file IN-FD as specified in the SELECT entry (Prog. 2.2, line 8) and the FD entry (lines 12 and 13). Each data record for this file (INPUT-RECORD as defined in lines 13 and 14) contains two fields (OLD-BALANCE-IR and CHECK-AMOUNT-IR, lines 15 and 17). For each INPUT-RECORD the content of OLD-BALANCE-IR is to be added to CHECK-AMOUNT-IR (the check amount is assumed to be a deposit) to produce the new balance.

The paragraph 100-MAIN-LOGIC in this program performs essentially the same function as did 100-MAJOR-PROCESSING in the file creation program. Compare the two paragraphs carefully; the only major difference is the writing of a heading line on the report (Prog. 2.2, lines 41 and 42) which precedes entering the loop to produce the body of the report.

The paragraph 200-SUB-LOGIC in this program performs a function similar to that of the paragraph 200-BUILD-FILE of the file creation program. In this case, data is moved one field at a time from the input record to a corresponding field in DETAIL-LINE (Prog. 2.2, lines 48 and 49). The required computation is performed (line 50) and the entire DETAIL-LINE is moved to the record associated with the output file (line 51) prior to writing a record onto the output file (line 52). As in Program 2.1, this paragraph terminates by reading the next record to be processed from the input file (line 53).

2.5 PREPARING A COBOL PROGRAM FOR COMPILATION

As noted in Chapter 1, Section 1.3, a COBOL program may be prepared and entered into the computer in a variety of ways. Regardless of the method used, a COBOL program initially may be written on coding sheets such as that shown in Figure 2.2 below. Each line of the coding sheet represents one input record. Each line is divided into fields used in entering COBOL statements. Positions 1 through 6 are used for a sequence number. The first record could be numbered 001010, the second record would then be 001020, and so on. Sequence numbers are optional; if sequence numbers are entered on COBOL statements, most compilers will check to ensure that the records are in proper sequence. Sequencing by tens allows statements to be added later.

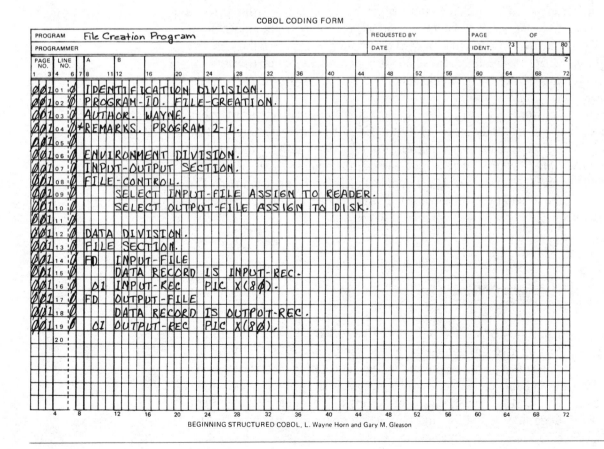

Figure 2.2 Sample COBOL coding sheet

Positions 73 through 80 are used for an identification sequence. The programmer may enter the program name here or choose to leave these positions blank. Position 7 (labeled CONT) is used in the continuation of a nonnumeric literal from one line to another (see chap. 5, section 5.8 for details). If the character "*" is entered in position 7, the entire line is treated by the compiler as a comment (i.e., the line is listed on the program listing but is not translated into machine language). Comments are useful to provide documentation regarding the function and purpose of a program. If it is not used for either of these purposes, position 7 is left blank. Most compilers allow the insertion of blank records in the program to provide for visual separation of various groups of statements in the final program listing.

Positions 8 through 72 are used for the content of the COBOL statement. There are two margins (A and B) delineated on the coding form. Some COBOL statements must begin in margin A (position 8), while others may not begin before margin B (position 12).

In summary, those entries which begin margin A are:

```
DIVISION headers
SECTION headers
paragraph names
FD  entries
01-49  entries
```

All other entries may not begin before margin B.

Note the placement of COBOL statements in Program 2.1 and 2.2. The rules for placement of statements permit a statement which may begin in margin B to be placed anywhere on the line after margin B. In a similar fashion, some entries which are listed above as beginning in margin A may begin anywhere to the right of margin A. In particular, record description entries (01 through 49) may begin anywhere on the line. However, it is common practice to show the breakdown of data records by indenting subordinate items as shown in Programs 2.1 and 2.2.

Many of the words used in a COBOL program are reserved words; they have a meaning automatically assumed by the COBOL compiler, and must be used only in a given context. A complete list of these words is included as Appendix D. Other words, such as file-names, data-names, and paragraph-names in the PROCEDURE DIVISION are defined solely by the programmer. The programmer should choose names which do not conflict with the COBOL reserved words.

2.6   IDENTIFICATION DIVISION ENTRIES

The general form of the IDENTIFICATION DIVISION is shown in Figure 2.3 below. This format is used throughout the text to represent the general form for COBOL program elements. All capitalized entries are COBOL reserved words. Entries which are underlined, if used, must be present as shown. All punctuation marks such as "−" and "." must be present as shown. Any entry which is capitalized but not underlined may be included at the programmer's discretion. Any entries described in lower case characters are supplied by the programmer. Any

```
IDENTIFICATION DIVISION.

PROGRAM-ID . program-name.

[AUTHOR . sentence. . . ]

[INSTALLATION. sentence. . . ]

[DATE-WRITTEN . sentence. . . ]

[DATE-COMPILED . sentence. . . ]

[SECURITY. sentence. . . ]
```

Figure 2.3   General form of the IDENTIFICATION DIVISION

entry enclosed in brackets ([]) is an optional entry. For example, a complete IDENTIFICATION DIVISION might be:

```
IDENTIFICATION DIVISION
PROGRAM-ID.  SAMPLE.
```

All other paragraphs in the division are optional. However, various operating systems place restrictions on the program-name specified in the PROGRAM-ID paragraph. Check with locally available documentation for further details. Ellipses (...) used on the general format specifications indicate that more than one element of the preceding type may be present. Note, for example, that all of the paragraphs except for PROGRAM-ID may contain as many sentences as desired.

The general purpose of the IDENTIFICATION DIVISION is to identify the program, programmer, when and where the program was written, and the purpose for writing the program.

1) The PROGRAM-ID paragraph specifies to the operating system a name for the program.
2) The AUTHOR paragraph specifies the name(s) of the programmer(s).
3) The INSTALLATION paragraph specifies where the program was written.
4) The DATE-WRITTEN paragraph specifies the date on which the program was written.
5) The DATE-COMPILED paragraph specifies when the program was compiled. Most compilers will insert an appropriate date into this paragraph replacing whatever entry was made by the programmer.
6) The SECURITY paragraph is used in sensitive application areas to specify the security level required for personnel to have access to the program.

Notice that an additional paragraph is used in Programs 2.1 and 2.2. The REMARKS paragraph is actually a comment because of the asterisk placed in column 7. ANSI-68 COBOL provided for a REMARKS paragraph at this point; the specification was omitted in ANSI-74 COBOL.

The REMARKS comments may be used for any purpose the programmer desires. They are typically used to describe in general terms the purpose served by the program. This paragraph also may be used to document changes made by subsequent programmers.

The ENVIRONMENT DIVISION describes the computing system and the files which will be required by the program. The ENVIRONMENT DIVISION may be

```
ENVIRONMENT DIVISION.

CONFIGURATION SECTION.

[SOURCE-COMPUTER . computer-name.]

[OBJECT-COMPUTER . computer-name.]

[SPECIAL-NAMES. special-names-entry.]

INPUT-OUTPUT SECTION.

[FILE-CONTROL. SELECT select-entry . . . ]

[I-O-CONTROL. i-o-control-entry . . . ]
```

Figure 2.4   *General form of the ENVIRONMENT DIVISION*

composed of two sections, CONFIGURATION SECTION and INPUT-OUTPUT SECTION, as shown in Figure 2.4. Note that both sections are optional. The CONFIGURATION SECTION is used to specify the SOURCE-COMPUTER which is the computer that will be used to compile the source program, the OBJECT-COMPUTER which is the computer which will be used to execute the object program, and SPECIAL-NAMES which will be recognized within the program. Entries in these paragraphs vary somewhat from one compiler to another.

All data to be processed and all output produced by a COBOL program must be organized into sets of data records called *files*. The FILE-CONTROL paragraph of the INPUT-OUTPUT SECTION is used to describe the files which the program will process. There will be one SELECT entry for each file. For example, refer to the two SELECT sentences defining the two files in program of Figure 2.1. The I-O-CONTROL paragraph of the INPUT-OUTPUT SECTION is used to describe special procedures to be used by the program in processing files.

The only entry that will be found in the ENVIRONMENT DIVISION of most COBOL programs will be the FILE-CONTROL paragraph of the INPUT-OUTPUT SECTION. Each file to be processed must be described in a SELECT sentence. The general form of the most useful parts of the SELECT sentence is

```
SELECT file-name ASSIGN TO system-name.
```

where the *file-name* is the name of the file which will be used within the COBOL program and the *system-name* is a description of the file which is communicated to the operating system. The general form of system-names varies from one computer installation to another; the manual for your installation will contain details.

2.7   DATA DIVISION ENTRIES

Data items which will be required in a program must be described in the DATA DIVISION. Generally programs require three distinct types of data items:

    1) Input—these items will be a part of an input record description;

DATA DIVISION.

FILE SECTION.

⎡ FD file-description-entry. . ⎤ . . .
⎢   ⎥
⎣ record-description-entry. . . ⎦ . . .

WORKING-STORAGE SECTION.

[working-data-item-description . . .]

[record-description . . .]

Figure 2.5   General form of the DATA DIVISION

2) Output—these items will be part of an output record description; and
3) Working—these items are required temporarily by the program but are not on an input record or an output record.

When a record from a file is read, data from the file is placed in the input record area. Before a record can be written onto an output file, that data must be placed in the output record. All other items needed by the program will be classified as working items.

File Section

The general form of the DATA DIVISION is shown in Figure 2.5 above. The FILE SECTION contains a description of each file to be processed and a description of each record to be found on the file. In Program 2.1 there is an input file description followed by a description of the input record and an output file description followed by an output record description. The WORKING-STORAGE section contains a description of working data items. In Program 2.2 there is a control variable (EOF-FLAG) and two detailed descriptions of sequences of data items (HEAD-LINE and DETAIL-LINE) which will ultimately be placed on the output file. Note that in each of these sequences there are literals (e.g., SPACES and ''OLD BALANCE'') as well as other data items which will become a part of an output line.

Figure 2.6 shows the general form of the most useful entries of the FD (*File Description*) entry. The use of { } indicates that one and only one of the entries contained within may be chosen.

The RECORDING MODE clause is an IBM extension of ANSI COBOL standards; it is required only by IBM compilers and may not be allowed by other compilers. The most common entry is RECORDING MODE IS F, which designates *fixed length* records. Each record in a file having fixed length records contains the same number of characters as all other records. (The entry V would designate variable length records.) The RECORD CONTAINS clause is used to describe the length of the record(s) associated with file; this clause is optional. If the RECORD CONTAINS clause is omitted, the compiler will assume a record length equal to the number of characters in the specified record name. The LABEL RECORDS clause usually is required; it describes to the COBOL compiler the way in which the program should process the first record in the file. If LABEL RECORD IS STANDARD is specified, the first record in the file is assumed to be a label record

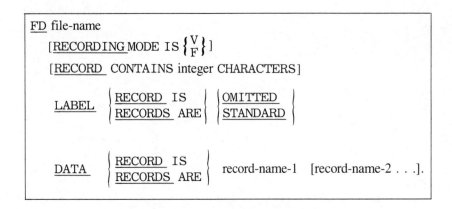

FD file-name

   [<u>RECORDING</u> MODE IS $\left\{ \begin{array}{c} V \\ F \end{array} \right\}$]

   [<u>RECORD</u> CONTAINS integer CHARACTERS]

   <u>LABEL</u> $\left\{ \begin{array}{l} \underline{RECORD} \ \underline{IS} \\ \underline{RECORDS} \ \underline{ARE} \end{array} \right\}$ $\left\{ \begin{array}{l} \underline{OMITTED} \\ \underline{STANDARD} \end{array} \right\}$

   <u>DATA</u> $\left\{ \begin{array}{l} \underline{RECORD} \ \underline{IS} \\ \underline{RECORDS} \ \underline{ARE} \end{array} \right\}$ record-name-1 [record-name-2 . . .].

Figure 2.6 General form of the FD entry. Note: The recording mode clause is an IBM extension not included in ANSI standards specification.

level-number $\left\{ \begin{array}{l} \text{data-name} \\ \underline{FILLER} \end{array} \right\}$ $\left\{ \begin{array}{l} \underline{PICTURE} \\ \underline{PIC} \end{array} \right\}$ IS picture   [<u>VALUE</u> IS literal].

Figure 2.7 General form of the RECORDING DESCRIPTION entry

containing a file identification, expiration date, file description, access keys and other such information. Label records are used to control access to a file to ensure that files are not destroyed by mistake and that unauthorized programs do not have access to the file. If LABEL RECORDS ARE OMITTED is specified, the first record on a file is assumed to be a data record. The DATA RECORD clause specifies the name of one or more records that will be found on the file. A detailed description of each type of record must follow the FD entry.

A record-description-entry has the form shown in Figure 2.7 where *level-number* is a two-digit number in the range 01 to 49; *data-name* is the name that identifies with the item; and *picture* is a description of the number and type of characters that will make up the item. The level-number 01 is classed as the highest level; level-numbers 02, 03, ... 49 are used on data items which are subdivisions of items with high level-numbers. In Program 2.2 the input record is given the overall name INPUT-RECORD and is subdivided into items (also called fields) which include OLD-BALANCE-IR and CHECK-AMOUNT-IR. The reserved word FILLER is used as the data-name for field which does not need to be referenced by any subsequent part of the program. The input record may be visualized as a sequence of 80 characters as follows:

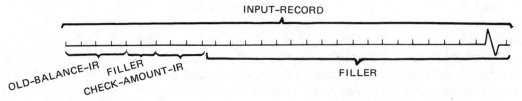

Any reference to the data-name INPUT-RECORD refers to the entire 80 characters; a reference to OLD-BALANCE-IR or CHECK-AMOUNT-IR refers to a specific subset of these characters. A record description entry which contains a PICTURE clause is an *elementary data item*; a record description entry which does not contain a PICTURE clause is a *group item*. Group data items may be subdivided; elementary data items may not. INPUT-RECORD is a group data item; OLD-BALANCE-IR and CHECK-AMOUNT-IR are elementary data items.

A data-name in COBOL must be composed only of the characters 0 through 9, A through Z, and - (hyphen). At least one character in the name must be alphabetic. Embedded hyphens are permitted; however, a hyphen may not be the first character nor the last character in a name. A name is terminated by a space or other mark of punctuation; embedded spaces are not permitted. The maximum length for a data-name is 30 characters. All other programmer defined names such as file-names, record-names, condition-names, paragraph-names, and so on are subject to the restrictions specified for data-names.

A requirement of structured programming is that data names be as descriptive as possible to aid the reader in understanding a program. A field which will contain the same data at some point in the program is customarily assigned essentially the same name. A suffix (or prefix) is used to provide unique data names (a requirement of COBOL) and to indicate which record contains the field. For example, in Program 2.2 the data item OLD-BALANCE is present both on INPUT-RECORD and DETAIL-LINE. The data-name OLD-BALANCE-IR is used for the field on INPUT-RECORD (IR is an abbreviation for INPUT-RECORD) while OLD-BALANCE-DL is used for the field on DETAIL-LINE.

A picture clause is made up of a sequence of characters called picture codes which are used to describe 1) the length of the field, and 2) the type of data contained in the field.

The picture code 9 is used to describe a numeric character; the picture code X is used to describe an alphanumeric character. (An alphanumeric character is any representable character (digit, letter or other); whereas a numeric character is any character 0 through 9.) The total number of 9s or Xs used in the picture defines the length of the field. Thus, in the Program in Figure 2.2 the field OLD-BALANCE-IR with a picture 9999 is described as a four-digit numeric item; the field CHECK-AMOUNT-IR with a picture 999 is a three-digit numeric field. All of the FILLER entries are given alphanumeric pictures of varying lengths. A repetition factor enclosed in parentheses may be used in a picture. When the repetition factor is used, the preceding character is repeated the specified number of time. For example, the entry PICTURE 9(4) is equivalent to PICTURE 9999.

Working-Storage Section

Entries in the WORKING-STORAGE SECTION are data items which are used in the program but are not specifically included in an input record or an output record. The VALUE clause may not be used in the FILE SECTION; its use is restricted to elementary data items in the WORKING-STORAGE SECTION. The VALUE clause is used to establish an initial value for a data item. For example, the initial value of EOF-FLAG in Program 2.2 is specified to be 0. The value of an item may be specified as any one of the following:

   1) Numeric constant (e.g., VALUE IS 0);
   2) Alphanumeric constant (e.g., VALUE IS "NO"); or
   3) Figurative constant (e.g., VALUE IS SPACES).

Numeric constants are written as a sequence of digits (e.g, 0, 123); alphanumeric constants are written as a sequence of characters enclosed in quotes; figurative constants are COBOL reserved words which represent a specific value such as ZERO and SPACES. (See Chap. 4, Fig. 4.5 for a complete list of figurative constants). In some systems alphanumeric constants are enclosed in single quotes (') rather than the double quotes (") used in this text. The reader must check locally available documentation to find out which character is accepted by his or her compiler.

2.8   SUMMARY OF PROCEDURE DIVISION ENTRIES

The PROCEDURE DIVISION describes the processing of the data files. It is the "action part" of any COBOL program. The PROCEDURE DIVISION of Program 2.2 has two paragraphs, 100-MAJOR-PROCESSING and 200-BUILD-FILE. Each sentence in the PROCEDURE DIVISION is made up of one or more statements. A statement begins with a COBOL reserved word describing the operation to be performed. Statements used in Program 2.2 include:

OPEN (line 40)
MOVE (lines 41,48,49,51)
WRITE (lines 42,52)
READ (lines 43,53)
PERFORM (line 44)
CLOSE (line 45)
STOP RUN (line 46)
ADD (line 50)

The OPEN statement causes the designated files to be opened (i.e., readied for processing). A file always must be opened before any READ or WRITE operations may be performed on it.

The MOVE statement causes data to be moved from one data item (the sending item) to another (the receiving item). A MOVE replaces the contents of the receiving item but does nothing to the sending item.

The WRITE statement causes the specified output record to be written onto the appropriate file. The AFTER clause designates the vertical spacing of paper for a printer file. A general form of the WRITE statement with the AFTER clause is shown in Figure 2.8.

When the AFTER clause is used, PAGE is used to skip to the top of a new page, 0 is used to skip no lines before printing, 1 is used to skip one line before printing, 2 is used to skip two lines before printing, and 3 is used to skip three lines before printing.

The READ statement causes a record to be read from the specified file. When the record is read, a check is made to determine if it is the system end-of-

$$
\underline{\text{WRITE}} \text{ record-name} \left[\underline{\text{AFTER}} \text{ ADVANCING} \begin{Bmatrix} 0 \\ 1 \\ 2 \\ 3 \end{Bmatrix} \left[\begin{Bmatrix} \text{LINE} \\ \text{LINES} \end{Bmatrix} \right] \text{[PAGE]} \right]
$$

Figure 2.8   General form of the WRITE/AFTER statement

file record. The purpose of the system end-of-file record is to mark the end of the data records so that a program will not inadvertently process data belonging to another file. When the end-of-file record is read, the statement(s) in the AT END clause of the READ statement will be executed. In Program 2.1 the READ statement

READ INPUT-FILE AT END MOVE "YES" TO END-OF-FILE.

will cause the contents of the data item END-OF-FILE to be set to "YES" when the end-of-file record for the file INPUT-FILE is read.

The PERFORM statement causes the sentences of the designated paragraph to be executed if the condition given in the UNTIL clause is *not* met. For example,

PERFORM 200-SUB-LOGIC UNTIL EOF-FLAG = 1

will cause a test of EOF-FLAG to be made. If EOF-FLAG = 1, the next statement will be executed. If EOF-FLAG $\neq$ 1, the paragraph 200-SUB-LOGIC will be executed. After execution of the paragraph, the condition is tested again and the procedure repeated. In Program 2.2 this logic is used to process each record of the input file and to stop processing when the end-of-file record has been read. The CLOSE statement is used to terminate processing of designated files. Any file which is opened should also always be closed before the program stops execution. The STOP RUN statement is used to terminate execution of the program. The ADD statement is used to perform the arithmetic operation of addition on designated data items and place the results in a location specified in the GIVING clause. For example,

ADD OLD-BALANCE-IR CHECK-AMOUNT-IR GIVING NEW-BALANCE-DL

IDENTIFICATION DIVISION.

The program, author, and other identifying information is given.

ENVIRONMENT DIVISION.

The computing system(s) to be used and the files to be processed are specified.

DATA DIVISION.
FILE SECTION.

The input and output files and the records for these files are described.

WORKING-STORAGE SECTION.

Other data items required by the program are described.

PROCEDURE-DIVISION.

The files are opened. Each record of the input file is processed and the appropriate line of output is written. When all the records have been processed, the files are closed and the execution of the program is terminated.

Figure 2.9 Summary of the COBOL program (Program 2.1)

causes the sum of OLD-BALANCE-IR and CHECK-AMOUNT-IR to be placed in NEW-BALANCE-DL. Commas may be used to separate data names or clauses in COBOL statements, but they are not required. They are used primarily to improve readability of programs.

2.9   DEBUG CLINIC

It is almost inevitable that there will be errors in COBOL programs when they are first submitted for compilation. Errors may be classed as either *syntax* errors or *logical* errors. A syntax error is an error in constructing a COBOL statement. The compiler will alert the programmer that syntax errors have been made by printing appropriate messages as part of the program listing. A logical error is an error in the logic of the program; the program does not perform the desired function. These errors become apparent as the programmer examines the output produced from the processing of sample data. *Debugging* is the process of removing syntax and logical errors from programs.

Syntax Errors

Program 2.3 is an example of a program with syntax errors. The error messages produced by the compiler follow the statement which contains the error. Usually the messages immediately follow the line of code which contains the error, but occasionally other lines of code may intervene. One error may produce one error message or several error messages. Common sources of syntax errors are omission of periods, omission or misspelling of reserved words and misspelling of data names.

> Line 27 in Program 2.3 is in error because of the omission of the reserved word PIC;   *Example*

        02   FILLER   X(3)   VALUE SPACES

This error caused the compiler to generate the error messages on lines 28, 30 and 31.

> Line 39 is in error because the period is omitted at the end of the line: *Example*

        02   FILLER   PIC X(7)   VALUE SPACES.

This error caused the error messages listed on lines 41 and 42. Because the period is missing on line 39, the compiler tried to interpret line 40 as a part of the statement which began on line 39.

Program 2.3 Program with syntax errors

```
Line
 1          IDENTIFICATION DIVISION.
 2          PROGRAM-ID. CHAPTER 2 EXAMPLE 2.
 3          AUTHOR. PAULA.
 4         *REMARKS. PROGRAM 2.3.
 5          ENVIRONMENT DIVISION.
 6          INPUT-OUTPUT SECTION.
 7          FILE-CONTROL.
 8              SELECT IN-FD ASSIGN TO DISK.
 9              SELECT PRINT ASSIGN TO PRINTER.
```
(continued)

Program 2.3 (continued)

```
10      DATA DIVISION.
11      FILE SECTION.
12      FD  IN-FD
13          DATA RECORD IS INPUT-RECORD.
14      01  INPUT RECORD.
15          02  OLD BALANCE-IR    PIC 9999.
16          02  FILLER            PIC XX.
17          02  CHECK-AMOUNT-IR   PIC 999.
18          02  FILLER            PIC X(71).
19      FD  PRINT
20          DATA RECORD IS OUTPUT-RECORD.
21      01  OUTPUT-RECORD         PIC X(132).
22      WORKING-STORAGE SECTION.
23      01  EOF-FLAG              PIC 9    VALUE 0.
24      01  HEAD-LINE.
25          02  FILLER           PIC X(3)    VALUE SPACES.
26          02  FILLER           PIC X(11)   VALUE "OLD BALANCE".
27          02  FILLER               X(3)    VALUE SPACES.
```
ERROR 000: UNRECOGNIZED CONSTRUCT*** X
```
29          02  FILLER           PIC X(12)   VALUE "CHECK AMOUNT".
```
ERROR 088: ELEMENTARY ITEM MUST HAVE SIZE*** 02
ERROR 168: ITEM CANNOT BE ZERO SIZE*** 02
```
32          02  FILLER           PIC X(3)    VALUE SPACES.
33          02  FILLER           PIC X(11)   VALUE "NEW BALANCE".
34      01  DETAIL-LINE.
35          02  FILLER           PIC X(5)    VALUE SPACES.
36          02  OLD-BALANCE-DL   PIC 9999.99.
37          02  FILLER           PIC X(9)    VALUE SPACES.
38          02  CHECK-AMOUNT-DL  PIC 9(3).99.
39          02  FILLER           PIC X(7)    VALUE SPACES
40          02  NEW-BALANCE-DL   PIC 9(4).99.
```
ERROR 000: UNRECOGNIZED CONSTRUCT*** 02
ERROR 027: DUPLICATE OR INCOMPATIBLE CLAUSE*** NEW-BALANCE-DL
```
43      PROCEDURE DIVISION.
44      100-MAIN-LOGIC.
45          OPEN INPUT IN-FD, OUTPUT PRINT.
46          MOVE HEAD-LINE TO OUTPUT-RECORD.
47          WRITE OUTPUT-RECORD AFTER ADVANCING PAGE.
48          READ IN-FD AT END MOVE 1 TO EOF-FLAG.
49          PERFORM 200-SUB-LOGIC UNTIL EOF-FLAG = 1.
```
ERROR 159: PROCEDURE-NAME DOES NOT OCCUR*** 200-SUB-LOGIC
```
51          CLOSE IN-FD, PRINT.
52          STOP RUN.
53      200-SUB-LOIGC.
54          MOVE OLD-BALANCE-IR TO OLD-BALANCE-DL.
55          MOVE CHECK-AMOUNT-IR TO CHECK-AMOUNT-DL.
56          ADD OLD-BALANCE-IR, CHECK-AMOUNT-IR GIVING NEW-BALANCE-DL.
```
ERROR 046: QUALIFIER OR NAME HAS NOT APPEARED BEFORE*** NEW-BALANCE-DL
ERROR 254: NUMERIC RECEIVING FIELD OPERAND EXPECTED*** NEW-BALANCE-DL
```
59          MOVE DETAIL-LINE TO OUTPUT-RECORD.
60          WRITE OUTPUT-RECORD AFTER ADVANCING 1 LINES.
61          READ IN-FD AT END MOVE 1 TO EOF-FLAG.
```

The error message on line 50 is produced because the paragraph referred to   *Example*
in the preceding line ''200-SUB-LOGIC'' does not exist. The probable
cause of this error is the misspelling of the paragraph name in line 53.

The error messages in lines 57 and 58 are caused by the omission of the   *Example*
period on line 39. Because of this error the data name ''NEW-BALANCE-
DL'' was never defined in the program.

Unfortunately there are no standards for error messages; each compiler uses
a different set. Usually a programmer's guide containing detailed information
about the error messages for the COBOL compiler used at a given computer
center is available.

Logical Errors

Even if a program is compiled without syntax errors, logical errors in the program may remain. The programmer must devise a set or sets of test data and
execute the program with the test data in order to assure that the program performs the function(s) specified for it correctly. It is a good idea to design the test
data very early in the program development process; when the expected output
with a set of test data is known in advance, the output actually produced by the
program can be analyzed easily.

2.10   SELF TEST EXERCISES

1. Matching

1. CODASYL
2. ANSI
3. DIVISION
4. ENVIRONMENT
5. DATA
6. IDENTIFICATION
7. PROCEDURE
8. sequence number
9. continuation
10. Margin A
11. MOVE
12. PROGRAM-ID
13. CONFIGURATION SECTION
14. INPUT-OUTPUT SECTION
15. SOURCE-COMPUTER
16. OBJECT-COMPUTER
17. SELECT
18. FILE SECTION
19. WORKING-STORAGE
    SECTION
20. FD
21. level-number
22. FILLER
23. OPEN
24. PERFORM
25. CLOSE
26. AFTER

a. Assigns name to a COBOL program
b. entry used in FILE SECTION of the DATA DIVISION
c. used on WRITE statements addressed to printer
d. computer used to compile the program
e. largest unit of subdivision of a COBOL program
f. column 7
g. column 8
h. assigns a file to a system component
i. columns 1-6
j. Conference on Data Systems Languages
k. terminates processing of a file by a COBOL program
l. section of DATA DIVISION in which record associated with files are defined
m. division of a COBOL program which defines data to be processed
n. American National Standards Institute
o. statement which readies a file for processing
p. computer used to execute the program
q. identifier used to indicate levels of subdivision of data
r. division of a COBOL program which identifies the program and the programmer
s. division of a COBOL program which specifies the computing environment in
   which the program will function
t. instruction used to copy data from one memory location to another
u. reserved word used to define unused positions of a record
v. command used to execute a COBOL paragraph
w. portion of the DATA DIVISION used to define data not directly a part of an input
   or out put record
x. portion of ENVIRONMENT DIVISION used to define the computing system
y. division used to describe the processing of data
z. portion of ENVIRONMENT DIVISION used to define files to be processed

2. Write a complete IDENTIFICATION DIVISION for Program 2.2.

3. Draw a program flowchart for Program 2.2.

4. List entries which must begin in Margin A.

5. Classify each of the following data-names as valid or invalid.
   a. INPUT-REC
   b. 100-32
   c. 300- PARA
   d. PARA-
   e. INPUT-DATA-TO-BE-PROCESSED-BY-THIS-PROGRAM
   f. INPUT REC

6. The following list of items were taken from Program 2.2. Match each item with the applicable terms from the list of descriptive terms below.

1. HEAD-LINE	a. division header
2. PROCEDURE DIVISION	b. section header
3. MOVE	c. paragraph header
4. IN-FD	d. group data name
5. INPUT-OUTPUT SECTION	e. elementary data name
6. CHECK-AMOUNT-DL	f. alphanumeric constant
7. 100-MAIN-LOGIC	g. figurative constant
8. ASSIGN	h. numeric constant
9. EOF-FLAG	i. reserved word
10. "OLD BALANCE"	j. picture code
11. 1	k. file name
12. SPACES	
13. X(5)	
14. 9999.99	
15. FILLER	
16. ADD	
17. AUTHOR	

7. Write DATA DIVISION entries to define a record containing the following fields:

positions	content
1 - 20	customer name
21 - 35	street address
36 - 45	city
46 - 47	state
48 - 52	zip code
53 - 80	unused

8. Classify each file-name, record-name and data-name defined in Program 2.2 using the following table:

Where Defined in DATA DIVISION

Type of Item	FILE SECTION Used for Input	FILE SECTION Used for Output	WORKING-STORAGE SECTION Used for Input	WORKING-STORAGE SECTION Used for Control	WORKING-STORAGE SECTION Used for Output
File					
Record					
Field					

2.11   PROGRAMMING EXERCISES[1]

1. Write a program to create a file on disk containing the data shown below:

CUSTOMER NAME	ADDRESS				CURRENT BALANCE
JONES, JAMES	123 A ST.	ANYWHERE	FL	32504	23.00
SMITH, MARY	100 MAIN PL.	SOMEWHERE	AL	34501	78.00
DOE, JANE	502 OAK RD.	ANYWHERE	FL	32504	2.90
JIMENEZ, JAMES	1000 JONES CT.	OVERTHERE	GA	49206	632.00
CHAI, LE	695 MAPLE	OVERHERE	LA	59600	.95

2. Write a program to list the data file created in Exercise 1 above. Include appropriate headings.

3. Write a program to produce address labels from the input data defined in Exercise 2 above. Output should be of the form

   Name
   Street Address
   City   State   Zip

4. Write a program to process a file containing records as follows:

position	
3-4	Grade-1
6-7	Grade-2
10-11	Grade-3

   Compute the sum of the grades and list them with appropriate headings.

5. Jones Furniture Co. maintains four warehouse facilities. Inventory records show the quantity of a given item on hand in each facility. The format for each record is:

Positions	
1-5	Inventory number
6-15	Item description
16-17	Quantity on hand warehouse 1
18-19	Quantity on hand warehouse 2
20-21	Quantity on hand warehouse 3
22-23	Quantity on hand warehouse 4

   Produce a report showing the total quantity of each item on hand.

---

[1]A supply of COBOL coding forms is included inside the back cover. Using these forms to code COBOL programs will help the reader avoid making careless errors when transcribing the program from written to machine readable form.

INTRODUCTION TO STRUCTURED PROGRAMMING IN COBOL

3

3.1   PROGRAM DEVELOPMENT

The task of developing a program involves much more than simply writing COBOL code, although this is of course a necessary step. In practice more time usually is spent in analyzing the problem at hand before writing the program and in testing the actual program than is spent in coding. The task of developing a program may be viewed as a seven-step process:

1) **Define the problem.** Answer the following questions: What is the purpose of the program? What data is to be processed? What output is desired? What is input? How will the program accomplish the desired goals?

2) **Design test data.** Only if the program is executed with an adequate amount of test data and the output produced is compared to the output desired, can the programmer be reasonably sure that his program is correct. At this step test data which will thoroughly test all aspects of the program should be designed.

3) **Design the program.** Decide on names for all files, records and fields that will be needed in the program. Draw a flowchart for the PRO-CEDURE DIVISION.

4) **Code the program.** Write the COBOL equivalent of the program designed in step 3 above.

5) **Compile the program.** Submit the program for compilation and correct any syntax errors.

6) **Test the program.** Run the program with the test data from step 2 above. If the output produced is not correct, revise the program and go to step 5.

7) **Document the program.** A properly written COBOL program has a great deal of built-in documentation; however, other forms of documentation such as structure diagrams, record layouts, and user and run manuals also may be needed.

3.2 WHY STRUCTURED PROGRAMMING?

When computers first were put into use the users tried to make them as efficient as possible to justify costs and prove the value of the systems. From the beginning, however, people who bought computers had to deal with not only cost of using the hardware to solve a problem (hardware cost), but also the cost of preparing programs for the machine to execute (program development costs). At first hardware costs were much greater than program development costs (Fig. 3.1). The emphasis on machine efficiency often forced programmers to use complicated logic and programming tricks that resulted in very efficient programs, but the programs were difficult to debug and also difficult for any other programmer to modify. Documentation (detailed explanations supplied with a program) provided a partial solution to the problem, but the documentation was often incomplete and sometimes incorrect.

In recent years hardware costs have become much lower than program development costs, and there has been a corresponding shift in programming philosophy. Programmer productivity has become a higher priority than the machine efficiency of the programs written. Programmers now are encouraged to develop straightforward solutions to problems and to concentrate on building programs in such a way that debugging, addition coding and future enhancements will require minimal effort.

Structured programming is a way of writing programs which, if followed carefully, will result in programs which are easy to

1) Read
2) Understand
3) Debug
4) Modify

A structured program can be understood clearly not only by its author but also by anyone else who needs to understand or change it. Structured programming decreases programming costs, particularly when applied to large programming projects. This cost decrease is apparent not only in the initial programming stages but also later on when the programs must be modified to suit new requirements. Also there tend to be fewer detected and undetected logical errors in structured

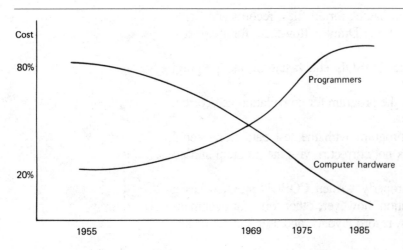

Figure 3.1 Relative costs of computing equipment and programming personnel

programs, so testing, debugging and maintenance times are reduced. Structured programming, in short, has gained wide acceptance as a standard programming technique.

3.3   WHAT IS STRUCTURED PROGRAMMING?

Structured programming is really a programming discipline. It encompasses techniques used to develop program logic and standards for the actual coding of the program. The technique used for program development generally is referred to as *top-down program design*. In top-down program design, a program is specified as a set of procedures to be executed in some chosen sequence; a procedure may be relatively simple (opening a file) or complex (accumulating the sum of a sequence of data items). A complex procedure will in turn be broken down into a sequence of simpler procedures until at last the COBOL code for the program can be written. For example, suppose we were to write a program to find the sum of a set of numbers. The entire program could be summarized as one rather complex procedure:

> Compute the sum of a set of data items.

This procedure must be respecified as a sequence of simpler procedures:

> Open the input and output files.
> Read first data record.
> Until there is no more data, accumulate the sum of each data item.
> Write the sum.
> Close the files.

The procedure ''accumulate the sum of each data item'' is still quite complex and must be respecified as follows:

> Add the data item to the sum.
> Read a data record.

Thus the complete program now has the form:

> Open the input and output files.
> Read first data record.
> Until there is no more data,
> > Add the data item to the sum
> > Read a data record.
> Write the sum.
> Close the files.

The procedures in this program are now specified in sufficiently simple form for easy implementation as a COBOL program as shown in Programs 3.3 and 3.4 on pages 48 and 50.

In programming, ''structure'' refers to the way in which statements are related to one another. In structured programming only three program structures are needed for program development:

1) Sequence
2) If/Then/Else (Decision)
3) Iteration (Loop)

In a Sequence structure, each statement is executed in succession. In flowchart form, a sequence structure is shown as:

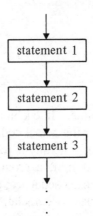

After statement 1 is executed, statement 2 is executed, followed by the execution of statement 3 and so on. The program specification

> Open the input and output files.
> Read first data record.
> Until there is no more data, accumulate the sum of each data item.
> Close the files.

makes use of a sequence structure. Each procedure is carried out in sequence; when one procedure is completed the next is executed. In a COBOL program every paragraph is a sequence structure (i.e., every paragraph is a sequence of sentences executed one after the other). For example, the paragraph 100-MAJOR-LOGIC in Program 3.3 (page 49, lines 34 through 43) contains nine sentences which are executed in succession. The paragraph 200-LOOP-CONTROL in the Program 3.3 (lines 45 through 49) contains five sentences executed one after the other.

The If/Then/Else structure describes a test condition and two possible resulting paths. Only one path is selected, and executed depending on the evaluation of the given test condition. In flowchart form the decision structure is shown as:

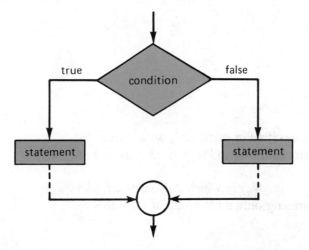

In COBOL this structure is implemented with the IF statement. We shall consider the If/Then/Else structure in great detail in Chapter 6.

The Iteration structure causes the repetition of one or more statements until a given condition is met. In flowchart form the iteration structure is shown as:

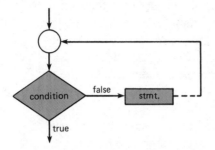

The program specification

> Until there is no more data, accumulate the sum of each data item.

is an example of an iteration structure. It involves a repetition of a procedure "accumulate the sum of the data items" so long as the test "no more data" is false. When the condition is true (i.e., when there is no more data to be processed) the loop is terminated and the next procedure is executed. In COBOL the PERFORM statement in Program 3.3 (line 33) on page 49 specifies the paragraph which contains the statements to be repeated (200-LOOP-CONTROL) and the condition (EOF-FLAG = 1). So long as the condition EOF-FLAG = 1 is false, the statements in 200-LOOP-CONTROL will be repeated. When the condition EOF-FLAG = 1 is true, the loop is terminated and the statement following the PERFORM statement is executed.

3.4 STRUCTURED PROGRAMMING STYLE

A major goal of structured programming is readability and ease of understanding. Unstructured programs sometimes get too complicated to be readable; one reason for this is the use of the unconditional branching statement GO TO. The GO TO statement causes a branch to a specified location within a program *with no provision for returning*. By contrast, the PERFORM statement causes a branch to a specified location, but when the paragraph is completed, control returns to the PERFORM statement. In a structured program, virtually all branching will be controlled by the PERFORM and IF statements. The GO TO statement, if used at all, is used in a very restricted and controlled manner, described later in this book. In fact, it is possible to write any program using only the three types of structures outlined above, and none of these structures requires the GO TO statement in COBOL implementation. For this reason structured programming is sometimes referred to as "go-to-less" programming; the avoidance of the use of the GO TO statement is an important principle of structured programming.

The goals of readability and ease of understanding lead to certain restrictions and practices in the coding of a structured COBOL program. For example, it is important to use meaningful names for data items, paragraphs and other names defined by the programmer. In COBOL, variable names and paragraph names may range in length from one to thirty characters, thus giving the programmer a wide latitude in the assignment of names. In a particular program, for example, a programmer might choose to call two variables X and Y, or he might choose PAY-RATE and HOURS-WORKED. It is obvious that the latter choice is more descriptive and would aid in understanding the type of data stored in each variable. In a similar spirit, the names of paragraphs should describe the functions performed in each paragraph. For example, in Program 3.4 on page 49 the paragraph names 100-MAJOR-LOGIC, 200-INITIALIZATION, 300-LOOP-CONTROL, 400-READ, 500-ACCUMULATE-SUM, 600-WRITE-DETAIL-LINE, and 700-END-OF-JOB were chosen to aid the reader in understanding the program. The paragraph numbers 100, 200, and so on help the reader to locate the paragraph quickly.

Comprehension and readability are enhanced considerably by the use of short single function paragraphs in a program. For example, Program 3.3 is rewritten in Program 3.4 to contain a number of short single function paragraphs. Note that Program 3.3 contains only two paragraphs, while Program 3.4 contains seven paragraphs. Which program do you find easier to read and understand? In this simple example you may prefer Program 3.3. However, as programs become longer and more complex the practice of coding reasonably short single function paragraphs can result in a more understandable and readable program. A rule of thumb is that no paragraph should be longer than one page of print or one screen of CRT display, whichever is appropriate. There is nothing to prevent paragraphs from being shorter to increase readability and understandability.

The discussion above suggests that there are good ways and not-so-good ways to write a correct COBOL program. Style is important in programming, as it is in writing reports, letters or novels. A good program is distinguished by more than correctness; the style in which it is written determines whether people can read and understand the program with ease. A well-written program is far more valuable than another program which, though it performs the same task, is written in a way which makes it unreadable and difficult to understand.

We cannot set down an exhaustive list of rules regarding style for writing a structured COBOL program, as there are no universally agreed-upon standards for style. You will find a number of programs in this text which, though imperfect, are written in "good" structured programming style. If you discover ways in which you can improve on our style, feel free to practice your improvements in your own programs. Any organization such as a large business which uses structured COBOL programming extensively will have a style book outlining rules and practices expected in coding programs at that installation.

In summary, the following rules form the bases for structured programming:

1) Use top-down program design techniques.

2) Use only the sequence, decision, and loop structures.

3) Use unconditional branching (the GO TO) with restraint if at all.

4) Follow standards of program readability and understandability.

By following the examples of structured COBOL programs in this text and applying the major rules above, you can become adept at writing structured COBOL programs. Although structured programming may place an added burden on you initially because you have to learn rules for structure as well as rules for COBOL language, the benefits of the structured approach far outweigh the disadvantages.

3.5 THE PERFORM Statement

The PERFORM statement causes a program to execute a paragraph and, when the paragraph is completed, to return either to the PERFORM statement itself or to the statement following the PERFORM statement. A general form for the PERFORM statement is:

> PERFORM   paragraph-name   [UNTIL condition   ]

Note the use of brackets ([ ]) in this general form. Brackets mean that the enclosed portion of the statement is optional.

If the UNTIL clause is omitted, the PERFORM statement causes the specified paragraph to be executed and, upon completion of that paragraph, control returns to the statement following the PERFORM statement. For example, in Program 3.1 the statement

        PERFORM 20-WRITE-SUMMARY-LINE

in the paragraph 10-MAIN-LOGIC causes the paragraph 20-WRITE-SUMMARY-LINE to be executed. The three sentences in the paragraph will be executed in sequential order; then, the statement immediately following the PERFORM statement will be executed. In flowchart form this structure would be shown as:

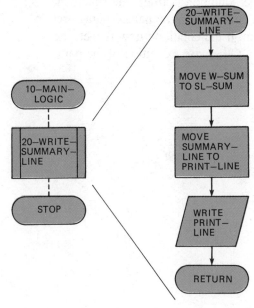

The result would be the same if the statements in the executed paragraph were inserted in place of the PERFORM statement. For example, consider the statement PERFORM 500-ACCUMULATE-SUM at line 43 of Program 3.4. The statement (line 49)

        ADD IR-NUMBER TO SUM-IT.

(which is the only statement in PERFORM 500-ACCUMULATION-SUM could be inserted in place of the statement PERFORM 500-ACCUMULATE-SUM) to give the same results. In general, if you wish to cause the execution of a paragraph one time, you will use the PERFORM statement without the UNTIL option.

Program 3.1   Example of the use of the PERFORM statement

```
10-MAIN-LOGIC
       .
       .
       .
      PERFORM 20-WRITE-SUMMARY-LINE.
       .
       .
       .
      STOP RUN.
20-WRITE-SUMMARY-LINE.
      MOVE W-SUM TO SL-SUM.
      MOVE SUMMARY-LINE TO PRINT-LINE.
      WRITE PRINT-LINE AFTER ADVANCING 2 LINES.
```

If, however, you desire to cause the execution of a paragraph to be repeated a number of times until some condition is satisfied, you include the UNTIL clause in the PERFORM statement. In this case the condition is tested before execution of the paragraph. If the condition is not met (the condition is false), the paragraph is executed. If the condition is met (the condition is true), the statement following the PERFORM statement is executed next. When the named paragraph has been executed, the condition is tested again; if the condition now is met, the statement following the PERFORM is executed. Otherwise execution of the paragraph is repeated.

Program 3.2   PERFORM/UNTIL program example

```
WORKING-STORAGE SECTION.
01 EOF-SWITCH PIC 9 VALUE ZERO.
      .
      .
      .
PROCEDURE DIVISION.
10-MAJOR-LOGIC.
      .
      .
      .
   PERFORM 20-LOOP-CONTROL UNTIL EOF-SWITCH = 1.
      .
      .
      .
   STOP RUN.
20-LOOP-CONTROL.
      .
      .
      .
   READ INPUT-FILE AT END MOVE 1 TO EOF-SWITCH
```

Program 3.2 illustrates the use of this version of the PERFORM statement. The condition being tested involves the value of a variable called EOF-SWITCH. A variable such as this is sometimes called a "program switch" because it has two values—0 and 1—in much the same way as a light switch has two positions—off and on. The value 0 corresponds to the switch being set in the "off" position; the value 1 represents the "on" position. Program switches are used as communications links among paragraphs of a program.

The program switch in Program 3.2 is used to detect when the last record from the input file has been read. So long as the last record has not been read, the switch remains in the "off" position. When the last record is read, the switch is turned to the "on" position. The occurrence of the reading of the last record is in the paragraph 20-LOOP-CONTROL; the fact that the last record has been read is communicated to the paragraph 10-MAJOR-LOGIC via the setting of the program switch EOF-SWITCH. The statement

```
PERFORM 20-LOOP-CONTROL UNTIL EOF-SWITCH = 1
```

will cause control to be passed to the paragraph 20-LOOP-CONTROL as long as the switch is "off" (i.e., it has value other than 1). The switch is in the "off" position in the WORKING-STORAGE SECTION where the data item is defined:

```
01 EOF-SWITCH PIC 9 VALUE ZERO.
```

The switch is turned to the "on" position in the paragraph 20-LOOP-CONTROL in the AT END clause of the READ statement. Figure 3.2 illustrates in flowchart form the logic of this use of the PERFORM statement. In general, any paragraph executed by a PERFORM/UNTIL statement must modify the condition being tested, or the program will enter an *infinite loop*. An infinite loop is formed when a sequence of statements is executed repeatedly with no possibility for the program to exit the sequence. Most computing systems contain provision for terminating programs after a reasonable period of time to protect the system from programs which are caught in an infinite loop.

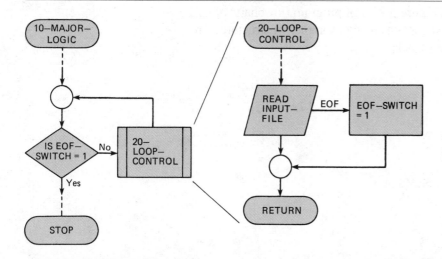

Figure 3.2 Flowchart of the PERFORM/UNTIL in Program 3.2

3.6   A COMPLETE EXAMPLE

The programs 3.3 and 3.4 list and calculate the sum of a sequence of values which are contained in a data file. Each record in the file contains one value.

Program 3.3 illustrates the process of accumulation, which is used to compute the sum of sequence of data items. The process essentially is one of maintaining a ''running'' total (i.e., adding one data item at a time into the total). In the beginning, a data item (SUM-IT) to be used to contain the total is assigned an initial value of zero; a data item used in this way is called an *accumulator*. When each data record is read, the data item from that record is added to the accumulator in the statement (line 45):

ADD IR-NUMBER TO SUM-IT

When all records have been read, the accumulator holds the accumulated sum of the values. A similar process can be used to count the occurrence of specific items, except that the value 1 is added to the accumulator. An accumulator used in this fashion is often referred to as a *counter*.

Program 3.4 contains Program 3.3 redone in an expanded modular form. Note that the PROCEDURE DIVISION of Program 3.3 contains two paragraphs, while Program 3.4 contains seven paragraphs. The 300-LOOP-CONTROL paragraph of Program 3.4 calls upon other paragraphs to do various functions, whereas in Program 3.3 instructions for these functions are written into the LOOP-CONTROL paragraph. For example, in place of the statement ADD IR-NUMBER TO SUM-IT (line 45 of Prog. 3.3) we find PERFORM 500-ACCUMULATE-SUM (line 43 of Prog. 3.4). The content of the paragraph 500-ACCUMULATE-SUM is the statement ADD IR-NUMBER TO SUM-IT (line 47 of Prog. 3.4).

The modular style used in Program 3.4 is the style preferred among most programmers. Each paragraph is concise and carries out a single well defined function; the name assigned to the paragraph is descriptive of the paragraph's function. The art of writing ''good'' structured programs begins with breaking down the task at hand into a manageable set of functions, each of which can be implemented in COBOL program by a paragraph of reasonable size and complexity. The result of this process is illustrated in terms of a program flowchart of each paragraph of Program 3.3 in Figure 3.7 by of program flowcharts of each paragraph. The remainder of this text contains many examples of structured programs which the reader should use as models.

Program 3.3   A Sample Accumulation

```
Line
  1     IDENTIFICATION DIVISION.
  2     PROGRAM-ID. PROGRAM 3.3
  3     AUTHOR. GARY GLEASON.
  4    *REMARKS. THIS PROGRAM SUMS A
  5    *          SERIES OF NUMBERS.
  6     ENVIRONMENT DIVISION.
  7     INPUT-OUTPUT SECTION.
  8     FILE-CONTROL.
  9         SELECT IN-FD ASSIGN TO DISK.
```

(continued)

Program 3.3 (continued)

```
10          SELECT PRINT ASSIGN TO PRINTER.
11     DATA DIVISION.
12     FILE SECTION.
13     FD  IN-FD
14          DATA RECORD IS INPUT-RECORD.
15     01   INPUT RECORD.
16          02  FILLER          PIC X(9).
17          02  IR-NUMBER       PIC 9(5).
18          02  FILLER          PIC X(66).
19     FD  PRINT
20          DATA RECORD IS PRINT-LINE.
21     01   PRINT-LINE          PIC X(132).
22     WORKING-STORAGE SECTION.
23     01   EOF-FLAG            PIC 9        VALUE ZERO.
24     01   SUM-IT             PIC 9(7)      VALUE ZERO.
25     01   DETAIL-LINE.
26          02  FILLER          PIC X(15)  VALUE SPACES.
27          02  DL-NUMBER       PIC ZZZZ9.
28     01   SUMMARY-LINE.
29          02  FILLER          PIC X(13)  VALUE SPACES.
30          02  SL-SUM          PIC ZZZZZ99.
31          02  FILLER          PIC X(7)   VALUE SPACES.
32          02  FILLER          PIC X(5)   VALUE SPACES.
33     PROCEDURE DIVISION.
34     100-MAIN-LOGIC.
35        OPEN INPUT IN-FD.
36        OPEN OUTPUT PRINT.
37        READ IN-FD AT END MOVE 1 TO EOF-FLAG.
38        PERFORM 200-LOOP-CONTROL UNTIL EOF-FLAG = 1.
39        MOVE SUM-IT TO SL-SUM.
40        MOVE SUMMARY-LINE TO PRINT-LINE.
41        WRITE PRINT-LINE AFTER ADVANCING 2 LINES.
42        CLOSE IN-FD, PRINT.
43        STOP RUN.
44     200-LOOP-CONTROL.
45        ADD IR-NUMBER TO SUM-IT.
46        MOVE IR-NUMBER TO SUM-T.
47        MOVE DETAIL-LINE TO PRINT-LINE.
48        WRITE PRINT-LINE AFTER ADVANCING 1 LINES.
49        READ IN-FD AT END MOVE 1 TO EOF-FLAG.
```

Program 3.4   Sample Accumulation in Modular Form

```
Line
 1     IDENTIFICATION DIVISION.
 2     PROGRAM-ID. PROGRAM 3.4
 3     AUTHOR. GARY GLEASON.
 4     *REMARKS.  THIS PROGRAM SUMS A
 5     *          SERIES OF NUMBERS.
 6     ENVIRONMENT DIVISION.
 7     INPUT-OUTPUT SECTION.
```

(continued)

Program 3.4   (continued)

```
 8     FILE-CONTROL.
 9          SELECT IN-FD ASSIGN TO DISK.
10          SELECT PRINT ASSIGN TO PRINTER.
11     DATA DIVISION.
12     FILE SECTION.
13     FD   IN-FD
14          DATA RECORD IS INPUT-RECORD.
15     01   INPUT RECORD.
16          02  FILLER           PIC X(9).
17          02  IR-NUMBER        PIC 9(5).
18          02  FILLER           PIC X(66).
19     FD   PRINT
20          DATA RECORD IS PRINT-LINE.
21     01   PRINT-LINE           PIC X(132).
22     WORKING-STORAGE SECTION.
23     01   EOF-FLAG             PIC 9        VALUE ZERO.
24     01   SUM-IT               PIC 9(7)     VALUE ZERO.
25     01   DETAIL-LINE.
26          02  FILLER           PIC X(15)    VALUE SPACES.
27          02  DL-NUMBER        PIC ZZZZ9.
28     01   SUMMARY-LINE.
29          02  FILLER           PIC X(13)    VALUE SPACES.
30          02  SD-SUM           PIC ZZZZZ99.
31          02  FILLER           PIC X(7)     VALUE SPACES.
32          02  FILLER           PIC X(5)     VALUE SPACES.
33     PROCEDURE DIVISION.
34     100-MAIN-LOGIC.
35          PERFORM 200-INITIALIZATION.
36          PERFORM 300-LOOP-CONTROL UNTIL EOF-FLAG = 1.
37          PERFORM 700-END-OF-JOB.
38     200-INITIALIZATION.
39          OPEN INPUT IN-FD.
40          OPEN OUTPUT PRINT.
41          PERFORM 400-READ.
42     300-LOOP-CONTROL.
43          PERFORM 500-ACCUMULATE-SUM.
44          PERFORM 600-WRITE-DETAIL-LINE.
45          PERFORM 400-READ.
46     400-READ.
47          READ IN-FD AT END MOVE 1 TO EOF-FLAG.
48     500-ACCUMULATE-SUM.
49          ADD IR-NUMBER TO SUM-IT.
50     600-WRITE-DETAIL-LINE.
51          MOVE IR-NUMBER TO DL-NUMBER.
52          MOVE DETAIL-LINE TO PRINT-LINE.
53          WRITE PRINT-LINE AFTER ADVANCING 1 LINES.
54     700-END-OF-JOB.
55          MOVE SUM-IT TO SL-SUM.
56          MOVE SUMMARY-LINE TO PRINT-LINE.
57          WRITE PRINT-LINE AFTER ADVANCING 2 LINES.
58          CLOSE IN-FD, PRINT.
59          STOP RUN.
```

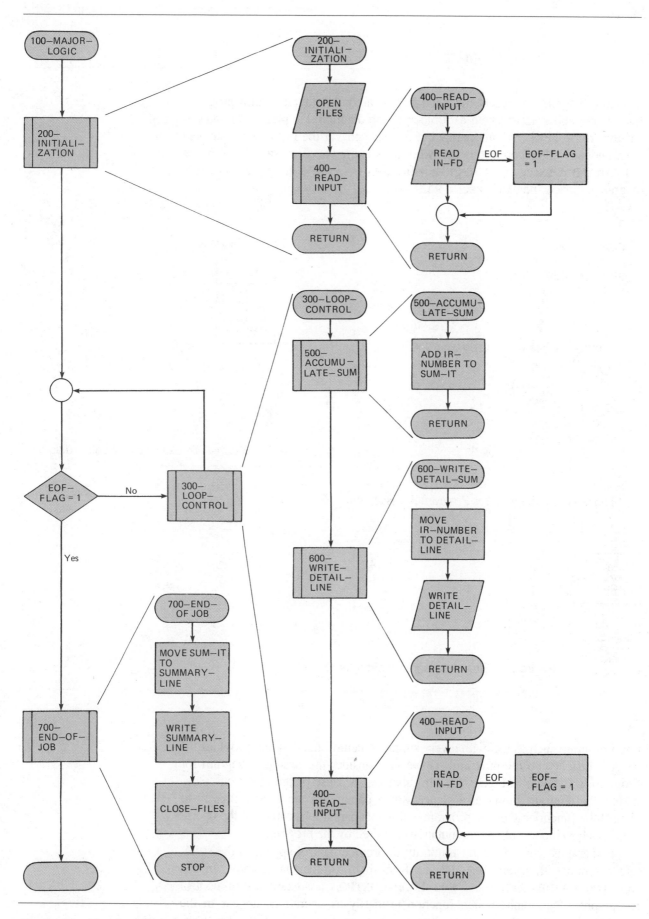

Figure 3.3 Flowchart for Program 3.3

3.7   STRUCTURE DIAGRAMS

Structure diagrams represent the relationships among paragraphs in a program. Each paragraph is represented as a block in the diagram; the paragraph name is written in the block. If one paragraph is executed via the PERFORM statement from another, a line connecting the two blocks is drawn. For example in Figure 3.4 PARA-B is executed (PERFORMed) from PARA-A, so a line in the structure diagram connects the block labeled PARA-B.

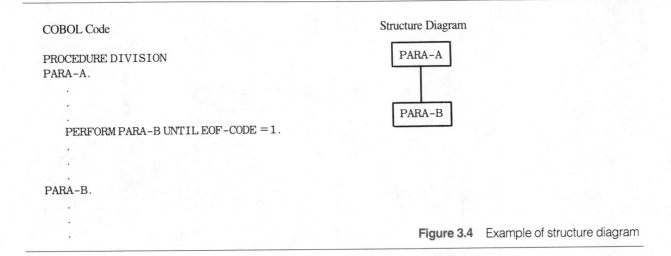

COBOL Code

PROCEDURE DIVISION
PARA-A.
    .
    .
    .

    PERFORM PARA-B UNTIL EOF-CODE = 1.
    .
    .

    .
PARA-B.
    .
    .
    .

Structure Diagram

Figure 3.4   Example of structure diagram

The structure diagram for Program 3.3 is shown in Figure 3.5.

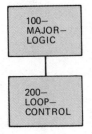

Figure 3.5   Structure diagram for Program 3.3

For a program such as this with a very simple structure, the diagram provides little new insight into the program. However, consider the structure diagram for Program 3.4 shown in Figure 3.6. In this case, because of the numerous paragraphs the diagram shows at a glance which paragraphs are used primarily to control the functioning of the program and which paragraphs carry out the operations (such as input, output, computation) required by the program.

Paragraphs which function primarily to provide control appear in the structure diagram with several lines leading from them to other paragraphs. In this case 100-MAJOR-LOGIC and 300-LOOP-CONTROL are examples of control paragraphs. Paragraphs which function primarily as operations appear in the structure diagram with few or no lines leading from them. In this case 200-

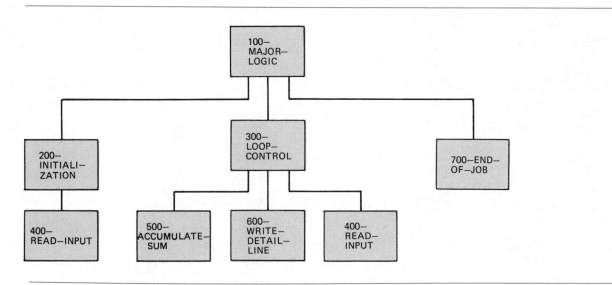

Figure 3.6 Structure diagram for Program 3.4

INITIALIZATION, 400-READ, 500-ACCUMULATE-SUM, 600-WRITE-DETAIL-LINE and 700-END-OF-JOB are operational paragraphs.

A structure diagram clearly shows the hierarchy into which paragraphs of a program are divided. A paragraph which is executed from a paragraph directly via a PERFORM, or indirectly by way of a paragraph which is PERFORMed, is *subordinate* to that paragraph. Thus, in Figure 3.5, it is clear that all other paragraphs are subordinate to 100-MAJOR-LOGIC while 500-ACCUMULATE-SUM, 600-WRITE-DETAIL-LINE, and 400-READ are subordinate to 300-LOOP-CONTROL.

3.8 DEBUG CLINIC

The PERFORM Statement

A fundamental restriction on the use of the PERFORM statement is that no paragraph may PERFORM itself. The following code would be invalid:

In general COBOL compilers will not detect violations of this rule; however, when the program is executed an infinite loop will result.

A more general restriction on the PERFORM statement is that no paragraph may PERFORM another paragraph which results in a PERFORM of the original paragraph. For example, consider the following code:

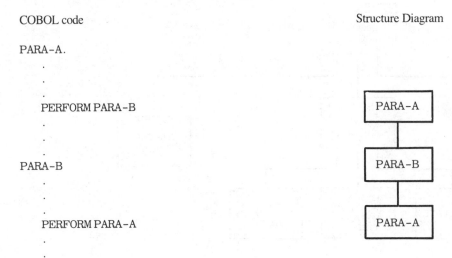

COBOL code

PARA-A.

    PERFORM PARA-B

PARA-B

    PERFORM PARA-A

PARA-A PERFORMs PARA-B which in turn PERFORMs PARA-A. As before, this code results in the creation of an infinite loop during execution. The error is perhaps more obvious from the structure diagram than from the COBOL code itself. This does not mean that a given paragraph may not occur several times in the structure diagram. For example, in Figure 3.5 400-READ occurs twice; the first time it is subordinate to 200-INITIALIZATION; the second time it is subordinate to 300-LOOP-CONTROL. However, note that in Figure 3.5, no paragraph is subordinate to itself.

Program Structure

As we discussed earlier, constructing "good" structured programs is as much an art as a science; however, certain guidelines should be observed. We have already discussed some of them: use of three fundamental structures; use of descriptive data-names and paragraph-names; segmentation of the program into control and operational paragraphs; and so on. The segmentation of a program has been the subject of a great deal of research, with the result that there is now general agreement on two principles, both of which have close analogs in organization theory.

In an organization, a manager should not be responsible for too many subordinates. The manager's "span of control" reaches an optimal limit; it is counterproductive to ask a manager to control more than that limit. In a similar way a control paragraph in a COBOL program has maximum "span of control". There is a limit to the number of subordinate paragraphs which a given paragraph should control directly. A structure diagram such as

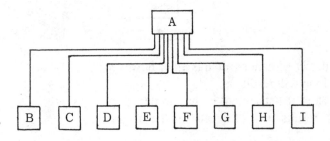

probably represents a paragraph with too many subordinates; its span of control is too large. It would be better to substitute an organization such as

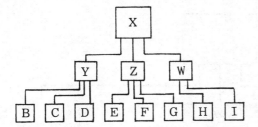

in which each control paragraph has a more restricted span of control.

There is no general agreement as to the number of paragraphs which represents an appropriate span of control in a COBOL program. It seems clear that ten subordinates are probably too many, but where the line is drawn is a matter of personal opinion.

In a management hierarchy there are levels ranging from the chief executive officer at the top through various levels of middle management to the lowest level employee. As the number of levels of bureaucracy grows, problems of communication and control may develop. In a similar way, problems of communication and control may develop within a COBOL program which has too many levels of subordination. Thus, a structure such as

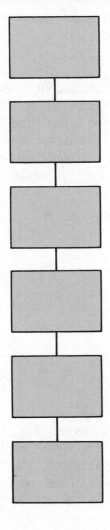

which has six levels should probably be redesigned to have fewer levels. A structure such as

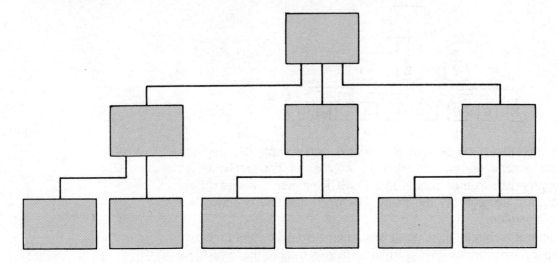

which has only three levels is preferable to the six-level structure above.

The COBOL programmer should analyze the structure diagrams of programs he or she writes to determine if each control paragraph has an appropriate span of control, and if there are an appropriate number of levels of subordination within the program. It is usually possible to redesign any program which fails either of these tests.

Loop Control

In a structured program, loops are created by the iteration structure implemented in COBOL by the PERFORM/UNTIL statement. Recall that PERFORM/UNTIL causes execution of the specified paragraph until a condition is met. There are three possible errors which may occur: the paragraph is never executed at all; the paragraph is execute exactly one time; and the paragraph is executed continuously without a proper end, creating an infinite loop. Consider the PERFORM/UNTIL statement from Program 3.4:

```
PERFORM 300-LOOP-CONTROL UNTIL EOF-FLAG = 1.
```

In flowchart form this would appear as

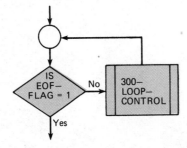

In one instance, suppose analysis of output from the program showed that the paragraph 300-LOOP-CONTROL was never executed at all. What would be the probable cause? The only reason is that EOF-FLAG is equal to 1. This could happen in one of two ways: either the initial value of EOF-FLAG was specified to be 1 in WORKING-STORAGE; or the program has caused the value of EOF-FLAG to become 1 prior to execution of the PERFORM/UNTIL statement. A probable cause of this latter condition is that there were no records in the file so that when 400-READ is PERFORMed in 200-INITIALIZATION (Prog. 3.4, line 45), the AT END clause on the READ statement causes the value 1 to be moved to EOF-FLAG. In the first case the programmer should rewrite the definition of EOF-FLAG in WORKING-STORAGE; in the second case he or she must ensure that there are records in the file to be processed.

On the other hand, suppose analysis of the output showed that the paragraph 300-LOOP-CONTROL was executed exactly one time. If there was only one record in the file being processed, this is obviously the way the program should behave. If, however, there was more than one record in the file, there is an error in the program. One likely source of error is the omission of the UNTIL clause on the PERFORM statement. The statement PERFORM 300-LOOP-CONTROL would cause 300-LOOP-CONTROL to be executed exactly one time. If the UNTIL clause is in its proper place, another cause for this error would be a statement within 300-LOOP-CONTROL which sets the value of EOF-FLAG to 1 by mistake.

Or, suppose analysis of the output from the program led us to believe that the program had entered an infinite loop. For example, the program has been terminated because of excessive elapsed time or a message has been produced indicating that an attempt has been made to read past end-of-file (i.e., an attempt to read more records than the file contained). If the value of EOF-FLAG never becomes 1, the PERFORM/UNTIL statement will cause 300-LOOP-CONTROL to be executed forever.

There are two possible causes for this condition; either the READ operation has been omitted within 300-LOOP-CONTROL; or the AT END clause on the READ statement does not set EOF-FLAG equal to 1. Omission of the READ operation within the loop will cause the program to appear to process the first record again and again. This is the most probable cause if the program terminates because of excessive time used. Failure of the program to set EOF-FLAG to 1 when end-of-file is reached will generally result in an attempt to read past end-of-file.

3.9 SELF TEST EXERCISES

1. List the three program structures used in structured programming and draw program flowcharts illustrating them.
2. What purpose do the numbers used with paragraph names have? Are the numbers required by COBOL syntax or are they a part of structured programming style?
3. What is a "switch"? Why are switches used?
4. What is an "accumulator"? Why are accumulators used?
5. Rewrite the PROCEDURE DIVISION of Program 2.1 in the modular form described in this chapter. Draw the associated structure diagram. Classify each paragraph as providing a control or operation function.
6. The PROCEDURE DIVISION of Program 2.1 has been rewritten in Program 3.5. Find logical errors in the code.

Program 3.5

```
Line
  1        PROCEDURE DIVISION.
  2        100-MAIN-LOGIC.
  3            PERFORM 200-INITIALIZATION.
  4            PERFORM 300-BUILD-FILE.
  5            PERFORM 500-TERMINATE.
  6        200-INITIALIZATION.
  7            OPEN INPUT INPUT-FILE
  8                 OUTPUT OUTPUT-FILE.
  9            PERFORM 400-READ-INPUT-FILE.
 10        300-BUILD-FILE.
 11            MOVE INPUT-REC TO OUTPUT-REC.
 12            WRITE OUTPUT-REC.
 13        400-READ-INPUT-FILE.
 14            READ INPUT-FILE
 15                 AT END MOVE "YES" TO END-OF-FILE
 16        500-TERMINATE.
 17            CLOSE INPUT-FILE
 18                  OUTPUT-FILE.
 19            STOP RUN.
```

3.10   PROGRAMMING EXERCISES

1. Rewrite the program assigned to you from Chapter 2 in the modular form described in this chapter.

2. A file contains daily sales records for a small retail business. The format for each record is

positions	
1-4	Department number
5-10	Date
11-15	Amount of sale

Write a program to list these records with appropriate headings. Compute the total of the sale amounts and print a line at the conclusion of the report containing this total.

3. A real estate office maintains a file containing a record for each property it handles. The records have the following format:

Positions	
1-10	Multiple Listing Service Number (MLS Number)
11-18	Sale price

Write a program to compute and print the total price for the properties, and the total number of properties. Use the following test data:

MLS Number	Sale Price
0123456789	$45,000.00
1111111111	$95,950.00
2222222222	$135,760.00

INPUT, OUTPUT, AND DATA MOVEMENT 4

4.1 PROGRAM EXAMPLE

The ABC Department Store maintains an inventory file showing the stock number, description, quantity on hand and unit cost for each item it stocks. The sales clerks need a listing of the file so that they can ascertain quickly the availability of items. The purchasing agent needs a listing of the file to aid in making decisions on which items should be reordered. The president of the store has expressed curiosity about the total number of different items carried by the store; he feels the information could be used in an advertising campaign he is planning.

Program 4.1 produces a report which could be used for all these purposes. Note that the report is made up of the following elements:

Major headings
Column headings
Detail lines
Summary line

Program 4.1 Monthly inventory program

```
Line
1         IDENTIFICATION DIVISION.
2         PROGRAM-ID. CHAPTER 4 EXAMPLE 1.
3         AUTHOR.  GARY GLEASON.
4         *REMARKS.
5         *         THIS PROGRAM COULD BE USED BY
6         *         A RETAIL STORE TO DETERMINE THE
7         *         INVENTORY OF SELECTED ITEMS
8         *         IN STOCK.
9         ENVIRONMENT DIVISION.
10        CONFIGURATION SECTION.
11        INPUT-OUTPUT SECTION.
12        FILE-CONTROL.
13            SELECT IN-FD ASSIGN TO DISK.
```

(continued)

Program 4.1 (continued)

```
14                SELECT PRINT ASSIGN TO PRINTER.
15        DATA DIVISION.
16        FILE SECTION.
17        FD  IN-FD
18            DATA RECORD IS INPUT-RECORD.
19        01  INPUT-RECORD.
20            02  IR-STOCK NUMBER  PIC 9(5).
21            02  IR-DESCRIPTION   PIC X(20).
22            02  IR-QUANTITY      PIC 9(3).
23            02  IR-UNIT-COST     PIC 999V99.
24            02  FILLER           PIC X(47).
25        FD  PRINT
26            DATA RECORD IS PRINT-LINE.
27        01  PRINT-LINE           PIC X(132).
28        WORKING-STORAGE SECTION.
29        01  EOF-FLAG             PIC 9   VALUE ZERO.
30        01  RECORDS-IN           PIC 9(5) VALUE ZERO.
31        01  MAJOR-HEADING.
32            02  FILLER  PIC X(27)  VALUE SPACES.
33            02  FILLER  PIC X(30)  VALUE
34            "ABC DEPARTMENT STORE INVENTORY".
35        01  MINOR-HEADING.
36            02  FILLER  PIC X(15)  VALUE SPACES.
37            02  FILLER  PIC X(12)  VALUE "STOCK NUMBER".
38            02  FILLER  PIC X(10)  VALUE SPACES.
39            02  FILLER  PIC X(11)  VALUE "DESCRIPTION".
40            02  FILLER  PIC X(10)  VALUE SPACES.
41            02  FILLER  PIC X(8)   VALUE "QUANTITY".
42            02  FILLER  PIC X(10)  VALUE SPACES.
43            02  FILLER  PIC X(9)   VALUE "UNIT COST".
44        01  DETAIL-LINE.
45            02  FILLER           PIC X(15)  VALUE SPACES.
46            02  DL-STOCK-NUMBER  PIC ZZZZ9.
47            02  FILLER           PIC X(17)  VALUE SPACES.
48            02  DL-DESCRIPTION   PIC X(20).
49            02  DL-QUANTITY      PIC ZZ9.
50            02  FILLER           PIC X(15)  VALUE SPACES.
51            02  DL-UNIT-COST     PIC $ZZZ.99.
52        01  TOTAL-LINE.
53            02  FILLER           PIC X   VALUE SPACES.
54            02  FILLER PIC X(27) VALUE "NUMBER OF ITEMS PROCESSED = ".
55            02  FILLER           PIC X(4)  VALUE SPACES.
56            02  RECORDS-IN-TL    PIC Z(5).
57        PROCEDURE DIVISION.
58        100-MAIN-LOGIC.
59            PERFORM 200-INITIALIZATION.
60            PERFORM 300-LOOP-CONTROL UNTIL EOF-FLAG = 1.
61            PERFORM 700-TERMINATION.
62        200-INITIALIZATION.
63            OPEN INPUT IN-FD.
64            OPEN OUTPUT PRINT.
65            MOVE MAJOR-HEADING TO PRINT-LINE.
```

(continued)

Program 4.1 (continued)

```
66              WRITE PRINT-LINE AFTER PAGE.
67              MOVE MINOR-HEADING TO PRINT-LINE.
68              WRITE PRINT-LINE AFTER 2 LINES.
69              PERFORM 400-READ.
70          300-LOOP-CONTROL.
71              ADD 1 TO RECORDS-IN.
72              PERFORM 500-RECORD-DETAIL-LINE.
73              PERFORM 600-WRITE-DETAIL-LINE.
74              PERFORM 400-READ.
75          400-READ.
76              READ IN-FD AT END MOVE 1 TO EOF-FLAG.
77          500-RECORD-DETAIL-LINE.
78              MOVE IR-STOCK-NUMBER   TO  DL-STOCK-NUMBER.
79              MOVE IR-DESCRIPTION    TO  DL-DESCRIPTION.
80              MOVE IR-QUANTITY       TO  DL-QUANTITY.
81              MOVE IR-UNIT-COST      TO  DL-UNIT-COST.
82          600-WRITE-DETAIL-LINE.
83              MOVE DETAIL-LINE TO PRINT-LINE.
84              WRITE PRINT-LINE AFTER 2.
85          700-TERMINATION.
86              MOVE RECORDS-IN TO RECORDS-IN-TL.
87              WRITE PRINT-LINE FROM TOTAL-LINE AFTER 2.
88              CLOSE IN-FD, PRINT.
89              STOP RUN.
```

Sample Output From Monthly Inventory Program

ABC DEPARTMENT STORE INVENTORY

STOCK NUMBER	DESCRIPTION	QUANTITY	UNIT COST
11111	SHIRTS	3	$ 15.00
22222	SHOES	10	$ 30.00
33333	SOCKS	50	$ 2.00

NUMBER OF ITEMS PROCESSED =   3

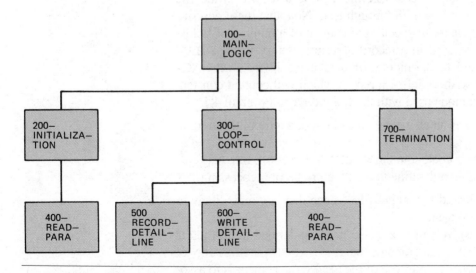

Figure 4.1   Structure diagram for monthly inventory program (Program 4.1)

This organization is quite typical of most reports written for business purposes.

Figure 4.1 shows the structure diagram for this program. Note that the output routines (600-WRITE-DETAIL-LINE and 500-RECORD-DETAIL-LINE) involve several statements. Structuring these routines as separate paragraphs aids in keeping the paragraphs containing the primary logic of the program (100-MAIN-LOGIC and 300-LOOP-CONTROL) simple, short and easy to understand.

4.2   THE FD AND SELECT ENTRIES

One FD entry is required in the FILE SECTION of the DATA DIVISION for each file to be processed. A general form for the FD entry is:

```
FD    file-name
      DATA  RECORD  IS record-name.
01    record-name [data-description-entry].
```

For example, Program 4.1 will process two files, so two FD entries are required: one for the file IN-FD (lines 17 through 24) and one for the file PRINT (lines 25 through 27). A record description must be provided in the FD entry. The record description may be quite simple, such as the description of the record PRINT-LINE (line 27) as a sequence of 132 characters, or complex such as the description of the record INPUT-RECORD (lines 19 through 24) which is subdivided into a number of fields.

In general a record will contain several fields. If the description of these fields is not written in the FD entry, then it is written as a part of WORKING-STORAGE. This approach is used with the file PRINT in Program 4.1. There are four different types of output records for this file. The description of these records MAJOR-HEADING (lines 31 through 34), MINOR-HEADING (lines 35 through 43), DETAIL-LINE (lines 44 through 51) and TOTAL-LINE (lines 52 through 56) is placed in the WORKING-STORAGE SECTION. The program moves the appropriate record to the output record before writing a record on the file PRINT (for example, lines 65, 67, and 78 through 81). Note that these descriptions make use of the VALUE clause to specify the content of a number of fields. The VALUE clause may *not* be used in a record-description-entry in the FILE-SECTION; its use is restricted to definitions of data items in the WORKING-STORAGE SECTION. If you wish to define a record which will contain constant data, you will employ the technique used with the file PRINT in Program 4.1:

1) Define the data-record as an elementary data item of appropriate length in the FD entry.
2) Define records and their content in the WORKING-STORAGE SECTION.
3) Move data to the data-record define in the FD entry before processing.

Usually this procedure is followed for output files, since they are most likely to contain records having constant data.

Every file to be processed by a program also must be defined in a SELECT statement in the FILE-CONTROL paragraph of the INPUT-OUTPUT SECTION of the ENVIRONMENT DIVISION. The purpose of the SELECT statement is to associate the file with a particular type of physical device. The general form of the

SELECT statement is:

> <u>SELECT</u> file-name <u>ASSIGN</u> TO system-name.

For example, in Program 4.1, the file `IN-FD` is associated with a disk file in the statement

    SELECT IN-FD ASSIGN TO DISK.

The particular system-names associated with particular devices vary from one compiler to another. The student must check with his instructor or with his local system manual to find out what system-names to use.

4.3   THE OPEN AND CLOSE STATEMENTS

Before any file in a program can be processed, it must be opened. The OPEN statement causes the computing system to perform various initialization procedures required before the file can be processed. The general form of the OPEN statement is:

> <u>OPEN</u> $\begin{Bmatrix} \underline{INPUT} \\ \underline{OUTPUT} \end{Bmatrix}$ file-name . . .

The programmer must specify whether a file is being opened as an INPUT or an OUTPUT file. It is permissible to READ records from a file opened as an INPUT file, and it is permissible to WRITE records onto a file opened as an OUTPUT file. It is not permissable to WRITE a record onto a file opened as INPUT or to READ a record from a file opened as OUTPUT; an attempt to perform either of these operations will result in an execution time diagnostic message and the program will be cancelled.

Example

To open the `INCOME-RECORDS` as in INPUT file, use the statement

    OPEN INPUT INCOME-RECORDS.

To open the file `PRINTED-OUTPUT` as an OUTPUT file, use the statement

    OPEN OUTPUT PRINTED-OUTPUT.

More than one file at a time may be opened by an OPEN statement. For example, the statement

    OPEN OUTPUT PRINT-OUTPUT, TAPE-OUTPUT.

will cause the files `PRINT-OUTPUT` and `TAPE-OUTPUT` to be opened as OUTPUT files.

The CLOSE statement causes a file to become unavailable for further processing. Any file which is opened in a program should also be closed before the program terminates. The general form of the CLOSE statement is:

> <u>CLOSE</u>   file-name . . .

One or more files may be closed in a CLOSE statement. Consider, for example the following CLOSE statements:

```
CLOSE INPUT-FILE OUTPUT-FILE.     (2 files are closed)
CLOSE PRINT. (1 file is closed)
```

Any file that has not been opened is assumed to be closed. A file may be opened and closed any number of times in a program. However, a file must be closed before it can be opened. In a typical file processing program such as the one shown in Program 4.1, files are opened (200-INITIALIZATION) and processed (300-LOOP-CONTROL). After all inputs and outputs have been performed, the files are closed (700-TERMINATION).

4.4   THE READ STATEMENT

A READ statement causes the computer to read one record from a specified file. The contents of the record are placed in the record area specified in the FD entry for the file. A general form for the READ statement is:

> READ   file-name { into DATA-NAME } AT   END   statement...

The file addressed in a READ statement must be currently opened as an INPUT file. When the end-of-file record is read, the statement(s) at the AT END clause of the statment are executed. For example, the statement

        READ IN-FD AT END CLOSE IN-FD STOP RUN.

will cause the statements CLOSE IN-FD and STOP RUN to be executed when the end-of-file record on IN-FILE is read. In a structured program a switch is often set when the end-of-file record is read. (A switch is a data item which has only two possible values, e.g., 1 and 0, "yes" and "no", "on" and "off.") A typical READ statement in a structured program would be:

        READ IN-FD AT END MOVE 1 TO EOF-FLAG.

The contents of the switch (EOF-FLAG in this case) can be tested in subsequent instructions to determine whether the record read should be processed (if it is not the end-of-file record) or whether processing should be terminated (if end-of-file has been reached). See, for example, the paragraph (100-MAIN-LOGIC) in Program 4.1.

When the INTO clause is included on a READ statement, data is placed in the record area specified in the FD entry for the file and also into the specified data-name. This feature often is used to allow the placement of a detailed description of an input record into the WORKING-STORAGE section. For example, in Program 4.1 the FD entry for the file IN-FD could be rewritten as:

```
FD   IN-FD
     DATA RECORD IS IN-RECORD.
01   IN-RECORD PICTURE X(80).
```

The following entries (which define the fields contained on the record) could be added to the WORKING-STORAGE section:

        01   IN-RECORD-DESCRIPTION.

```
02   IR-STOCK-NUMBER      PICTURE 9(5).
02   IR-DESCRIPTION       PICTURE X(20).
02   IR-QUANTITY          PICTURE 9(3).
02   IR-UNIT-COST         PICTURE 999V99.
02   IR-FILLER            PICTURE X(47).
```

With these changes, the READ statement at line 76 in (Prog. 4-1) would be changed to:

    READ IN-FD INTO IN-RECORD-DESRIPTION AT END MOVE 1 TO EOF-FLAG.

Data would be placed into the input record IN-RECORD *and* into IN-RECORD-DESCRIPTION.

4.5   THE MOVE STATEMENT

The MOVE statement causes the transfer of data from one location in memory to another. The general form of the MOVE statement is:

> MOVE   data-name TO data-name. . .

The data at the location from which the information is moved (the sending item) is not changed; the data at the target location (the receiving item) is replaced by new data. For example, suppose FLDA and FLDB are as shown in Figure 4.2 below. After execution of the statement

    MOVE FLDA TO FLDB
           ↗   ↖
        sending   receiving
        item   item

the contents of FLDA is unchanged; the contents of FLDB is the same as FLDA. More than one item may be designated as a receiving item. In this case the contents of the sending item are moved to each of the receiving items. For example, the statement

        MOVE FLDA TO FLDB, FLDC, FLDD.

will cause FLDB, FLDC and FLDD to receive identical data from FLDA.

Contents before MOVE

    FLDA   FLDB

    |J|O|E| | | |X|Y|Z|W| |

Contents after MOVE

    FLDA   FLDB

Figure 4.2   Results of the execution of MOVE FLDA TO FLDB

    |J|O|E| | | |J|O|E| | |

4.6   THE WRITE STATEMENT

The WRITE statement causes one record to be written onto an output file. The general form of the WRITE statement is shown in Figure 4.3.

WRITE   record-name   [FROM   data-name] $\begin{Bmatrix} \text{AFTER} \\ \text{BEFORE} \end{Bmatrix}$ ADVANCING $\begin{Bmatrix} \text{integer LINES} \\ \text{PAGE} \end{Bmatrix}$

Figure 4.3   General form of the WRITE statement

Remember that the WRITE statement always addresses a record, while a READ statement addresses a file. The *record-name* used in the WRITE statement must be the same as the record declared in the FD entry for the file. The contents of the record are transferred to the appropriate file. The file addressed in a WRITE statement must be currently open.

If the printer is the device assigned to the file, the AFTER/BEFORE clause is used to specify the vertical spacing of the printed output line. The AFTER option causes vertical spacing to be performed prior to writing a new line. The BEFORE option causes the line to be written first, and then the vertical spacing is performed. In either case the PAGE entry will cause the advancement of paper to the top of a new page; the use of an integer (such as 0, 1, 2, 3) causes the printer to skip the specified number of lines.

Data to be written onto a file must be present in the output record area before the WRITE statement is executed. In Program 4.1 there are four types of output lines defined in the WORKING-STORAGE SECTION: MAJOR-HEADING (line 31), MINOR-HEADING (line 38), DETAIL-LINE (line 44) and TOTAL-LINE (line 52). Prior to the WRITE operation for the first three types of lines, the contents of each appropriate output line are moved to the output record area. For example, in lines 65 and 66 one finds:

```
MOVE MAJOR-HEADING TO PRINT-LINE.
WRITE PRINT-LINE AFTER PAGE.
```

Use of the FROM clause can simplify output operations of this type. When the FROM clause is included, the contents of the designated data-name are automatically moved to the output record area before the WRITE operation is performed. For example, the two statements above could be combined as follows:

```
WRITE PRINT-LINE FROM MAJOR-HEADING AFTER PAGE.
```

The contents of MAJOR-HEADING are moved to PRINT-LINE before the output record is written. The FROM clause is used in Program 4.1 in writing the TOTAL-LINE (line 87):

```
WRITE PRINT-LINE FROM TOTAL-LINE AFTER 2.
```

4.7   DATA TYPES

Any field may be classified either 1) alphabetic, 2) numeric, 3) alphanumeric, or 4) report, depending on the type of picture codes used in the PICTURE clause associated with the field. An alphabetic field must contain only alphabetic characters or blanks. An alphabetic field is defined using the picture code A. Examples are:

```
03  CITY  PIC AAAAAAAAAA.
03  NAME  PIC A(20).
```

Both CITY and NAME are defined to be alphabetic data items; CITY is a field containing ten characters, while NAME contains twenty characters.

A numeric field may contain only numeric data. A numeric field is defined using the picture codes 9, V, and S. The 9 specifies a numeric digit, (i.e., a single number). The V specifies the position of the decimal point. The S specifies that the item is to be signed (i.e., may become negative).

Example

```
03 SAL-CODE PIC 9.
```

SAL-CODE is a one-digit numeric field. For instance salary paid for a particular project is coded as a single-digit ''6''.

```
03 SALARY PIC 999V99.
```

SALARY is a five-digit field such as 423.78 (dollars). The decimal point is assumed to be placed between the third and fourth digits. Note that such salaries cannot be negative.

```
01 AMOUNT PIC S9(4)V9(3).
```

AMOUNT is a seven-digit field. The decimal point is placed between the fourth and fifth digits. The item may become negative since the S is present. (If an S is not present in the picture codes of a numeric item, then the item is assumed always to be positive.) If used, an S must precede other codes used in describing the item. In Program 4.1, IR-QUANTITY (line 22), IR-UNIT-COST (line 23), EOF-FLAG (line 29), and RECORDS-IN (line 30) are numeric items.

An alphanumeric field may contain any string of numeric, alphabetic, or special characters. Alphanumeric fields may be defined in two ways:

1) All group items are considered as alphanumeric regardless of the definition of the elementary items in the group. Recall that a group item is an item which is subdivided into one or more elementary data items. The specification of group items does not contain a PICTURE clause. For example, in Program 4.1 MAJOR-HEADING, MINOR-HEADING, DETAIL-LINE, TOTAL-LINE and INPUT-RECORD are group items and, hence, are classed as alphanumeric.

2) Fields defined using the picture code X are alphanumeric. The X represents an alphanumeric character. For example, in Program 4.1 IR-DESCRIPTION (line 21), PRINT-LINE (line 27), and all of the FILLER entries are alphanumeric because of the picture code X.

Fields defined using the picture codes Z, ., $, and so on are report-type items. The purpose of these codes is to prepare a numeric item for readability on a report. For example, in Program 4.1, the items DL-STOCK-NUMBER (line 46), DL-QUANTITY (line 49), DL-UNIT-COST (line 51) and RECORDS-IN-TL (line 56) are given report-type pictures and hence are nonnumeric items. The Z provides for the substitution of a blank in place of a nonsignificant leading zero.

The decimal point is inserted in place of the assumed position of the decimal point. The $ is printed to label items which represent dollar amounts.

Arithmetic operations can be performed only on numeric type data items. Arithmetic operations, therefore, cannot be performed on data items which are alphabetic or alphanumeric.

4.8 DATA MOVEMENT

Programming involves moving a lot of data around. Sometimes you have to move alphanumeric data from one data item to another; more often you have to move numeric data to a report-type field. All would be easy enough if the receiving fields always have as many characters (or elements, or numbers, or letters) as did the data, but that does not always happen. For instance, a check writing machine in a major Blue Cross plan does not have very many spaces assigned for the name of the person receiving the check. So instead of his full name, which the computer has in its subscriber file—properly spelled and listed with his address and policy number—Alphonse Hornswogger will get a check made out to HORNS, A. Clearly, the data item in the check writing program has fewer spaces than the name file in the program feeding it.* The rules for fitting data into spaces too large or too small depend on the kind of data you are dealing with, as detailed below.

When alphabetic and alphanumeric data are moved from one field to another, characters are moved from left to right. If the sending field and receiving field have exactly the same length, the receiving field becomes an exact duplicate of the sending field.

Example

```
MOVE FLDA TO FLDB.

 A  B  C  D              A  B  C  D 

FLDA PIC A(4)        FLDB PIC A(4)
```

If the receiving field is longer than the sending field, blanks are added to the right most positions of the receiving field.

Example

```
MOVE FLDA TO FLDB.

 1  A  3  B              1  A  3  B         These blanks are inserted
                                            because FLDB is longer
FLDA PIC X(4)        FLDB PIC X(6)      than FLDA
```

If the receiving field is shorter than the sending field, the *rightmost* characters are truncated.

---

*Hornswogger endorses his check by writing HORNS, A. first; then underneath it, he writes his full and correct name. Can truncating (cutting off) a name lead to confusion? No, because the Blue Cross computer is really reading the subscriber account number-for which there are always enough data spaces. It does not pay much attention to Mr. Hornswogger's name.

Example

MOVE FLDA TO FLDB.

⌐1‚A‚3‚B¬   ⌐1‚A¬

FLDA PIC X(4)   FLDB PIC XX

When numeric data is moved to a numeric type data item, the digits to
the left of the decimal point are moved from right to left. If the receiving
field is too short, truncation of excess *leftmost* digits will be performed. If
the receiving field is too long, zeros will be inserted in the unused leftmost
digits.

Example

MOVE FLDA TO FLDB.

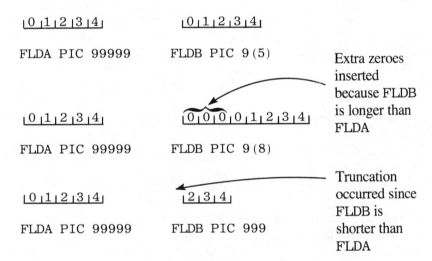

⌐0‚1‚2‚3‚4¬   ⌐0‚1‚2‚3‚4¬

FLDA PIC 99999   FLDB PIC 9(5)   Extra zeroes
                                           inserted
                                           because FLDB
⌐0‚1‚2‚3‚4¬   ⌐0‚0‚0‚0‚1‚2‚3‚4¬   is longer than
                                           FLDA
FLDA PIC 99999   FLDB PIC 9(8)

                                           Truncation
⌐0‚1‚2‚3‚4¬   ⌐2‚3‚4¬   occurred since
                                           FLDB is
FLDA PIC 99999   FLDB PIC 999   shorter than
                                           FLDA

Digits to the right of the decimal point are moved from left to right. If
the receiving field is too short, truncation of excess *rightmost* digits will be
performed. If the receiving field is too long, zeroes will be inserted in the
unused leftmost digits.

Example

MOVE FLDA TO FLDB.

⌐1‚2‚3‚0¬   ⌐1‚2‚3‚0¬

FLDA PIC V9999   FLDB PIC V9(4)   Extra zeroes
                                           inserted since
                                           FLDB is
⌐1‚2‚3‚0¬   ⌐1‚2‚3‚0‚0‚0¬   longer than
                                           FLDA
FLDA PIC V9999   FLDB PIC V9(6)

                                           Truncation of
                                           rightmost digits
⌐1‚2‚3‚0¬   ⌐1‚2¬   occurred since
                                           FLDB is
FLDA PIC V9999   FLDB PIC V99   shorter than
                                           FLDA

Decimal points in two numeric fields are aligned before transferring digits in the MOVE operation. Transfers of digits to the left and to the right of the decimal point are carried out independently.

MOVE FLDA TO FLDB

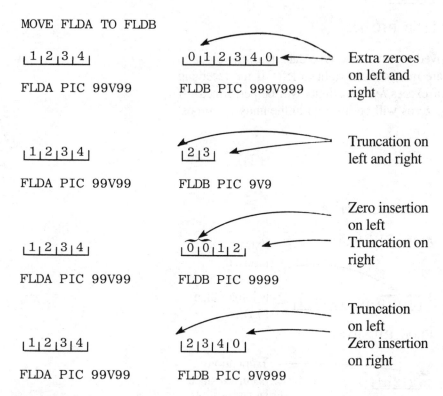

| $\lfloor 1_\vert 2_\vert 3_\vert 4 \rfloor$ | $\lfloor 0_\vert 1_\vert 2_\vert 3_\vert 4_\vert 0 \rfloor$ | Extra zeroes on left and right |
| FLDA PIC 99V99 | FLDB PIC 999V999 | |

$\lfloor 1_\vert 2_\vert 3_\vert 4 \rfloor$ $\qquad$ $\lfloor 2_\vert 3 \rfloor$ $\qquad$ Truncation on left and right

FLDA PIC 99V99 $\qquad$ FLDB PIC 9V9

$\qquad\qquad\qquad\qquad\qquad\qquad$ Zero insertion on left

$\lfloor 1_\vert 2_\vert 3_\vert 4 \rfloor$ $\qquad$ $\lfloor 0_\vert 0_\vert 1_\vert 2 \rfloor$ $\qquad$ Truncation on right

FLDA PIC 99V99 $\qquad$ FLDB PIC 9999

$\qquad\qquad\qquad\qquad\qquad\qquad$ Truncation on left

$\lfloor 1_\vert 2_\vert 3_\vert 4 \rfloor$ $\qquad$ $\lfloor 2_\vert 3_\vert 4_\vert 0 \rfloor$ $\qquad$ Zero insertion on right

FLDA PIC 99V99 $\qquad$ FLDB PIC 9V999

Internally, the sign of a data item is expressed as a code in the rightmost digit of the item. For purposes of illustration in this book we shall show the sign by a raised − or + above the rightmost digit.

MOVE FLDA TO FLDB.

$\lfloor 1_\vert 2_\vert 3_\vert 4_\vert \bar{5} \rfloor$

FLDA PIC S999V99 $\qquad\qquad$ The value of FLDA is negative.

$\lfloor 0_\vert 0_\vert 1_\vert 2_\vert \overset{+}{3} \rfloor$

FLDB PIC S999V99 $\qquad\qquad$ The value of FLDB is positive.

If a signed data item is moved to an unsigned data item the sign is lost. The value of the resulting field is unsigned and hence positive.

MOVE FLDA TO FLDB

$\lfloor 1_\vert 2_\vert 3_\vert 4_\vert 5 \rfloor$ $\qquad\qquad$ $\lfloor 1_\vert 2_\vert 3_\vert 4_\vert 5 \rfloor$

FLDA PIC S999V99 $\qquad$ FLDB PIC 999V99

If an unsigned data item is moved to a signed item the resulting value is assumed to be positive.

Example

```
MOVE FLDA TO FLDB
```

| 1 | 2 | 3 | 4 | 5 | | 1 | 2 | 3 | 4 | 5̄ |

```
FLDA PIC 999V99        FLDB PIC S999V99
```

4.9 EDITING

The only time that numeric data is moved into a nonnumeric field is for purposes of editing the data for report output. The receiving field is described using report type picture codes. Report-type picture codes such as Z, $, and . react with the numeric digits moved into the field, resulting in an appropriately edited character string.

Decimal Point Insertion (.)

The use of the decimal point (.) in a report-type picture causes the decimal point to be inserted in the indicated position in the item. The implied position of the decimal point in the numeric sending item is aligned with the indicated position in the report-type receiving item. Zeroes will be inserted into the resulting field on the left or right if the receiving item is longer than the sending item. Digits also may be truncated on the left or right if the receiving item is too short to receive all of the digits of the sending field.

Example

```
MOVE FLDA TO FLDB
```

| 0 | 1 | 2 | 3 | 4 | | 0 | 1 | 2 | . | 3 | 4 |

```
FLDA PIC 999V99        FLDB PIC 999.99`
```

| 0 | 1 | 2 | 3 | 4 | | 0 | 0 | 1 | 2 | . | 3 |

```
FLDA PIC 999V99        FLDB PIC 9999.9
```

| 0 | 1 | 2 | 3 | 4 | | 2 | . | 3 | 4 | 0 |

```
FLDA PIC 999V99        FLDB PIC 9.999
```

Zero Suppression (Z)

The character Z in a report-type picture will cause substitution of blanks in place of leading zeroes in the sending item. When a nonzero digit is encountered, that digit and all subsequent digits (zero or nonzero) are moved to the receiving field.

Example

```
MOVE FLDA TO FLDB
```

| 0 | 1 | 0 | 3 | 4 | | | 1 | 0 | . | 3 | 4 |

Blank is inserted in place of leading zero

```
FLDA PIC 999V99        FLDB PIC ZZZ.99
```

|0|0|0|0|0| |_|_|_|_.|0|0| Decimal point
                                                       will be inserted
FLDA PIC 999V99   FLDB PIC ZZZ.99   if the digit to
                                                       the immediate
                                                       right is not
                                                       suppressed.

|0|0|0|0|0| |_|_|_|_|_|_| Decimal point
                                                       is not inserted
FLDA PIC 999V99   FLDB PIC ZZZ.ZZ   since digit to
                                                       right is
                                                       suppressed

|1|0|0|0|0| |1|0|0|.|0|0|

FLDA PIC 999V99   FLDB PIC ZZZ.ZZ

Dollar Sign Insertion ($)

The character $ used as the first character in a report-type picture will cause the $ to be the first character in the receiving item.

Example

        MOVE FLDA TO FLDB

        |0|1|0|3|4| |$|_|1|0|.|3|4|

        FLDA PIC 999V99   FLDB PIC $ZZZ.99

If more than one $ is used in the report type picture, the character will cause zero suppression in each position in which it occurs, and the $ will be inserted immediately in front of the first nonsuppressed character.

Example

        MOVE FLDA TO FLDB

        |0|1|0|3|4| |_|$|1|0|.|3|4|

        FLDA PIC 999V99   FLDB PIC $$$$.99

        |0|0|0|0|0| |_|_|_|$|.|0|0|

        FLDA PIC 999V99   FLDB PIC $$$$.99

Check Protection (*)

The character * used in a report-type picture will cause the asterisk to be inserted in place of each leading zero or other suppressed character. The * is used chiefly in prefacing the dollar amount on checks.

Example

MOVE FLDA TO FLDB

| 0 | 0 | 0 | 1 | 2 | 3 | 4 | | * | * | * | 1 | 2 | . | 3 | 4 |

FLDA PIC 99999V99   FLDB PIC *****.99

| 1 | 2 | 3 | 4 | 5 | 6 | 7 | | $ | 1 | 2 | 3 | 4 | 5 | . | 6 | 7 |

FLDA PIC 99999V99   FLDB PIC $*****.99

| 0 | 0 | 0 | 0 | 0 | | $ | * | * | * | * | * | * |

FLDA PIC 999V99   FLDB PIC $***.**

Comma Insertion (,)

The character ",", used in a report-type picture will cause the comma to be inserted in the appropriate position in the receiving field if the character immediately preceding is not a suppressed zero.

Example

MOVE FLDA TO FLDB

| 0 | 0 | 1 | 2 | 3 | 4 | 5 | | 0 | , | 0 | 1 | 2 | , | 3 | 4 | 5 |

FLDA PIC 9(7)   FLDB PIC 9,999,999

| 0 | 0 | 1 | 2 | 3 | 4 | 5 | | | | | 1 | 2 | , | 3 | 4 | 5 |

FLDA PIC 9(7)   FLDB PIC Z,ZZZ,ZZZ

| 0 | 0 | 0 | 0 | 1 | 2 | 3 | | | | | | | | 1 | 2 | 3 |

FLDA PIC 9999999   FLDB PIC Z,Z(3),Z(3)

| 0 | 0 | 1 | 2 | 3 | 4 | | | | | | 1 | , | 2 | 3 | 4 |

FLDA PIC 9999999   FLDB PIC Z,ZZZ,ZZZ

| 0 | 0 | 1 | 2 | 3 | 4 | 5 | 6 | 7 | | | | | $ | 1 | 2 | , | 3 | 4 | 5 | . | 6 | 7 |

FLDA PIC 9(7)V99   FLDB PIC $$,$$$,$$$.99

| 0 | 0 | 1 | 2 | 3 | 4 | 5 | 6 | 7 | | $ | * | * | * | 1 | 2 | , | 3 | 4 | 5 | . | 6 | 7 |

FLDA PIC 9999999V99   FLDB PIC $*,***,***.99

Sign Insertion (+ and −)

The character "−" used as the first or last character in a report-type picture will cause the minus sign to be inserted in the appropriate position of the receiving field if the sending item is negative. If the sending field is positive or unsigned, a blank is inserted.

Example

MOVE FLDA TO FLDB

| 1 | 2 | 3 | 4 | 5̄ | | − | 1 | 2 | 3 | . | 4 | 5 |

FLDA PIC S999V99   FLDB PIC −999.99

| 0 | 1 | 2 | 3 | 4̄ | | 0 | 1 | 2 | . | 3 | 4 | − |

FLDA PIC S999V99   FLDB PIC ZZZ.99−

| 1 | 2 | 3 | 4 | 5̇ | | 1 | 2 | 3 | . | 4 | 5 | |

FLDA PIC 999V99   FLDB PIC ZZZ.ZZ−

The character "+" may be used in exactly the same way as the character "−" except that the plus sign will be inserted whenever the sending item is positive or unsigned, and the minus sign will be inserted if the sending item is negative.

Example

MOVE FLDA TO FLDB.

| 1 | 2 | 3 | 4 | 5̇ | | + | 1 | 2 | 3 | . | 4 | 5 |

FLDA PIC S999V99   FLDB PIC +ZZZ.ZZ

| 0 | 1 | 2 | 3 | 4̄ | | | − | | 1 | 2 | . | 3 | 4 |

FLDA PIC S999V99   FLDB PIC +ZZZ.ZZ

| 0 | 0 | 0 | 1 | 2 | | | | | . | 1 | 2 | + |

FLDA PIC 999V999   FLDB PIC ZZZ.99+

The use of more than one − (or +) as the first characters in a report type picture will cause zero suppression. It will also give you the appropriate sign preceding the first nonsuppressed character.

Example

MOVE FLDA TO FLDB

| 0 | 0 | 0 | 1 | 2 | 3 | 4̄ | | | | | − | 1 | 2 | . | 3 | 4 |

FLDA PIC S99999V99   FLDB PIC −(6).99

| 0 | 0 | 0 | 0 | 0 | 1 | 2̄ | | | | | | | − | . | 1 | 2 |

FLDA PIC S99999V99   FLDB PIC +++++.99

Credit and Debit Insertion (CR and DB)

The characters CR and DB used as the last two characters in a report-type picture will cause CR or DB to be inserted in the receiving field if the sending field is negative. Otherwise, blanks will be inserted.

Example

```
MOVE FLDA TO BLDB
```

| 0 | 1 | 2 | 3 | 4̄ | | | | 1 | 2 | . | 3 | 4 | C | R |

FLDA PIC S999V99   FLDB PIC ZZZ.99CR

| 0 | 1 | 2 | 3 | 4̇ | | | | 1 | 2 | . | 3 | 4 | | |

FLDA PIC S999V99   FLDB PIC ZZZ.99CR

| 0 | 0 | 0 | 1 | 2̄ | | | | | $ | . | 1 | 2 | D | B |

FLDA PIC S999V99   FLDB PIC $$$$.99DB

Blank Insertion (B)

The character B used in a report-type picture will cause a blank to be inserted in the receiving field.

Example

| 1 | 2 | 3 | 4 | 5 | 6 | 7 | 8 | 9 | | 1 | 2 | 3 | | 4 | 5 | | 6 | 7 | 8 | 9 |

FLDA PIC 9(0)   FLDB PIC 999B99B9999

| 0 | 1 | 2 | 3 | 4̄ | | | | 1 | 2 | . | 3 | 4 | | C | R |

FLDA PIC S999V99   FLDB PIC ZZZ.99BCR

Slash Insertion (/)

The character slash (/) used in a report-type picture will cause the character to be inserted in the receiving field. The primary use for this code is for editing date fields.

Example

```
MOVE DATE-IN TO DATE-OUT
```

| 0 | 3 | 0 | 5 | 8 | 2 | | 0 | 3 | / | 0 | 5 | / | 8 | 2 |

DATE-IN PIC 9(6)   DATE-OUT PIC 99/99/99.

4.10   SUMMARY OF DATA MOVEMENT

A summary of all possible cases of data movement is shown in Figure 4.4. The result of a data movement operation in those cases described as ''not permitted'' depends on the system in use. In most cases the compiler will treat such MOVE

RECEIVING FIELD TYPE

		Alphabetic or Alphanumeric	Numeric	Report
SENDING FIELD TYPE	Alphabetic or Alphanumeric	Characters moved left to right with truncation and padding on right	Not permitted	Not permitted
	Numeric	Same as alphanumeric to alphanumeric	Decimal points in fields are aligned. Digits right of decimal point are moved left to right. Digits left of decimal point are moved right to left. Truncation/padding of leading/trailing digits in receiving field.	Same as numeric to numeric except editing of numeric digits is performed
	Report	Same as alphanumeric to alphanumeric	Not permitted	Not permitted

Figure 4.4 Summary of MOVEs by data type

instructions as syntax errors. In any case these types of moves are most likely logical errors because the result will be of no value to the program. While the movement of a numeric field to a field described as alphanumeric is permitted and handled in the same way as an alphanumeric to alphanumeric move, this type of movement is performed rarely in practice. Numeric data is usually moved to another numeric field or to a report-type field in preparation for output.

4.11 FIGURATIVE CONSTANTS

The COBOL language provides a number of *figurative constants* which are assigned reserved word names (Fig. 4.5). Any of these figurative constants may be used in any place the corresponding nonfigurative constant would be appropri-

Reserved Word	Value
ZERO ZEROS ZEROES	0
HIGH-VALUE HIGH-VALUES	the largest value which can be represented in the computer (binary 1's)
SPACE SPACES	one or more blanks
LOW-VALUE LOW-VALUES	the smallest value which can be represented in the computer (binary 0's)
ALL "character"	a string of appropriate length consisting entirely of the specified character
QUOTE QUOTES	quotation mark(s)

Figure 4.5 Figurative constants

ate. Examples of using the figurative constants ZERO and SPACES are abundant
in Program 4.1.

The following are equivalent: *Example*

```
03 DATA PIC X(5) VALUE ALL "*".
03 DATA PIC X(5) VALUE "*****".
```

In both cases the content of DATA will be:

```
 |*|*|*|*|*|
    DATA
```

Suppose you desire to describe the character string "XYZ" for inclusion on   *Example*
an output line. The following code could be used:

```
02   DATA.
     03   FILLER   PIC X     VALUE QUOTE.
     03   FILLER   PIC XXX   VALUE "XYZ".
     03   FILLER   PIC X     VALUE QUOTE.
```

The content of DATA will be:

```
 |"|X|Y|Z|"|
    DATA
```

Use of the figurative constant QUOTE is the only way to specify this character
(the ") in the string since quotes are used in coding nonnumeric constants in
COBOL.

The following statements are equivalent: *Example*

```
              MOVE 0     TO FLD.
```
and
```
              MOVE ZERO TO FLD.
```

The figurative constants HIGH-VALUE (S) and LOW-VALUES (S) are used
in certain instances for passing values between a program and the operating system (see Chapter 10, Section 10.4 for an example of the use of these constants).

4.12 SIGNED NUMBERS

As noted earlier, the picture code S must be the first code in the picture of any
variable which may be negative. For example, the following DATA division
declarations specify FLD-B as signed variables:

```
01   REC-DESC.
     03   FLD-A    PIC S9999.
     03   FLD-B    PIC S9V99.
     03   FILLER   PIC X(73).
```

Suppose REC-DESC specified in the preceding example is the description of a
data record. FLD-A and FLD-B may be positive or negative. If a value is entered
in a field in the ordinary fashion, it is stored as an unsigned value (i.e. positive).
But what about a negative quantity? There are two ways to enter negative data:
entering the sign as a part of the rightmost digit in the field, and entering the sign
as a separate character.

Sign in Rightmost Digit

As discussed in Section 4.8 above, the sign of a value is associated with the rightmost digit in the field. When using punched card input, the sign may be punched in conjunction with the rightmost digit in the field. An 11 zone together with the digit in the rightmost position is used for a negative value. A 12 zone and the appropriate digit is used for a positive value. If the data card shown in Figure 4.6 is read using the above record description, the value of FLD-A and FLD-B will be:

$$\lfloor 0 \mid 0 \mid 3 \mid \bar{4} \rfloor \qquad\qquad \lfloor 4 \mid 0 \mid \overset{+}{1} \rfloor$$

FLD-A   FLD-B

The absence of any zone punch will also signify a positive value. When output is produced for a signed field, the character equivalent of the punch combination will be used.

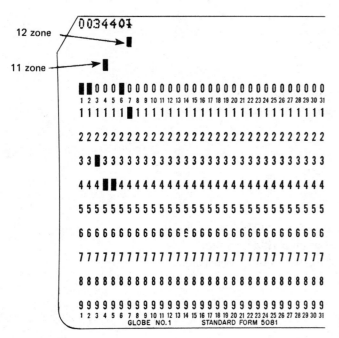

Figure 4.6   Data card with signed values

For example, if the content of FLD-A and FLD-B were printed without editing, the output would appear as:

0   0   3   N   4   0   A

FLD-A   FLD-B

The appearance of alphabetic characters in the rightmost position of the fields is caused by the inclusion of zones in the output. (11-4 is the code for N and 12-1 is the code for A.) The movement of a signed field to an edited field is necessary to suppress this inclusion of a sign zone along with the digit in the rightmost position.

Example

MOVE FLDA TO FLDB, FLDC.

$$\lfloor 0 \mid 3 \mid \overset{+}{4} \rfloor \qquad\qquad \lfloor 0 \mid 3 \mid 4 \rfloor \qquad\qquad \lfloor \;\; \mid 3 \mid 4 \rfloor$$

FLDA PIC S999   FLDB PIC 999   FLDC PIC ZZZ

Those who use terminals and diskettes to enter data must perform the logical equivalent of supplying a 12 or 11 zone in the rightmost position of a signed numeric field. This is done by using the character equivalent of the punch combination (Fig. 4.7).

Punched card code	Character	Meaning For Signed Data
12-1	A	$\overset{+}{1}$
12-2	B	$\overset{+}{2}$
12-3	C	$\overset{+}{3}$
12-4	D	$\overset{+}{4}$
12-5	E	$\overset{+}{5}$
12-6	F	$\overset{+}{6}$
12-7	G	$\overset{+}{7}$
12-8	H	$\overset{+}{8}$
12-9	I	$\overset{+}{9}$
11-1	J	$\overline{1}$
11-2	K	$\overline{2}$
11-3	L	$\overline{3}$
11-4	M	$\overline{4}$
11-5	N	$\overline{5}$
11-6	O	$\overline{6}$
11-7	P	$\overline{7}$
11-8	Q	$\overline{8}$
11-9	R	$\overline{9}$

Figure 4.7

Thus, in order to enter FLDB and FLDC with values -34 and $+4.01$ respectively, the terminal or diskette user would enter:

0 0 3 N   4 0 A

FLD-A   FLD-B

Note that characters representing $\overset{+}{0}$ and $\overset{-}{0}$ are omitted from the list above. Details as to how these characters are to be entered vary from one system to another. The reader must check the user's manual or other local documentation to determine the appropriate procedure.

The SIGN IS Clause

The sign of a data item may be entered as a leading or trailing character in the field if the item is defined using the SIGN IS clause (Fig. 4.8.).

SIGN IS $\begin{Bmatrix} \underline{\text{LEADING}} \\ \text{TRAILING} \end{Bmatrix}$ [SEPARATE CHARACTER]

Figure 4.8 General form of the SIGN IS clause

When this clause is used in the definition of the item, the S picture code, which must be present, is counted as a position in the field.

A field A is 4 characters in length and the user desires to enter the sign of the field as a leading character. The field would be defined by   *Example*

         A   PIC S999   SIGN IS LEADING SEPARATE.

If the characters $-1,0,2$ are entered on the input record, the value of A will be -102. If the characters are -3 are entered, the value of A will be -3.

A field B is 6 characters in length; the user will enter the sign in the right-   *Example*
most character of the field. The field would be defined by

         B   PIC S99999   SIGN IS TRAILING.

If the characters $1,0,2,-$ are entered on the input record, the value of B will be -102.

4.13   DEBUG CLINIC

File, Record, Field References

A very common mistake made by beginning programmers is to reference a file, record or field by two different names in the same program. It is important to remember that all references to the same file, record or field must use the same data-name.

For example, consider the following lines taken from Program 4.1:

```
line
13        SELECT IN-FD  ASSIGN TO DISK.
  .          .
  .          .
  .          .
17        FD  IN-FD
18            DATA RECORD IS INPUT-RECORD.
19        01  INPUT-RECORD.
  .          .
  .          .
  .          .
63            OPEN INPUT IN-FD.
  .          .
  .          .
  .          .
```

76   READ IN-FD AT END MOVE 1 TO EOF-FLAG.
     .   .
     .   .
     .   .
88   CLOSE IN-FD, PRINT.

Note that the name IN-FD is used in the SELECT entry, FD entry, OPEN statement, READ statement and CLOSE statement, and also that the name INPUT-
RECORD is used both in the DATA RECORD clause and the following 01 entry.

Failure to use the same file, record or field name in each reference will be
treated by the compiler as a syntax error.

Mixing WRITE/BEFORE and WRITE/AFTER

Care must be exercised in utilizing both options of the WRITE statement in the
same program. Recall that the BEFORE option causes lines to be printed prior to
advancing the paper (WRITE . . . BEFORE ADVANCING) while the AFTER option
cause paper to be advanced prior to writing the line (WRITE . . . AFTER
ADVANCING).

In a given program, if WRITE/BEFORE is used for all WRITE statements the
printer normally will be on a new line for each output. The same observation is
true if WRITE/AFTER is used for all WRITE statements. If a program uses a
WRITE/AFTER followed by a WRITE/BEFORE, the WRITE/AFTER leaves the
paper on the line printed. The following WRITE/BEFORE causes another line to
be printed and then the paper is advanced. The second line of print will be printed on top of the first one!

In order to avoid problems of this kind, most COBOL programmers employ
only WRITE/AFTER or WRITE/BEFORE in a given program.

Editing

When performing editing of numeric data, make sure the receiving field contains
a sufficient number of positions for all digits in the sending field. In general,
when a numeric field is moved to an edited field, the decimal points are aligned.
Leading and trailing digits are truncated or padded with zeroes depending on
number of positions in the edited field.

Suppose the instruction   *Examples*

MOVE FLDA TO FLDB.

is executed.

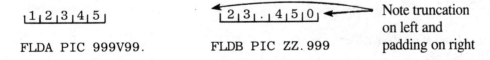

FLDA PIC 999V99.   FLDB PIC ZZ.999

Note truncation
on left and
padding on right

In this case, FLDB contains too few digits on the left to accommodate all
digits of FLDA, resulting in truncation of the leading digit. FLDB contains
more digits on the right of the decimal point than FLDA; hence, FLDB is padded on the right with a zero.

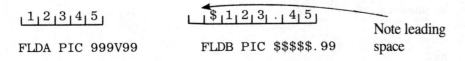

FLDA PIC 999V99   FLDB PIC $$$$.99

Note leading
space

FLDB contains space for four digits to the left of the decimal point. Since FLDA has only three digits left of the decimal point, FLDA is padded on the left with a zero. Because of the editing function the leading zero is then suppressed.

$$\boxed{1\,|\,2\,|\,3\,|\,4\,|\,5}\qquad\qquad\boxed{\$\,|\,2\,|\,3\,|\,.\,|\,4\,|\,5}\qquad\text{Note}$$

FLDA PIC 999V99   FLDB PIC \$\$\$.99   truncation

FLDB contains space for only two digits left of the decimal point because the dollar sign uses one space and is never suppressed. This results in the truncation of the leading digit of FLDA.

The programmer must be careful to construct edit pictures which are sufficiently long to accommodate all digits of the field to be edited.

Signed Fields

Recall that a field which will be signed (i.e., may become negative) must be described in the DATA DIVISION by a picture which contains the picture code S as its first character. Thus if the data 032J is read into a field described as S9999, the resulting value is -321. Suppose signed data is entered into a field which is not described using the S picture code: for example, the data 032J is read into a field described as 9999. In this case the value stored will be 321—a positive value! In order for a field to store a negative value it *must* be described using the S picture code.

Remember also that when a signed field is specified without the SIGN IS clause, S is *not* counted as a part of the number of characters in the field. If the SIGN IS clause is used, the S *is* counted as a character in the field.

Example

    Q PIC S999.

The size of the field is three.

    R PIC S999 SIGN IS LEADING.

The size of the field is four.

4.14   SELF TEST EXERCISES

1. Consider the following information about a file:
    File-name: SALES-RECORD
    Device type: disk
    Record-name: SALESMAN
   a. Write an FD entry for the file.
   b. Write an OPEN statement for the file.
   c. Write a READ statement for the file.
   d. Write a CLOSE statement for the file.

2. Consider the following information about a file:
    File-name: PAYROLL
    Device type: printer
    Record-name: NET-PAY

a. Write an FD entry for the file.
b. Write an OPEN statement for the file.
c. Write a READ statement for the file.
d. Write a CLOSE statement for the file.

3. Show the result of the statement MOVE ITM1 TO ITM2 for ITM1 and ITM2 as shown below:

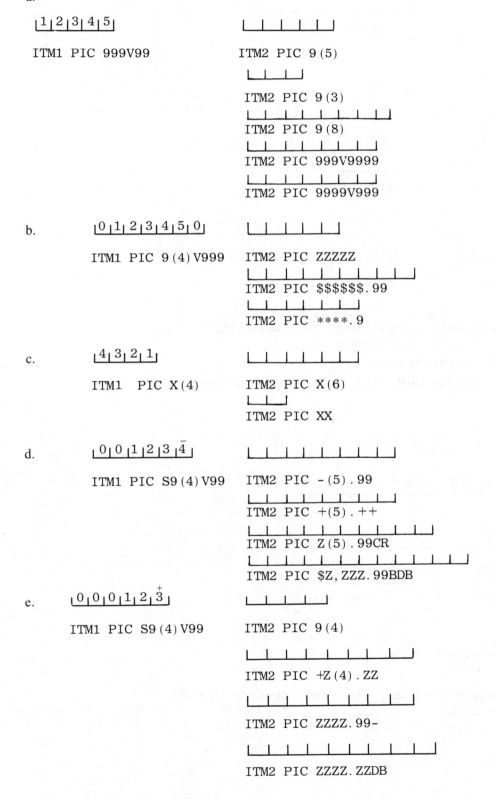

a.

| 1 | 2 | 3 | 4 | 5 |

ITM1 PIC 999V99 ITM2 PIC 9(5)

ITM2 PIC 9(3)

ITM2 PIC 9(8)

ITM2 PIC 999V9999

ITM2 PIC 9999V999

b.

| 0 | 1 | 2 | 3 | 4 | 5 | 0 |

ITM1 PIC 9(4)V999 ITM2 PIC ZZZZZ

ITM2 PIC $$$$$.99

ITM2 PIC ****.9

c.

| 4 | 3 | 2 | 1 |

ITM1 PIC X(4) ITM2 PIC X(6)

ITM2 PIC XX

d.

| 0 | 0 | 1 | 2 | 3 | 4̄ |

ITM1 PIC S9(4)V99 ITM2 PIC -(5).99

ITM2 PIC +(5).++

ITM2 PIC Z(5).99CR

ITM2 PIC $Z,ZZZ.99BDB

e.

| 0 | 0 | 0 | 1 | 2 | 3⁺ |

ITM1 PIC S9(4)V99 ITM2 PIC 9(4)

ITM2 PIC +Z(4).ZZ

ITM2 PIC ZZZZ.99-

ITM2 PIC ZZZZ.ZZDB

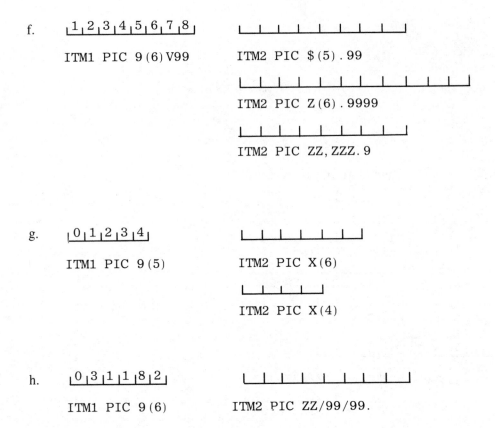

f. | 1 | 2 | 3 | 4 | 5 | 6 | 7 | 8 |

ITM1 PIC 9(6)V99   ITM2 PIC $(5).99

ITM2 PIC Z(6).9999

ITM2 PIC ZZ,ZZZ.9

g. | 0 | 1 | 2 | 3 | 4 |

ITM1 PIC 9(5)   ITM2 PIC X(6)

ITM2 PIC X(4)

h. | 0 | 3 | 1 | 1 | 8 | 2 |

ITM1 PIC 9(6)   ITM2 PIC ZZ/99/99.

4. Draw a program flowchart for the paragraph of Program 4.1 which will terminate the processing of the loop. What will cause this termination?

5. List types of output lines found in most reports.

6. In each cell of the following table classify each type of move as permitted or not permitted

		Receiving Field		
		Alphabetic or Alphanumeric	Numeric	Report
Sending Field	Alphabetic or Alphanumeric			
	Numeric			
	Report			

4.15 PROGRAMMING EXERCISES

1. Write a program to produce an appropriately edited report listing each item from data records in the following format:

positions
  1-20   Name
  21-34   Street address

35-41	City
42-46	ZIP code
47	Marital status code
50-60	Yearly salary (two decimal places implied)

Write a line at the conclusion of your report specifying the total number of records processed.

Use the following data to test your program:

Name	Street address	City	ZIP	Marital Status Code	Yearly Salary
JOHN DOE	123 A ST.	MOBILE	34712	S	$16,000.00
MARY SMITH	1400 MAPLE	NEW ORLEANS	51760	M	$27,500.00
JAMES BROWN	72 MAIN AVE.	JACKSONVILLE	32571	W	$17,895.85
SUSY QUEUE	1900 OAK ST.	TROY	47501	M	$15,970.00

2. Write a program to process a file containing records in the following format and produce a report listing sales in each department. The last line of the report should contain the totals for each column of the report.

Positions	
1-6	Date
10-19	Sales in shoe department
20-29	Sales in ladies' clothing
30-39	Sales in men's clothing
40-49	Sales in children's clothing
50-59	Sales in jewelry department

3. A real estate company maintains the following records for each listed property.

Positions	
1-8	Multiple listing number
9-10	Zone
11-25	Address
26	Number of bedrooms
27-28	Number of baths (9V9)
29	Total number of rooms
30	Number of cars in carport
31	Number of cars in garage
32-40	Elementary school name
41-49	Junior high school name
50-58	High school name
59-63	Taxes (9999)
64.68	Price (999999)
69-74	Amount of existing mortgage (999999)
75-77	Amount of payment on existing mortgage (999)
78-80	Interest rate on existing mortgage (V999)

Write a program to list this file using a format similar to the following:

```
MULTILE LISTING NUMBER xxxxxxxx    ZONE xx
ADDRESS         xxxxxxxxxxxxxxxx   PRICE $xxxxxx
ROOMS x    BEDROOMS x     BATHS x.x
CARPORT x    GARAGE x
  .
  .
  .
etc.
```

4. The managers of Burgers, Inc. which operates a franchise system of hamburger restaurants, are concerned with the profitability of a number of the company's outlets. They have requested a report showing basic data about each store. The format for the

input records is:

Positions
  1-10   Franchise number
11-25   Location
26-40   Manager's name
41-48   Previous year's profits (S999999V99)
               (Field could be negative if the store
               lost money.)

The manager of the computer at ABC Furniture, Inc. prepares a record in the following format for each supply requisition he makes:

Positions
1-6   Date
7-25   Description
26-31   Amount (9999V99)

At the end of each month, he collects all the requisitions and runs a program to list each requisition and the total for the month. Write a program for the manager to use for this task.

ARITHMETIC STATEMENTS 5

Arithmetic statements are used to perform computations in a COBOL program. Two types of arithmetic statements can be used. One type uses the verbs ADD, SUBTRACT, MULTIPLY and DIVIDE to specify the arithmetic operation to be performed; the other type uses the verb COMPUTE and allows the programmer to specify arithmetic operations using the symbols + (for add), − (for subtract), ∗ (for multiply) and / (for divide). The programmer may chose whichever type of statement he or she finds most advantageous.

5.1 THE ADD STATEMENT

The ADD statement is used to perform addition of numeric data items. Figure 5.1 shows a general form for the ADD statement.

$$\underline{\text{ADD}} \quad \left\{ \begin{array}{l} \text{data-name} \\ \text{constant} \end{array} \right\} \quad \cdots \quad \left\{ \begin{array}{l} \underline{\text{TO}} \\ \underline{\text{GIVING}} \end{array} \right\} \quad \text{data-name}.$$

Figure 5.1 General form of the ADD statement

Any number of data items may be added; the result is placed in the last *data-name* specified. If the TO option is used, the receiving item participates as an addend. If the GIVING option is used, the calculated sum is moved to the receiving item and does not participate in the addition.

Add credit to present balance to get new balance.   *Example*

    ADD CREDIT, BAL GIVING NEW-BAL.

| 0 | 3 | 2 | 0 | 0 | | 0 | 0 | 4 | 0 | 0 | 0̄ | | 0 | 0 | 0 | 8 | 0 | 0̄ |

CREDIT PIC 999V99   BAL PIC S9999V99   NEW-BAL PIC S9999V99

   Calculation: 32.00 + (−40.00) = −8.00

Example

Add the constant 3.2 to the two variables X and Y to get Z. In this case, X = 23.0 and Y = 123.

ADD 3.2, X, Y, GIVING Z

|_2_|_3_|_0_| |_1_|_2_|_3_| |_0_|_1_|_4_|_9_|_2_|

X PIC 99V9   Y PIC 999   Z PIC 9(4)V9

Calculation: 3.2 + 23.0 + 123 = 149.2

Example

Add 1 to the present value of the variable KOUNT.

ADD 1 TO KOUNT

Before Execution   *After Execution*

|_0_|_0_|_3_| |_0_|_0_|_4_|

KOUNT PIC 999   KOUNT PIC 999

Example

Add the constant 3.2 and the variables X, Y, to Z, whose values in this case are 23.0, 123 and 149.2.

ADD 3.2, X, Y TO Z

Before Execution
|_2_|_3_|_0_| |_1_|_2_|_3_| |_0_|_1_|_4_|_9_|_2_|

X PIC 99V9   Y PIC 999   Z PIC 9(4)V9

After Execution
|_2_|_3_|_0_| |_1_|_2_|_3_| |_0_|_2_|_9_|_8_|_4_|

X PIC 99V9   Y PIC 999   Z PIC 9(4)V9

Calculation: 3.2 + 23.0 + 123 + 149.2 = 298.4
Note that this example could be rewritten as

ADD 3.2, X, Y, Z GIVING Z.

The results would be exactly the same.

When the computer executes the ADD (and SUBTRACT) instruction, data items are adjusted to align decimal positions; the operation is performed, taking into account the sign of the field (if any); and the result is placed in the receiving fields. In all arithmetic instructions (as in the MOVE instruction), data is moved to the receiving field from the decimal point to the right and also from the decimal point to the left. *Truncation* occurs on the leftmost digits of the integer portion and of the rightmost digits of the fractional portion if the receiving field is too short. Padding with zeroes occurs on the left and right if the receiving field is too long.

Add the regular hours (40) to overtime hours (6.5) to get total hours. The   *Example*
regular and overtime hours may contain fractions, but total hours does not.

ADD REG-HR, OV-HR GIVING TOT-HR

| 4 | 0 | 0 | | 0 | 6 | 5 | | 0 | 4 | 6 |

REG-HR PIC 99V9   OV-HR PIC 99V9   TOT-HR PIC 999

Calculation: 40.0 + 6.5 = 46.5 ← Truncated when result is moved to TOT-
HR.

Add regular sales (30.40) to special sales (245.00) to get total sales.   *Example*

ADD REG-SALES, SPECIAL-SALES GIVING TOTAL-SALES.

| 0 | 3 | 0 | 4 | 0 | | 2 | 4 | 5 | 0 | 0 |

REG-SALES PIC 999V99   SPECIAL-SALES PIC 999V99

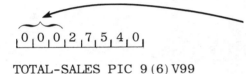

| 0 | 0 | 0 | 2 | 7 | 5 | 4 | 0 | The first three
                                                     zeroes pad out
TOTAL-SALES PIC 9(6)V99   the field of
                                                     whole dollars.

5.2   THE SUBTRACT STATEMENT

The SUBTRACT statement is used to perform subtraction of numeric data items,
as shown in general form in Figure 5.2.

SUBTRACT $\begin{Bmatrix} \text{data-name} \\ \text{constant} \end{Bmatrix}$ .. FROM $\begin{Bmatrix} \text{data-name [\underline{GIVING} data-name]} \\ \text{constant} \quad \underline{GIVING} \text{ data-name} \end{Bmatrix}$.

Figure 5.2   General form of the SUBTRACT statement

The result is placed in the last *data-name* specified. The GIVING clause is
optional when the subtrahend (the value subtracted from) is specified as a data-
name, but required when it is specified as a constant.
   Subtract FICA tax (26.00) from pay (400.00) to get net pay.   *Example*

SUBTRACT FICA FROM PAY GIVING NET-PAY.

| 0 | 2 | 6 | 0 | 0 | | 0 | 4 | 0 | 0 | 0 | 0 | | 0 | 3 | 7 | 4 | 0 | 0 |

FICA PIC 999V99   PAY PIC 9999V99   NET-PAY PIC 9999V99

Calculation: 400.00 − 26.00 = 374.00

Subtract FICA tax (26.00) from pay (400.00).   *Example*

SUBTRACT FICA FROM PAY

Before Execution

0	2	6	0	0

FICA PIC 999V99

0	4	0	0	0	0

PAY PIC 9999V99

After Execution

0	2	6	0	0

FICA PIC 999V9

0	3	7	4	0	0

PAY PIC 9999V99

    Any number of items may be subtracted. The sign (if any) is considered in the operation.

Subtract 3.2 and X (-1.2) from Y (3.2) to get Z.   *Example*

SUBTRACT 3.2, X FROM Y GIVING Z

0	1	2	0̄

X PIC S99V99

0	0	3	2̟⁺

Y PIC S99V99

0	1	6	8̄

Z PIC S99V99

Calculation: $.32 - 3.2 - (-1.2) = -1.68$

When you subtract from a constant, the GIVING clause *must* be specified, since it is not permissible to store a different value into a constant.

Subtract contents of Field A (20) from 25. The following statement is   *Example* *invalid*:

SUBTRACT FLDA FROM 25

The following statement is *valid*:

SUBTRACT FLDA FROM 25 GIVING FLDB

2	0	0	0

FLDA PIC 99V99

0	5	0	0

FLDB PIC 99V99

5.3   THE MULTIPLY STATEMENT

The MULTIPLY statement is used to perform multiplication of two numeric items (Fig. 5.3).

$$\underline{MULTIPLY} \begin{Bmatrix} \text{data-name} \\ \text{constant} \end{Bmatrix} \text{BY} \begin{Bmatrix} \text{data-name} & [\underline{GIVING} \text{ data-name}] \\ \text{constant} & \underline{GIVING} \text{ data-name} \end{Bmatrix}.$$

Figure 5.3   General form of the MULTIPLY statement

The result is placed in the last *data-name* specified.

Example Multiply pay (400.00) by the constant .065 to get FICA tax. (Note that you are multiplying by a constant, so the GIVING clause is required.)

```
MULTIPLY PAY BY .065 GIVING FICA
```

| 0 | 4 | 0 | 0 | 0 | 0 |

PAY PIC 9999V99

| 0 | 2 | 6 | 0 | 0 |

FICA PIC 9999V99

Computation: $400 \times .065 = 26.00$

Example Multiply price (20.00) times percent (25%) to get sale price. (Note that most sales are based on a percent-off figure, not a direct percent as in this example.)

```
MULTIPLY PRICE BY PCT GIVING SALE-PRICE
```

| 0 | 2 | 0 | 0 | 0 |

PRICE PIC 999V99

| 2 | 5 | 0 |

PCT PIC V999

| 0 | 0 | 5 | 0 | 0 |

SALE-PRICE PIC 999V99

Computation: $20.00 \times .250 = 5.00$

Example Multiply the contents of Field A (12.3) by the contents of Field B (2.3) and store the results in FLDB.

```
MULTIPLY FLDA BY FLDB
```

Before Execution

| 1 | 2 | 3 |

FLDA PIC 99V9

| 0 | 2 | 3 |

FLDB PIC 99V9

After Execution

| 1 | 2 | 3 |

FLDA PIC 99V9

| 2 | 8 | 2 |

FLDB PIC 99V9

Computation: $12.3 \times 2.3 = 28.29$ ← This last digit will be truncated when the result is moved to FLDA

5.4   THE DIVIDE STATEMENT

Recall the terminology used in arithmetic division:

```
                2  ←——— Quotient

Divisor ——→  7)15  ←——— Dividend

               14

                1  ←——— Remainder
```

The DIVIDE statement has two formats as shown in Figure 5.4.

Format 1

DIVIDE {data-name / constant} <u>INTO</u> data-name.

Format 2

DIVIDE {data-name / constant} {<u>INTO</u> / <u>BY</u>} {data-name / constant} <u>GIVING</u> data-name [<u>REMAINDER</u> data-name].

Figure 5.4 General form of the DIVIDE statement

When the INTO option is specified, the divisor is specified first and the dividend is specified next. If the GIVING clause is omitted, then the quotient replaces the dividend.

Divide the kount (20) into a total (100) to get the average.   *Example*

DIVIDE KOUNT INTO TOTAL GIVING AVERAGE
       Divisor   Dividend   Quotient

| 2 0 | | 0 1 0 0 | | 0 5 |

KOUNT PIC 99   SUM PIC 9999   AVERAGE PIC 99

Divide the contents of Field A (12.3) into Field B (4.6).   *Example*

DIVIDE FLDA INTO FLDB
      Divisor   Dividend   Quotient

Before Execution

| 1 2 3 | | 0 4 6 |

FLDA PIC 99V9   FLDB PIC 99V9

Computation: $4.6 \div 12.3 = .3$

After Execution

| 1 2 3 | | 0 0 3 |

FLDA PIC 99V9   FLDB PIC 99V9

When the BY option is specified, the dividend is specified first and the divisor is specified next. The GIVING clause *must* be used in this case.

Divide the total (100) by the kount (20) to get the average.   *Example*

DIVIDE TOTAL BY KOUNT GIVING AVERAGE
  Dividend   Divisor   Quotient

```
  0  1  0  0          2  0              0  5
|__|__|__|__|      |__|__|          |__|__|

SUM PIC 9999    COUNT PIC 99    AVERAGE PIC 99
```

If the REMAINDER option is included, the remainder after the division will be
placed in the specified data name.

Divide the dividend (62.8) by the contents of Field A to get Field B, and   *Example*
place any remainder in Field C.

DIVIDE 62.8 BY FLDA GIVING FLDB REMAINDER FLDC
      ↑   ↑   ↗   ↗
   Dividend   Divisor   Quotient   Remainder

```
   0  1  3            4  8  3              0  1
 |__|__|__|        |__|__|__|          |__|__|

 FLDA PIC 9V99      FLDB PIC 999      FLDC PIC Z99
```

Computation:

```
                        4 83.
          .13.      )62.80.
                     52
                     ────
                     10.8
                     10.4
                     ────
                       .40
                       .39
                       ───
                       .01
```

Divide 16.3 into 4.36; store the quotient in Field A and record any   *Example*
remainder in Field C.

DIVIDE 16.3 INTO 4.36 GIVING FLDA REMAINDER FLDB
       ↑   ↑   ↗   ↗
   Divisor   Dividend   Quotient   Remainder

```
   0  2  6              0  1  2
 |__|__|__|          |__|__|__|

 FLDA PIC 9V99        FLDB PIC 9V99
```

Computation:

```
                     .26
           16.3  )4.3 60

                  3.2 6
                  ─────
                  1.1 00
                   .9 78
                  ─────
                   .1 22
```

Note placement of decimal point in remainder.

5.5   THE COMPUTE STATEMENT

The COMPUTE statement is used to perform any desired sequence of arithmetic
operations. The symbols used for operations are:

+   Add
−   Subtract
*   Multiply
/   Divide
** Exponentiation

The general form of the COMPUTE statement is

> COMPUTE data-name = expression.

The value of the expression is placed in the location specified by the *data-name*. An *expression* is either a constant, a variable or any valid combination of constants and/or variables linked by arithmetic operations. Arithmetic operation symbols, and the "=" sign must be preceded and followed by at least one blank.

Move the value 42 to FLDA.   *Example*

```
COMPUTE FLDA = 42
```

Place the value of FLDA into FLDB.

```
COMPUTE FLDB = FLDA
```

Multiply content of FLDA by 3 and place the result in FLDC.

```
COMPUTE FLDC = 3 * FLDA
```

Divide the TOTAL by KOUNT and place the result in AV.

```
COMPUTE AV = TOTAL / KOUNT
```

Add A and B; subtract C from the result.

```
COMPUTE VALUE = A + B − C
```

Multiply A times itself three times to get the cube of A or A^3.

```
COMPUTE X = A ** 3
```

Parentheses may be used to control the order in which operations are carried out. Expressions within parentheses are evaluated first. For some compilers a left parenthesis "(" must be preceded by a blank and a right parenthesis ")" must be followed by a blank or a period.

Add 3 to the contents of Field B. Then multiply the sum by 6.   *Example*

Note absence of blanks in these positions.

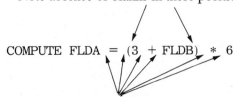

COMPUTE FLDA = (3 + FLDB) * 6

Note presence of blanks in these positions. Thus 3 is added to FLDB and the result is multiplied by 6.

As many sets of parentheses as are necessary may be used.

Compute the result of adding Z to Q; then subtract that sum from Y; then   *Example*
multiply what is left by 6.

```
COMPUTE X = (Y - (Z + Q)) * 6
```

The expression in the innermost set of parentheses is evaluated first.

In the absence of parentheses, an expression is evaluated by performing operations in order of precedence (Fig. 5.5).

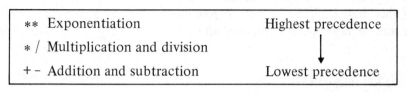

** Exponentiation	Highest precedence
* / Multiplication and division	
+ – Addition and subtraction	Lowest precedence

Figure 5.5 Precedence of arithmetic operations

Operations with equal precedence (such as multiplication and division or addition and subtraction) are performed in a left-to-right order.

Compute B × C first. Then add A.

Example

COMPUTE X = A + B * C

Multiplication has higher precedence than addition; therefore, B and C are multiplied first and only then is the result added to A.

Compute the exponential 2^3 first. Then divide the result into the product of 4 × 2.

Example

COMPUTE FLDA = 4 * 2 / 2 ** 3

Exponentiation has highest precedence; hence, the first operation to be performed is 2^3. Then, since multiplication precedes division and they are both of the same order of precedence, the next operation is 4 × 2. Finally the division is performed, giving 1 as a value of the expression.

Compute 3 × 2 and add it to 4. Then compute 3 × 3 × 3 and multiply that result by 2. Subtract the last answer from the first (3 × 2 plus 4). (Your answer will be −8.)

Example

COMPUTE A = 4 + 3 * 2 − 3 ** 2 * 2

This is equivalent to COMPUTE A = (4 + (3 * 2)) − ((3 ** 2) * 2).

5.6 THE ROUNDED OPTION

The ROUNDED option may be used with any of the arithmetic statements. When it is specified, rounding of the computed result will be performed by the computer before it places the value in the receiving field. Rounding is performed by adding 5 to the digit immediately following the rightmost decimal digit to be stored, and then truncating excess decimal digits as usual.[1] For example, suppose

---

[1]Negative quantities are rounded by first taking the absolute value of the field, performing the rounding operation, and then making the resulting field negative. For example,

12.347	absolute value	12.347
		+5
12.35	result is negative	12.352

1 2 3 5

PIC S99V99

the calculated result for an arithmetic operations is 12.347, and this value will be stored in a location with picture 99V99. Rounding will be performed as follows:

12.347   If this last digit is 0, 1, 2, 3, or 4, rounding has no effect on
+   5   the value stored. If this digit is 5, 6, 7, 8 or 9, rounding
———   causes a carry of one into the next position and does affect the
12.352   value stored.

 1 2 3 5

PIC 99V99   2 is lost due to truncation

If the receiving field had picture 99V99, the rounding would result in

12.345   This digit is less than 5; rounding has no effect on the value
+   5   stored.
———
12.395   95 is lost due to truncation

PIC 99V9

The placement of the ROUNDED option in each of the arithmetic statements is shown below in general formats (Fig. 5.6):

$$\underline{\text{ADD}} \left\{ \begin{array}{l} \text{data-name} \\ \text{constant} \end{array} \right\} \cdots \left\{ \begin{array}{l} \underline{\text{TO}} \\ \underline{\text{GIVING}} \end{array} \right\} \text{data-name} \; [\; \underline{\text{ROUNDED}} \;]$$

$$\underline{\text{SUBTRACT}} \left\{ \begin{array}{l} \text{data-name} \\ \text{constant} \end{array} \right\} \cdots \underline{\text{FROM}} \left\{ \begin{array}{l} \text{data-name} \; [\underline{\text{GIVING}} \; \text{data-name}] \\ \text{constant} \quad \underline{\text{GIVING}} \; \text{data-name} \end{array} \right\} \; [\; \underline{\text{ROUNDED}} \;]$$

$$\underline{\text{MULTIPLY}} \left\{ \begin{array}{l} \text{data-name} \\ \text{constant} \end{array} \right\} \underline{\text{BY}} \left\{ \begin{array}{l} \text{data-name} \; [\underline{\text{GIVING}} \; \text{data-name}] \\ \text{constant} \quad \underline{\text{GIVING}} \; \text{data-name} \end{array} \right\} \; [\; \underline{\text{ROUNDED}} \;]$$

$$\underline{\text{DIVIDE}} \left\{ \begin{array}{l} \text{data-name} \\ \text{constant} \end{array} \right\} \underline{\text{INTO}} \; \text{data-name} \; [\; \underline{\text{ROUNDED}} \;]$$

$$\underline{\text{DIVIDE}} \left\{ \begin{array}{l} \text{data-name} \\ \text{constant} \end{array} \right\} \begin{array}{l} \underline{\text{INTO}} \\ \underline{\text{BY}} \end{array} \left\{ \begin{array}{l} \text{data-name} \\ \text{constant} \end{array} \right\} \underline{\text{GIVING}} \; \text{data-name} \; [\; \underline{\text{ROUNDED}} \;] [\; \underline{\text{REMAINDER}} \; \text{data-name}]$$

$$\underline{\text{COMPUTE}} \; \text{data-name} \; [\; \underline{\text{ROUNDED}} \;] = \text{expression}$$

Figure 5.6   General form of arithmetic statements

Add 6.2, 4.52, and 7.892 to get an answer rounded to the nearest whole   *Example*
number.

ADD 6.2, 4.52, 7.892 GIVING X ROUNDED

Computation: 6.2
                      4.52
                    +7.892
                    ───────
                     18.612
                    +   5
                    ───────
                     19.112

After Execution

|_1_|_9_|

X PIC 99

Multiply the contents of Field A (12.3) times the contents of Field B (3.4)   *Example*
and round the answer to tenths.

MULTIPLY FLDA BY FLDB ROUNDED

Before Execution

|_1_|_2_|_3_| |_0_|_3_|_4_|

FLDA PIC 99V9   FLDB PIC 99V9

Computation: 12.3
                    × 3.4
                    ───────
                      492
                    369
                    ───────
                    41.82
                    +   5
                    ───────
                    41.87

After Execution

|_4_|_1_|_8_|

FLDB PIC 99V9

Add 4.2 to 8.97 and round the answer to tenths.   *Example*

COMPUTE XYZ ROUNDED = 4.2 + 8.97

Computation: 4.2
                    +8.97
                    ───────
                    13.17
                    +   5
                    ───────
                    13.22

|_1_|_3_|_2_|

XYZ PIC 99V9

Program 5.1   Payroll register program

```
1        IDENTIFICATION DIVISION
2        PROGRAM-ID. CHAPTER 5 EXAMPLE 1.
3        AUTHOR. HORN.
4        ENVIRONMENT DIVISION.
5        INPUT-OUTPUT SECTION.
6        FILE-CONTROL.
7            SELECT IN-FD ASSIGN TO DISK.
8            SELECT PRINT ASSIGN TO PRINTER.
9        DATA DIVISION.
10       FILE SECTION.
11       FD   IN-FD
12            DATA RECORD IS INPUT RECORD.
13       01   INPUT-RECORD.
14            03   EMPLOYEE-NUMBER-IR          PIC 9(9).
15            03   EMPLOYEE-NAME-IR            PIC X(20).
16            03   REG-HRS-IR                  PIC 99V9.
17            03   OT-HRS-IR                   PIC 99V9.
18            03   PAY-RATE-IR                 PIC 99V99.
19            03   WITH-RATE-IR                PIC V999.
20            03   OTHER-DEDUCTIONS-IR         PIC 999V99.
21            03   FILLER                      PIC X(33).
22       FD PRINT
23            DATA RECORD IS PRINT-LINE.
24       01   PRINT-LINE                  PIC X(132).
25       WORKING-STORAGE SECTION.
26       01   EOF-FLAG                    PIC 9 VALUE 0.
27       01   FICA-FACTOR                 PIC 9V9999 VALUE 0.0665.
28       01   COMPUTED-AMOUNTS.
29            03 WITH-AMT                 PIC 999V99.
30            03 NET-PAY                  PIC 9999V99.
31            03 GROSS-PAY                PIC 9999V99.
32            03 FICA                     PIC 999V99.
33       01   ACCUMULATED-TOTALS.
34            03 TOTAL-NET                PIC 9(6)V99 VALUE 0.
35            03 TOTAL-WITH               PIC 9(4)V99 VALUE 0.
36            03 TOTAL-OTHER              PIC 9(5)V99 VALUE 0.
37            03 TOTAL-FICA               PIC 9(5)V99 VALUE 0.
38            03 TOTAL-GROSS              PIC 9(6)V99 VALUE 0.
40       01   HEADING-LINE.
41            03   FILLER                 PIC X(54) VALUE SPACES.
42            03   FILLER                 PIC X(28) VALUE "XYZ COMPANY
43                 "PAYROLL REGISTER".
44       01   SUB-HEAD-1.
45            03   FILLER                 PIC X VALUE SPACES.
46            03   FILLER                 PIC X(8) VALUE "EMPLOYEE".
47            03   FILLER                 PIC X(6) VALUE SPACES.
48            03   FILLER                 PIC X(8) VALUE "EMPLOYEE".
49            03   FILLER                 PIC X(11) VALUE SPACES.
50            03   FILLER                 PIC X(7) VALUE "REGULAR".
51            03   FILLER                 PIC X(2) VALUE SPACES.
52            03   FILLER                 PIC X(9) VALUE "OVER-TIME".
53            03   FILLER                 PIC X(3) VALUE SPACES.
```

(continued)

Program 5.1 (continued)

```
54          03  FILLER                      PIC X(3) VALUE "PAY".
55          03  FILLER                      PIC X(2) VALUE SPACES.
56          03  FILLER                      PIC X(12) VALUE "WITH-HOLDING".
57          03  FILLER                      PIC X(5) VALUE SPACES.
58          03  FILLER                      PIC X(4) VALUE "FICA".
59          03  FILLER                      PIC X(5) VALUE SPACES.
60          03  FILLER                      PIC X(5) VALUE "OTHER".
61          03  FILLER                      PIC X(6) VALUE SPACES.
62          03  FILLER                      PIC X(5) VALUE "GROSS".
63          03  FILLER                      PIC X(7) VALUE SPACES.
64          03  FILLER                      PIC X(3) VALUE "NET".
65      01  SUB-HEAD-2.
66          03  FILLER                      PIC X(2) VALUE SPACES.
67          03  FILLER                      PIC X(6) VALUE "NUMBER".
68          03  FILLER                      PIC X(9) VALUE SPACES.
69          03  FILLER                      PIC X(4) VALUE "NAME".
70          03  FILLER                      PIC X(14) VALUE SPACES.
71          03  FILLER                      PIC X(5) VALUE "HOURS".
72          03  FILLER                      PIC X(5) VALUE SPACES.
73          03  FILLER                      PIC X(5) VALUE "HOURS".
74          03  FILLER                      PIC X(4) VALUE SPACES.
75          03  FILLER                      PIC X(4) VALUE "RATE".
76          03  FILLER                      PIC X(2) VALUE SPACES.
77          03  FILLER                      PIC X(4) VALUE "RATE".
78          03  FILLER                      PIC X(2) VALUE SPACES.
79          03  FILLER                      PIC X(6) VALUE "AMOUNT".
80          03  FILLER                      PIC X(12) VALUE SPACES.
81          03  FILLER                      PIC X(10) VALUE "DEDUCTIONS".
82          03  FILLER                      PIC X(4) VALUE SPACES.
83          03  FILLER                      PIC X(3) VALUE "PAY".
84          03  FILLER                      PIC X(8) VALUE SPACES.
85          03  FILLER                      PIC X(3) VALUE "PAY".
86      01  DETAIL-LINE.
87          03  FILLER                      PIC X    VALUE SPACES.
88          03  EMPLOYEE-NUMBER-OUT         PIC 9(9).
89          03  FILLER                      PIC X(2) VALUE SPACES.
90          03  EMPLOYEE-NAME-OUT           PIC X(20).
91          03  FILLER                      PIC X(3) VALUE SPACES.
92          03  REG-HRS-OUT                 PIC ZZ.9.
93          03  FILLER                      PIC X(6) VALUE SPACES.
94          03  OT-HRS-OUT                  PIC ZZ.9.
95          03  FILLER                      PIC X(3) VALUE SPACES.
96          03  PAY-RATE-OUT                PIC $ZZ.99.
97          03  FILLER                      PIC X(2) VALUE SPACES.
98          03  WITH-RATE-OUT               PIC .999.
99          03  FILLER                      PIC X VALUE SPACES.
100         03  WITH-AMT-OUT                PIC $ZZZ.99.
101         03  FILLER                      PIC X(3) VALUE SPACES.
102         03  FICA-OUT                    PIC $ZZZ.99.
103         03  FILLER                      PIC X(3) VALUE SPACES.
104         03  OTHER-DEDUCTIONS-OUT        PIC $ZZZ.99.
105         03  FILLER                      PIC X(3) VALUE SPACES.
```

(continued)

Program 5.1   (continued)

```
106            03  GROSS-PAY-OUT           PIC $Z(4).99.
107            03  FILLER                  PIC X(3) VALUE SPACES.
108            03  NET-PAY-OUT             PIC $Z(4).99.
109            03  FILLER                  PIC X    VALUE SPACES.
110        01  TOTAL-LINE.
111            03  FILLER                  PIC X(54) VALUE SPACES.
112            03  FILLER                  PIC X(6) VALUE "TOTALS".
113            03  FILLER                  PIC X(4) VALUE SPACES.
114            03  TOTAL-WITH-OUT          PIC $Z(4).99.
115            03  FILLER                  PIC X VALUE SPACES.
116            03  TOTAL-FICA-OUT          PIC $Z(5).99.
117            03  FILLER                  PIC X VALUE SPACES.
118            03  TOTAL-OTHER-OUT         PIC $Z(5).99.
119            03  FILLER                  PIC X VALUE SPACES.
120            03  TOTAL-GROSS-OUT         PIC $Z(6).99.
121            03  FILLER                  PIC X VALUE SPACES.
122            03  TOTAL-NET-OUT           PIC $Z(6).99.
123        PROCEDURE DIVISION.
124        100-MAIN-LOGIC.
125            PERFORM 200-INITIALIZATION.
126            PERFORM 400-READ.
127            PERFORM 300-PROCESS-READ UNTIL EOF-FLAG = 1.
128            PERFORM 700-TERMINATION.
129        200-INITIALIZATION.
130            OPEN INPUT IN-FD, OUTPUT PRINT.
131            WRITE PRINT-LINE FROM HEADING-LINE AFTER PAGE.
132            WRITE PRINT-LINE FROM SUB-HEAD-1 AFTER 2.
133            WRITE PRINT-LINE FROM SUB-HEAD-2 AFTER 1.
134            MOVE SPACES TO PRINT-LINE.
135            WRITE PRINT-LINE AFTER 1.
136        300-PROCESS-READ.
137            PERFORM 500-COMPUTATIONS.
138            PERFORM 600-DETAIL-OUTPUT.
139            PERFORM 400-READ.
140        400-READ.
141            READ IN-FD AT END MOVE 1 TO EOF-FLAG.
142        500-COMPUTATIONS.
143            COMPUTE GROSS-PAY ROUNDED = REG-HRS-IR * PAY-RATE-IR +
144                OT-HRS-IR * PAY-RATE-IR * 1.5.
145            MULTIPLY WITH-RATE-IR BY GROSS-PAY GIVING WITH-AMT ROUNDED.
146            MULTIPLY FICA-FACTOR BY GROSS-PAY GIVING FICA ROUNDED.
147            SUBTRACT WITH-AMT, FICA, OTHER-DEDUCTIONS-IR
148                FROM GROSS-PAY GIVING NET-PAY.
149            ADD WITH-AMT              TO TOTAL-WITH
150            ADD FICA                 TO TOTAL-FICA.
151            ADD OTHER-DEDUCTIONS-IR   TO TOTAL-OTHER.
152            ADD GROSS-PAY            TO TOTAL-GROSS.
153            ADD NET-PAY             TO TOTAL-NET.
154        600-DETAIL-OUTPUT.
155            MOVE EMPLOYEE-NUMBER-IR   TO EMPLOYEE-NUMBER-OUT.
156            MOVE EMPLOYEE-NAME-IR     TO EMPLOYEE-NAME-OUT.
157            MOVE REG-HRS-IR          TO REG-HRS-OUT.
158            MOVE OT-HRS-IR           TO OT-HRS-OUT.
```

(continued)

Program 5.1 (continued)

```
159          MOVE  PAY-RATE-IR          TO PAY-RATE-OUT.
160          MOVE  WITH-RATE-IR         TO WITH-RATE-OUT.
161          MOVE  OTHER-DEDUCTIONS-IR  TO-OTHER-DEDUCTIONS-OUT.
162          MOVE  WITH-AMT             TO WITH-AMT-OUT.
163          MOVE  FICA                 TO FICA-OUT.
164          MOVE  GROSS-PAY            TO GROSS-PAY-OUT.
165          MOVE  NET-PAY              TO NET-PAY-OUT.
166          WRITE PRINT-LINE FROM DETAIL-LINE AFTER 1.
167      700-TERMINATION.
168          MOVE  TOTAL-WITH   TO TOTAL-WITH-OUT.
169          MOVE  TOTAL-FICA   TO TOTAL-FICA-OUT.
170          MOVE  TOTAL-OTHER  TO TOTAL-OTHER-OUT.
171          MOVE  TOTAL-GROSS  TO TOTAL-GROSS-OUT.
172          MOVE  TOTAL-NET    TO TOTAL-NET-OUT.
173          WRITE PRINT-LINE FROM TOTAL-LINE AFTER 2.
174          CLOSE IN-FD, PRINT.
175          STOP RUN.
```

Sample Output

```
                          XYZ COMPANY PAYROLL REGISTER

EMPLOYEE    EMPLOYEE    REGULAR OVER-TIME   PAY    WITH-HOLDING   FICA     OTHER       GROSS     NET
 NUMBER       NAME       HOURS   HOURS     RATE   RATE   AMOUNT          DEDUCTIONS     PAY      PAY

300000000 JOE  JONES      40.0     4.0    $12.00  .010 $  5.52  $ 32.02   $125.00   $ 552.00  $ 389.46
200000000 TOM  JONES      40.0     5.0    $20.00  .050 $ 47.50  $ 55.10   $150.00   $ 950.00  $ 697.40
100000000 PINK PANTHER    40.0      .0    $10.00  .050 $ 20.00  $ 23.20   $100.00   $ 400.00  $ 256.80
400000000 AMY  SMITH      40.0      .0    $25.00  .100 $100.00  $ 58.00   $300.00   $1000.00  $ 542.00

                                           TOTALS  $173.02  $168.32   $675.00  $2902.00  $1885.66
```

5.7 PROGRAM EXAMPLE

Program 5.1 is a solution to the following problem:

The XYZ Company requires a payroll register to be constructed showing gross pay and net pay for its employees. Input consists of records containing the following fields:

Employee number
Employee name
Regular hours worked
Overtime hours worked
Pay rate
Federal withholding rate
Other deductions

The program must calculate and print:

Gross pay
Amount of federal income tax to withhold
Amount of FICA taxes to withhold
Net pay

The program must also accumulate and print appropriate totals.

Program 5.1 makes extensive use of the arithmetic statements described in this chapter, particularly in the paragraph 500-COMPUTATIONS (lines 141 through 152). The program also illustrates several new COBOL features and structured programming practices.

Continuation of Nonnumeric Literals

Lines 41 and 42 of the program illustrate the procedure for continuing nonnumeric literals from one line to the next.

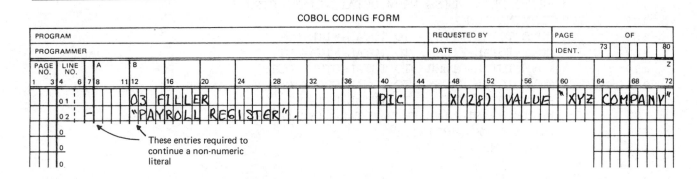

Figure 5.7 Continuation of non-numeric literals

As shown in Figure 5.7 above, the literal XYZ COMPANY PAYROLL REGISTER is broken into two parts; the first part on line 41 extends from positions 61 through 72; the second part is on line 42 positions 13 through 28. The two parts are connected by placing a dash ("−") in position 7 and quotes in margin B (position 12) of the continuation line. In general, the placement of a "−" in position 7 of a line will cause the content of that line to be treated as a continuation of the preceding line. When using this mechanism to continue nonnumeric literals,[2] the remaining characters of the literal must be preceded by a quote in margin B. Note that there are no quotes following the literal on the first line; all of the characters from the opening quote (position 60 in Figure 5.7) through position 72 are treated as part of the literal.

Grouping of Related Fields in WORKING-STORAGE

A number of variables in addition to the usual output records are defined in WORKING-STORAGE (lines 28 through 38). All of the variables could be defined as 01 items; however, current structured programming practice requires that related items which describe the relation be grouped under 01 items. Thus, under COMPUTED-AMOUNTS the items WITH-AMT, NET-PAY, GROSS-PAY and FICA are defined, and under TOTALS all the variables which are used as accumulators are defined. This practice makes the program easier to read.

VALUE Clause For All Variables

In Program 5.1 the variables listed under TOTALS are all accumulators. The VALUE clause is used to ensure that the initial value of each variable is zero so that the accumulation process will function properly. The variables listed under COMPUTED-AMOUNTS are also initialized to zero. This is not a requirement of

---

[2]Although other COBOL elements including data-names, numeric-constants and reserved words can be continued by use of a "−" in position 7, the continuation facility is recommended only for non-numeric literals.

the logic of the program since the value in each of them is replaced by appropriate statements in 500-COMPUTATIONS (see lines 142, 144, 145 and 147). The VALUE clause is used in these cases because of the general principle of structured programming:

> All elementary non-report items defined in WORKING-STORAGE should be given an initial value.

The reason for this practice lies not in an absolute requirement for logical correctness but in making the program easier to debug and update.

Suppose, for example, that a programmer omits the initialization of some variable such as FICA-AMT. Suppose further that the statement computing FICA-AMT is omitted in the PROCEDURE DIVISION. In this case the first reference to FICA-AMT usually will cause the program to terminate because of invalid data. The source of such errors usually is difficult to locate. However, if FICA-AMT had been initialized, the reference to the variable would have been processed with a value zero and the program would have continued in a normal fashion. When the programmer noted that the value of FICA-AMT was zero on the sample output, he or she could surmise that the computation in the PROCEDURE DIVISION was either incorrect or omitted. The debugging process thus is simplified considerably.

This practice also results in programs which are easier to update. If a subsequent revision of the program results in the deletion of the statement which computes a value for the variable, the remaining statements can be left unaltered because the variable will have no effect on the computations.

Constants in WORKING-STORAGE

Consider the data item FICA-FACTOR defined in line 27 of Program 5.1. This value is used in the computation of the FICA withholding amount at line 145. The practice of defining constants such as this in WORKING-STORAGE makes programs easier to change when the value of the constant changes. If this practice is followed, a programmer performing maintenance only has to make a single change in a well defined, easily located WORKING-STORAGE entry. Otherwise, the maintenance programmer must search through the PROCEDURE DIVISION and change every instance where the constant is used. This is a particular burden if the constant is used more than once. There is always the chance that one value will be changed but another will not be resulting in a potentially difficult debugging problem.

5.8 THE ON SIZE ERROR OPTION

The ON SIZE ERROR option causes the program to test for error and to take appropriate action when two types of errors are found during execution of an arithmetic statement:

1) Division by a divisor having value zero.
2) A receiving field which is too small to accept all the significant digits to the left of the decimal point of the calculated result.

The programmer is responsible for specifying data items which are sufficiently large to hold any valid results. The programmer also needs to ensure that the computer is not asked to attempt the impossible operation of dividing by zero. However, such errors do occur due to errors in data and/or programmer oversight. The ON SIZE ERROR option allows the program to take appropriate action when such errors are detected during execution of a program. If the ON SIZE ERROR option is included in the arithmetic statement, the statement in that clause will be executed if either of the errors is detected. The general form of the clause is

> ON <u>SIZE</u> <u>ERROR</u> statement. . .

Any number of statements may be included in an ON SIZE ERROR clause. The clause is placed after the main body of each of the arithmetic statements.

Add X (78.3) and Y (87.2) to get Z; also, if a size error appears write an appropriate message.   *Example*

```
ADD X, Y GIVING Z
    ON SIZE ERROR
        WRITE OUTLINE FROM ERROR-MISC-LINE AFTER 1.
```

Before Execution

  7 8 3   8 7 2

X PIC 99V9   Y PIC 99V9   Z PIC 99V9

Computation:

	78.3
	+87.2
Size error	
detected	165.5

Since a size error has occurred, the WRITE statement will be executed; that is, the program will now print a message explaining that the answer field is too small.

After Execution

  6 5 5

Z PIC 99V9

The content of ERROR-MSG-LINE will be written on the printer. An appropriate message would be "ARITHMETIC OVERFLOW HAS OCCURRED."

Divide the contents of FLDA (2.3) by the contents of FLDB (0) to get FLDC.   *Example*
Also, if a size error occurs, move both FLDA and FLDB to a report line that explains the error.

```
DIVIDE FLDA BY FLDB GIVING FLDC
    ON SIZE ERROR
        MOVE FLDA TO FLDA-OUT
        MOVE FLDB TO FLDB-OUT
        WRITE OUT-LINE FROM ERR-LINE AFTER 1.
```

Another option for this statement would be

```
DIVIDE FLDA BY FLDB GIVING FLDC
    ON SIZE ERROR
        PERFORM ERROR-MESSAGE-OUTPUT.
```

The paragraph ERROR-MESSAGE-OUTPUT would contain the required statements to produce the error message.

Before Execution

0	2	3

0	0

FLDA PIC 99V9   FLDB PIC 99

Since the value of the divisor is zero, the statements in the ON SIZE ERROR clause will be executed; the division will not be performed.

In each of the above examples, the sentence following the arithmetic statement will be executed next after the ON SIZE ERROR statements have been executed. In flowchart form the ON SIZE ERROR option is shown as:

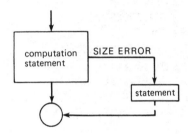

If a division by zero is attempted by a statement and the ON SIZE ERROR clause is not a part of the statement, the program is halted by the operating system, which prints an appropriate error message. If a receiving field is too small to accept the significant digits to the left of the decimal point and the ON SIZE ERROR clause is not a part of the statement, the results are moved to the receiving field and the leftmost digits will be truncated.

Add one variable X, to another, Y, to get the result Z.   *Example*

ADD X, Y GIVING Z.

Before Execution

7	8	3

8	7	2

X PIC 99V9   Y PIC 99V9   Z PIC 99V9

Computation: 78.3
                87.2
             165.5

After Execution

7	8	3

8	7	2

left most digits
of receiving field

6	5	5

X PIC 99V9   Y PIC 99V9   have been truncated.   Z PIC 99V9

One area in programming in which size errors are particularly prevalent is in the accumulation of totals. The programmer has little control over the number of records the program will process or the size of the values that fields will contain. Inflation, which causes values to increase, is a partial cause of this problem; a program which performed adequately in the past may be faced with an overflow in accumulation of totals because of newly inflated values.

One way in which the programmer can warn the user of a report that overflow has occurred is by placement of flags beside fields in which there has been overflow. For example, suppose the TOTAL-LINE from Program 5.1 (lines 109 through 121) is replaced with the following:

```
01   TOTAL LINE.
     03   FILLER                 PIC  X(54)   VALUE  SPACES.
     03   FILLER                 PIC  X(6)    VALUE  "TOTALS".
     03   FILLER                 PIC  X(4)    VALUE  SPACES.
     03   TOTAL-WITH-OUT         PIC  $Z(4).99.
     03   ERROR-IN-WITH-FLAG     PIC  X   VALUE  SPACES.
     03   TOTAL-FICA-OUT         PIC  $Z(5).99.
     03   ERROR-IN-FICA-FLAG     PIC  X   VALUE  SPACES.
     03   TOTAL-OTHER-OUT        PIC  $Z(5).99.
     03   ERROR-IN-OTHER-FLAG    PIC  X   VALUE  SPACES.
     03   TOTAL-GROSS-OUT        PIC  $Z(6).99.
     03   ERROR-IN-GROSS-FLAG    PIC  X   VALUE  SPACES.
     03   TOTAL-NET-OUT          PIC  $Z(6).99.
     03   ERROR-IN-NET-FLAG      PIC  X   VALUE  SPACES.
```

Each accumulated total has been provided with a field into which an appropriate character such as "*" can be placed if overflow occurs. The statements which compute these totals in the PROCEDURE DIVISION (lines 148 through 152) can be replaced by.

```
ADD WITH-AMT TO TOTAL-WITH
    ON SIZE ERROR MOVE "*" TO ERROR-INT-WITH-FLAG.
ADD FICA TO TOTAL-FICA
    ON SIZE ERROR MOVE "*" TO ERROR-IN-FICA-FLAG.
ADD OTHER-DEDUCTIONS-IR TO TOTAL-OTHER
    ON SIZE ERROR MOVE "*" TO ERROR-IN-OTHER-FLAG.
ADD GROSS-PAY TO TOTAL-GROSS
    ON SIZE ERROR MOVE "*" TO ERROR-IN-GROSS-FLAG.
ADD NET-PAY TO TOTAL-NET
    ON SIZE ERROR MOVE "*" TO ERROR-IN-NET-FLAG.
```

If a size error occurs in any of the accumulation statements, the character "*" will be moved to the appropriate output field. Output from this program might appear as

```
TOTALS     $1129.30 $304.00    $3222.19   $5241.14*$1035.91*
```

in which overflow has occurred in accumulation of the last two items— TOTAL-GROSS and TOTAL-NET.

5.9   DEBUG CLINIC

Computation With Nonnumeric Items

Note that in Program 5.1, several data items appear to be defined twice. For example, consider GROSS-PAY (line 105). GROSS-PAY is defined as a numeric item (PIC 9999V99) while GROSS-PAY-OUT is defined as a report item (PIC $Z(4).99). This dual definition is necessary because after GROSS-PAY is computed (line 142), it is required for further computations (lines 147 and 151). In general a computation statement may place results in a report item. For example,

```
COMPUTE GROSS-PAY-OUT ROUNDED =
   REG-HRS-IR * PAY-RATE-IR +
   OT-HRS-IR * PAY-RATE-IR * 1.5
```

would be a valid statement. The result would be computed and the value would be edited when placed in GROSS-PAY-OUT. But GROSS-PAY-OUT is a nonnumeric item because of the editing process. Because it is nonnumeric, it cannot be a part of a numeric operation. Thus, a statement such as

```
ADD GROSS-PAY-OUT TO TOTAL-GROSS
```

would be invalid.

Items used as accumulators are used both as the receiving field and as a part of the computation, so accumulators must be defined as numeric fields as well as edited output fields. In preparation for output, the numeric field which has acted as an accumulator is moved to an appropriately edited output field. Any other item which will be used in further computations after a value is placed in it must be defined both as a numeric field and as an edited field. Computations cannot be performed on nonnumeric edited data items.

Testing Programs

As programs become longer and more complex, the job of providing adequate test data becomes more demanding. In fact, it may be necessary to test programs with more than one set of data records to make sure that the program will function properly in all sets of circumstances. A common practice is to test each program at least three times: once with no data (that is, with an input file which contains no data records); again with "good" data (data which results in no error conditions); and finally with "bad" data (data which tests the program's ability to handle error conditions). The development of a set of data records which provides a thorough test of a program's logic should be started early in the program development cycle. This task is one that beginning programmers often do not perform adequately because it can be tedious and time consuming; however, the success or failure of a programming project often hinges as much on thorough testing of the finished product as it does on imaginative program design or meticulous coding. Placing a program into production before it has been adequately tested surely will be embarrassing for the programmer and perhaps expensive for the organization. The old engineering maxim "there is never time to do it right but always time to do it over" often applies to programming.

5.10 SELF TEST EXERCISES

1. Write COBOL statements for each of the following:
   a. Add A and B
   b. Subtract EXPENSE from INCOME and store result in BALANCE
   c. Store the product of A and D in A
   d. Divide SALES by 12 and store the quotient in MONTHLY-AVERAGE
   e. Compute the volume of a sphere ($V = 4/3\,\pi\,r^3$)
   f. $I = P \times R \times T$
   g. $a = 25\%$ of b
   h. $A = P(1 + r)^n$

2. Show the contents of each data item after execution of each of the following statements:

a. ADD A, B GIVING C ROUNDED

| 0 2 3 | 0 4 5 6 | ___ |

A PIC 99V9   B PIC 99V99   C PIC 99

b. SUBTRACT A FROM C GIVING B

| 0 3 $\bar{2}$ | 1 7 $\bar{0}$ | ___ |

A PIC 99V9   C PIC S99V9   B PIC 99

c. MULTIPLY C BY B

| 0 3 2 $\overset{+}{1}$ | 0 4 $\bar{2}$ |

C PIC S99V99   B PIC S999

d. DIVIDE C BY B GIVING A ROUNDED REMAINDER D

| 0 6 $\bar{0}$ | 1 2 0 | ___ | ___ |

C PIC S99V9   B PIC S999   A PIC S99V9   D PIC S99

e. COMPUTE A = B ** 3

| 0 $\bar{3}$ | ___ |

B PIC S99   A PIC S999

f. COMPUTE A ROUNDED = C + B * A ON SIZE ERROR MOVE 0 TO A

| 0 5 | 1 2 3 | 1 6 |

C PIC 99   B PIC 99V9   A PIC V99

g. COMPUTE A = A + (B - C) / B
       ON SIZE ERROR
          MOVE 0 TO A.

| 3 2 0 | 0 0 | 0 1 2 |

A PIC 99V9   B PIC 99   C PIC 999

h. MULTIPLY A BY B GIVING C ROUNDED.

| 3 2 $\bar{0}$ | 0 1 0 2 | ___ |

A PIC S99V9   B PIC 99V99   C PIC 99

i. DIVIDE A INTO B.

| 3 2 $\bar{0}$ | 6 4 $\overset{+}{0}$ |

A PIC S99V9   B PIC S99V9

3. Draw a structure diagram for Program 5.1. Identify each paragraph as a control or operation paragraph.

4. With respect to the operation of Program 5.1, what purpose is served by each of the following:
   a. line 28
   b. The VALUE clause on line 9.
   c. The "−" in position 7 of line 42.
   d. line 27
   e. The ROUNDED option on line 142.
5. Given a date in the form m/d compute the equivalent approximate Julian date. Julian date refers to the day of the year: Jan. 1 has Julian date 1, Dec. 31 has Julian date 365, and so on.

5.11 PROGRAMMING EXERCISES

1. Write a program to compute the amount of money one will earn if he or she invests P dollars at an interest rate R for N years with interest compounded daily. The formula required is:

   $$A = P \times (1 + R / 360)^{360 \times N}$$

2. Write a program to produce an end-of-year sales summary for a retail store. Input consists of records containing the following fields:

   Department name and number
   Amount of sales in first quarter
   Amount of ales in second quarter
   Amount of sales in third quarter
   Amount of sales in fourth quarter

   Output should consist of all input data and the total sales for each department as well as the total yearly sales for the store.

3. Write a program that could be used by a department store to determine the value of items in stock. Input consists of records containing:

   Quantity
   Item (including stock number and name)
   Unit cost

   Output should consist of all data read in and the value of each item (quantity * unit cost) as well as the total value of all items in stock.

4. An inventory file contains records in the following format:

Positions	
1-6	Item number
7-20	Description
21-26	Cost
27-32	Selling price

   A sale is planned with progressive discounts from selling price of 10%, 15% and 20%. Write a program to list all of the input data and the three discounted selling prices.

5. A daily sales file contains records with the following fields:

   Department number (1, 2, 3, or 4)
   Date
   Item description
   Selling price for each item
   Cost of each item

   Write a program to list all input data and compute total amount of sale and profit for each sale. Accumulate and print totals of sales and profits.

6. A check digit is an extra digit of an account number which is computed as a function of the other digits. Its purpose is to enable the verification of valid account numbers. If any digits are mispunched or transposed, the check digit computed by the program will not match the check digit of the account number, thus enabling the identification of an invalid account number. There are a number of schemes for computation of check digits. One of the most effective methods uses the following sequence of steps:

  a. Suppose the account number contains 5 digits and a sixth check digit:

$$d_1d_2d_3d_4d_5d_{ck}$$

  b. Compute $S = d_1 + 2 \times d_2 + 3 \times d_3 + 5 \times d_4 + 7 \times d_5$ (the multipliers are purposely chosen to be prime numbers; this system has been shown to yield very good error detection capabilities).

  c. The check digit d_{ck} is the one's digit of S.

Suppose the account number is 23576.   *Example*

$$S = 2 + 2 \times 3 + 3 \times 5 + 5 \times 7 + 7 \times 6 = 100$$

The ones digit of 100 is 0, hence $d_{ck} = 0$. The complete account number is 235760. Suppose that in the transcription process two digits of the account number are transposed (a very common error); for example, 237560 is entered instead of 235760. The check digit computation for 235760 is $S = 2 + 2 \times 3 + 3 \times 7 + 5 \times 5 + 7 \times 6 = 96$; hence, the check digit for this account number would be 6, not 0: The erroneous account number has been detected.

Write a program to input a sequence of account numbers and compute the check digit.

7. Write a program to generate seven-digit account numbers beginning with 1000001 using the method for check digit computation described in Exercise 6 above. Often the check digit is inserted as middle digit in the account number, e.g., 10001000. check digit. Modify your program to list the account numbers in this fashion.

8. Write a program to list the number of bills of each denomination required make up the pay envelopes for a payroll. Input consists of the net amount to be paid in dollars. Output should consist of the number of twenties, tens, fives and ones required for that amount. Compute and list the total number of bills of each denomination which will be required. For example, $273 would be made up of

$$
\begin{array}{ll}
13 \text{ twenties} & = \$260 \\
1 \text{ ten} & = \$\ 10 \\
0 \text{ fives} & = \$\ \ 0 \\
3 \text{ ones} & = \underline{\$\ \ \ 3} \\
& \$273
\end{array}
$$

9. Write a program to calculate the amount of monthly payment required to pay a mortgage based on the following input data:

Principal (P)   The required formula is

Interest rate (R)

Time in years (T)

$$\dfrac{P \times \dfrac{R}{12}}{1 - \left[\dfrac{1}{1 + \dfrac{R}{12}}\right]^{(T\times12)}}$$

Use the following test data:

P	R	I	Expected Value of Monthly Payment
$10,000	.08	20	$83.64
$65,000	.16	30	$874.09
$105,000	.175	25	$1551.41

Note: Your computed values may vary slightly from those shown due to internal differences among computers.

THE IF STATEMENT AND CONDITIONS 6

6.1 PROGRAM EXAMPLE

Program 6.1 shows a solution to the following problem:

A company maintains a personnel file, each record of which contains

employee identification number
employee name
sex (M=male, F=female)
age of the employee
year employee was hired

The personnel manager needs a list of employees hired prior to 1960. Write a program to process the personnel file and generate the report.

Program 6.1 Employee report

```
Line
1        IDENTIFICATION DIVISION.
2        PROGRAM-ID. CHAPTER 6 EXAMPLE 1.
3        AUTHOR. PAULA.
4        ENVIRONMENT DIVISION.
5        INPUT-OUTPUT SECTION.
6        FILE-CONTROL.
7            SELECT PERSONNEL-DATA-FILE ASSIGN TO DISK.
8            SELECT PRE-1960-EMPLOYEE-REPORT ASSIGN TO PRINTER.
9        DATA DIVISION.
10       FILE SECTION.
11       FD PERSONNEL-DATA-FILE
12           DATA RECORD IS PERSONNEL-DATA-RECORD.
13       01   PERSONNEL-DATA-RECORD.
14            03   ID-NUM-PDR        PIC X(9).
15            03   NAME-PDR          PIC X(15).
16            03   SEX-PDR           PIC X.
17            03   AGE-PDR           PIC 99.
```

(continued)

Program 6.1   (continued)

```
18              03   DATE-HIRED-PDR   PIC 9999.
19              03   FILLER           PIC X(59).
20         FD   PRE-1960-EMPLOYEE-REPORT
21              DATA RECORD IS OUTPUT-RECORD.
22         01   OUTPUT-RECORD         PIC X(132).
23         WORKING-STORAGE SECTION.
24         01   EOF-FLAG              PIC 9 VALUE ZERO.
25         01   HEAD-LINE.
26              03   FILLER           PIC X(35) VALUE SPACES.
27              03   FILLER           PIC X(29) VALUE
28                   "EMPLOYEES HIRED PRIOR TO 1960".
29              03 FILLER             PIC X(53) VALUE SPACES.
30         01   PRE-1960-EMPLOYEES-OUT.
31              03   FILLER           PIC X(21) VALUE SPACES.
32              03   ID-NUM-OUT       PIC X(9).
33              03   FILLER           PIC X(5)  VALUE SPACES.
34              03   NAME-OUT         PIC X(15).
35              03   FILLER           PIC X(5)  VALUE SPACES.
36              03   SEX-OUT          PIC X.
37              03   FILLER           PIC X(5)  VALUE SPACES.
38              03   AGE-OUT          PIC 99.
39              03   FILLER           PIC X(5)  VALUE SPACES.
40              03   DATE-HIRED-OUT   PIC 9999.
41         PROCEDURE DIVISION.
42         100-MAIN-ROUTINE.
43            PERFORM 200-INITIALIZATION.
44            PERFORM 300-SERVICE-LENGTH-DECISION UNTIL EOF-FLAG = 1.
45            PERFORM 700-TERMINATION.
46         200-INITIALIZATION.
47            OPEN INPUT PERSONNEL-DATA-FILE
48                   OUTPUT PRE-1960-EMPLOYEE-REPORT.
49            MOVE HEAD-LINE TO OUTPUT-RECORD.
50            WRITE OUTPUT-RECORD AFTER PAGE.
51            READ PERSONNEL-DATA-FILE AT END MOVE 1 TO EOF-FLAG.
52         300-SERVICE-LENGTH-DECISION.
53            IF DATE-HIRED-PDR < 1960
54               PERFORM 400-EMPLOYEE-REPORT
55            ELSE
56               NEXT SENTENCE.
57            READ PERSONNEL-DATA-FILE AT END MOVE 1 TO EOF-FLAG.
58         400-EMPLOYEE-REPORT.
59            MOVE ID-NUM-PDR      TO ID-NUM-OUT.
60            MOVE NAME-PDR        TO NAME-OUT.
61            MOVE SEX-PDR         TO SEX-OUT.
62            MOVE AGE-PDR         TO AGE-OUT.
63            MOVE DATE-HIRED-PDR TO DATE-HIRED-OUT.
64            MOVE PRE-1960-EMPLOYEES-OUT TO OUTPUT-RECORD.
65            WRITE OUTPUT-RECORD AFTER 2.
66         700-TERMINATION.
67            CLOSE PERSONNEL-DATA-FILE.
68            CLOSE PRE-1960-EMPLOYEE-REPORT.
69            STOP RUN.
```

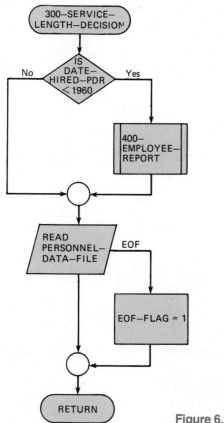

Figure 6.1   Flowchart of decision example.

This program makes use of the IF statement to select those employees to be listed in the report (lines 53 through 56). For each employee record read, the content of DATE-HIRED-PDR is compared to 1960. If DATE-HIRED-PDR is less than 1960, the paragraph 400-EMPLOYEE-REPORT is executed. If DATE-HIRED-PDR is greater than or equal to 1960, execution of 400-EMPLOYEE-REPORT is bypassed. In either case the next record from the file is read. The flowchart of the paragraph 300-SERVICE-LENGTH-DECISION is shown in Figure 6.1.

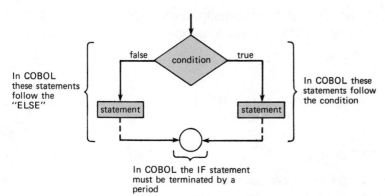

Figure 6.2   Flowchart of the IF/THEN/ELSE structure.

The IF/THEN/ELSE structure along with the sequence and iteration structures are the fundamental constructions required in structured programming. Figure 6.2 illustrates the flowchart form of this structure. In COBOL, the IF statement is used to implement the IF/THEN/ELSE structure. Notice that COBOL syntax omits the word THEN. Those statements following the condition are executed if the condition is true; those statements following ELSE are executed if the condition is false.

6.2 THE IF STATEMENT

The general form of the IF statement is shown in Figure 6.3.

IF condition $\begin{Bmatrix} \text{statement.} . . \\ \underline{\text{NEXT SENTENCE}} \end{Bmatrix} \begin{bmatrix} \underline{\text{ELSE}} & \begin{Bmatrix} \text{statement.} . . \\ \underline{\text{NEXT SENTENCE}} \end{Bmatrix} \end{bmatrix}$.

Figure 6.3 General from of the IF statement.

If the condition is true, only the statement(s) before the ELSE clause will be executed. If the condition is false, the statements following ELSE will be executed; the statements preceding ELSE will *not* be executed.

When the statement(s) either before the ELSE clause or in the ELSE clause are completed, control is given to the sentence following the IF statement. In Figure 6.1, the READ statement will be executed next regardless of which path is taken in the IF statement:

```
IF DATE-HIRED-PDR < 1960
     PERFORM 400-EMPLOYEE-REPORT
ELSE
     NEXT SENTENCE.
READ PERSONNEL-DATA-FILE ...
```

If the value of HOURS is greater than 40, execute OVERTIME-PAY; otherwise, execute REGULAR-PAY.   *Example*

```
IF HOURS > 40
     PERFORM OVERTIME-PAY
ELSE
     PERFORM REGULAR-PAY.
```

If A = B, then execute COMPUTE-PROC and OUTPUT-1 sequentially, and   *Example*
then execute the next sentence. If A ≠ B, perform OUTPUT-2 four times and
then execute the next sentence.

```
IF A = B
     PERFORM COMPUTE-PROC
     PERFORM OUTPUT-1
ELSE
     COMPUTE KOUNT = 1
     PERFORM OUTPUT-2 UNTIL KOUNT > 4.
```

If no action needs to be taken when a true (or false) condition is encountered, the statement NEXT SENTENCE is used to pass control to the sentence following the IF statement.

If the value of the variable CODE is equal to 0, the next sentence is executed; *Example* otherwise, one is added to KOUNT and OUTPUT-ROUTINE is executed and then the next sentence is executed.

```
IF CODE EQUAL 0
    NEXT SENTENCE
ELSE
    ADD 1 TO KOUNT
    PERFORM OUTPUT-ROUTINE.
```

The above example is equivalent to adding one to KOUNT and executing OUTPUT-ROUTINE when the value of CODE is *not* equal to zero. The following statement is thus equivalent to the preceding sentence:

```
IF CODE NOT EQUAL 0
    ADD 1 TO KOUNT
    PERFORM OUTPUT-ROUTINE
ELSE
    NEXT SENTENCE.
```

The ELSE clause of the IF statement is optional. If the ELSE clause is omitted and the condition is false, the sentence following the IF statement is executed. (The statements following the condition are executed only when the condition is true.)

If AGE is greater than 25, move AGE and NAME to an output record and write *Example* the output record.

```
IF AGE IS GREATER THAN 25
    MOVE AGE TO AGE-OUT
    MOVE NAME TO NAME-OUT
    WRITE OUT-REC AFTER 1.
```

If the value of CODE is not equal to 0, add 1 to KOUNT and execute *Example* OUTPUT-ROUTINE.

```
IF CODE NOT EQUAL 0
    ADD 1 TO KOUNT
    PERFORM OUTPUT-ROUTINE.
```

This code is equivalent to

```
IF CODE NOT EQUAL 0
    ADD 1 TO KOUNT
    PERFORM OUTPUT-ROUTINE
ELSE
    NEXT SENTENCE.
```

The rules of COBOL syntax do not require that each statement in an IF statement be placed on a separate line, nor that the word ELSE be aligned with IF as shown in the above examples. However, this placement does aid in readability, and it is a recommended structured programming practice.

6.3 RELATIONAL CONDITIONS

The preceding examples contained many examples of the use of relational conditions. Relational conditions are used to compare two entities (Fig. 6.4).

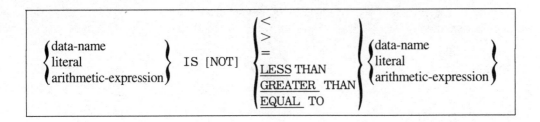

Figure 6.4   General form of relational conditions.

Note that the relation being tested may be expressed either symbolically using the symbol $<$, $>$, or $=$, or verbally as LESS THAN, GREATER THAN, or EQUAL TO. (The use of the words THAN and TO in the verbal expressions is optional.) The meaning of the symbols is shown below:

Symbol	Verbal Expression
$<$	LESS THAN
$>$	GREATER THAN
$=$	EQUAL TO

When writing a condition a programmer may choose a symbol or the corresponding verbal expression at his or her option; the meaning of the resulting condition will be the same.

> The following conditions are equivalent: *Example*
>
> ```
> HOURS > 40
> HOURS GREATER THAN 40
> HOURS GREATER 4
> ```

The word "IS" may be included in a condition at the option of the programmer; the purpose of the word is to aid in readability.

> The following conditions are equivalent to each other and to those in the pre-   *Example*
> vious example:
>
> ```
> HOURS IS > 40
> HOURS IS GREATER THAN 40
> HOURS IS GREATER 40
> ```

To negate any of the relations you will write NOT before the type of relation. For example, the condition

> HOURS IS NOT GREATER THAN 40

is true for values of HOURS 0, 1, 2, 3, . . . , 38, 40 and false if HOURS has value of 41 or larger.

The programmer has a number of alternative ways in which to express the data items he or she wishes to compare. The following examples illustrate some of the possibilities:

Example

```
4  IS EQUAL TO  CODE
```
literal   data-name

This condition will
be true when the
value of CODE is 4
and false otherwise.

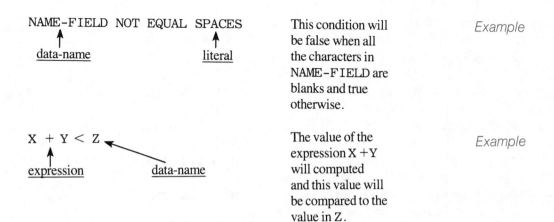

Example

This condition will
be false when all
the characters in
NAME-FIELD are
blanks and true
otherwise.

Example

The value of the
expression X +Y
will computed
and this value will
be compared to the
value in Z.

Occasionally it is necessary to write conditions of the form A ≤ B (A less than or
equal to B) or A ≥ B (A greater than or equal to B) This can be done easily by
using the NOT option. The COBOL equivalent of A ≤ B is

```
A NOT GREATER THAN B
or
A NOT > B
```

If the value of SALES is 600 or greater compute COMMISSION as 10% of *Example*
SALES.

```
IF SALES NOT LESS THAN 600
    MULTIPLY 0.10 BY SALES GIVING COMMISSION.
```

The values 600, 601, 602, ... satisfy the condition SALES NOT LESS THAN 600.

6.4   NESTED IF STATEMENTS

In many instances, actions will depend on conditions being satisfied. For example, suppose we want to count the number of males and females in a set of data
which contains a SEX-CODE having value M for males and F for females. If the
value of SEX-CODE is neither M nor F, the data record contains an error, and we
shall perform an error routine to take appropriate action. This error routine is
performed when the sequence of conditions SEX-CODE = "M" and SEX-CODE =
"F" are both false. The flowchart for this task would be:

The following COBOL code could be used to perform this task.

```
IF  SEX-CODE  =  "M"
    ADD 1 TO MALE-COUNT
ELSE
    IF SEX-CODE  =  "F"
        ADD 1 TO FEMALE-COUNT
    ELSE
        PERFORM ERROR-ROUTINE.
```

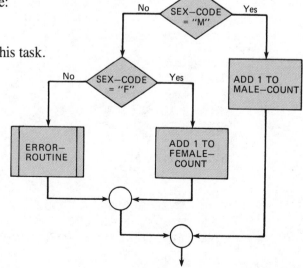

Note that the terminal collector blocks in the above flowchart correspond to the period which terminates the IF statement in the COBOL code. In this example, the ELSE clause of the IF statement which tests the condition SEX-CODE = "M" contains another IF statement which tests the condition SEX-CODE = "F". If both of these conditions are false, then ERROR-ROUTINE will be executed. This is an example of an IF statement which contains another IF statement; statements of this sort are called *nested* IF statements. This example also shows a useful way to test conditions that exclude one another; a person is either male or female, but not both. When an IF statement is nested, an ELSE clause must be included for each IF. For example, suppose we wish to obtain a list of the names of males and females who are over 20 years of age together with the notation OVER 20 and MALE or FEMALE. The flowchart for this task would be:

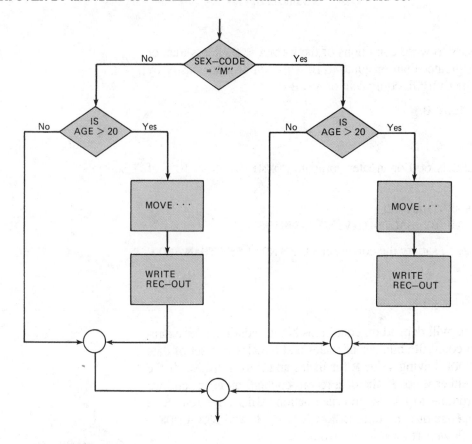

This flowchart would be translated into COBOL as:

```
IF  SEX-CODE  =  "M"
    IF  AGE > 20
        MOVE  "OVER 20"  TO  AGE-OUT
        MOVE  NAME  TO  NAME-OUT
        MOVE  "MALE"  TO  SEX-OUT
        WRITE  REC-OUT  AFTER  1
    ELSE
        NEXT  SENTENCE
ELSE
    IF  AGE > 20
        MOVE  "OVER 20"  TO  AGE-OUT
        MOVE  NAME  TO  NAME-OUT
        MOVE  "FEMALE"  TO  SEX-OUT
```

```
        WRITE REC-OUT AFTER 1
    ELSE
        NEXT SENTENCE.
```

Note the importance of the ELSE clause after WRITE REC-OUT AFTER 1. If this clause were omitted, the next ELSE clause would have been associated with the test on AGE rather than the test on SEX-CODE. The preceding coding could be simplified (and improved) as follows:

```
IF AGE > 20
    MOVE "OVER 20" TO AGE-OUT
    MOVE NAME TO NAME-OUT
    IF SEX-CODE = "M"
        MOVE "MALE" TO SEX-OUT
        WRITE OUT-REC AFTER 1
    ELSE
        MOVE "FEMALE" TO SEX-OUT
        WRITE OUT-REC AFTER 1.
```

The flowchart for this code would be:

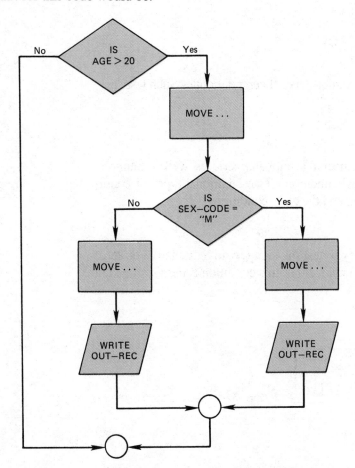

In the preceding example the statement WRITE OUT-REC AFTER 1 occurs in both clauses of the SEX-CODE test. We might wonder if this could not be simplified by placing the common statement after the IF statement, so that no matter which branch of the test is taken, the common statement will still be executed. This is not the case at all, because after either clause of an IF statement is concluded, the *sentence* following is executed next. In the above example, the output is to be performed only if AGE is greater than 20. If the output statement followed the entire IF statement, it would be produced for all values of AGE. If the logic of a problem makes this type of structure necessary, the entire sequence of statements should be placed into a separate paragraph. The preceding code could be written as:

```
    IF AGE > 20 PERFORM OVER-20-ROUTINE.
    .
    .

    .
OVER-20-ROUTINE.
    MOVE "OVER 20" TO AGE-OUT.
    MOVE NAME TO NAME-OUT.
    IF SEX-CODE = 1
        MOVE "MALE" TO SEX-OUT
    ELSE
        MOVE "FEMALE" TO SEX-OUT.
    WRITE OUT-REC AFTER 1.
```

6.5 SIGN AND CLASS CONDITIONS

Thus far all conditions used in our examples have been relational. Such tests as

```
    IF KOUNT IS GREATER THAN 13...
    IF AMOUNT < 0...
    IF SEX-CODE = "M"...
```

use conditions of this type. Remember that alphanumeric as well as numeric tests may be made with the relational condition. Two additional types of conditions may be used: the sign condition and the class condition.

Sign Condition

The sign condition is convenient way to test the sign (positive, negative or zero) of a variable or expression. The general form of this condition is demonstrated in Figure 6.5.

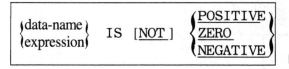

Figure 6.5   General form of the sign condition.

Example

```
    IF KODE IS ZERO...

    PERFORM PARA-X UNTIL A + B IS POSITIVE...

    IF AMOUNT-DUE NEGATIVE...

    IF BALANCE IS NOT NEGATIVE...
```

Note that NOT NEGATIVE is equivalent to testing for greater than or equal to zero, and NOT POSITIVE is equivalent to testing for less than or equal to zero. If a field tested for sign has not been defined using the S picture code, it will never be negative.

Class Condition

The class condition is used to test whether a variable contains alphabetic data or numeric data. Figure 6.6 shows the general form of this condition.

data-name   IS   [NOT] $\begin{cases} \text{NUMERIC} \\ \text{ALPHABETIC} \end{cases}$

Figure 6.6   General form of the class condition.

The numeric test can be performed on fields with numeric or alphanumeric pictures. If the variable contains any characters other than 0, 1, 2, ..., 9 then the numeric test will be false.

Example

```
IF IN-FLD IS NUMERIC..
ELSE...
```

|1|2|3|4| | |1|2|3|

IN-FLD PIC X(4)   IN-FLD PIC X(4)

Numeric test is true.   Numeric test is false because the field contains a blank — a non-numeric character.

The ALPHABETIC test may be performed on fields with alphanumeric or alphabetic pictures. If the field contains solely characters A, B, C, ..., Z or blank, then an ALPHABETIC test will be true; otherwise it will be false.

Example

```
IF NAME IS ALPHABETIC...
ELSE...
```

|J|O|H|N| |J|O|N|E|S|

NAME PIC X(10)
Alphabetic test is true.

|1|2|3|4|A|B|C| | | |

NAME PIC X(10)
Alphabetic test is false

Fields which should contain only numeric characters but do not, and fields which should contain only alphabetic characters or spaces but do not, may occur because of error in data preparation or entry. It is important that data processing systems be provided with error-free data. The class condition is a useful tool to enable the COBOL program to take alternate action when it encounters data containing errors.

6.6 COMPOUND CONDITIONS

All of the conditions described to this point—relational, sign and class—are called *simple* conditions. The logical operations NOT, AND and OR may be used to construct *compound* conditions based on simple conditions.

NOT

The NOT operation acts on a single condition with the general form:

NOT condition

The resulting compound condition is true when the condition is false and false when the condition is true.

Write a condition which will be true when the value of HRS is not greater   *Example*
than forty:

NOT HRS > 40

⌐3¡2⌐

HRS PIC 99   Since HRS > 40 is false, NOT HRS > 40
                    is true.

Write a condition which will be true when NET-PAY is nonnegative (i.e.,   *Example*
greater than or equal to zero).

NOT NET-PAY IS NEGATIVE

⌐0¡0¡3¡6̄¡0¡0⌐

NET-PAY PIC S9999V99 The condition NET-PAY IS NEGA-
                      TIVE is true; therefore, NOT NET-
                      PAY IS NEGATIVE is false.

AND

The AND operation connects two conditions with the general form:

condition-1   AND   condition-2

The resulting compound condition is true only in the case when both condition-1 and condition-2 are true. It is false in all three other cases (that is, it is false if either condition-1 or condition-2 or both are false).

Write a condition which will be true when both A < 10 and B = 4.   *Example*

A < 10 AND B = 4

⌐0¡6⌐   ⌐0¡3⌐

A PIC 99   B PIC 99

The condition A < 10 is true but B = 4 is false.

Write a condition which will check the validity of both HRS and RATE,   *Example*
which are numeric fields.

```
HRS IS NUMERIC AND RATE IS NUMERIC
```

Both HRS and RATE must be NUMERIC for the compound condition to be true.

OR

The OR operation, which connects two conditions, has the general form:

condition-1 OR condition-2

The resulting compound condition is true when either condition-1 or condition-2 (or both) are true (three cases), and false only in the one case when both condition-1 and condition-2 are false.

Write a condition which will be true when either A < 10 or B =4 or both: *Example*

```
A < 10 OR B = 4

 0 6        0 3

A PIC 99   B PIC 99
```

Write a compound condition which will be true if either HRS or RATE is not numeric. *Example*

```
HRS IS NOT NUMERIC OR RATE IS NOT NUMERIC
```

For both the AND and OR operations there are four possible combinations: both conditions being true; either one being false; or both conditions being false. These together with the value of resulting compound conditions are summarized in Figure 6.7. The operation NOT acts only on one condition hence there are only two possibilities—the condition is true or false. The value of the resulting compound condition is summarized in Figure 6.8.

Compound conditions may be used either in IF statements or in the PERFORM statement. For example, suppose we wish to repeat execution of a routine continually until either of two conditions is met. The following code illustrates

condition-1	condition-2	condition-1 AND condition-2	condition-1 OR condition-2
true	true	true	true
true	false	false	true
false	true	false	true
false	false	false	false

Figure 6.7 Summary of logical operations AND and OR.

condition	NOT condition
true	false
false	true

Figure 6.8 Summary of the logical operation NOT.

the use of a compound condition in the PERFORM statement to accomplish this objective:

```
PERFORM ROUTINE
    UNTIL CONDITION-1-FLAG = 1 OR CONDITION-2-FLAG = 1.
```

Similarly, if repetition of a routine is desired until both of two conditions are true the following code could be used:

```
PERFORM ROUTINE
    UNTIL CONDITION-1-FLAG = 1 AND CONDITION-2-FLAG = 1.
```

Suppose, for example, we want to produce a listing of employees with more than thirty years of experience based on a personnel file. The program must process the entire data file. When a record which meets the specified condition is found, the content of that record is listed. The following COBOL code could be used:

```
MAIN-ROUTINE.
    .
    .
    .
    PERFORM LOOP-CONTROL UNTIL EOF = 1.
    .
    .
    .
LOOP-CONTROL.
    PERFORM READ-ROUTINE
        UNTIL EOF = 1 OR YRS-EXPERIENCE > 29.
    IF EOF NOT = 1
        PERFORM OUTPUT-ROUTINE.
READ-ROUTINE.
    READ INPUT-FILE AT END MOVE 1 TO EOF.
OUTPUT-ROUTINE.
    WRITE OUTPUT-RECORD FROM INPUT-RECORD AFTER 1.
```

If more than one logical operation is present in a compound condition, the order in which the operations are evaluated will determine the value of the condition. The same problem arose in the evaluation of arithmetic expressions containing more than one arithmetic operation. Recall that arithmetic operations are assigned precedence. In evaluating an arithmetic expression, arithmetic operations with higher precedence are performed before operations with lower precedence. In a similar fashion, logical operations are assigned precedence to control the order of evaluation in compound conditions. Figure 6.9 gives the rules of precedence for logical operations.

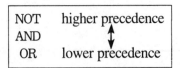

Figure 6.9   Precedence for logical operations.

For example, suppose a variable A has a value 6 and B has value 3. Consider the compound condition:

```
NOT A < 10 AND B = 4
```

Since NOT has higher precedence than AND, the condition NOT A < 10 is evaluated before the condition involving AND. The entire condition will be evaluated as follows:

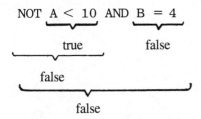

In evaluating a compound condition, the simple conditions which may be relational, class or sign conditions are evaluated first. In this example, the simple conditions are A < 10 and B =4, which are evaluated as true and false respectively. Then the logical operation with highest precedence is evaluated. In this case NOT has highest precedence so the NOT condition is evaluated next. Finally the next highest operation is evaluated, in this case an AND condition which results in the final value of the entire condition.

Consider the following condition with the values of variables as shown: *Example*

A < 10 OR B = 4 AND A IS NOT POSITIVE

⌊0⌊6⌋   ⌊0⌊3⌋

A PIC 99   B PIC 99

The above condition is evaluated as follows:

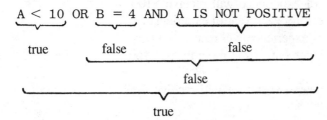

The AND condition is evaluated before the OR condition because AND has higher precedence than OR.

If two or more operators with equal precedence are present (two or more ORs, for example), the conditions are evaluated in order from left to right.

Consider the following condition with the values of variables as shown: *Example*

AGE < 29 AND YRS-EXPERIENCE > 5 AND DEPT-CODE = 3

⌊2⌊8⌋   ⌊0⌊7⌋   ⌊4⌋

AGE PIC 99   YEARS-EXPERIENCE PIC 99   DEPT-CODE PIC 9

The above condition is evaluated as follows:

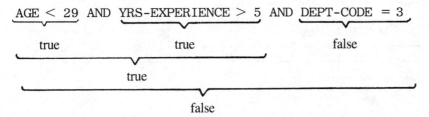

If you want to write a logical expression which requires an order of evaluation different from the normal order, use parentheses. Conditions within parentheses are evaluated before conditions outside parentheses.

Consider the following condition with contents of variables as shown: *Example*

```
NOT  (A < 10  AND  B = 4)
      |0|6|              |0|3|

      A PIC 99          B PIC 99
```

The above expression is evaluated as follows:

```
    NOT  (A < 10  AND  B = 4)
         _____/      \____/
          true          false
         _____/
                   false
   _____/
                true
```

Note that the AND condition is evaluated first in this case because of the parentheses.

The XYZ Department Store has decided to give a Christmas bonus to its   *Example*
employees. The amount of the bonus is subject to the following considerations:

- Employees with less than one year of experience will be given a flat $100 bonus.
- Employees with one to three years of experience will receive $100 plus 10 percent of their monthly paycheck for each year of experience.
- Employees with three to twenty years experience will receive 20 percent of their monthly paycheck plus 5 percent of the monthly pay for each year of experience.
- Employees with more than twenty years experience will receive the same bonus as twenty-year employees.

Let us assume that data records are to be processed containing the following fields:

```
YEARS          number of years experience
MONTHLY-PAY    amount of monthly pay
```

```
IF YEARS = 0
   COMPUTE BONUS = 100.
IF YEARS > 0 AND YEARS NOT > 3
   COMPUTE BONUS = 100 + YEARS * 0.1 * MONTHLY-PAY.
IF YEARS > 3 AND YEARS NOT > 20
   COMPUTE BONUS = .2 * MONTHLY-PAY +
                   YEARS * 0.05 * MONTHLY-PAY.
IF YEARS > 20
   COMPUTE BONUS = 1.2 * MONTHLY-PAY.
```

Figure 6.10   Christmas bonus computation.

The routine required to compute the amount of the Christmas bonus is shown in Figure 6.10. Notice that by use of compound conditions, it is possible to perform the computations without the use of nested IF statements, which would otherwise be required.

6.7   STRUCTURE DIAGRAMS

Recall that structure diagrams represent the relationships among paragraphs in a program. Each paragraph is represented as a block in the diagram; the paragraph name is written in the block. If one paragraph is executed via the PERFORM statement from another, a line connecting the two blocks is drawn.

If the execution of a paragraph is conditional (controlled by an IF statement), the line connecting the two blocks is joined to the block representing the executing paragraph by a diamond-shaped symbol (Fig. 6.11). In this case the left-hand branch of the connecting line represents the paragraph to be executed when the condition is true; the right-hand branch represents the paragraph to be executed when the condition is false. Occasionally a branch on the line may be empty (Fig. 6-12).

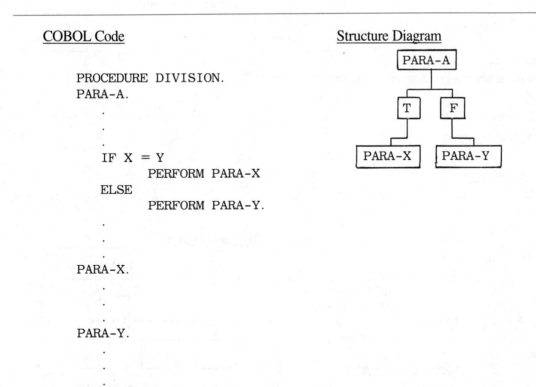

Figure 6.11   Structure diagram reflecting conditional branching.

<u>COBOL Code</u>

```
PROCEDURE DIVISION.
MAIN-LOGIC.
       .
       .
       .
       IF X = Y
                     PERFORM EQUAL-ROUTINE
       ELSE
       .             NEXT SENTENCE.
       .

       .
       IF CODE = 1
                     NEXT SENTENCE.
       ELSE
       .             PERFORM CODE-ROUTINE.
       .

       .
PARA-X.
       .
       .
       .
CODE-ROUTINE.
       .
       .
       .
```

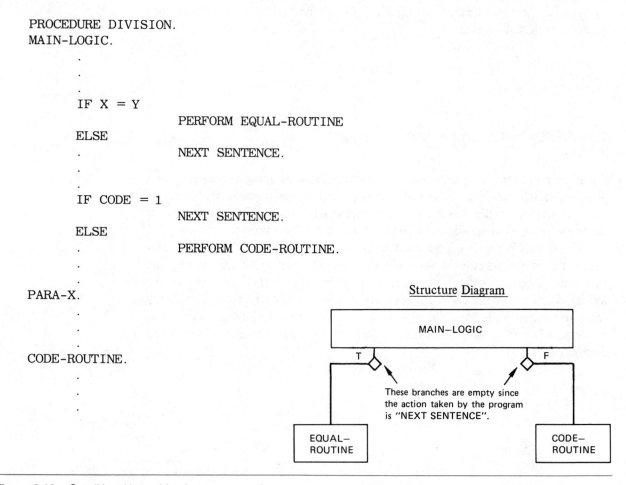

<u>Structure Diagram</u>

Figure 6.12   Conditional branching in a structure diagram.

<u>COBOL Code</u> <u>Structure Diagram</u>

```
PROCEDURE DIVISION.
MAIN-LOGIC.
       .
       .
       .
       IF SW = 0
                     IF A = B
                            PERFORM X
                            PERFORM Y
                     ELSE
                            PERFORM Z
       ELSE
       .             NEXT SENTENCE.
       .

       .
```

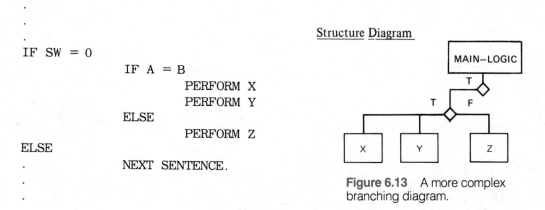

<u>Structure Diagram</u>

Figure 6.13   A more complex branching diagram.

A slightly more complex IF statement and the associated structure diagram are shown in Figure 6.13. Note that along the *true* branch the blocks are placed in the order of the execution of the associated paragraphs from left to right.

6.8 ERROR CHECKING

Errors can enter a data processing system in many ways. Wrong values for data fields can be entered at the source of the data. For example, a clerk sells an item for $10 but writes $9 on the sales ticket. Another source of error occurs at the point that someone generates a machine-readable document that will ultimately be processed by the computing system. In traditional data processing systems, data from a sales ticket would be punched onto cards which could be processed directly by the computer. The key punch operator could make any number of errors in punching the data: digits within a field could be transposed, an alphabetic character could be punched in what should be a numeric field, or a numeric character could be punched in what should be an alphabetic field, to list a few examples. Modern data processing systems often make use of key-to-tape or key-to-disk systems through which the operator records data directly on a tape or disk. However, many of the same kinds of errors are possible. A well-written program will attempt to test the data it processes to detect as many errors as possible in the data items.

Data fields which contain characters of an inappropriate type (i.e., a numeric field which contains an alphabetic character or an alphabetic field which contains a numeric character) are said to contain *invalid* data. The class test is a convenient means for checking the validity of input data fields. Each data item on an input record can be checked using the appropriate class test. If the item does not contain the correct type of data, an error message concerning the record can be written, and processing of the data can be bypassed. For example, consider the following input record description:

```
01    INPUT-RECORD.
      03 EMP-NUM-IR      PIC 9(9).
      03 EMP-NAME-IR     PIC X(20).
      03 HRS-WORKED-IR   PIC 99V99.
      03 PAY-RATE-IR     PIC 99V99.
      03 FILLER          PIC X(43).
```

The code required to check the validity of data in this record might be as shown in Program 6.2. The structure diagram for this program is illustrated in Figure 6.14.

In this program note the use of the switch ERROR-FLAG. The switch is set to value 0 or 1 in 40-ERROR-CHECK-ROUTINE. It is then used by 30-PROCESS-READ to determine the appropriate action to take for the record.

Error checking also may take the form of checking that data in fields is within valid ranges. For example, suppose the maximum and minimum pay-rates are defined in WORKING-STORAGE as:

```
01    PAY-RATES.
      03 MAXIMUM-RATE  PIC 99V99 VALUE 30.00.
      03 MINIMUM-RATE  PIC 99V99 VALUE 3.35.
```

To detect a field outside this range the following statements could be added to

Program 6.2   Validity check program example.

```
10-MAIN-LOGIC
      PERFORM 20-INITIALIZATION.
      PERFORM 30-PROCESS-READ UNTIL EOF = 1.
      PERFORM 80-TERMINATION.
20-INITIALIZATION
      .
      .
      .

30-PROCESS-READ.
      PERFORM 40-ERROR= CHECK-ROUTINE.
      IF ERROR-FLAG = 0
          PERFORM 50-NORMAL-PROCESS
      ELSE
          PERFORM 60-ERROR-PROCESS.
      PERFORM 70-READ-INPUT-FILE.
40-ERROR-CHECK-ROUTINE.
      MOVE 0 TO ERROR-FLAG.
      IF EMP-NUM-IR NOT NUMERIC
          MOVE 1 TO ERROR-FLAG.
      IF EMP-NAME-IR NOT ALPHABETIC
          MOVE 1 TO ERROR-FLAG.
      IF HOURS-WORKED-IR NOT NUMERIC
          MOVE 1 TO ERROR-FLAG.
      IF PAY-RATE NOT NUMERIC
          MOVE 1 TO ERROR-FLAG.
50-NORMAL-PROCESS.
      .
      .
      .

60-ERROR-PROCESS.
      .
      .
      .

70-READ-INPUT-FILE
      .
      .
      .

80-TERMINATION.
```

```
40-ERROR-CHECK-ROUTINE:

      IF PAY-RATE-IR > MAXIMUM-RATE
          MOVE 1 TO ERROR-FLAG.
      IF PAY-RATE-IR < MINIMUM-RATE
          MOVE 1 TO ERROR-FLAG.
```

The use of a simple two-value switch will result in a record being flagged as an error, although no indication will be given as to which field is in error or the type of error which may be present. It is indeed possible to write a complete description of the errors encountered in a data record; it is also possible to generate a code which would indicate which fields are in error and what type of error was encountered. For example, in this case there are four items to be tested, so let's

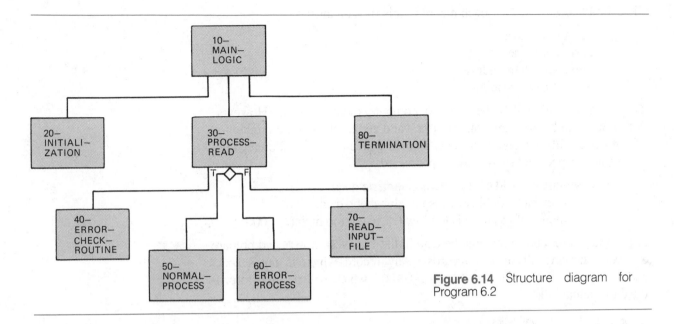

Figure 6.14 Structure diagram for Program 6.2

assume that ERROR-CODE is a four-digit number. The first digit would indicate an error in the first field; the second digit would indicate an error in the second field, and so on. Assume that 1 in a given position would indicate that the wrong type of data is present. A 2 would mean that the value of the data item is out of range. (If there were more types of errors we could easily extend the list of codes.) The 40-ERROR-CHECK-ROUTINE could now be coded as:

```
40-ERROR-CHECK-ROUTINE.
    MOVE 0 TO ERROR-CODE.
    IF EMP-NUM-IR NOT NUMERIC
        ADD 1000 TO ERROR-CODE.
    IF EMP-NUM-IR NOT ALPHABETIC
        ADD 100 TO ERROR-CODE.
    IF HRS-WORKED-IR NOT NUMERIC
        ADD 10 TO ERROR-CODE.
    IF PAY-RATE-IR NOT NUMERIC
        ADD 1 TO ERROR-CODE
    ELSE
        IF PAY-RATE-IR > MAXIMUM-RATE
            ADD 2 TO ERROR-CODE
        ELSE
            ADD 2 TO ERROR-CODE.
```

Naturally, the out-of-range test does not apply to alphabetic information. Therefore, if PAY-RATE-IR is NOT NUMERIC, the testing for an out-of-range value should not be performed. Thus, if EMP-NUM-IR is NOT NUMERIC and the PAY-RATE is out of range, the ERROR-CODE generated would be 1002. The value of ERROR-CODE could be written out along with the data in the 60-ERROR-PROCESS. A programmer-prepared guide for the user (commonly called an operations manual) could explain the meaning of the code used in the flag. In the following example more detailed descriptions of errors are produced.

Program 6.3 represents a solution to the following problem:

Example

At the XYZ Gas Company data gathered by meter readers is loaded into a file called "GAS-USAGE." Each record in this file contains:

> account number
> customer name
> previous meter reading
> present meter reading

This data will ultimately be used to compute monthly bills. However, before this can be done the data must be validated to prevent the production of erroneous bills. In particular, data records with any of the following conditions are suspect and should not be processed:

> any numeric field containing nonnumeric data.
> customer-name field contains nonalphabetic data.
> the amount of gas used is too low (< 10) or too high (> 1000).

A program is needed to process the data in the file GAS-USAGE and prepare a report showing all suspect records. Any record which is not suspect should be written to a file VALID-GAS-USAGE which will be used to produce the actual bills.

Program 6.3   Data validation example

```
1         IDENTIFICATION DIVISION.
2         PROGRAM-ID. CHAPTER 6 EXAMPLE 2.
3         AUTHOR. PAULA.
4         ENVIRONMENT DIVISION.
5         INPUT-OUTPUT SECTION.
6         FILE-CONTROL.
7              SELECT GAS-USAGE ASSIGN TO DISK.
8              SELECT INVALID-DATA-REPORT ASSIGN TO PRINTER.
9              SELECT VALID-GAS-USAGE ASSIGN TO DISK.
10        DATA DIVISION.
11        FILE SECTION.
12        FD   GAS-USAGE
13             DATA RECORD IS GAS-USAGE-RECORD.
14        01   GAS-USAGE-RECORD.
15             02 ACCOUNT-NUMBER      PIC 9(6).
16             02 NAME                PIC X(20).
17             02 PREVIOUS-READING    PIC 9(6).
18             02 PRESENT-READING     PIC 9(6).
19        FD   INVALID-DATA-REPORT
20             DATA RECORD IS PRINT-LINE.
21        01   PRINT-LINE             PIC X(132).
22        FD   VALID-GAS-USAGE
23             DATA RECORD IS VALID-GAS-RECORD.
24        01   VALID-GAS-RECORD       PIC X(38).
25        WORKING-STORAGE SECTION.
26        01   EOF-FLAG               PIC 9 VALUE ZERO.
27        01   ERROR-FLAG             PIC 9 VALUE ZERO.
28        01   USAGE-X                PIC 9(6) VALUE ZERO.
29        01   USAGE-LIMITS.
30             03 LOWER-LIMIT         PIC 9(6) VALUE 10.
31             03 UPPER-LIMIT         PIC 9(6) VALUE 100000.
32        01   HEADING-LINE-1.
33             02 FILLER              PIC X(43) VALUE SPACES.
```

(continued)

Program 6.3   (continued)

```
34                 02 FILLER              PIC X(15)  VALUE
35                     "XYZ GAS COMPANY".
36                 02 FILLER              PIC X(74)  VALUE SPACES.
37          01  HEADING-LINE-2.
38                 02 FILLER              PIC X(14)  VALUE "ACCOUNT NUMBER".
39                 02 FILLER              PIC X(12)  VALUE SPACES.
40                 02 FILLER              PIC X(4)   VALUE "NAME".
41                 02 FILLER              PIC X(12)  VALUE SPACES.
42                 02 FILLER              PIC X(22)  VALUE "PREVIOUS METER READING".
43                 02 FILLER              PIC X(4)   VALUE SPACES.
44                 02 FILLER              PIC X(21)  VALUE "PRESENT METER READING".
45                 02 FILLER              PIC X(4)   VALUE SPACES.
46                 02 FILLER              PIC X(10)  VALUE "USAGE".
47          01  AMOUNT-USED.
48                 03 FILLER                       PIC X(4)  VALUE SPACES.
50                 03 ACCOUNT-NUMBER-OUT           PIC 9(6).
51                 03 FILLER                       PIC X(8)  VALUE SPACES.
52                 03 NAME-OUT                      PIC X(20).
53                 03 FILLER                       PIC X(12) VALUE SPACES.
54                 03 PREVIOUS-READING-OUT          PIC 9(6).
55                 03 FILLER                       PIC X(19) VALUE SPACES.
56                 03 PRESENT-READING-OUT           PIC 9(6).
57                 03 FILLER                       PIC X(12) VALUE SPACES.
58                 03 USAGE-OUT                     PIC Z,ZZZ,ZZ9.
59          01  MESSAGE-LINE-1.
60                 02 FILLER              PIC X(69)  VALUE
61                     "***CHECK FOR NONNUMERIC IN FIELDS 1,3,4 ABOVE ***".
62          01  MESSAGE-LINE-2.
63                 02 FILLER              PIC X(65)  VALUE
64                     "***CHECK FOR NONALPHABETIC IN FIELD 2 ABOVE ***".
65          01  MESSAGE-LINE-3.
66                 02 FILLER  PIC X(28) VALUE "***USAGE AMOUNT TOO SMALL***".
67          01  MESSAGE-LINE-4.
68                 02 FILLER  PIC X(28) VALUE "***USAGE AMOUNT TOO LARGE***".
69      PROCEDURE DIVISION.
70      10-MAIN-ROUTINE.
71          PERFORM 20-INITIALIZATION.
72          PERFORM 30-CHECK-COMPUTE-WRITE-READ UNTIL EOF-FLAG = 1.
73          PERFORM 100-TERMINATION.
74      20-INITIALIZATION.
75          OPEN INPUT GAS-USAGE.
76          OPEN OUTPUT INVALID-DATA-REPORT.
77          OPEN OUTPUT VALID-GAS-USAGE.
78          WRITE PRINT-LINE FROM HEADING-LINE-1 AFTER PAGE.
79          WRITE PRINT-LINE FROM HEADING-LINE-2 AFTER 2.
80          PERFORM 70-READ.
81      30-CHECK-COMPUTE-WRITE-READ.
82          PERFORM 40-CHECK.
83          PERFORM 50-COMPUTE.
84          PERFORM 55-RANGE-CHECK.
85          PERFORM 60-WRITE-IF-VALID.
86          PERFORM 70-READ.
```

(continued)

Program 6.3   (continued)

```
87      40-CHECK.
88          MOVE ZERO TO ERROR-FLAG.
89          IF ACCOUNT-NUMBER NUMERIC
90                  AND PREVIOUS-READING NUMERIC
91                          AND PRESENT-READING NUMERIC
92              NEXT SENTENCE
93          ELSE
94              PERFORM 75-ERROR-LOCATE-1.
95          IF NAME ALPHABETIC
96              NEXT SENTENCE
97          ELSE
98              PERFORM 80-ERROR-LOCATE-2.
99      50-COMPUTE.
100         IF PRESENT-READING > PREVIOUS-READING
101             SUBTRACT PREVIOUS-READING FROM PRESENT READING
102                 GIVING USAGE-X
103         ELSE
104             COMPUTE USAGE-X = PRESENT-READING + 100000
105             - PREVIOUS-READING.
106     55-RANGE-CHECK.
107         IF USAGE-X < LOWER-LIMIT
108             PERFORM 82-ERROR-LOCATE-3
109         ELSE
110             NEXT SENTENCE.
111         IF USAGE-X > UPPER-LIMIT
112             PERFORM 84-ERROR-LOCATE-4
113         ELSE
114             NEXT SENTENCE.
115     60-WRITE-IF-VALID.
116         IF ERROR-FLAG = 0
117             PERFORM 65-WRITE
118         ELSE
119             NEXT SENTENCE.
120     65-WRITE.
121         MOVE GAS-USAGE-RECORD TO VALID-GAS-RECORD.
122         WRITE VALID-GAS-RECORD.
123     70-READ.
124         READ GAS-USAGE AT END MOVE 1 TO EOF-FLAG.
125     75-ERROR-LOCATE-1.
126         PERFORM 90-MOVE.
127         MOVE MESSAGE-LINE-1 TO PRINT-LINE.
128         WRITE PRINT-LINE AFTER 2.
129         MOVE 1 TO ERROR-FLAG.
130     80-ERROR-LOCATE-2.
131         PERFORM 90-MOVE.
132         MOVE MESSAGE-LINE-2 TO PRINT-LINE.
133         WRITE PRINT-LINE AFTER 2.
134         MOVE 1 TO ERROR-FLAG.
135     82-ERROR-LOCATE-3.
136         PERFORM 90-MOVE.
137         MOVE MESSAGE-LINE-3 TO PRINT-LINE.
138         WRITE PRINT-LINE AFTER 2.
```

(continued)

Program 6.3 (continued)

```
139          MOVE 1 TO ERROR-FLAG.
140      84-ERROR-LOCATE-4.
141          PERFORM 90-MOVE.
142          MOVE MESSAGE-LINE-4 TO PRINT-LINE.
143          WRITE PRINT-LINE AFTER 2.
144          MOVE 1 TO ERROR-FLAG.
145      90-MOVE.
146          MOVE ACCOUNT-NUMBER TO ACCOUNT-NUMBER-OUT.
147          MOVE NAME            TO NAME-OUT.
148          MOVE PREVIOUS-READING TO PREVIOUS-READING-OUT.
149          MOVE PRESENT-READING TO PRESENT-READING-OUT.
150          MOVE USAGE-X         TO USAGE-OUT.
151          MOVE AMOUNT-USED TO PRINT-LINE.
152          WRITE PRINT-LINE AFTER 2.
153      100-TERMINATION.
154          CLOSE GAS-USAGE.
155          CLOSE INVALID-DATA-REPORT.
156          CLOSE VALID-GAS-USAGE.
157          STOP RUN.
```

```
                              XYZ GAS COMPANY
ACCOUNT NUMBER        NAME        PREVIOUS METER READING    PRESENT METER READING    USAGE
   111111     JOSEPH R JONES          100300                   000600             900,300
***USAGE AMOUNT TOO LARGE***
   511555        JOHN DOE             000010                   000090                 102
***CHECK FOR NONNUMERIC IN FIELDS 1,3,4 ABOVE***
   666666       SUSIE R202            000010                   000090                  80
***CHECK FOR NONALPHABETIC IN FIELD 2 ABOVE***
   777777       MARY JANE2            000010                   000015                  80
***CHECK FOR NONALPHABETIC IN FIELD 2 ABOVE***
   777777       MARY JANE2            000010                   000015                   5
***USAGE AMOUNT TOO SMALL***
```

Programs encountered thus far in this text always have processed two files—an input file and an output file. This is not, however, a general rule. The program in Figure 6.15 processes three files—one input file and two output files. In general a program may process any number of input and/or output files.

The computation of the amount of gas used in Program 6.3 is not as straightforward as we might initially expect. At first glance there is a temptation to compute the amount of usage by subtracting the previous reading from the present reading. This procedure is fine most of the time; however, meters count only up to some maximum (999999 in our example) before they *roll over* and begin again at zero. If this happens the present reading will actually appear to be less than the previous reading. For example, suppose the previous reading was 999980 and the present reading is 000020. The amount of usage is actually 40. To handle this case, the formula for computing usage is:

$$usage = (present\text{-}reading + 1000000) - previous\text{-}reading$$

For the above data the computation would yield:

$$usage = (20 + 1000000) - 999980$$
$$= 1000020 - 999980$$
$$= 40$$

Note that in the paragraph 50-COMPUTE (lines 98 through 104) in Program 6.3, which implements this procedure for computing the amount of usage, one of these two methods of computing usage is selected based on the relation of PRESENT-READING to PREVIOUS-READING. When nonnumeric characters are present in a numeric field, the computer will use the numeric equivalent of the character in any computations with that field. The numeric equivalent is based on the internal representation of character. When the field is edited for output, the content of the field will appear to be numeric. Thus, in the sample output for Program 6.3 record two had at least one nonnumeric character in a numeric field, yet the values listed in these fields all appear to be numeric. This problem can be solved by treating each numeric field as both numeric and alphanumeric, since in an alphanumeric field each character is preserved. We shall return to this problem after discussion of the REDEFINES clause (Chapter 8).

6.9 DEBUG CLINIC

The Case of the Missing Period

One of the most common errors made when using the IF statement is the omission of the period which is required to terminate the statement. For example, suppose we want to write code to implement the following flowchart:

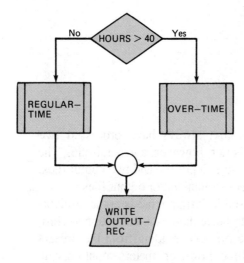

The correct code is:

```
IF HOURS > 40
    PERFORM OVER-TIME
ELSE
    PERFORM REGULAR-TIME.
WRITE OUTPUT-REC AFTER 1.
```

However, suppose the program is coded (erroneously) as:

```
IF HOURS > 40
    PERFORM OVERTIME
ELSE
    PERFORM REGULAR-TIME   (note missing period)
WRITE OUTPUT-REC AFTER 1.
```

The result will be to include the WRITE statement as a part of the ELSE clause of the IF statement, as though the flowchart had been written:

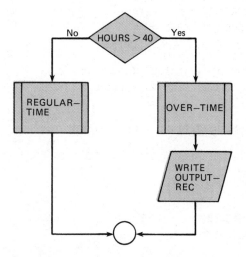

The alignment of the WRITE statement in the same column as the IF and ELSE entries indicates to the reader that the WRITE statement is not a part of the ELSE clause of the IF statement, but the compiler ignores the placement of statements. The period is required to terminate the IF statement.

Conditional and Imperative Statements

A *conditional* statement is a statement which

1) contains one or more statements in a clause, and
2) selects the action(s) to be taken next depending on the evaluation of some condition.

It is clear that the IF statement is a conditional statement. Other statements also are classed as conditional, including:

- any arithmetic statement with the ON SIZE ERROR option
- READ statement with the AT END option

In all of these statements the action to be taken depends on the evaluation of some condition. In the case of the arithmetic statement with the ON SIZE ERROR option, the statements in the ON SIZE ERROR clause are executed if there is overflow or division by zero; otherwise, execution continues with the next sentence. The statement(s) in the AT END clause of a READ statement are executed at end-of-file; otherwise, the next sentence is executed. Conditional statements are always terminated by a period.

Any statement which is not a conditional statement is an *imperative* statement. Examples of imperative statements include:

- arithmetic statements without the clause ON SIZE ERROR
- WRITE statement

- PERFORM statement
- MOVE statement

Imperative statements are terminated either by a period or a COBOL verb signifying the start of another statement.

A single COBOL PROCEDURE DIVISION sentence may be made up of many imperative statements.

The following two coding sequences are equivalent: *Example*

```
MOVE A TO A-OUT          MOVE A TO A-OUT.
MOVE B TO B-OUT          MOVE B TO B-OUT.
COMPUTE-OUT = A + B      COMPUTE-OUT = A + B.
WRITE OUT-REC AFTER 1.   WRITE OUT-REC AFTER 1.
```

On the left there is a single sentence composed of four imperative statements. On the right there are four sentences; each sentence contains a single imperative statement.

Clauses within conditional statements may be made up of any number of imperative statements.

Example

```
COMPUTE A = B + C
   ON SIZE ERROR
      MOVE "ERROR IN COMP" TO MSG-OUT
      WRITE OUT-REC FROM ERR-REC AFTER 1
      MOVE 0 TO A.
```

In the example above the ON SIZE ERROR clause is made up of three imperative statements.

```
READ IN-FILE
   AT END
      MOVE 999 TO A
      MOVE "YES" TO EOF.
```

In this example the AT END clause is made up of two imperative statements.

Care must be taken that every conditional statement ends with a period. If the period is omitted, succeeding statements will be erroneously included as a part of a clause of the conditional statement.

Example

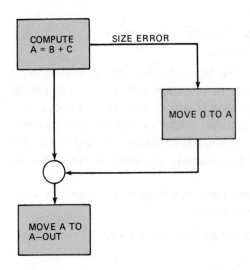

The correct code terminates the conditional COMPUTE statement with a period:

```
COMPUTE A = B + C
    ON SIZE ERROR
        MOVE 0 TO A.
MOVE A TO A-OUT.
```

If the conditional COMPUTE statement is not terminated with a period, as in

```
COMPUTE A = B + C
    ON SIZE ERROR
        MOVE 0 TO A
MOVE A TO A-OUT.
```

the result is to include the statement MOVE A TO A-OUT as a part of the ON SIZE ERROR clause as though the flowchart had been written

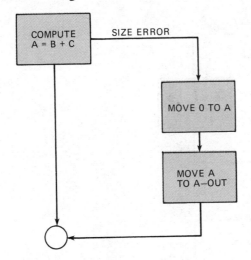

Embedding a conditional statment into a clause of another conditional statement is possible only if the embedded conditional statement is the last one in a clause.

Suppose we wish to implement the following flowchart: *Example*

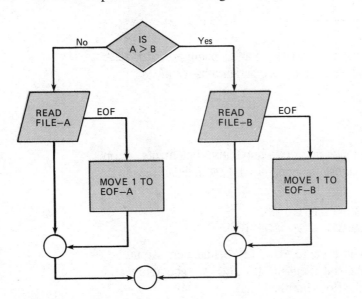

It would be correct to code this flowchart as

```
IF A > B
    READ FILE-B AT END MOVE 1 TO EOF-B
ELSE
    READ FILE-A AT END MOVE 1 TO EOF-A.
```

The conditional statement READ FILE-B is terminated by ELSE; the conditional statment READ FILE-A and the IF statement itself are terminated by the period.

Suppose we wish to implement the following flowchart: *Example*

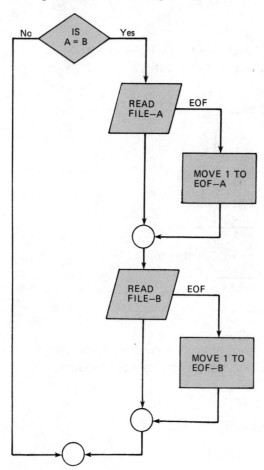

The best way to code this logic is to write separate paragraphs for READ FILE-A and READ FILE-B and PERFORM these paragraphs, as in:

```
IF A = B
    PERFORM READ-FILE-A
    PERFORM READ-FILE-B.
```

This IF statement has a clause made up of two imperative statements. If one attempts to embed two conditional statements into the IF statement, as in

```
IF A = B
    READ FILE-A AT END MOVE 1 TO EOF-A
    READ FILE-B AT END MOVE 1 TO EOF-B.
```

the code would be in error because the READ FILE-B statement would be a part of the AT END clause of the statement READ FILE-A. The above code would be executed as thought the flowchart had read:

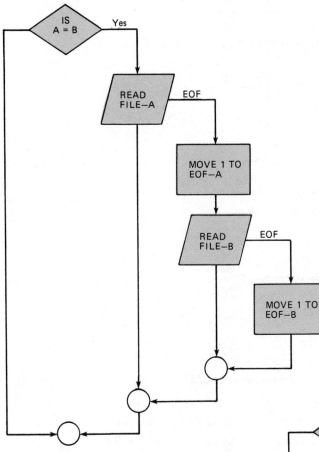

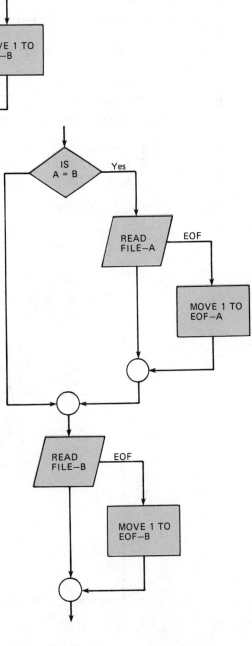

Note that a clause in a conditional statement is made up of statements, *not* sentences. If a programmer tried to salvage the above code by placing a period at the end of the first READ statement, as in

```
IF  A  =  B
    PERFORM READ-FILE-A.
    PERFORM READ-FILE-B.
```

the coding would be in error because the added period would terminate not only the READ statement but also the IF statement. The result would be as though the flowchart read as shown at the right.

The programmer should break a program into paragraphs to avoid inclusion of conditional statements in a clause of another conditional statement.

6.10   SELF TEST EXERCISES

1. Evaluate each of the following conditions based on the following variables:

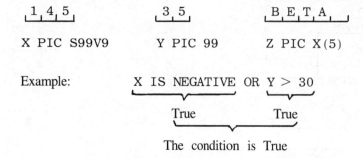

X PIC S99V9   Y PIC 99   Z PIC X(5)

Example: X   IS   NEGATIVE   OR   Y > 30

                      True   True

                  The   condition   is   True

    a. X < Y OR Y IS NEGATIVE
    b. Z IS ALPHABETIC
    c. X IS NUMERIC AND Z IS NOT ALPHABETIC
    d. NOT Y IS POSITIVE
    e. NOT X IS ZERO OR Y IS NOT NEGATIVE
    f. NOT (X > 25 OR Y < 39)
    g. X > Y OR X IS ZERO AND Y > 1
    h. X < Y AND (Y < OR X > 30)

2. Write an IF statement to compute minimum payment defined by:

$$\text{minimum payment} = \begin{cases} \text{balance, if balance} \leq \$20 \\ \$20 + 10\% \text{ of (balance} - \$20, \text{ if } \$20 < \text{balance} \leq \$100 \\ \$36 + 20\% \text{ of (balance} - \$100), \text{ if balance} > \$100 \end{cases}$$

3. Write COBOL code to implement each of the following flowcharts.
    a.

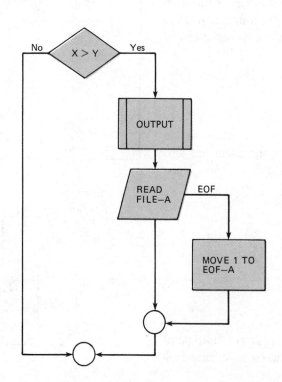

b.

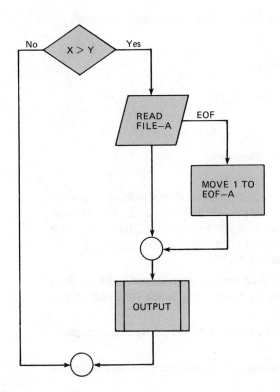

c.

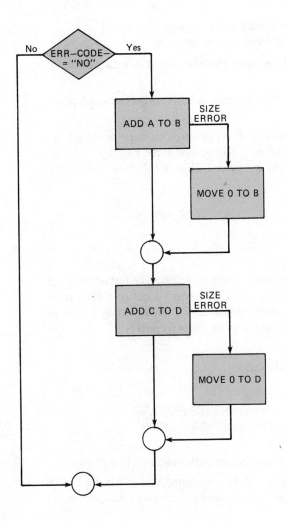

4. Write a data validation routine to check the validity of the following data record:

```
01   DATA-REC
     03   ACCOUNT-NUM-DR  PIC 9(9).
     03   CUSTOMER-NAME-DR  PIC X(20).
     03   CUSTOMER-ADDRESS-DR
          05   STREET-ADDRESS-DR  PIC X(15).
          05   CITY-DR  PIC X(8).
          05   STATE-DR  PIC XX.
          05   ZIP-DR  PIC 9(9).
     03   BALANCE-FORWARD-DR  PIC 9999V99.
```

   The fields ACCOUNT-NUM-DR, ZIP-DR and BALANCE-FORWARD-DR must be numeric. The fields CUSTOMER-NAME-DR, CITY-DR and STATE-DR must be non-blank and contain only alphabetic data. MOVE "YES" to a field VALIDITY-ERROR if errors are found; otherwise, MOVE "NO" to VALIDITY-ERROR. Why is it not possible to check the validity of STREET-ADDRESS-DR?

5. The PERFORM UNTIL statement is classed as an imperative statement, yet it involves checking a condition and taking alternative actions. Why is the PERFORM UNTIL statement classed as imperative?

6. How would the program of Program 6.1 be modified to list all women employees over 40 but under 65 years of age?

7. Write the PROCEDURE DIVISION and necessary additional DATA DIVISION entries to modify the program of Program 6.1 to

   - list all female employees
   - count and print the number of male and female employees
   - compute and print the average age for males and females.

8. In the program in Program 6.1, should the valve 1960 be placed in a data-name in working storage? Why?

9. Draw a structure diagram of Program 6.3. Identify control and operational paragraphs.

10. Consider the sample output for Program 6.3. The first error message produced for account number 777777 shows usage of 80. The second error message for this account shows usage of 5. What caused this error? How would you correct the problem?

6.11   PROGRAMMING EXERCISES

1. The managers of Burgers, Inc., a franchise system of hamburger restaurants, are concerned with the profitability of a number of the company's outlets. They have requested a report showing basic data about each store and having a flag for stores showing profits less than $20,000. The format for the input records is:

Positions	
1-10	Franchise number
11-25	Location
26-40	Manager's name
41-48	Previous year's profits (S999999V99) (Field could be negative if the store lost money.)

   Print a row of asterisks (e.g., "*****") as a flag for each store with low profits.

2. At ABC Furniture store, Inc. the manager of the computing center has separately budgeted amounts for computer supplies, office supplies, computer equipment and

office equipment. He needs to keep track of his cumulative expenditures in each of these categories. He has created a data file with records in the following format:

position
1-6   date of purchase
7-25   description of purchase
26-32   amount (2 decimal places)
33   account code
         1 = computer supplies
         2 = office supplies
         3 = computer equipment
         4 = office equipment

Write a program to list each purchase in an appropriately labeled column. Accumulate and print totals for each account.

Sample Data:

Date	Description	Amount	Account code
1/1/82	office chair	95.00	4
1/2/82	calculator	259.50	4
1/2/82	continuous paper	593.00	1
1/13/82	typewriter ribbons	9.00	2
1/14/82	terminal	3000.00	3
1/15/82	ribbon	359.00	1

3. The FHA insures home mortgages up to $85,000. The downpayment schedule is as follows:

   3% of the first $45,000
   10% of the next $10,000
   20% of the remainder

Write a program to accept input records containing an applicant's name and the amount of the loan requested. Output should consist of all input fields and the amount of the downpayment required. Reject any application that is for more than $85,000. Also compute the total amounts of loans and downpayments.

4. Using the file described in Program 6.3, write a program to compute the amount of the monthly bill. Output should consist of all input data and the amount of the bill based on the following schedule:

   $ 6.00, if amount used is less than 50
   $ 6.00 + .10 × (amount used - 50), if 50 ≤ amount used ≤ 200
   $21.00 + .08 × (amount used - 200), if amount > 200

5. Write a program that could be used to determine a weekly payroll. The input file contains one record per employee with the following fields: employee name, employee number, hourly rate of pay and hours worked. Have your program list the employee name, employee number, hourly rate of pay, number of hours worked and gross pay. Remember to pay time and one-half for all hours over 40 worked in the week.

6. Jones Hardware, Inc. maintains an accounts receivable file with records of the following format:

Positions
1-6   Account number
7-25   Customer name
26-31   Date of last purchase (month, day, year)
32-37   Date of last payment (month, day, year)
38-43   Balance of account
44-55   Address
55-65   City

66-67   State
68-73   Zip Code

Write a program to produce a report which will be used by clerks who will write letters to customers requesting either their continued business for inactive accounts or payment of a past due balance. If the date of last purchase indicates that no purchase has been made in the past three months and the balance is zero, indicate that a letter requesting continued patronage should be written. If the balance of the account is greater than $1 and no payment has been made in the previous two months indicate a letter requesting payment. If the balance is greater than $100 and no payment has been made in the previous four months, indicate a stronger letter threatening that legal action will be taken if payment is not forthcoming. For purposes of this program, assume that the current date is 02/30/83. (A method for handling current date input will be covered in Chapter 12.)

7. Write a program to list all three-bedroom houses with more than one bath in the price range $65,000 to $95,000 using the file described in Chapter 4, Exercise 3.

8. Write a program to list all accounts with a past due balance using the file described in Exercise 6 above. Count the number of accounts which have had no payment made in the previous month, the previous two months, the previous three months and the previous four or more months. Write these amounts after processing the entire file.

9. When a house is listed and sold by real estate brokers, the commission is divided among four people: the listing broker (firm which lists and advertises the house), the listing salesman (person who secures the listing from the owner), the selling salesman (person who sells the house) and the selling broker (firm for whom the selling salesman works).

    In Happy Valley, which has six real estate brokers and many salesmen, commissions are divided as follows: When the listing salesman and selling salesman work for the same broker, the commission is divided 25 percent to the listing salesman, 30 percent to the selling salesman and 45 percent to the broker. When the listing salesman and selling salesman work for different brokers, the commission is divided 25 percent to the listing salesman, 35 percent to the listing broker, 20 percent to the selling salesman and 20 percent to the selling broker.

    Design the input record and write a program to calculate real estate commissions for the city of Happy Valley.

10. Modify the program written for Chapter 5, Exercise 9 to produce an amortization schedule for the loan. There should be one line of output for each month's payment showing:

    Payment number
    Payment to interest
    Payment to principal
    Total monthly payment
    New balance

Accumulate and print the total of the interest payments. (The last month's payment may be slightly more or less than the other payments.) For example, for principal of $105,000, interest rate of 17.5 percent and time of 25 years, the expected output would be similar to:

NUMBER	PRINCIPAL	INTEREST	PMT	AMT BALANCE
1	20.16	1531.25	1551.41	104980.00
2	20.45	1530.96	1551.41	104959.00
3	20.75	1530.66	1551.41	104939.00
4	21.05	1530.36	1551.41	104918.00
5	21.36	1530.05	1551.41	104896.00

6	21.67	1529.74	1551.41	104875.00
7	21.99	1529.42	1551.41	104853.00
8	22.31	1529.10	1551.41	104830.00
9	22.64	1528.77	1551.41	104806.00
.				
.				
.				
295	1422.56	128.85	1551.41	7413.10
296	1443.3	108.11	1551.41	5969.80
297	1464.35	87.06	1551.41	4505.45
298	1485.71	65.70	1551.41	3019.74
299	1507.37	44.04	1551.41	1512.37
300	1512.37	22.06	1534.43	0.00
TOTAL INTEREST	$360,406.00			

REPORTS AND CONTROL BREAKS 7

7.1 REPORT REQUIREMENTS

Businesses require many reports, so it is no surprise that many COBOL programs are written to produce reports, which summarize and make available the data in files. There are several features shared by such report writing programs which require special logic. Among these features and requirements are:

FEATURE	REQUIREMENT
1. Headings	Is there a major heading? What column headings are required? Is a date required?[1]
2. Page Numbers	Are pages to be numbered?
3. Page Totals	Are page totals required for some items?
4. Subtotals	Are subtotals required for segments of data? How many levels of subtotals are required?
5. Grand Totals	What items require grand totals?

Management of the ABC Company desires a report showing each *Example* employee's name, employee number, department and salary. The report should have appropriate headings on each page and pages should be numbered. Each page should list the total of the salaries of the employees on that page; the final page should list the total number of employees and the total salaries of all employees. The data for the required report is contained in the file INFD which contains records in alphabetic sequence for all employees of the company. The structure diagram for the required program is given in Figure 7.1 and the program itself with a sample of the output produced is Program 7.1.

---

[1]Logic for including dates is discussed in Chapter 12.

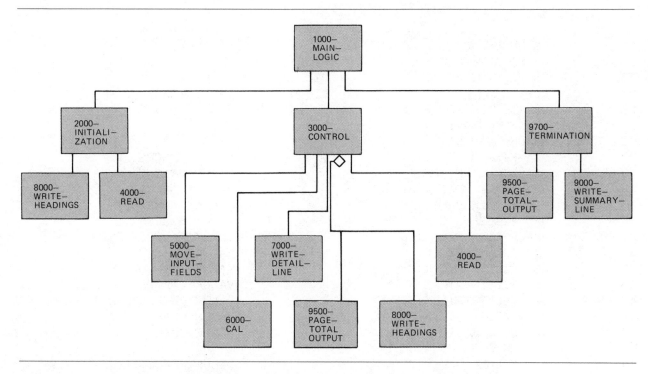

Figure 7.1   Structure diagram of Alphabetic employee report program.

Program 7.1   Alphabetic employee report program.

```
1        IDENTIFICATION DIVISION.
2        PROGRAM-ID. CHAPTER 7 EXAMPLE 1.
3        AUTHOR. GARY GLEASON.
4        ENVIRONMENT DIVISION.
5        INPUT-OUTPUT SECTION.
6        FILE-CONTROL.
7            SELECT INFD ASSIGN TO DISK.
8            SELECT PRNT ASSIGN TO PRINTER.
9        DATA DIVISION.
10       FILE SECTION.
11       FD   INFD
12           DATA RECORD IS INPUT-RECORD.
13       01   INPUT-RECORD.
14           02   IR-NAME              PIC X(16).
13           02   IR-INITIAL           PIC X.
14           02   IR-EMPLOYEE-NUMBER    PIC X(9).
15           02   IR-DEPARTMENT         PIC X(3).
16           02   IR-SALARY            PIC 9(6).
17           02   FILLER               PIC X(45).
18       FD   PRNT
19           DATA RECORD IS PRINT-LINE.
20       01   PRINT-LINE              PIC X(132).
21       WORKING-STORAGE SECTION.
22       01   ACCUMULATED-TOTALS.
23           03 PAGE-COUNT                PIC 999      VALUE ZERO.
24           03 LINE-COUNT                PIC 999      VALUE ZERO.
```
(continued)

Program 7.1 (continued)

```
25            03  NUMBER-OF-EMPLOYEES       PIC 999      VALUE ZERO.
26            03  SALARY-TOTAL              PIC 9(8)     VALUE ZERO.
27            03  PAGE-TOTAL                PIC 9(6)V99  VALUE ZERO.
28     01  EOF-FLAG                         PIC 9        VALUE ZERO.
29            88  NOT-END-OF-FILE                        VALUE 0.
30            88  END-OF-FILE                            VALUE 1.
31     01  MAJOR-HEADING.
32            02  FILLER PIC X(47)                       VALUE SPACES.
33            02  FILLER PIC X                           VALUE SPACES.
34            02  FILLER PIC X(3)                        VALUE "ABC".
35            02  FILLER PIC X(7)                        VALUE "COMPANY".
36            02  FILLER PIC X                           VALUE SPACES.
37            02  FILLER PIC X(10)                       VALUE "ALPHABETIC".
38            02  FILLER PIC X                           VALUE SPACES.
39            02  FILLER PIC X(8)                        VALUE "EMPLOYEE".
40            02  FILLER PIC X                           VALUE SPACES.
41            02  FILLER PIC X(6)                        VALUE "REPORT".
42            02  FILLER PIC X(15)                       VALUE SPACES.
43            02  FILLER PIC X(4)                        VALUE "PAGE".
44            02  MH-PAGE-COUNTER PIC ZZZ.
45            02  FILLER PIC X(25)                       VALUE SPACES.
46     01  SUBHEADING.
47            02  FILLER  PIC X(26)                      VALUE SPACES.
48            02  FILLER PIC X(9)                        VALUE "LAST NAME".
49            02  FILLER PIC X(8)                        VALUE SPACES.
50            02  FILLER PIC X(7)                        VALUE "INITIAL".
51            02  FILLER PIC X(8)                        VALUE SPACES.
52            02  FILLER PIC X(15)                       VALUE "EMPLOYEE NUMBER".
53            02  FILLER PIC X(8)                        VALUE SPACES.
54            02  FILLER PIC X(10)                       VALUE "DEPARTMENT".
55            02  FILLER PIC X(8)                        VALUE SPACES.
56            02  FILLER PIC X(6)                        VALUE "SALARY".
57            02  FILLER PIC X(27)                       VALUE SPACES.
58     01  DETAIL-LINE.
59            02  FILLER             PIC X(26)           VALUE SPACES.
60            02  DL-NAME            PIC X(16).
61            02  FILLER             PIC X(3)            VALUE SPACES.
62            02  DL-INITIAL         PIC X.
63            02  FILLER             PIC X(14)           VALUE SPACES.
64            02  DL-EMPLOYEE-NUMBER PIC X(9).
65            02  FILLER             PIC X(16)           VALUE SPACES.
66            02  DL-DEPARTMENT      PIC X(3).
67            02  FILLER             PIC X(10)           VALUE SPACES.
68            02  DL-SALARY          PIC $ZZZ,ZZZ.
69            02  FILLER             PIC X(25)           VALUE SPACES.
70     01  SUMMARY-LINE.
71            02  FILLER                     PIC X(70)   VALUE SPACES.
72            02  SL-NUMBER-OF-EMPLOYEES     PIC ZZZ9.
73            02  FILLER                     PIC X(5)    VALUE SPACES.
74            02  FILLER                     PIC X(9)    VALUE "EMPLOYEES".
75            02  FILLER                     PIC X(7)    VALUE SPACES.
76            02  SL-SALARY-TOTAL            PIC $**,***,**9.
77            02  FILLER                     PIC X(25)   VALUE SPACES.
```

(continued)

Program 7.1   (continued)

```
78      01  PAGE-TOTAL-LINE.
79          02  FILLER               PIC X(88)        VALUE SPACES.
80          02  PTL-PAGE-TOTAL       PIC $ZZZ,ZZZ.99.
81      PROCEDURE DIVISION.
82      1000-MAIN-LOGIC.
83          PERFORM 2000-INITIALIZATION.
84          PERFORM 3000-CONTROL UNTIL END-OF-FILE.
85          PERFORM 9700-TERMINATION.
86      2000-INITIALIZATION.
87          OPEN INPUT INFD, OUTPUT PRNT.
88          PERFORM 8000-WRITE-HEADINGS.
89          PERFORM 4000-READ.
90      3000-CONTROL.
91          PERFORM 5000-MOVE-INPUT-FIELDS.
92          PERFORM 6000-CAL.
93          PERFORM  7000-WRITE-DETAIL-LINE.
94          IF LINE-COUNT > 46
95              PERFORM 9500-PAGE-TOTAL-OUTPUT
96              PERFORM 8000-WRITE-HEADINGS
97          ELSE
98              NEXT SENTENCE.
99          PERFORM 4000-READ.
100     4000-READ.
101         READ INFD AT END MOVE 1 TO EOF-FLAG.
102     5000-MOVE-INPUT-FIELDS.
103             MOVE IR-NAME             TO DL-NAME.
104             MOVE IR-INITIAL          TO DL-INITIAL.
105             MOVE IR-EMPLOYEE-NUMBER TO DL-EMPLOYEE-NUMBER.
106             MOVE IR-SALARY           TO DL-SALARY.
107             MOVE IR-DEPARTMENT       TO DL-DEPARTMENT.
108     6000-CAL.
109         ADD 1 TO NUMBER-OF-EMPLOYEES.
110         ADD IR-SALARY TO SALARY-TOTAL.
111         ADD IR-SALARY TO PAGE-TOTAL.
112     7000-WRITE-DETAIL-LINE.
113         MOVE DETAIL-LINE TO PRINT-LINE.
114         WRITE PRINT-LINE AFTER 2 LINES.
115         ADD 2 TO LINE-COUNT.
116     8000-WRITE-HEADINGS.
117         ADD 1 TO PAGE-COUNT.
118         MOVE PAGE-COUNT               TO MH-PAGE-COUNTER.
119         MOVE MAJOR-HEADING            TO PRINT-LINE.
120         WRITE PRINT-LINE AFTER PAGE.
121         MOVE SUBHEADING               TO PRINT-LINE.
122         WRITE PRINT-LINE AFTER 2 LINES.
123         MOVE 3 TO LINE-COUNT.
124     9000-WRITE-SUMMARY-LINE.
125         MOVE NUMBER-OF-EMPLOYEES      TO SL-NUMBER-OF-EMPLOYEES.
126         MOVE SALARY-TOTAL            TO SL-SALARY-TOTAL.
127         MOVE SUMMARY-LINE            TO PRINT-LINE.
128         WRITE PRINT-LINE AFTER 3 LINES.
129     9500-PAGE-TOTAL-OUTPUT.
130         MOVE PAGE-TOTAL TO PTL-PAGE-TOTAL.
```

(continued)

Program 7.1 (continued)

```
131        WRITE PRINT-LINE FROM PAGE-TOTAL-LINE AFTER 2.
132        MOVE 0 TO PAGE-TOTAL.
133     9700-TERMINATION.
134        PERFORM  9500-PAGE-TOTAL-OUTPUT.
135        PERFORM  9000-WRITE-SUMMARY-LINE.
136        CLOSE INFD, PRNT.
137        STOP RUN.
```

<pre>
                ABCCOMPANY ALPHABETIC EMPLOYEE REPORT   PAGE 1
LAST NAME   INITIAL   EMPLOYEE NUMBER   DEPARTMENT   SALARY
ABNER   L   987654321   654 $ 90,000
ACHER   W   011907260   001 $ 57,000
ADAMS   S   123456789   234 $ 75,300
ALDRIDGE   M   159763548   222 $ 14,000
ALSIP   J   762158345   222 $ 10,000
AMORE   M   562160536   042 $ 17,000
ANDERSON   J   123456789   123 $ 10,000
ARD   S   745213214   298 $ 13,000
BROXTON   D   987987987   042 $ 30,000
BUTTER   B   036028036   203 $125,000
CADENHEAD   J   142753869   241 $ 50,000
CALDWELL   W   654654654   072 $ 10,000
CANDY   D   320220290   542 $ 24,000
CANTRELL   S   980250026   555 $ 14,000
CARTER   T   345678901   456 $ 85,000
CARTOLER   V   028099812   021 $ 75,000
CHRISTOPHER   B   024631205   216 $ 19,000
CHRISTY   C   421360380   777 $ 35,000
COOPER   R   019876536   438 $ 15,000
CUNNINGHAM   C   439726158   555 $ 12,000
DAEHNKE   M   153248765   423 $ 14,000
DAVIDSON   D   325986431   132 $ 40,000
                                                        $834,300.00

                ABCCOMPANY ALPHABETIC EMPLOYEE REPORT   PAGE 4
LAST NAME   INITIAL   EMPLOYEE NUMBER   DEPARTMENT   SALARY
RUSHING   R   901125544   998 $ 14,000
SELLERS   P   312312312   052 $ 30,000
SIMPSON   D   412578525   652 $ 10,000
SMITH   R   320120354   012 $ 7,000
SPRINGER   S   452831429   701 $ 16,000
THOMPSON   S   262373155   215 $ 10,000
VINCENT   W   212345226   217 $ 12,000
WARD   T   321321321   032 $ 11,000
WATKINS   S   545116355   544 $ 12,000
WESTINGHOUSE   M   456253255   215 $ 12,000
WILSON   A   632547328   777 $ 10,000
                                                        $144,000.00

                          77   EMPLOYEES $*2,291,300
</pre>

7.2 REPORT WRITING TECHNIQUES

When you write a program to generate a report, you will want to give the reader guidance in interpreting the information contained in the report. Usually you will want to print a heading at the top of every page. Occasionally a major heading—the company name and the report title, for example—is required on the first page but not on succeeding pages. Generally there will be column headings on every page to identify the data contained on the lines of the report.

A very useful technique to control the generation of headings is *line counting*. A typical page of computer output contains 64 lines of print, although this varies greatly among computing systems. (Check the size of the printed page generated on your computer. In Program 7.1 we have assumed that the page contains 46 lines.) The program uses a line counter to keep track of the number of lines of print generated. When a line is written, an appropriate value (1 for single spacing, 2 for double spacing, and so on) is added to the line counter. After each output operation, the value of the line counter is tested against the maximum number of lines allowed on a page. If the page is full, headings are written at the top of a new page, the line counter is re-initialized, and processing proceeds. This approach is used in Program 7.1. The paragraph 3000-CONTROL (lines 90 through 99) contains the test:

```
IF LINE-COUNT > 46
   PERFORM 8000-WRITE-HEADINGS
```

The paragraph 8000-WRITE-HEADINGS takes care of re-initializing the LINE-COUNT (line 123).

Page numbers often are required in reports. The writing of page numbers can be accomplished by the routine which is used to print the report headings. A page counter is initialized to value zero. Each time the heading routine is entered, the page counter is incremented by 1, and the value is moved to the appropriate field on the page heading line. In Program 7.1, the paragraph 8000-WRITE-HEADINGS contains the sentence (line 117)

```
              ADD 1 TO PAGE-COUNT.
```

which performs this function.

Page totals are totals of data items occurring on a page. Variables used to accumulate page totals should be re-initialized in the page total routine. Page totals should be printed when the program detects that a page is *full* before page headings for a new page are printed. Program 7.1 also shows an example of this technique. The paragraph 3000-CONTROL (lines 90 through 99) contains the following statements:

```
IF LINE-COUNT > 46
   PERFORM 9500-PAGE-TOTAL-OUTPUT
     .
     .
     .
```

The paragraph 9500-PAGE-TOTAL-OUTPUT contains logic required to write page totals and re-initialize the appropriate variable (lines 129 through 132).

Grand totals are printed after all data has been processed. As each record is processed, items are added to appropriate totals. When end-of-file is detected, both page totals (if any) and grand totals should be printed. The last page is usually not a full page of data; hence, page totals would not have been printed at the usual point (i.e., when LINE-COUNT > 46) in the program. Program 7.1 illustrates the logic required for the accumulation and printing of a grand total. The grand total is accumulated in 6000-CAL (lines 108 through 111) which contains the statements:

```
ADD 1 TO NUMBER-OF-EMPLOYEES.
ADD IR-SALARY TO SALARY-TOTAL.
```

The grand total is produced after end-of-file has been reached. The paragraph 9700-TERMINATION executes both 9500-PAGE-TOTAL-OUTPUT and 9000-WRITE-SUMMARY-LINE (lines 134 and 135) which performs the desired output after end-of-file.

7.3   NAMED CONDITIONS

Named conditions are useful in documenting the meaning of a programmer written test. Suppose, for example, that data being processed contains a code having value 1 if sex is male and 2 if sex is female. The PROCEDURE division statement

```
IF  CODE  = 1
     PERFORM MALE-ROUTINE
ELSE
     IF  CODE  = 2
         PERFORM FEMALE-ROUTINE
     ELSE
         PERFORM ERROR-ROUTINE.
```

could be used to differentiate in the processing of males and females. The meaning of the tests CODE = 1 and CODE = 2 is not apparent from the statement of the condition itself. It is possible to assign a name to the conditions CODE = 1 and CODE = 2. The 88 level used in the DATA division defines these names as follows:

```
03   CODE   PIC 9.
     88   SEX-IS-MALE VALUE 1.
     88   SEX-IS-FEMALE VALUE 2.
```

The condition SEX-IS-MALE is true if CODE has a value of 1 and false otherwise. The condition SEX-IS-FEMALE is true when the CODE has a value of 2 and false otherwise. The PROCEDURE division code above could now be rewritten as:

```
IF  SEX-IS-MALE
     PERFORM MALE-ROUTINE
ELSE
     IF  SEX-IS-FEMALE
         PERFORM FEMALE-ROUTINE
     ELSE
         PERFORM ERROR-ROUTINE
```

The general form of the 88 level entry is shown in Figure 7.2. Any number 88 level entries may follow an elementary data item definition in the DATA division.

$$88 \text{ condition -name } \begin{Bmatrix} \underline{VALUE} & IS \\ \underline{VALUES} & ARE \end{Bmatrix} \text{literal} -1 \left[\begin{Bmatrix} \underline{THROUGH} \\ \underline{THRU} \end{Bmatrix} \text{literal} -2 \right] \ldots$$

Figure 7.2 General form of the 88 level entry.

A common usage of the named condition in a structured program is in the *Example* end-of-file testing as shown in Program 7.1 (lines 28 through 30):

```
01  EOF-FLAG  PIC 9 VALUE ZERO.
    88  NOT-END-OF-FILE  VALUE 0.
    88  END-OF-FILE  VALUE 1.
```

The PERFORM statement in the paragraph 1000-MAIN-LOGIC which con- *Example* trols the loop (line 84) is written as

```
        PERFORM 3000-CONTROL UNTIL END-OF-FILE.
```

This statement is much more descriptive than its equivalent, which we have used in previous programs:

```
PERFORM 3000-CONTROL UNTIL EOF-FLAG = 1.
```

Note that more than one value can be included in a VALUE clause.

Suppose a company has numbered its stores 1, 2, 3, 7, 10 and 20. The pro- *Example* gram which checks the validity of the store-number on an input record could use the following code:

```
03  STORE-NUMBER  PIC 99.
    88  VALID-STORE-NUMBER
        VALUES ARE 1, 2, 3, 7, 10, 20.
```

The condition VALID-STORE-NUMBER will be true when the value of STORE-NUMBER is 1, 2, 3, 7, 10 or 20.

The THROUGH clause is useful for including a sequence of values. For example, the above 88 level entry could also be written as:

```
88  VALID-STORE-NUMBER
        VALUES ARE 1 THROUGH 3, 7, 10, 20.
```

The clause 1 THROUGH 3 is equivalent to 1, 2, 3.

The following code could be used to define a condition INVALID-STORE- *Example* NUMBER which would include all possible values of STORE-NUMBER except 1, 2, 3, 7, 10 and 20:

```
03  STORE-NUMBER  PIC 99.
    88  INVALID-STORE-NUMBER
        VALUES ARE 0, 4 THRU 6, 8, 9,
                11 THRU 19, 21 THRU 99.
```

7.4 CONTROL BREAKS

Often, subtotals are required for related subsets of data within a report. For example, suppose the data processed by Program 7.1 has been sorted into order by department number. Program 7.2 below processes this data and generates a report showing salary totals for each department. The structure diagram for Program 7.2 is given in Figure 7.3.

The basic problem encountered in writing such a program is the recognition of breaks within the data (called *control breaks*). A control break occurs, for example, when a data record is read for an employee in a department whose number differs from the preceding employee's department number. At this point the program must produce the totals for the preceding department before processing the current data record. The technique used to detect a break requires a holding location (HOLD-DEPARTMENT). The content of this location is compared with the value of IR-DEPARTMENT when each record is processed (lines 111 and 112):

```
IF  IR-DEPARTMENT NOT  = HOLD-DEPARTMENT
    PERFORM 6000-DEPARTMENT-BREAK.
```

If the two values are the same, the current employee belongs to the same department as the previous employee. If the two values differ, the current employee belongs to a different department and a control break is recognized. The control break processing routine (6000-DEPARTMENT-BREAK, lines 126 through 136), in addition to writing the required totals, must move IR-DEPARTMENT to HOLD-DEPARTMENT (line 136) so that the next control break can be determined. A basic problem occurs in using this scheme for the first record processed, since there is no preceding record with which to compare. This problem is solved by moving the value of IR-DEPARTMENT to HOLD-DEPARTMENT (line 109) after the first record is read and before processed. Of course, this action should be done only for the first record; Program 7.2 uses a switch FIRST-RECORD-FLAG to bypass this initialization after the first record is processed. The data item FIRST-RECORD-FLAG is defined with value zero so that the named condition is initially true (lines 35 through 36). In order to initialize the value of HOLD-DEPARTMENT, the following code is used (lines 108 through 110):

```
IF  FIRST-RECORD
    MOVE IR-DEPARTMENT TO HOLD-DEPARTMENT
    MOVE 1 TO FIRST-RECORD-FLAG.
```

After execution of this code for the first record, the value of FIRST-RECORD-FLAG is set to one, so that when processing subsequent records the value of FIRST-RECORD will be false and the initialization will not be performed.

When end-of-file is encountered, a group of data records for the last department will have been processed but no totals will have been produced for that department. It is therefore necessary to recognize a control break after end-of-file has been reached. This is done in Program 7.2 in the paragraph 9000-TERMINATION (lines 147 through 151):

```
8000-TERMINATION.
    PERFORM 6000-DEPARTMENT-BREAK.
    PERFORM 8000-WRITE-SUMMARY-LINE.
    .
    .
    .
```

Note that the control break routine is executed before the final total routine so that the output lines appear in the proper sequence on the report.

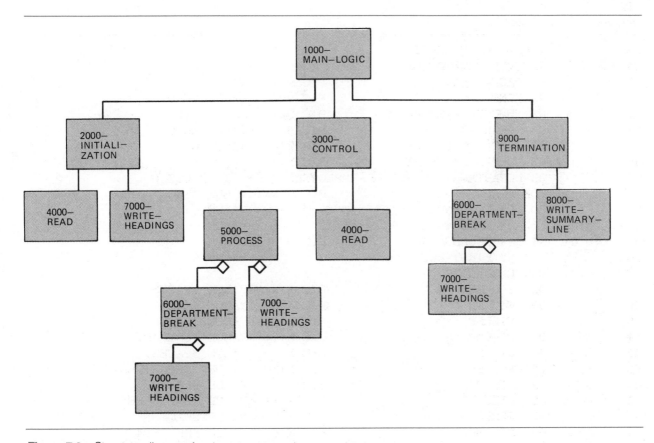

Figure 7.3 Structure diagram for department employee report.

Program 7.2 Department employee report program.

```
1        IDENTIFICATION DIVISION
2        PROGRAM-ID.  CHAPTER 7 EXAMPLE 2.
3        AUTHOR.  HORN.
4        ENVIRONMENT DIVISION.
5        INPUT-OUTPUT SECTION.
6        FILE-CONTROL.
7            SELECT INFD ASSIGN TO DISK.
8            SELECT PRNT ASSIGN TO PRINTER.
9        DATA DIVISION.
10       FILE SECTION.
11       FD   INFD
12           DATA RECORD IS INPUT-RECORD.
13       01   INPUT-RECORD.
14           02   IR-NAME              PIC X(16).
15           02   IR-INITIAL           PIC X.
16           02   IR-EMPLOYEE-NUMBER    PIC X(9).
17           02   IR-DEPARTMENT         PIC X(3).
18           02   IR-SALARY            PIC 9(6).
19           02   FILLER               PIC X(45).
20       FD   PRNT
21           DATA RECORD IS PRINT-LINE.
22       01   PRINT-LINE                       PIC X(132).
```

(continued)

Program 7.2   (continued)

```
23        WORKING-STORAGE SECTION.
24        01    ACCUMULATED-TOTALS.
25              03 PAGE-COUNT                 PIC 999     VALUE ZERO.
26              03 LINE-COUNT                 PIC 999     VALUE ZERO.
27              03 NUMBER-OF-EMPLOYEES        PIC 999     VALUE ZERO.
28              03 SALARY-TOTAL               PIC 9(8)    VALUE ZERO.
29              03 DEPT-TOTAL-SALARY          PIC 9(8)    VALUE 0.
30              03 HOLD-DEPARTMENT            PIC X(3).
31              03 DEPARTMENT-NUMBER-OF-EMPLOYEES    PIC 99 VALUE 0.
32        01    EOF-FLAG                      PIC 9       VALUE ZERO.
33                    88 NOT-END-OF-FILE                  VALUE 0.
34                    88 END-OF-FILE                       VALUE 1.
35        01    FIRST-RECORD-FLAG             PIC 9       VALUE 0.
36                    88 FIRST-RECORD                      VALUE 0.
37        01    MAJOR-HEADING.
38              02    FILLER                  PIC X(47) VALUE SPACES.
39              02    FILLER                  PIC X(3)    VALUE "ABC".
40              02    FILLER                  PIC X       VALUE SPACES.
41              02    FILLER                  PIC X(7)    VALUE "COMPANY".
42              02    FILLER                  PIC X       VALUE SPACES.
43              02    FILLER                  PIC X(10) VALUE "DEPARTMENT".
44              02    FILLER                  PIC X       VALUE SPACES.
45              02    FILLER                  PIC X(8)    VALUE "EMPLOYEE".
46              02    FILLER                  PIC X       VALUE SPACES.
47              02    FILLER                  PIC X(6)    VALUE "REPORT".
48              02    FILLER                  PIC X(15) VALUE SPACES.
49              02    FILLER                  PIC X(4)    VALUE "PAGE".
50              02    MH-PAGE-COUNTER         PIC ZZZ.
51              02    FILLER                  PIC X(25) VALUE SPACES.
52        01    SUBHEADING.
53              02    FILLER                  PIC X(26) VALUE SPACES.
54              02    FILLER                  PIC X(9)    VALUE "LAST NAME".
55              02    FILLER                  PIC X(8)    VALUE SPACES.
56              02    FILLER                  PIC X(7)    VALUE "INITIAL".
57              02    FILLER                  PIC X(8)    VALUE SPACES.
58              02    FILLER                  PIC X(15) VALUE
59                                            "EMPLOYEE NUMBER".
60              02    FILLER                  PIC X(8)    VALUE SPACES.
61              02    FILLER                  PIC X(10) VALUE "DEPARTMENT".
62              02    FILLER                  PIC X(8)    VALUE SPACES.
63              02    FILLER                  PIC X(6)    VALUE "SALARY".
64              02    FILLER                  PIC X(27) VALUE SPACES.
65        01    DETAIL-LINE.
66              02    FILLER                  PIC X(26) VALUE SPACES.
67              02    DL-NAME                 PIC X(16).
68              02    FILLER                  PIC X(3)    VALUE SPACES.
69              02    DL-INITIAL              PIC X.
70              02    FILLER                  PIC X(14) VALUE SPACES.
71              02    DL-EMPLOYEE-NUMBER      PIC X(9).
72              02    FILLER                  PIC X(16) VALUE SPACES.
73              02    DL-DEPARTMENT           PIC X(3).
74              02    FILLER                  PIC X(10) VALUE SPACES.
```

(continued)

Program 7.2   (continued)

```
75              02   DL-SALARY               PIC $ZZZ,ZZZ.
76              02   FILLER                  PIC X(25) VALUE SPACES.
77         01   DEPARTMENT-TOTAL-LINE.
78              02   FILLER                  PIC X(70) VALUE SPACES.
79              02   DTL-NUMBER-OF-EMPLOYEES PIC Z9.
80              02   FILLER                  PIC X(5)   VALUE SPACES.
81              02   FILLER                  PIC X(9)   VALUE "EMPLOYEES".
82              02   FILLER                  PIC X(7)   VALUE SPACES.
83              02   DTL-TOTAL-SALARY        PIC $**,***,***.
84              02   FILLER                  PIC X(28) VALUE SPACES.
85         01   SUMMARY-LINE.
86              02   FILLER                  PIC X(70) VALUE SPACES.
87              02   SL-NUMBER-OF-EMPLOYEES  PIC ZZZ9.
88              02   FILLER                  PIC X(5)   VALUE SPACES.
89              02   FILLER                  PIC X(9)   VALUE "EMPLOYEES".
90              02   FILLER                  PIC X(7)   VALUE SPACES.
91              02   SL-SALARY-TOTAL         PIC $**,***,***.
92              02   FILLER                  PIC X(25) VALUE SPACES.
93         PROCEDURE DIVISION.
94         1000-MAIN-LOGIC.
95              PERFORM 2000-INITIALIZATION.
96              PERFORM 3000-CONTROL UNTIL END-OF-FILE.
97              PERFORM 9000-TERMINATION.
98         2000-INITIALIZATION.
99              OPEN INPUT INFD OUTPUT PRNT.
100             PERFORM 4000-READ.
101             PERFORM 7000-WRITE-HEADINGS.
102        3000-CONTROL.
103             PERFORM 5000-PROCESS.
104             PERFORM 4000-READ.
105        4000-READ.
106             READ INFD AT END MOVE 1 TO EOF-FLAG.
107        5000-PROCESS.
108             IF FIRST-RECORD
109                 MOVE IR-DEPARTMENT TO HOLD-DEPARTMENT
110                 MOVE 1 TO FIRST-RECORD-FLAG.
111             IF IR-DEPARTMENT NOT = HOLD-DEPARTMENT
112                 PERFORM 6000-DEPARTMENT-BREAK.
113             MOVE IR-NAME            TO DL-NAME.
114             MOVE IR-INITIAL         TO DL-INITIAL.
115             MOVE IR-EMPLOYEE-NUMBER TO DL-EMPLOYEE-NUMBER.
116             MOVE IR-SALARY          TO DL-SALARY.
117             MOVE IR-DEPARTMENT      TO DL-DEPARTMENT.
118             ADD IR-SALARY           TO DEPT-TOTAL-SALARY.
119             ADD 1                   TO DEPARTMENT-NUMBER-OF-EMPLOYEES.
120             ADD IR-SALARY           TO SALARY-TOTAL.
121             ADD 1                   TO NUMBER-OF-EMPLOYEES.
122             WRITE PRINT-LINE FROM DETAIL-LINE AFTER 2.
123             ADD 2                   TO LINE-COUNT.
124             IF LINE-COUNT > 46
125                 PERFORM 7000-WRITE-HEADINGS.
126        6000-DEPARTMENT-BREAK.
```

(continued)

Program 7.2   (continued)

```
127              MOVE DEPARTMENT-NUMBER-OF-EMPLOYEES TO
128                  DTL-NUMBER-OF-EMPLOYEES.
129              MOVE DEPT-TOTAL-SALARY TO DTL-TOTAL-SALARY.
130              WRITE PRINT-LINE FROM DEPARTMENT-TOTAL-LINE AFTER 2.
131              ADD 2 TO LINE-COUNT.
132              IF LINE-COUNT > 46
133                  PERFORM 7000-WRITE-HEADINGS.
134              MOVE 0 TO DEPARTMENT-NUMBER-OF-EMPLOYEES.
135              MOVE 0 TO DEPT-TOTAL-SALARY.
136              MOVE IR-DEPARTMENT TO HOLD-DEPARTMENT.
137          7000-WRITE-HEADINGS.
138              ADD 1 TO PAGE-COUNT.
139              MOVE PAGE-COUNT TO MH-PAGE-COUNTER.
140              WRITE PRINT-LINE FROM MAJOR-HEADING AFTER CHANNEL 1.
141              WRITE PRINT-LINE FROM SUBHEADING AFTER 2.
142              MOVE 3 TO LINE-COUNT.
143          8000-WRITE-SUMMARY-LINE.
144              MOVE NUMBER-OF-EMPLOYEES TO SL-NUMBER-OF-EMPLOYEES.
145              MOVE SALARY-TOTAL TO SL-SALARY-TOTAL.
146              WRITE PRINT-LINE FROM SUMMARY-LINE AFTER 3.
147          9000-TERMINATION.
148              PERFORM 6000-DEPARTMENT-BREAK.
149              PERFORM 8000-WRITE-SUMMARY-LINE.
150              CLOSE INFD, PRNT.
151              STOP RUN.
```

	ABC COMPANY DEPARTMENT EMPLOYEE REPORT			PAGE
LAST NAME	INITIAL	EMPLOYEE NUMBER	DEPARTMENT	SALARY
SMITH	R	320120354	012	$ 7,000
KILLINGER	D	901234567	012	$ 2,000
HENDRIX	R	123456789	012	$ 16,500
		3	EMPLOYEES	$****25,500
CARTOLER	V	028099812	021	$ 75,000
ROBERTSON	M	326985412	021	$ 30,000
		2	EMPLOYEES	$***105,000
WARD	T	321321321	032	$ 11,000
		1	EMPLOYEES	$****11,000
NOBLES	C	987987987	042	$ 9,000
BROXTON	O	987987987	042	$ 30,000
AMORE	M	562160536	042	$ 17,000
		3	EMPLOYEES	$****56,000
SELLERS	P	312312312	052	$ 30,000
FRANKLIN	R	321321321	052	$ 20,000
		2	EMPLOYEES	$****50,000
HORNING	B	963963963	062	$100,000
PARKER	L	147147147	062	$ 20,000
		2	EMPLOYEES	$***120,000
CALDWELL	W	654654654	072	$ 10,000
ELMORE	N	321321321	072	$ 40,000
LONG	M	456456456	072	$ 12,000
		3	EMPLOYEES	$****62,000
HIX	G	865423567	111	$ 20,000
FARMER	J	320154208	111	$ 8,000
		2	EMPLOYEES	$****28,000
CHRISTY	C	421360380	777	$ 35,000
WILSON	A	632547328	777	$ 10,000
		2	EMPLOYEES	$****45,000
		20	EMPLOYEES	$***502,500

7.5 MULTILEVEL CONTROL BREAKS

Often reports require subtotals for more than one type of subset of the data. For example, suppose the department number of the data processed by Program 7.2 is coded with the division number of the company as the first digit of the department within the division. Division totals as well as department totals are produced by Program 7.3 below. This program requires the recognition of two levels of control breaks: a break in department number, and a break in division number.

A break in division number must automatically result in a break in department number, since departments are subordinate to divisions. This task is performed in Program 7.3 by the paragraph 6500-DIVISION-BREAK (lines 158 through 167). The first action taken in this paragraph is:

PERFORM 6000-DEPARTMENT-BREAK.

When more than one level of control break is to be recognized within a program, hold areas for each of the break fields are required. The hold areas must be initialized after reading the first record and then must be replaced with the new value after each break has occurred. The handling of the hold field initialization is carried out as part of the paragraph 2000-INITIALIZATION (Prog. 7.3, lines 111 through 115). After the first record is read (line 113) the values of IR-DEPARTMENT and IR-DIVISION are moved to respective hold fields (lines 114 through 115).

Program 7.3 Division/department report program.

```
1        IDENTIFICATION DIVISION.
2        PROGRAM-ID. CHAPTER 7 EXAMPLE 3.
3        AUTHOR. HORN.
4        ENVIRONMENT DIVISION.
5        INPUT-OUTPUT SECTION.
6        FILE-CONTROL.
7            SELECT INFD ASSIGN TO DISK.
8            SELECT PRNT ASSIGN TO PRINTER.
9        DATA DIVISION.
10       FILE SECTION.
11       FD   INFD
12            DATA RECORD IS INPUT-RECORD.
13       01   INPUT-RECORD.
14            02   IR-NAME              PIC X(16).
15            02   IR-INITIAL           PIC X.
16            02   IR-EMPLOYEE-NUMBER    PIC X(9).
17            02   IR-DIVISION          PIC X.
18            02   IR-DEPARTMENT        PIC X(2).
19            02   IR-SALARY            PIC 9(6).
20            02   FILLER               PIC X(45).
21       FD   PRNT
22            DATA RECORD IS PRINT-LINE.
23       01   PRINT-LINE               PIC X(132).
24       WORKING-STORAGE SECTION.
25       01   COUNTERS.
26            03 PAGE-COUNT            PIC 999    VALUE ZERO.
```

(continued)

```
27                  03 LINE-COUNT                  PIC 999      VALUE 46.
28                     88 PAGE-FULL       VALUE 46 THRU 99.
29          01   ACCUMULATED-TOTALS.
30                  03 NUMBER-OF-EMPLOYEES      PIC 999      VALUE ZERO.
31                  03 SALARY-TOTAL            PIC 9(8)    VALUE ZERO.
32                  03 DEPARTMENT-NUMBER-OF-EMPLOYEES   PIC 99 VALUE 0.
33                  03 DEPT-TOTAL-SALARY        PIC 9(8)   VALUE 0.
34                  03   DIVISION-NUMBER-OF-EMPLOYEES   PIC 99 VALUE 0.
35                  03   DIVISION-TOTAL-SALARY        PIC 9(8) VALUE 0.
36          01   HOLD-FIELDS.
37                  03 HOLD-DEPARTMENT          PIC X(2)    VALUE SPACES.
38                  03 HOLD-DIVISION            PIC X       VALUE SPACES.
39          01   EOF-FLAG                       PIC 9       VALUE ZERO.
40                     88 NOT-END-OF-FILE       VALUE 0.
41                     88 END-OF-FILE           VALUE 1.
42          01   MAJOR-HEADING.
43                  02   FILLER                 PIC X(44) VALUE SPACES.
44                  02   FILLER                 PIC X(3)   VALUE "ABC".
45                  02   FILLER                 PIC X       VALUE SPACES.
46                  02   FILLER                 PIC X(7)   VALUE "COMPANY".
47                  02   FILLER                 PIC X       VALUE SPACES.
48                  02   FILLER                 PIC X(19) VALUE
49                  "DIVISION/DEPARTMENT".
50                  02   FILLER                 PIC X       VALUE SPACES.
51                  02   FILLER                 PIC X(8)   VALUE "EMPLOYEE".
52                  02   FILLER                 PIC X       VALUE SPACES.
53                  02   FILLER                 PIC X(6)   VALUE "REPORT".
54                  02   FILLER                 PIC X(10) VALUE SPACES.
55                  02   FILLER                 PIC X(4)   VALUE "PAGE".
56                  02   MH-PAGE-COUNTER        PIC ZZZ.
57          01   SUBHEADING.
58                  02   FILLER                 PIC X(26) VALUE SPACES.
59                  02   FILLER                 PIC X(9)   VALUE "LAST NAME".
60                  02   FILLER                 PIC X(8)   VALUE SPACES.
61                  02   FILLER                 PIC X(7)   VALUE "INITIAL".
62                  02   FILLER                 PIC X(8)   VALUE SPACES.
63                  02   FILLER                 PIC X(15) VALUE
64                  "EMPLOYEE NUMBER".
65                  02   FILLER                 PIC X(8)   VALUE SPACES.
66                  02   FILLER                 PIC X(10) VALUE "DEPARTMENT".
67                  02   FILLER                 PIC X(8)   VALUE SPACES.
68                  02   FILLER                 PIC X(6)   VALUE "SALARY".
69          01   DETAIL-LINE.
70                  02   FILLER                 PIC X(26) VALUE SPACES.
71                  02   DL-NAME                PIC X(16).
72                  02   FILLER                 PIC X(3)   VALUE SPACES.
73                  02   DL-INITIAL             PIC X.
74                  02   FILLER                 PIC X(14) VALUE SPACES.
75                  02   DL-EMPLOYEE-NUMBER     PIC X(9).
76                  02   FILLER                 PIC X(15) VALUE SPACES.
77                  02   DL-DIVISION            PIC X
78                  02   FILLER                 PIC X       VALUE SPACES.
```

(continued)

Program 7.3 (continued)

```
79              02   DL-DEPARTMENT            PIC X(2).
80              02   FILLER                   PIC X(10) VALUE SPACES.
81              02   DL-SALARY                PIC $ZZZ,ZZZ.
82         01   DEPARTMENT-TOTAL-LINE.
83              02   FILLER                   PIC X(70) VALUE SPACES.
84              02   DTL-NUMBER-OF-EMPLOYEES  PIC Z9.
85              02   FILLER                   PIC X(5)  VALUE SPACES.
86              02   FILLER                   PIC X(9)  VALUE "EMPLOYEES".
87              02   FILLER                   PIC X(7)  VALUE SPACES.
88              02   DTL-TOTAL-SALARY         PIC $**,***,***.
89         01   DIVISION-TOTAL-LINE.
90              02   FILLER  PIC X(23) VALUE "**** DIVISION TOTAL ***".
91              02   FILLER                   PIC X(47) VALUE SPACES.
92              02 DVT-NUMBER-OF-EMPLOYEES    PIC Z9.
93              02   FILLER                   PIC X(5)  VALUE SPACES.
94              02   FILLER                   PIC X(9)  VALUE "EMPLOYEES".
95              02   FILLER                   PIC X(7)  VALUE SPACES.
96              02 DVT-TOTAL-SALARY           PIC $**,***,***.
97         01   SUMMARY-LINE.
98              02   FILLER                   PIC X(15) VALUE SPACES.
99              02   FILLER  PIC X(23) VALUE "**** COMPANY TOTAL ****".
100             02   FILLER                   PIC X(30) VALUE SPACES.
101             02   SL-NUMBER-OF-EMPLOYEES   PIC ZZZ9.
102             02   FILLER                   PIC X(5)  VALUE SPACES.
103             02   FILLER                   PIC X(9)  VALUE "EMPLOYEES".
104             02   FILLER                   PIC X(7)  VALUE SPACES.
105             02   SL-SALARY-TOTAL          PIC $**,***,***.
106        PROCEDURE DIVISION.
107        1000-MAIN-LOGIC.
108            PERFORM 2000-INITIALIZATION.
109            PERFORM 3000-CONTROL UNTIL END-OF-FILE.
110            PERFORM 9000-TERMINATION.
111        2000-INITIALIZATION.
112            OPEN INPUT INFD OUTPUT PRNT.
113            PERFORM 4000-READ.
114                MOVE IR-DEPARTMENT  TO HOLD-DEPARTMENT
115                MOVE IR-DIVISION    TO HOLD-DIVISION.
116        3000-CONTROL.
117            PERFORM 4050-CONTROL-BREAK-CHECK.
118            PERFORM 5000-PROCESS.
119            PERFORM 4000-READ.
120        4000-READ.
121            READ INFD AT END MOVE 1 TO EOF-FLAG.
122        4050-CONTROL-BREAK-CHECK.
123            IF IR-DIVISION NOT = HOLD-DIVISION
124                PERFORM 6500-DIVISION-BREAK
125            ELSE
126                IF IR-DEPARTMENT NOT = HOLD-DEPARTMENT
127                PERFORM 6000-DEPARTMENT-BREAK
128            ELSE
129                NEXT SENTENCE.
130        5000-PROCESS.
```

(continued)

Program 7.3   (continued)

```
131           MOVE IR-NAME               TO DL-NAME.
132           MOVE IR-INITIAL            TO DL-INITIAL.
133           MOVE IR-EMPLOYEE-NUMBER TO DL-EMPLOYEE-NUMBER.
134           MOVE IR-SALARY             TO DL-SALARY.
135           MOVE IR-DIVISION           TO DL-DIVISION.
136           MOVE IR-DEPARTMENT         TO DL-DEPARTMENT.
137           ADD IR-SALARY              TO DEPT-TOTAL-SALARY.
138           ADD IR-SALARY              TO DIVISION-TOTAL-SALARY.
139           ADD 1                      TO DEPARTMENT-NUMBER-OF-EMPLOYEES.
140           ADD 1                      TO DIVISION-NUMBER-OF-EMPLOYEES.
141           ADD IR-SALARY              TO SALARY-TOTAL.
142           ADD 1                      TO NUMBER-OF-EMPLOYEES.
143           IF PAGE-FULL
144               PERFORM 7000-WRITE-HEADINGS.
145           WRITE PRINT-LINE FROM DETAIL-LINE AFTER 2.
146           ADD 2                      TO LINE-COUNT.
147      6000-DEPARTMENT-BREAK.
148           IF PAGE-FULL
149               PERFORM 7000-WRITE HEADINGS.
150           MOVE DEPARTMENT-NUMBER-OF-EMPLOYEES TO
151               DTL-NUMBER-OF-EMPLOYEES.
152           MOVE DEPT-TOTAL-SALARY  TO DTL-TOTAL-SALARY.
153           WRITE PRINT-LINE FROM DEPARTMENT-TOTAL-LINE AFTER 2.
154           ADD 2                      TO LINE-COUNT.
155           MOVE 0                     TO DEPARTMENT-NUMBER-OF-EMPLOYEES.
156           MOVE 0                     TO DEPT-TOTAL-SALARY.
157           MOVE IR-DEPARTMENT         TO HOLD-DEPARTMENT.
158      6500-DIVISION-BREAK.
159           PERFORM 6000-DEPARTMENT-BREAK.
160           IF PAGE-FULL
161               PERFORM 7000-WRITE-HEADINGS.
162           MOVE DIVISION-TOTAL-SALARY TO DVT-TOTAL-SALARY.
163           MOVE DIVISION-NUMBER-OF-EMPLOYEES TO DVT-NUMBER-OF-EMPLOYEES.
164           WRITE PRINT-LINE FROM DIVISION-TOTAL-LINE AFTER 3.
165           MOVE 0                     TO DIVISION-NUMBER-OF-EMPLOYEES.
166           MOVE 0                     TO DIVISION-TOTAL-SALARY.
167           MOVE IR-DIVISION TO HOLD-DIVISION
168      7000-WRITE-HEADINGS.
169           ADD 1 TO PAGE-COUNT.
170           MOVE PAGE-COUNT TO MH-PAGE-COUNTER.
171           WRITE PRINT-LINE FROM MAJOR-HEADING AFTER PAGE 1.
172           WRITE PRINT-LINE FROM SUBHEADING AFTER 2.
173           MOVE 3 TO LINE-COUNT.
174      8000-WRITE-SUMMARY-LINE.
175           MOVE NUMBER-OF-EMPLOYEES TO SL-NUMBER-OF-EMPLOYEES.
176           MOVE SALARY-TOTAL TO SL-SALARY-TOTAL.
177           WRITE PRINT-LINE FROM SUMMARY-LINE AFTER 3.
178      9000-TERMINATION.
179           PERFORM 6500-DIVISION-BREAK.
180           PERFORM 8000-WRITE-SUMMARY-LINE.
181           CLOSE INFD, PRNT.
182           STOP RUN.
```

(continued)

Program 7.3 (continued)

```
                    ABC COMPANY DIVISION-DEPARTMENT EMPLOYEE REPORT           PAGE    1
LAST NAME           INITIAL       EMPLOYEE NUMBER            DEPARTMENT          SALARY
SMITH               R             320120354                    0 12       $   7,000
KILLINGER           D             901234567                    0 12       $   2,000
HENDRIX             R             123456789                    0 12       $  16,000
                                            3        EMPLOYEES         $****25,000
CARTOLER            V             028099812                    0 21       $  75,000
ROBERTSON           M             326985412                    0 21       $  30,000
                                            2        EMPLOYEES         $***105,000
WARD                T             321321321                    0 32       $  11,000
                                            1        EMPLOYEES         $****11,000
NOBLES              C             987987987                    0 42       $   9,000
BROXTON             O             987987987                    0 42       $  30,000
AMORE               M             562160536                    0 42       $  17,000
                                            3        EMPLOYEES         $****56,000
SELLERS             P             312312312                    0 52       $  30,000
FRANKLIN            R             321321321                    0 52       $  20,000
                                            2        EMPLOYEES         $****50,000
HORNING             B             963963963                    0 62       $100,000
PARKER              L             147147147                    0 62       $  20,000
                                            2        EMPLOYEES         $***120,000
CALDWELL            W             654654654                    0 72       $  10,000
ELMORE              N             321321321                    0 72       $  40,000
LONG                M             456456456                    0 72       $  12,000
                    ABC COMPANY DIVISION DEPARTMENT EMPLOYEE REPORT          PAGE    2
                    LAST NAME     INITIAL    EMPLOYEE NUMBER        DEPARTMENT     SALARY
                                            3        EMPLOYEES         $****62,000
**** DIVISION TOTAL ***                    16        EMPLOYEES         $***429,000
                    CHRISTY       C          421360380               7 77       $  35,000
                    WILSON        A          632547328               7 77       $  10,000
                                            2        EMPLOYEES         $****45,000
**** DIVISION TOTAL ***                     2        EMPLOYEES         $****45,000
            **** COMPANY TOTAL ****        18        EMPLOYEES         $***474,000
```

The logic used for generation of page headings in Program 7.3 differs somewhat from that used in preceding programs in this chapter. A line counter is defined and initialized in the DATA DIVISION (lines 27 and 28):

```
03   LINE-COUNT   PIC 99 VALUE 46.
     88   PAGE-FULL   VALUE 46 THRU 99.
```

Note that initially PAGE-FULL is true. Just before any output to the printer the condition PAGE-FULL is tested (lines 143 and 144, 148 and 149, 160 and 161). If PAGE-FULL is true, the paragraph 7000-WRITE-HEADINGS (lines 168 through 173) is executed. This paragraph produces the required headings and resets LINE-COUNT (line 173). Thus, because PAGE-FULL is initially true before the first output to the printer, the page headings will be produced. This makes it unnecessary to produce page headings in the initialization procedure, as required by the method used in Programs 7.1 and 7.2.

7.6 DEBUG CLINIC

Programs requiring line counting, page numbers, and subtotals are somewhat more complex than programs which have been encountered previously in this text. It is, therefore not uncommon for programmers to encounter logical errors during the debugging of such programs. The following list presents some of the most common problems and some suggestions as to what the possible causes of the problem may be.

Logical Problem	*Possible causes*
No headings	Page heading paragraph not included
	PERFORM of page heading paragraph omitted
Headings on first page only	PERFORM of page heading paragraph not included in processing of body of report
	Line counter not incremented
Page headings occur on all pages but first	PERFORM of page heading paragraph not included in initialization
	Line counter not initialized properly
Page headings do not occur at top of every physical page of output	Line counter not incremented after each output Amount added to line counter not equal to number lines produced
	Number of lines per page used in program exceeds actual number of lines per page
Page headings occur in the middle of physical pages of output	Computer operator failed to align paper in printer properly
	Skipping to top of a new page is not a feature of the printer in use
	Skipping to top of a new page has been disallowed (this is sometimes done to save paper)
Page number is same on all pages	Page counter not incremented in page heading paragraph
Page totals are cumulative	Subtotal field not reinitialized to zero after production of subtotal output
Subtotal with value zero occurs before first detail output	Hold field has not been initialized for first input record
Subtotals occur after every detail output line	Hold field is not replaced with a new value in the control break routine

Logical Problem	Probable Causes
No totals at end of report	Program does not perform control break routines as part of termination
A group includes an output line which should be included in the following group	Program is checking for control break after detail processing rather than before processing.

7.7   SELF TEST EXERCISES

1. Evaluate each of the following conditions:

```
  2                                      A B

03 FLDA PIC 9.                  03 FLDB PIC XXX.
    88 ITEM-TYPE-1 VALUE 1.         88 XYZ VALUE "ABC", "AB".
    88 ITEM-TYPE-2 VALUE 2.
    88 ITEM-TYPE-OTHER VALUE 0, 3 THRU 9.
```

Example   NOT ITEM-TYPE-1

False

True

   a. ITEM-TYPE-1
   b. ITEM-TYPE-1 OR ITEM-TYPE-2
   c. XYZ
   d. NOT XYZ
   e. NOT (ITEM-TYPE-1 OR ITEM-TYPE-2)
   f. XYZ AND NOT ITEM-TYPE-1
   g. NOT XYZ AND ITEM-TYPE-1 OR NOT ITEM-TYPE-2
   h. NOT ITEM-TYPE-OTHER

2. Which method of initialization of hold areas—the one in Program 7.2 using a switch or the one in Program 7.3—seems to be best? Why?

3. In Programs 7.1, and 7.2, the line counter is initialized to value 0. Each output operation forwards the counter. After each output the counter is tested to see if the page is full. If the page is full a new page is initiated with headings and page number. Using this scheme, what would happen if the last line in the report happened to fall on the last line of a page? What would happen if there are no records in the file?

4. In Program 7.3 an alternative method for handling line counting is used. The line counter is initialized to a value greater than the number of lines on a page. For example, if there are 45 lines on a page, the line counter is defined with initial value 46. The program then tests the line counter for full page before each output operation. Because of the initial value of the line count, page headings will be produced in advance of the first output operation and each time thereafter that the page becomes full. What advantages are there to this scheme? What would happen if
   1) there are no records in the file?
   2) the last line of the report falls on the last line of a page?

   Which method for line counting seems best?

5. *Should the number of lines per page be defined as a data item in* WORKING-STORAGE? Why?

6. For the program of Figure 7.5, suppose we want to include the department number as a part of the output line showing each department total. Which of the following should be moved to the output record: IR–DEPARTMENT or HOLD–DEPARTMENT? Why?

7.8 PROGRAMMING EXERCISES

1. Write a program to determine the inventory value of stock items. Input consists of data records containing:

> Quantity
> Item stock number and name
> Unit cost

There may be more than one input record per item. For example, baseballs may have been purchased as follows: 5 baseballs at a unit cost of $2.00, and 4 baseballs at a unit cost of $2.25. The program should list the quantity, stock number and name, item weighted average unit cost, and total dollar value of each stock item in appropriately spaced columns. Headings on each page are required, as are page numbers. Also write the total value of all items in the inventory.

2. The XYZ Wholesale Supply Company has prepared records containing the following items:

> Department number
> Transaction date
> Amount of order

Write a program to list each record and produce totals for each department as well as overall totals. List the department number only once for each department's group of records. Use the following test data:

Department Number	Transaction Date	Amount of Order
100	1/10/82	6.75
100	1/10/82	14.85
100	1/11/82	7.00
100	1/13/82	19.50
102	1/10/82	7.95
102	1/11/82	9.95
102	1/11/82	18.50
103	1/12/82	19.70
103	1/13/82	6.50
104	1/11/82	4.50

Your output should be similar to

XYZ WHOLESALE SUPPLY COMPANY

DEPARTMENT NUMBER	TRANSACTION DATE	AMOUNT OF ORDER
100	1/10/82	6.75
	1/10/82	14.85
	1/11/82	7.00
	1/13/82	19.50
	TOTAL	$48.10*
102	1/10/82	7.95
	1/11/82	9.95

	1/11/82	18.50
	TOTAL	$36.40*
103	1/12/82	9.70
	1/13/82	6.50
	TOTAL	$16.20*
104	1/11/82	4.50
	TOTAL	$4.50*
	GRAND TOTAL	$105.20***

3. Modify the program written for Exercise 2 above to produce daily totals within each department. Assume that the data is in sequence by transaction date within each department group.

4. Write a program to alert top management of the XYZ Corporation when sales in its department are outside certain limits (abnormally high or abnormally low). Input records contain the department number, year, and total sales for that year. You may assume that the records are in ascending sequence by year and that all records for a given department are grouped together (the most recent year is the last record in the department group). If the most recent year's sales are more than 10 percent greater than the average for the entire period, then sales are high. If the most recent year's sales are less than 90 percent of the average for the period, then sales are low. Output should be one line per department consisting of department number, most recent year's sales, average sales and a flag HIGH or LOW if appropriate.

5. You have been hired as a programmer for the Harris Hardware Co. Harris makes nuts, bolts and washers. At the end of each day a record is prepared for each employee with the following format:

Positions	
1-20	NAME
21-25	EMPLOYEE NO.
26-27	HOURS WORKED
28-30	RATE OF PAY
31-32	NUMBER OF DOZEN STAINLESS STEEL BOLTS MADE
33-34	NUMBER OF DOZEN STAINLESS STEEL NUTS MADE
35-36	NUMBER OF DOZEN STAINLESS STEEL WASHERS MADE
37-38	NUMBER OF DOZEN BRASS BOLTS MADE
39-40	NUMBER OF DOZEN BRASS NUTS MADE
41-42	NUMBER OF DOZEN BRASS WASHERS MADE
43-44	NUMBER OF DOZEN FIBER WASHERS MADE
45-80	BLANK

The cost of production *per item* is as follows:

	NUTS	BOLTS	WASHERS
Stainless Steel	$0.07	$0.07	$0.07
Brass	$0.04	$0.05	$0.02
Fiber	—	—	$0.005

At the end of the week, all records for the week are processed. You may assume that prior to processing, the entire file has been sorted and all the records for each employee are together. There will be one to five records per employee. When each employee's records are processed, write out under appropriate headings his or her name, employee number, total production by category, total hours worked for the week, and pay for the week, counting any hours worked in one day in excess of eight hours as time and one half. When all records are processed, skip to a new page and give total production cost for each category as well as grand total cost of production for the week.

6. Write a program to perform an edit of the data described in Exercise 5 above. Your program should check for the following conditions:
   a. More than 5 records for one employee
   b. Record out of sequence
   c. HOURS-WORKED is blank or HOURS-WORKED > 18
   d. RATE-OF-PAY is blank
   e. All of the fields positions 31-44 are blank

   Write appropriate messages when each condition is found.

7. Assume that the data described in Chapter 4, Exercise 3 (page 85) has been sorted into order by zone. Write a program to list the number of homes in each of the following categories for each zone:

   Selling price ≤ $40,000
   $40,000 < selling price ≤ $70,000
   $70,000 < selling price ≤ $95,000
   $95,000 < selling price

8. Assume that the data described in Chapter 6, Exercise 2 has been sorted into sequence by account code. Write a program to list and summarize expenditures for each account.

TABLES AND PERFORM/VARYING

8

8.1 WHAT IS A TABLE?

A *table* is a sequence of consecutive storage locations (each location of which is called an *element*) having a common name. The elements can be accessed using the table name and a specific subscript to point to the particular element to be referenced. For example, suppose we wish to store seventy-five values representing student grades. One approach would be to create individually named data items to store the values. Another approach would be to create a table and store the values in elements of the table. Such a table might be visualized as:

GRADE (1)	45
GRADE (2)	92
GRADE (3)	70
.	.
.	.
.	.
GRADE (75)	80

The elements of the table are referenced by a name GRADE and a subscript value enclosed in parentheses.[1] The value of GRADE (1) is 45; the value of GRADE (75) is 80; and so on. The subscript points to a particular value in the

---

[1]Some compilers require that at least one space must precede a left parenthesis and one space must follow a right parenthesis. Also, a space must not follow a left parenthesis nor precede a right parenthesis. For example, the following table references are invalid for these compilers:

GRADE(1)	No space preceding left parenthesis
GRADE (1)	Space following left parenthesis
GRADE (1)	Space preceding right parenthesis

table. A subscript must be either a constant or a data-name.[2] When a data-name is used, its value determines the particular element of the table being referenced. For example, the following are valid references:

GRADE (IND)   The value of IND at the time of execution
will determine which element of GRADE is
referenced.

GRADE (35)   The 35th element of GRADE is referenced.

The ability to use a variable as a subscript accounts for the utility of tables. For example, suppose we want to compute the sum of grades. If the grades had not been stored in a table, then a very long computational statement (involving seventy-five different variable names) would have to be used. However, with tables the sum can be accumulated using the following code:

```
    .
    .
    .

    MOVE  0  TO  TOTAL-X.
    MOVE  1  TO  IND.
    PERFORM ADD-ROUTINE UNTIL IND > 75.

    .
    .
    .

ADD-ROUTINE.
    ADD  GRADE  (IND)  TO  TOTAL-X.
    ADD  1  TO  IND.
```

At the first repetition of ADD-ROUTINE, the value of IND will be 1, and the contents of GRADE (1) will be added to TOTAL-X. Then the value of IND will become 2 and the contents of GRADE (2) will be added to TOTAL-X, and so on. The process terminates when the value of IND exceeds 75 at which time all of the grades will have been added into TOTAL-X.

8.2 THE OCCURS CLAUSE

The OCCURS clause is used in the DATA division to define a table. Figure 8.1 shows a general form for usage of the OCCURS clause. In the OCCURS clause *integer* specifies the number of elements to be contained in the table.

The OCCURS clause cannot be used on an 01 level data item. For example, the following code would create the table for storing 75 grades:

```
01  GRADE-TABLE.
    02   GRADE OCCURS 75 TIMES PIC 99.
```

The data-name GRADE-TABLE is a group data item; it is the overall name for the entire set of seventy-five data items. A data-name used with an OCCURS clause may be an elementary data item, as in the above example, or it may be a group data item. For example, suppose we wish to store the names and

---

[2]Some compilers permit any expression to be used as a subscript. For such compilers the following would be a valid table reference:

GRADE (IND + 3)   The expression IND + 3 will be evaluated to determine which element of
GRADE is referenced.

---

level-number data-name <u>OCCURS</u> integer TIMES

Figure 8.1   General form of the OCCURS clause

---

addresses of one hundred people in such a way that one element of the table corresponds to the data being stored about one person. The following code could be used:

```
01   NAME-ADDRESS-TABLE.
     02   NAME-AND-ADDRESS OCCURS 100 TIMES.
          03   NAME PIC X(20).
          03   ADDRESS PIC X(30).
```

In this case NAME-AND-ADDRESS is a group data item; each NAME-AND-ADDRESS is composed of two fields. The data stored for the fifth person then could be referenced by:

NAME-AND-ADDRESS (5)

When the OCCURS clause is used on a group data item, a subscript may be used not only on the group data item name but also on any subordinate field. In the above example it would also be valid to reference

NAME (5)

in order to obtain the name only, and

ADDRESS (5)

in order to obtain the address only. The data structure defined above may be visualized as follows:

Subscripts may be associated only with subordinate parts, not with the overall name of the data structures. For example: NAME-ADDRESS-TABLE (3) would be invalid, since NAME-ADDRESS-TABLE occurs exactly one time; it is a name for $100(20 + 30) = 5000$ characters of data.

An alternative form for storing the above data would be

```
01   ALTERNATE-NAME-ADDRESS-TABLE.
     02   NAME OCCURS 100 TIMES PIC X(20).
     02   ADDRESS OCCURS 100 TIMES PIC X(30).
```

This structure may be visualized as:

In this case both NAME (5) and ADDRESS (5) would have to be referenced to access all data stored for person number 5. This is less desirable than the other approach if both name and address are desired at the same time.

The subscript used in any reference to an element of a table must have a value in the range one to the size of the table specified in the OCCURS clause. Any reference involving a subscript having a value outside this range will result in an execution time error message. For example, for the NAME-ADDRESS-TABLE discussed above, the following references would be invalid:

NAME (0)	Zero is not in the range 1 to 100
NAME (101)	101 is too large

8.3   LOADING AND PROCESSING A TABLE

The OCCURS clause is required to define a table. Data then can be placed into the table. Usually it is not known exactly how many items are to be stored in a table, so the number of elements reserved in the OCCURS clause must be at least as large as the largest number of items anticipated. The program can use a counter to indicate the location into which the item is to be stored and to ensure that the maximum capacity of the table is not exceeded inadvertently. A program segment which could be used to store data into the NAME-ADDRESS-TABLE is shown below:

```
    .
    .
    .

    MOVE ZERO TO ERROR-FLAG.
    MOVE ZERO TO NUM-ELEMENTS.
    READ INFD AT END MOVE "YES" TO EOF-FLAG.
    PERFORM STORE-AND-READ UNTIL
    EOF-FLAG = "YES" OR ERROR-FLAG = 1.

    .
    .
    .

STORE-AND-READ.
    ADD 1 TO NUM-ELEMENTS.
    IF NUM-ELEMENTS > 100
        MOVE 1 TO ERROR-FLAG
    ELSE
        MOVE NAME-IN TO NAME (NUM-ELEMENTS)
        MOVE ADDRESS-IN TO ADDRESS (NUM-ELEMENTS)
        READ INFO AT END MOVE "YES" TO EOF-FLAG.
```

Note that in the above program segment the value contained in NUM-ELEMENTS after loading the data into the table reflects the actual number of elements contained in the table. Subsequent processing of the table would use this value for termination. For example, the following code could be used to produce a listing of the elements of NAME-ADDRESS-TABLE:

```
    .
    .
    .
```

```
    MOVE ZERO TO TABLE-INDEX.
      PERFORM TABLE-OUTPUT
      UNTIL TABLE-INDEX = NUM-ELEMENTS.
    .
    .
    .
    TABLE-OUTPUT.
      ADD 1 TO TABLE-INDEX.
      MOVE NAME (TABLE-INDEX) TO NAME-OUT.
      MOVE ADDRESS (TABLE-INDEX) TO ADDRESS-OUT.
      WRITE OUTPUT-REC FROM NAME-AND-ADDRESS-OUT AFTER 1.
```

Numeric data contained in a table may be processed by any desired arithmetic statement. A subscript must be included to indicate which element of the table is to be operated on. Usually table elements are processed within a loop in order to perform similar operations on all or any of the elements of the table. For example, the following code could be used to calculate the average of the elements contained in the GRADE-TABLE defined above:

```
    MOVE 0 TO SUM-OF-GRADES.
    MOVE 1 TO IND.
    PERFORM SUMMATION-ROUTINE UNTIL IND > NUM-OF-ELEMENTS.
    COMPUTE AVERAGE = SUM-OF-GRADES / NUM-OF-ELEMENTS.
    .
    .
    .
    SUMMATION-ROUTINE.
      ADD GRADE (IND) TO SUM-OF-GRADES.
      ADD 1 TO IND.
```

In this example, the first time SUMMATION-ROUTINE is entered, the value of IND will be 1, so GRADE (1) will be added to SUM-OF-GRADES; the second time, GRADE (2) will be added to SUM-OF-GRADES, and so on until the sum of all of the elements has been accumulated.

8.4 OCCURS/DEPENDING ON

In cases where an entire table is not always utilized, it is advantageous to use the DEPENDING ON clause with the OCCURS. The DEPENDING ON clause specifies a data-name which will contain the number of table elements used. A general form of the OCCURS clause is given in Figure 8.2.

level-number	data-name-1	<u>OCCURS</u> integer <u>TO</u> integer-2 TIMES <u>DEPENDING</u> ON data-name-2

Figure 8.2 General form of OCCURS/DEPENDING ON

The content of *data-name-2* is treated as the upper limit of the table. Any reference to a table element using a subscript value larger than the content of data-name-2 is treated as invalid. When the DEPENDING ON clause is included, you must specify the smallest number of table elements to be used (*integer-1*) and the maximum number of elements (*integer-2*). It is an error for the content of *data-name-2* to be less than *integer-1* or greater than *integer-2*.

Consider the table NAME-ADDRESS-TABLE defined above. An alternate way to create this table would be *Example*

```
01    NAME-ADDRESS-TABLE.
      02   NAME-AND-ADDRESS
               OCCURS 0 TO 100 TIMES
               DEPENDING ON NUM-ELEMENTS.
           03   NAME  PIC X(20).
           03   ADDRESS  PIC X(30).
```

The variable NUM-ELEMENTS is used in exactly the same way as before; it stores the location of the last table element in use.

Sometimes the value of *data-name-2* is included as an input item rather than calculated by counting.

Each record in a data file contains registration data for a student enrolled at XYZ College. Students may enroll for a maximum of ten courses. A field within the record specifies the number of courses in which the student is enrolled. The following DATA DIVISION entries could be used to define this record: *Example*

```
01    STUDENT-RECORD.
      03   STUDENT-NUM-SR   PIC 9(9).
      03   STUDENT-NAME-SR   PIC X(20).
        .
        .
        .
      03   NUM-COURSES-SR   PIC 99.
      03   COURSE-ENROLLMENT-SR
               OCCURS 0 TO 10 TIMES
               DEPENDING ON NUM-COURSES-SR.
           05   COURSE-NUM-SR   PIC X(6).
           05   COURSE-NUM-SR   PIC X(20).
```

The advantage in using the DEPENDING ON clause is that the system will automatically check each subscript reference against the actual number of elements in use as opposed to the maximum number of elements allocated. Thus, in the example above, if the value of NUM-COURSES-SR is 4, a reference such as COURSE-NUM (5) would be treated as invalid even though 5 is less than 10. It is strongly recommended that the programmer use the DEPENDING ON clause for any table which may be only partially used.

8.5   PERFORM **WITH THE** VARYING **OPTION**

The PERFORM statement with the VARYING option is used to initialize and move a counter automatically. For example:

```
PERFORM PARA VARYING INDX FROM 1 BY 1 UNTIL INDX > 10.
```

would cause the variable INDX to have values of 1, 2, 3, ... 9, 10 for successive executions of PARA. The execution of this statement proceeds as follows:

1) Move the initial value to the variable (move 1 to INDX in this example).
2) If condition is *not* met, execute the paragraph; otherwise go on to the next statement (compare INDX to 10 in this example).

3) After execution of the paragraph add the increment to the variable (add 1 to INDX in this example).
4) Go to Step 2.

Note that the incrementation of the variable is performed *before* the test is made; hence, the value of INDX after exit from the loop would be 11, the first value of INDX to satisfy the condition.

Figure 8.3 illustrates the general form of the PERFORM statement with the VARYING option.

PERFORM paragraph-name ___VARYING___ data-name
___FROM___ initial-value ___BY___ increment-value ___UNTIL___ condition.

Figure 8.3 General form of PERFORM/VARYING

In the PERFORM/VARYING *initial-value* and *increment-value* may be a data-name or constant.[3]

A flowchart of the steps taken automatically in the execution of this version of the PERFORM statement will help you understand how it works (Fig. 8.4).

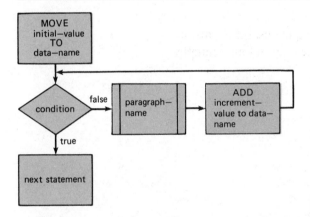

Figure 8.4 Flowchart form of PERFORM/VARYING

For example, for the statement

PERFORM VARYING INDX FROM 1 BY 1 UNTIL INDX > 10.

The corresponding flowchart would be

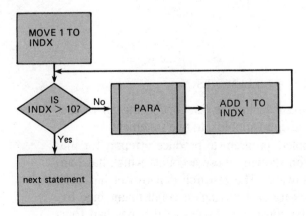

---

[3]Some compilers will allow any arithmetic expression to be used to specify initial-value and increment-value.

Example

```
PERFORM PARA-A VARYING A FROM 10 BY -1 UNTIL A = 0.
```

The values of A for successive executions of PARA-A will be 10, 9, 8, ... 2,
1. The final value of A is 0, resulting in an exit from the loop.

```
PERFORM PARA-B
   VARYING B FROM 4 BY 0.5 UNTIL B > 6.
```

The values of B for successive executions of PARA-B will be 4, 4.5, 5, 5.5,
6. The final value of B is 6.5, resulting in an exit from the loop.

Example

```
PERFORM PARA-C VARYING C FROM X BY Y
   UNTIL C > 13 OR C + Q > 43.
```

Note that a data-name may be used to specify an initial-value and an
increment-value. Also, note that the condition may be any compound condition. The results of execution of this statement cannot be determined
without knowing values of X, Y and Q.

```
MOVE 10 TO Y.
PERFORM PARA-X
   VARYING X FROM Y BY 2 UNTIL X > 4.
```

Example

In this example, PARA-X will not be executed since the condition is satisfied
by the initial value of X.

The PERFORM statement with the VARYING option is quite useful for manip-
ulating table elements. For example, compare the following coding examples
which compute the sum of the elements of a table:

Example

```
MOVE 0 TO SUM-OF-ELEMENTS.
MOVE 1 TO INDX.
PERFORM SUM-ROUTINE UNTIL INDX > 10.
   .
   .
   .
SUM-ROUTINE.
   ADD TABLE (INDX) TO SUM-OF-ELEMENTS.
   ADD 1 TO INDX.
```

Example

```
MOVE 0 TO SUM-OF-ELEMENTS.
PERFORM SUM-ROUTINE VARYING INDX
   FROM 1 BY 1 UNTIL INDX > 10.
   .
   .
   .
SUM-ROUTINE.
   ADD TABLE (INDX) TO SUM-OF-ELEMENTS.
```

The VARYING option offers a very useful technique for condensing all of the
required steps for handling the table indexing variable into one statement.

Example

Program 8.1 below shows a complete program to produce a report for the
ABC Savings and Loan Association showing those accounts which have an
unusually high number of withdrawals. The research department has collected data regarding the frequency for each savings account maintained by
the institution. An account will be considered excessive if it has had four
more withdrawals than the average number of withdrawals for all accounts.

A table is very useful in this problem because the data must be processed twice; once in order to find the average and a second time to find accounts to be included on the report.

In the 3000-CONTROL paragraph (lines 77 through 82), the data is stored in the tables (lines 80 and 81) each time a record is read. When all the records have been read, the average is computed (4000-AVERAGE, lines 87 through 91); then the data contained in the tables is searched (6000-DECISION-PRINT, lines 100 through 106) for accounts showing an excessive number of withdrawals. PERFORM/VARYING is used (lines 63 and 64) to generate values of the index IND from 1 to KOUNT so that the search will include all of the data contained in the tables.

Program 8.1   Excess withdrawal report program

```
Line
1          IDENTIFICATION DIVISION.
2          PROGRAM-ID.   CHAPTER 8 EXAMPLE 1.
3          AUTHOR.   GARY GLEASON.
4          ENVIRONMENT DIVISION.
5          INPUT-OUTPUT SECTION.
6          FILE-CONTROL.
7             SELECT INFD ASSIGN TO DISK.
8             SELECT PRINT ASSIGN TO PRINTER.
9          DATA DIVISION.
10         FILE SECTION.
11         FD   INFD.
12             DATA RECORD IS INPUT-RECORD.
13         01   INPUT-RECORD.
14             02   NAME-IR     PIC X(20).
15             02   FILLER      PIC X(10).
16             02   NUMBER-IR   PIC 999.
17             02   FILLER      PIC X(47).
18         FD   PRINT
19             DATA RECORD IS PRINT-LINE.
20         01   PRINT-LINE     PIC X(132).
21         WORKING-STORAGE SECTION.
22         01   EOF-FLAG       PIC 9         VALUE ZERO.
23         01   KOUNT          PIC 99        VALUE ZERO.
24         01   IND            PIC 99        VALUE ZERO.
25         01   SUM-IT         PIC 9(5)      VALUE ZERO.
26         01   AVERAGE        PIC 9(5)V99 VALUE ZERO.
27         01   HEADER-1-LINE.
28             02   FILLER     PIC X(30)     VALUE SPACES.
29             02   FILLER     PIC X(16)     VALUE "C U S T O M E R ".
30             02   FILLER     PIC X(16)     VALUE " L I S T I N G ".
31         01   HEADER-2-LINE.
32             02   FILLER     PIC X(25)     VALUE SPACES.
33             02   FILLER PIC X(13)         VALUE "E X C E S S ".
34             02   FILLER PIC X(22)         VALUE " W I T H D R A W A L S".
35             02   FILLER     PIC X(65)     VALUE SPACES.
36         01   HEADER-3-LINE.
37             02   FILLER     PIC X(25)     VALUE SPACES.
```

(continued)

Program 8.1   (continued)

```
38              02   FILLER     PIC X(13)     VALUE "CUSTOMER NAME".
39              02   FILLER     PIC X(10)     VALUE SPACES.
40              02   FILLER     PIC X(23)     VALUE " NO   TRANSACTIONS".
41         01   AVERAGE-LINE.
42              02   FILLER     PIC X(25)     VALUE SPACES.
43              02   FILLER PIC X(26)         VALUE "AVERAGE NO  OF  WITHDRAWALS".
44              02   AVERAGE-OUT PIC Z(4)9.99.
45         01   SPACE-LINE    PIC X(132)  VALUE SPACES.
46         01   DETAIL-LINE.
47              02   FILLER     PIC X(25)     VALUE SPACES.
48              02   NAME-DL    PIC X(20).
49              02   FILLER     PIC X(20)     VALUE SPACES.
50              02   NUMBER-DL  PIC 999.
51         01   TABLE-OF-WITHDRAWALS.
52              02   NAME-AND-NUMBER-OF-WITHDRAWALS
53                   OCCURS 0 TO 25 TIMES
54                   DEPENDING ON KOUNT.
55                   03   NAME   PIC X(20).
56                   03   NUMBER-OF-WITHDRAWALS PIC 999.
57     PROCEDURE DIVISION.
58     1000-MAJOR-LOGIC.
59         PERFORM 2000-INITIALIZATION.
60         PERFORM 3000-CONTROL UNTIL EOF-FLAG = 1.
61         PERFORM 4000-AVERAGE.
62         PERFORM 5000-WITHDRAWS-HEADING.
63         PERFORM 6000-DECISION-PRINT VARYING IND FROM 1 BY 1
64             UNTIL IND' > KOUNT.
65         PERFORM 9000-TERMINATION.
66     2000-INITIALIZATION.
67         OPEN INPUT INFD.
68         OPEN OUTPUT PRINT.
69         PERFORM 2500-DETAIL-HEADING.
70         PERFORM 1500-READ.
71     1500-READ.
72         READ INFD AT END MOVE 1 TO EOF-FLAG.
73     2500-DETAIL-DEADING.
74         WRITE PRINT-LINE FROM HEADER-1-LINE AFTER 0.
75         WRITE PRINT-LINE FROM HEADER-3-LINE AFTER 1.
76         PERFORM 5100-CARRIAGE-CONTROL 2 TIMES.
77     3000-CONTROL.
78         ADD 1 TO KOUNT.
79         PERFORM 3500-DETAIL-LISTING.
80         MOVE NAME-IR TO NAME (KOUNT).
81         MOVE NUMBER -IR TO NUMBER-OF-WITHDRAWALS (KOUNT).
82         PERFORM 1500-READ.
83     3500-DETAIL-LISTING.
84         MOVE NAME-IR TO NAME-DL.
85         MOVE NUMBER-IR TO NUMBER-DL.
86         WRITE PRINT-LINE FROM DETAIL-LINE AFTER 1.
87     4000-AVERAGE.
88         PERFORM 4500-CROSS-FOOT VARYING IND FROM 1 BY 1
```

(continued)

Program 8.1 (continued)

```
89              UNTIL IND > KOUNT.
90          DIVIDE SUM-IT BY KOUNT GIVING AVERAGE.
91          MOVE AVERAGE TO AVERAGE-OUT.
92      4500-CROSS-FOOT.
93          ADD NUMBER-OF-WITHDRAWS (IND) TO SUM-IT.
94      5000-WITHDRAWS-HEADING.
95          WRITE PRINT-LINE FROM HEADER-2-LINE AFTER 3
96          WRITE PRINT-LINE FROM HEADER-3-LINE AFTER 1
97          PERFORM 5100-CARRIAGE-CONTROL 2 TIMES.
98      5100-CARRIAGE-CONTROL.
99          WRITE PRINT-LINE FROM SPACE-LINE AFTER 1.
100     6000-DECISION-PRINT.
101         IF NUMBER-OF-WITHDRAWS (IND) > AVERAGE + 4
102             MOVE NAME (IND) TO NAME-DL
103             MOVE NUMBER-OF-WITHDRAWS (IND) TO NUMBER-DL
104             WRITE PRINT-LINE FROM DETAIL-LINE AFTER 1
105         ELSE
106             NEXT SENTENCE.
107     9000-TERMINATION.
108         WRITE PRINT-LINE FROM AVERAGE-LINE AFTER 2.
109         CLOSE INFD PRINT.
110         STOP RUN.
```

```
        C U S T O M E R   L I S T I N G
CUSTOMER NAME           NO TRANSACTIONS

ALLEN, JAMES                015
BARRON, TED                 012
CARDWELL, MIKE              017
DYKES, DAVID                019
ETHERIDGE, M                024
FRANKLIN, KAREN             024
GIORGIO, MIKE               028
HARRELL, CRAIG              036
INGRAM, DANIEL              085
JONES, FRANK                055
KELLY, MICHEAL              032
LOWE, SHERRY                021
MARVIN, GEORGE              021
NADEN, NELLY                065
OSBORN, JAMIE               028
PETERS, PAUL                027
QUEBEC, OSCAR               014
ROMERO, JULIUS              021
SMITH, ALLEN                052
TANGENT, EVAN               011
UNITY, JOEY                 045
VICKERY, LARRY              025
WATERS, SARAH               034
YOUNG, SHARON               025
ZENNER, MIKE                014
```

(continued)

Program 8.1   (continued)

```
E X C E S S        W I T H D R A W A L S
CUSTOMER NAME               NO TRANSACTIONS

HARRELL, CRAIG                  036
INGRAM, DANIEL                  085
JONES, FRANK                    055
NADEN, NELLY                    065
SMITH, ALLEN                    052
UNITY, JOEY                     045
AVERAGE NO   OF WITHDRAWALS   30.00
```

When using the PERFORM with the VARYING option, take care that the program does not enter an endless loop. The specified condition *must* occur for exiting from the loop; that is, the loop is repeated until the condition is found. For example, the following statements could cause an endless loop:

```
PERFORM PARA-D VARYING D FROM 1 BY 2 UNTIL D = 4.
```

The values of D will be 1, 3, 5, 7, ... D will never have value 4; thus, the loop never will terminate. The following statement, while syntactically correct, could cause an infinite loop or other execution time error depending on the values of a table Q:

```
PERFORM PARA-E VARYING E FROM 1 BY 1 UNTIL Q (E) = 0.
```

If an element of the array Q has value 0, the loop will terminate; otherwise, an execution time error will result. The above statement is useful for searching for a specified value in a table but it would be better to write:

```
PERFORM PARA-E VARYING E
    FROM 1 BY 1 UNTIL E > 10 OR Q (E) = 0.
```

Assuming that 10 is the number of elements in the table, the above statement will cause an exit when an element of the table Q having value 0 is found or when all the elements of Q have been compared.

8.6   THE EXIT STATEMENT

What should be the content of PARA-E referred to in Program 8.1 above? There is no need to increment the indexing variable; that is done by the VARYING option on the PERFORM statement. There is no need to compare an element of the table to the search value; that is done in the condition of the PERFORM statement. In fact there is no work to be done in PARA-E, yet the syntax of COBOL requires at least one sentence in every paragraph. The EXIT sentence is provided for this contingency. The general form of the EXIT statement is:

$$\boxed{\text{EXIT}.}$$

When used, the EXIT statement must be the *only* statement in the paragraph.

The search routine now can be written:

```
PERFORM PARA-E VARYING E
    FROM 1 BY 1 UNTIL E > 10 OR Q (E) = 0.
IF E > 10
    PERFORM ELEMENT-NOT-FOUND
ELSE
    PERFORM ELEMENT-FOUND.
    .
    .
    .
PARA-E.
    EXIT.
```

The EXIT statement is used in paragraphs which are required by COBOL syntax but which otherwise serve no function. When large programs are designed and developed in parts, it is often necessary to include in early versions of the program paragraphs which will be developed later. In order to begin testing the program at early stages of development programmers frequently include unfinished paragraphs with an EXIT statement as their only content. In this way the program can be compiled and tested without syntax errors resulting from references to missing paragraphs. Of course, the program will not perform all of its required functions until all dummy paragraphs have been replaced with code required to perform their designated functions.

8.7 PERFORM WITH THE TIMES OPTION

Program 8.1 includes another form of the PERFORM statement which can be used to execute a paragraph any number of times without varying a specific variable. Figure 8.5 shows the general form of the PERFORM statement with the TIMES option:

$$\underline{\text{PERFORM}}\ \text{paragraph-name}\ \left\{ \begin{array}{l} \text{data-name} \\ \text{integer} \end{array} \right\}\ \underline{\text{TIMES}}$$

Figure 8.5 General form of PERFORM/TIMES statement

The number of repetitions is specified using either an *integer*, as in

```
PERFORM PROCESS 10 TIMES.
```

or with a *data-name*, as in

```
PERFORM PROCESS N TIMES.
```

When a data-name is used, its value determines the number of repetitions. Thus, if the value of N is 10, the preceding two PERFORM statements are equivalent.

In Program 8.1, this version of the PERFORM statement is used to space a specified number of lines after headings have been printed (lines 76 and 97).

8.8   THE REDEFINES CLAUSE

In some instances there is a need to define the same data item with different names and differing characteristics. For example, suppose a product classification code contains eight digits, with the first two digits representing the division of the company which manufactures the item. For some purposes, it is useful to use one eight-digit numeric field; for others, it may be useful to have the field broken down into two fields. The REDEFINES clause is used in the DATA division to accomplish this:

```
03   PRODUCT-CLASSIFICATION-CODE PIC 9(8).
03   P-C-CODE REDEFINES PRODUCT-CLASSIFICATION-CODE.
     05   DIVISION PIC 9(2).
     05   PRODUCT PIC 9(6).
```

Both PRODUCT-CLASSIFICATION-CODE and P-C-CODE refer to the same eight characters:

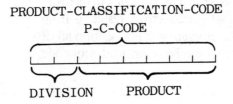

The REDEFINES clause is necessary because of the numeric nature of the data. At first glance the following code would seem to accomplish the same result:

```
03   PRODUCT-CLASSIFICATION-CODE.
     05   DIVISION PIC 9(2).
     05   PRODUCT PIC 9(6).
```

However, the PRODUCT-CLASSIFICATION-CODE is a group item and hence an alphanumeric item, and cannot in general be used in computations or edited output.

The general form of the REDEFINES clause is shown in Figure 8.6.

| level-number   data-name   <u>REDEFINES</u>   preceding-data-name. |

Figure 8.6   General form of the REDEFINES clause

The *level-number* used on the REDEFINES entry must be the same as the level-number on the *preceding-data-name* which is being "redefined." The REDEFINES clause may be used on a group data item as in the above example, or on an elementary data item as in the following example:

```
01   XYZ PIC X(5).
01   ZYW  REDEFINES XYZ PIC 9(5).
```

The above coding could be used when you want to reference the same field as both a numeric item and an alphanumeric item.

8.9   TABLE LOOK-UP

The REDEFINES clause often is used to create a table of constants to be processed by a program. Consider the following example: XYZ Manufacturing Corporation manufactures five types of widgets.

Code	Description
1	MIDGET
2	REGULAR
3	KING
4	SUPER
5	GIANT

A data record contains an item PRODUCT-CODE having value 1, 2, 3, 4 or 5;
a program must output the corresponding verbal description.

One approach to the problem is to create a table of constants as follows:

```
DESCRIPTION (1)   MIDGET
DESCRIPTION (2)   REGULAR
DESCRIPTION (3)   KING
DESCRIPTION (4)   SUPER
DESCRIPTION (5)   GIANT
```

The following code could be used to create this table:

```
01  DESCRIPTION-CONSTANTS.
    02  FILLER PIC X(7) VALUE "MIDGET".
    02  FILLER PIC X(7) VALUE "REGULAR".
    02  FILLER PIC X(7) VALUE "KING".
    02  FILLER PIC X(7) VALUE "SUPER".
    02  FILLER PIC X(7) VALUE "GIANT".
01  DESCRIPTION-TABLE REDEFINES DESCRIPTION-CONSTANTS.
    02  DESCRIPTION OCCURS 5 TIMES PIC X(7).
```

The data layout created by the above may be visualized as:

The data item PRODUCT-CODE from an input record can be used as a subscript to access the appropriate item from the table:

```
MOVE DESCRIPTION (PRODUCT-CODE) TO OUTPUT-DESCRIPTION.
```

If the value of PRODUCT-CODE is 1, 2, 3, 4 or 5, the above code will cause
no problems; however, if some other value is contained in PRODUCT-CODE, the
reference DESCRIPTION (PRODUCT-CODE) will produce an execution time
error. A better statement for accessing the table would be:

```
IF PRODUCT-CODE = 0 OR PRODUCT-CODE > 5
    MOVE "INVALID" TO OUTPUT-DESCRIPTION
ELSE
    MOVE DESCRIPTION (PRODUCT-CODE) TO OUTPUT-DESCRIPTION.
```

In this example the look-up process was exceedingly simple, since there was a one-to-one correspondence between the PRODUCT-CODE and the table element containing the desired data DESCRIPTION (PRODUCT-CODE). If this correspondence does not exist, it may be necessary to search a table to find the desired element. The search may take the form of accessing elements of the table sequentially until the desired element is found, as in the following example: The XYZ Company uses a four digit inventory code for its five products:

Inventory Code	Description
1234	MIDGET
2314	REGULAR
8978	KING
8900	SUPER
7892	GIANT

The numeric data item INV-CODE is contained on an input-record. The program must output the corresponding word description.

The following code could be used to establish the table of constants:

```
01   INVENTORY-DESCRIPTION-CONSTANTS.
     03   FILLER PIC X(11) VALUE "1234 MIDGET".
     03   FILLER PIC X(11) VALUE "2314 REGULAR".
     03   FILLER PIC X(11) VALUE "8978 KING".
     03   FILLER PIC X(11) VALUE "8900 SUPER".
     03   FILLER PIC X(11) VALUE "7892 GIANT".
01   INVENTORY-DESCRIPTION-TABLE REDEFINES
     INVENTORY-DESCRIPTION-CONSTANTS.
     03   INVENTORY-DESCRIPTION-ITEM OCCURS 5 TIMES.
          05   INVENTORY PIC 9(4).
          05   DESCRIPTION PIC X(7).
```

The above coding yields the following data structures:

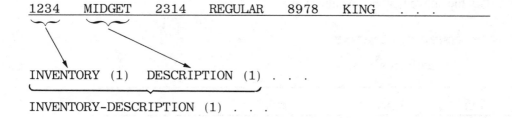

```
1234   MIDGET   2314   REGULAR   8978   KING   . . .
```

```
INVENTORY (1)   DESCRIPTION (1) . . .

INVENTORY-DESCRIPTION (1) . . .
```

The program must search for an element of INVENTORY which is the same as INV-CODE and use the corresponding element of DESCRIPTION. The following code could be used:

```
PERFORM SEARCH-EXIT VARYING IND FROM 1 BY 1
    UNTIL IND > 5 OR INVENTORY (IND) = INV-CODE.
IF IND > 5
    MOVE "INVALID" TO OUTPUT-DESCRIPTION
ELSE
    MOVE DESCRIPTION (IND) TO OUTPUT-DESCRIPTION.
    .
    .
    .
SEARCH-EXIT.
    EXIT.
```

8.10 COUNTING AND ACCUMULATION

Tables may be used for a variety of purposes. In previous examples, tables have been used to store both data and constants. Another usage for a table is in counting.

Example

A survey has been made of customer arrival times in the XYZ Department Store. One record has been prepared for each arrival, showing in coded form the hour during which the customer arrived. The following code was used in preparing the data records:

Hour	Code
9-10 A.M.	1
10-11 A.M.	2
11-12 A.M.	3
12-1 P.M.	4
1-2 P.M.	5
2-3 P.M.	6
3-4 P.M.	7
4-5 P.M.	8
5-6 P.M.	9

The output desired is a frequency distribution showing the number of customers who arrived during each hour.

A table of nine elements (to be utilized as counters) can be used to accumulate the desired counts. The elements of the table must be initialized to have value of zero. This process is complicated somewhat by the fact that the VALUE clause may not be used with an OCCURS clause in the DATA division; that is, the following code is invalid:

```
01   COUNTERS.
     03   KOUNT OCCURS 9 TIMES PIC 99 VALUE 0.
```

One approach to initialization is to use the REDEFINES option as though a table of constants were being created:

```
01   CONSTANTS.
     03   FILLER PICTURE X(18) VALUE ALL "0".
01   COUNTERS REDEFINES CONSTANTS.
     03   KOUNT OCCURS 9 TIMES PIC 99.
```

For a large table this approach will become quite cumbersome and impractical. An alternative is to initialize the table in the PROCEDURE division prior to utilizing the variables for counting. For example:

```
     PERFORM INITIALIZE VARYING K FROM 1 BY 1 UNTIL K > 9.
     .
     .
     .
     INITIALIZE.
       MOVE ZERO TO KOUNT (K).
```

Once the table of counters has been initialized, the process of accumulating the required totals can begin. Suppose the data-name associated with the code on the data record is HOUR-CODE. The contents of this variable can be used to select which element of KOUNT is to be incremented. The basic code could be:

```
     ADD 1 TO KOUNT (HOUR-CODE).
```

If HOUR-CODE has value 1, KOUNT (1) will be incremented; if HOUR-CODE has value 2, one will be added to KOUNT (2), and so forth.

Tables also may be used for accumulation. For example, the XYZ Department store wants to determine which day of the week is on average its busiest day. A record for each date in the previous 52 weeks has been prepared with a code 1, 2, 3, ..., 7 showing the day of the week (DAY-CODE) and the amount of sales (SALES-AMOUNT) for that day.

A table containing seven elements can be used to accumulate the desired totals. Each element of the table must be initialized to have value zero; then as each data record is processed, the value of SALES-AMOUNT is added to the appropriate element of the table, as in the following code:

```
        .
        .
        .

    PERFORM INITIALIZATION VARYING K FROM 1 BY 1 UNTIL K > 7.
    PERFORM READ-AND-PROCESS UNTIL END-OF-FILE.
        .
        .
        .

INITIALIZATION.
    MOVE 0 TO TOTAL (K).
READ-AND-PROCESS.
    READ INPUT-FILE AT END MOVE 1 TO EOF-SWITCH.
    IF NOT END-OF-FILE
        ADD SALES-AMOUNT TO TOTAL (DAY-CODE).
```

8.11 TWO-DIMENSIONAL TABLES

A two-dimensional table is a sequence of storage locations (elements) having a common name and requiring two subscripts in order to access a particular element. For example, suppose we wish to store grades for four tests for up to seventy-five students. We could use a data structure such as:

	Test #1	Test #2	Test #3	Test #4
Student #1	GRADE (1,1)	GRADE (1,2)	GRADE (1,3)	GRADE (1,4)
Student #2	GRADE (2,1)	GRADE (2,2)	GRADE (2,3)	GRADE (2,4)
.				
.				
.				
Student #75	GRADE (75,1)	. . .		GRADE (75,4)

The elements of the table are referenced by the data-name GRADE and two subscripts. The first subscript refers to the student (the row). The second subscript refers to the test number for that student (the column).

Two usages of the OCCURS clause are required to create a two dimensional table. For example, the data structure could be created with the following DATA

DIVISION entries:

```
01   NUM-STUDENTS  PIC 99 VALUE 0.
01   GRADE-TABLE.
     02   STUDENT OCCURS 0 TO 75 TIMES DEPENDING ON NUM-STUDENTS.
          03   GRADE OCCURS 4 TIMES PIC 99.
```

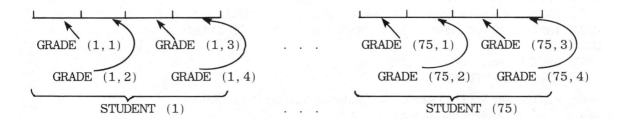

Note that the data-name STUDENT may be subscripted. Thus STUDENT (1) is a reference to all four grades of student number 1. However, STUDENT is a group item and, hence, is an alphanumeric field. Any reference to the data name GRADE must always include two subscripts.

The table could be expanded to store additional data such as the student's name and average grade. Consider the following code:

```
01   NUM-STUDENTS  PIC 99  VALUE 0.
01   STUDENT-DATA-TABLE
     02   STUDENT OCCURS 0 TO 75 TIMES DEPENDING ON NUM-STUDENTS.
          03   NAME PIC X(20).
          03   GRADE OCCURS 4 TIMES PIC 99.
          03   AVERAGE PIC 99.
```

The structure created by this code can be visualized as:

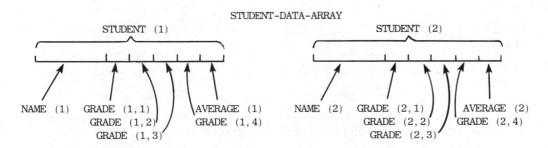

Suppose the data record containing the students' names and grades has the following description:

```
01   DATA-RECORD.
     02   STUDENT-NAME PIC X(20).
     02   STUDENT-GRADE OCCURS 4 TIMES PIC 99.
```

The following code would be used to input this data and store it into STUDENT-DATA-TABLE:

```
          .
          .
          .

     READ INFO INTO DATA-RECORD AT END MOVE 1 TO EOF-CODE.
```

```
        PERFORM STORE-AND-READ UNTIL
            END-OF-FILE OR NUM-STUDENTS = 75.
        .
        .
        .
    STORE-AND-READ.
        ADD 1 TO NUM-STUDENTS.
        MOVE STUDENT-NAME TO NAME (NUM-STUDENTS).
        PERFORM GRADE-MOVE VARYING INX FROM 1 BY 1 UNTIL INX > 4.
        READ INFO INTO DATA-RECORD AT END MOVE 1 TO EOF-CODE.
    GRADE-MOVE.
        MOVE STUDENT-GRADE (INX) TO
            GRADE (NUM-STUDENTS, INX).
```

Assuming that the data has been stored, the following code could be used to compute the averages for each of the students:

```
    PERFORM AVERAGE-ROUTINE
        VARYING INX FROM 1 BY 1 UNTIL INX > NUM-STUDENTS.
    AVERAGE ROUTINE.
        COMPUTE SUM-X = 0.
        PERFORM SUMMATION VARYING J FROM 1 BY 1 UNTIL J > 4.
        COMPUTE AVERAGE (INX) = SUM-X / 4.
    SUMMATION.
        ADD GRADE (INX, J) TO SUM-X.
```

Two-dimensional tables may be used for storing tables of constants which will be used by a program. Consider, for example, the following table showing the prices of various grades of petroleum products at four refineries:

	REFINERY			
	1	2	3	4
GRADE 1 Diesel	.98	.95	1.01	1.11
GRADE 2 Regular	1.10	1.20	1.15	1.19
GRADE 3 Unleaded	1.20	1.25	1.26	1.30

The number of gallons purchased, the refinery number and the type of fuel number have been stored on data records. A program which will look up the

Program 8.2   Table look-up program

```
1        IDENTIFICATION DIVISION.
2        PROGRAM-ID. CHAPTER 8 EXAMPLE 2.
3        AUTHOR. GARY GLEASON.
4        ENVIRONMENT DIVISION.
5        INPUT-OUTPUT SECTION.
6        FILE-CONTROL.
7            SELECT INFD ASSIGN TO DISK.
8            SELECT PRINT ASSIGN TO PRINTER.
```

(continued)

Program 8.2   (continued)

```
9          DATA DIVISION.
10         FILE SECTION.
11         FD   INFD
12              DATA RECORD IS INPUT-RECORD.
13         01   INPUT-RECORD.
14              02   GALLON-IR       PIC 9(5).
15              02   FUEL-TYPE-IR    PIC 9.
16              02   COMPANY-CODE-IR PIC 9.
17              02   FILLER          PIC X(73).
18         FD   PRINT
19              DATA RECORD IS PRINT-LINE.
20         01   PRINT-LINE           PIC X(132).
21         WORKING-STORAGE SECTION.
22         01   EOF-FLAG             PIC 9 VALUE ZERO.
23         01   FUEL-PRICING-TABLE.
24              02   DIESEL.
25                   03   FILLER PIC 9V99 VALUE 0.98.
26                   03   FILLER PIC 9V99 VALUE 0.95.
27                   03   FILLER PIC 9V99 VALUE 1.01.
28                   03   FILLER PIC 9V99 VALUE 1.11.
29              02   REGULAR.
30                   03   FILLER PIC 9V99 VALUE 1.10.
31                   03   FILLER PIC 9V99 VALUE 1.20.
32                   03   FILLER PIC 9V99 VALUE 1.15.
33                   03   FILLER PIC 9V99 VALUE 1.19.
34              02   UN-LEADED.
35                   03   FILLER PIC 9V99 VALUE 1.20.
36                   03   FILLER PIC 9V99 VALUE 1.25.
37                   03   FILLER PIC 9V99 VALUE 1.26.
38                   03   FILLER PIC 9V99 VALUE 1.30.
39         01   FUEL-PRICES REDEFINES FUEL-PRICING-TABLE.
40              02   FUEL-TYPE OCCURS 3 TIMES.
41                   03   PRICE OCCURS 4 TIMES PIC 9V99.
42         01   DETAIL-LINE.
43              02   FILLER          PIC X(35) VALUE SPACES.
44              02   FUEL-COST-DL    PIC  $**,***.99.
45              02   FILLER          PIC X(87) VALUE SPACES.
46         PROCEDURE DIVISION.
47         1000-MAJOR-LOGIC.
48              OPEN INPUT INFD OUTPUT PRINT.
49              PERFORM 4000-READ.
50              PERFORM 3000-CONTROL UNTIL EOF-FLAG = 1.
51              CLOSE INFD PRINT.
52              STOP RUN.
53         3000-CONTROL.
54              MULTIPLY PRICE (FUEL-TYPE-IR, COMPANY-CODE-IR) BY
55                   GALLON-IR GIVING FUEL-COST-DL.
56              MOVE DETAIL-LINE TO PRINT-LINE.
57              WRITE PRINT-LINE AFTER 1.
58              PERFORM 4000-READ.
59         4000-READ.
60              READ INFD AT END MOVE 1 TO EOF-FLAG.
```

appropriate price per gallon and output the total amount of the purchase is needed. Program 8.2 makes use of a table of constants created in the DATA DIVI-
SION (lines 23 through 38) as a two-dimensional table and *looks-up* the appropriate value from the table. (line 54):

        MULTIPLY PRICE (FUEL-TYPE-IR, COMPANY-CODE-IR) ...

The variables FUEL-TYPE-IR and COMPANY-CODE-IR are used as subscripts to
reference the appropriate element of the table PRICE.

8.12 THE PERFORM/VARYING/AFTER STATEMENT

There are many instances, particularly when processing two-dimensional tables
in which it is necessary to alter two variables over specified ranges. The
PERFORM/VARYING/AFTER statement is an extension of the ideas utilized in
PERFORM/VARYING and allows automatic control over two variables in one
statement (Fig. 8.7). When one AFTER clause is used, *data-name$_1$* is varied
through its range of values for each value of *data-name$_2$* (Fig. 8.8).

<u>PERFORM</u> paragraph-name
    <u>VARYING</u> data-name$_1$ <u>FROM</u> initial-value$_1$ <u>BY</u> increment-value$_1$ <u>UNTIL</u> condition$_1$
    [<u>AFTER</u> data-name$_2$ <u>FROM</u> initial-value$_2$ <u>BY</u> increment-value$_2$ <u>UNTIL</u> condition$_2$]
    [<u>AFTER</u> data-name$_3$ <u>FROM</u> initial-value$_3$ <u>BY</u> increment-value$_3$ <u>UNTIL</u> condition$_3$]

Figure 8.7 General form of the PERFORM/VARYING/AFTER statement

---

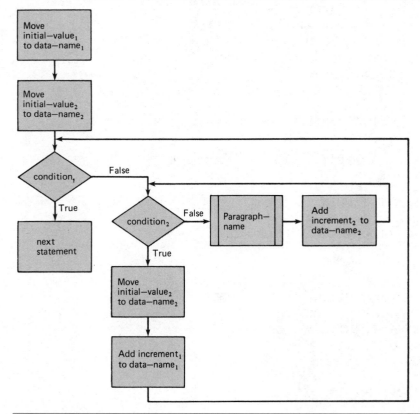

Figure 8.8 Flowchart of PERFORM/
VARYING with one AFTER clauses

Consider the statement: *Example*

```
PERFORM PARA-A
    VARYING X FROM 1 BY 1 UNTIL X > 4
    AFTER   Y FROM 1 BY 1 UNTIL Y > 3.
```

PARA-A would be executed $3 \times 4 = 12$ times with the following values of X and Y:

X	1	1	1	2	2	2	3	3	3	4	4	4
Y	1	2	3	1	2	3	1	2	3	1	2	3

For each new value of the first variable X, the second variable Y is re-initialized to its starting value and continues to be incremented until the second condition (Y > 3) is satisfied. The flowchart for this statement would be:

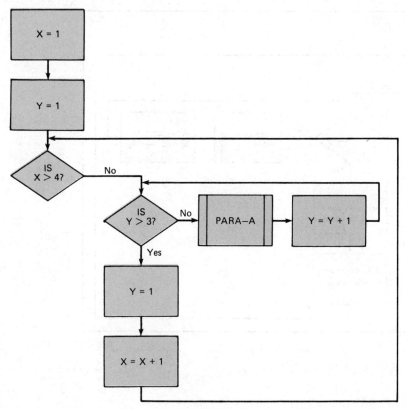

When two AFTER clauses are used, *data-name₃* is varied through its range of values for each value of *data-name₂*, and *data-name₂* is varied through its range of values for each value of *data-name₁* (Fig. 8.9).

Consider the statement: *Example*

```
PERFORM PARA-B
    VARYING X FROM 1 BY 1 UNTIL X > 3
    AFTER   Y FROM 1 BY 1 UNTIL Y > 4
    AFTER   Z FROM 1 BY 1 UNTIL Z > 2.
```

PARA-B would be executed $3 \times 4 = 24$ times with the following values of X, Y and Z:

X	1	1	1	1	1	1	1	1	2	2	2	2	2	2	2	2	3	3	3	3	3	3	3	3
Y	1	1	2	2	3	3	4	4	1	1	2	2	3	3	4	4	1	1	2	2	3	3	4	4
Z	1	2	1	2	1	2	1	2	1	2	1	2	1	2	1	2	1	2	1	2	1	2	1	2

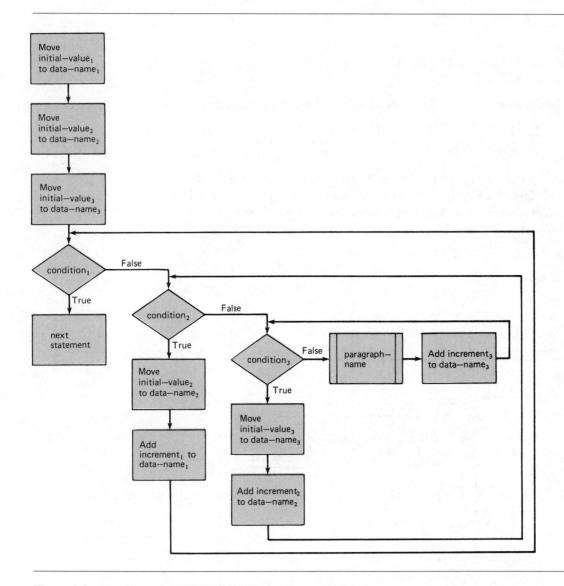

Figure 8.9 Flowchart of PERFORM/VARYING with two AFTER clauses

Example

A data file contains production data for each working day at Widgets Mfg., Inc. Each record contains the total number of units produced for each of the five production lines at the factory for a working day. At most the file contains one year's data. For a program which will store this data into a table, the following DATA DIVISION entries could be used:

```
01   NUM-DAYS PIC 999 VALUE 0.
01   PRODUCTION-DATA.
     02   DAILY-DATA
          OCCURS 0 TO 366 TIMES
          DEPENDING ON NUM-DAYS.
          03   PRODUCTION PIC 9(5) OCCURS 5 TIMES.
```

Suppose that the program has read and stored the data and that it is required to calculate the average daily production for all production lines. The following code could be used:

```
        .
        .
        .
    MOVE 0 TO PRODUCTION-TOTAL.
    PERFORM SUMMATION
        VARYING DAY-INDEX
            FROM 1 BY 1 UNTIL DAY-INDEX > NUM-DAYS
        AFTER LINE-INDEX
            FROM 1 BY 1 UNTIL LINE-INDEX > 5.
    COMPUTE AVERAGE-PRODUCTION =
        PRODUCTION-TOTAL / (NUM-DAYS * 5)
        .
        .
        .

SUMMATION.
    ADD PRODUCTION (DAY-INDEX, LINE-INDEX)
        TO PRODUCTION-TOTAL.
```

8.13   THREE-DIMENSIONAL TABLES

Tables of up to three dimensions may be created and processed by a COBOL program. A three-dimensional table may be visualized as a series of two-dimensional tables. For example, suppose an instructor has five classes, each class containing a maximum of seventy-five students each of whom takes five tests. A table to store this data could be defined as:

```
01   GRADE-TABLE.
    02   CLASS-ENTRY OCCURS 5 TIMES.
        03   STUDENT-ENTRY OCCURS 75 TIMES.
            04   TEST-ENTRY OCCURS 5 TIMES.
                05   GRADE PIC 99.
```

This structure may be visualized as shown in Figure 8.10.

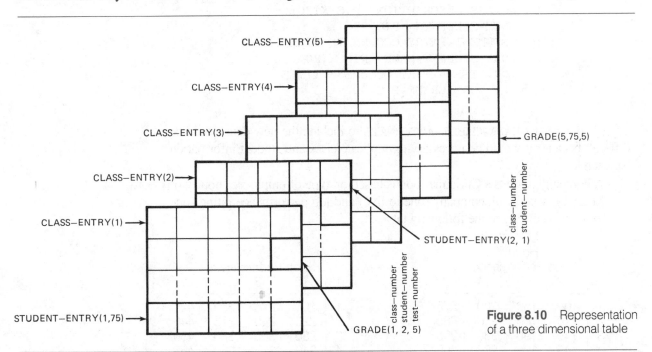

Figure 8.10   Representation of a three dimensional table

Each CLASS-ENTRY is composed of a table of size 75 × 5; the entire structure contains 5 × 75 × 5 = 750 elements. References to CLASS-ENTRY require one subscript. References to STUDENT-ENTRY require two subscripts; the first indicates the class and the second indicates the student within the class. References to TEST-ENTRY and GRADE require three subscripts; the first indicates the class, the second indicates the student, and the third indicates the test.

Note that the order of subscripts from left to right corresponds to the order in which the OCCURS clauses are nested. It would be possible to create storage for this data in a number of different ways. So long as the subscripts used to reference the data correspond to the way in which the structure was created, the same processing steps can be accomplished. For example, suppose the following DATA DIVISION entry is made:

```
01   GRADE-TABLE-ALTERNATE.
     02   TEST-ENTRY OCCURS 5 TIMES.
          03   CLASS-ENTRY OCCURS 5 TIMES.
               04   STUDENT-ENTRY OCCURS 75 TIMES.
                    05   GRADE PIC 99.
```

Reference to GRADE (4, 1, 2) would mean test number 4, class number 1, student number 2.

The way in which a table should be created will be governed to some extent by the way data is organized on input and also by the type of processing to be performed. For example, suppose it is necessary to include a description of each class, the number of students in each class and the name of each student in the data structure. The first way in which the data was defined can be modified easily to include this data as shown below:

```
01   GRADE-TABLE-EXTENDED.
     02   CLASS-ENTRY OCCURS 5 TIMES.
          03   CLASS-DESCRIPTION  PIC X(20).
          03   NUM-STUDENTS  PIC 99.
          03   STUDENT-ENTRY OCCURS 75 TIMES.
               04   STUDENT-NAME  PIC X(20).
               04   TEST-ENTRY OCCURS 5 TIMES.
                    05   GRADE PIC 99.
```

Trying to modify GRADE-TABLE-ALTERNATE to include the new data would be difficult because it would be necessary to duplicate class and student information for each test.

Example

A company assigns a Christmas bonus based on type of employee (hourly or salaried), years with company (one to five) and job performance rating (one to four) according to the following tables:

	Hourly Job Performance					Salaried Job Performance		
1	2	3	4		1	2	3	4
1	100	150	200	275	1	200	275	350	425
2	110	160	210	285	2	220	245	375	440
3	140	190	230	295	3	230	305	380	450
4	145	195	235	300	4	240	315	395	465
5	160	200	240	305	5	250	325	400	475

A data structure to store this data for a program which will look up the appropriate bonus value could be defined as:

```
01   BONUS-CONSTANTS.
     02   HOURLY-CONSTANTS.
          03   FILLER PIC X (12) VALUE "100150200275".
          03   FILLER PIC X (12) VALUE "110160210285".
          03   FILLER PIC X (12) VALUE "140180230295".
          03   FILLER PIC X (12) VALUE "145195235300".
          03   FILLER PIC X (12) VALUE "160200240305".
     02   SALARIED-CONSTANTS.
          03   FILLER PIC X (12) VALUE "200275350425".
          03   FILLER PIC X (12) VALUE "220295375440".
          03   FILLER PIC X (12) VALUE "230305380450".
          03   FILLER PIC X (12) VALUE "240315395465".
          03   FILLER PIC X (12) VALUE "250325400475".
01   BONUS-TABLE REDEFINES BONUS-CONSTANTS.
     02   EMPLOYEE-LEVEL-ENTRY OCCURS 2 TIMES.
          03   YEARS-WITH-CO-ENTRY OCCURS 5 TIMES.
               04   JOB-PERFORMANCE-ENTRY OCCURS 4 TIMES.
                    05   BONUS-AMOUNT PIC 999.
```

Assume that the variable EMPLOYEE-LEVEL contains a value 1 if the employee is hourly, and 2 if the employee is salaried. Also assume the JOB-PERFORMANCE contains a value 1 to 4 and that YEARS-WITH-CO contains the employee length of service. The following code could be used to compute CHRISTMAS-BONUS:

```
IF YEARS-WITH-CO < 1
    MOVE BONUS-AMOUNT (EMPLOYEE-LEVEL, JOB-PERFORMANCE, 1)
    TO CHRISTMAS-BONUS.
IF YEARS-WITH-CO > 5
    MOVE BONUS-AMOUNT (EMPLOYEE-LEVEL, JOB-PERFORMANCE, 5)
    TO CHRISTMAS-BONUS.
IF YEARS-WITH-CO > 0 AND YEARS-WITH-CO < 6
    MOVE BONUS-AMOUNT (EMPLOYEE-LEVEL, JOB-PERFORMANCE, YEARS-WITH-CO)
    TO CHRISTMAS-BONUS.
```

8.14   DEBUG CLINIC

Errors in utilizing tables most commonly result from problems with out-of-range subscript values. If a subscript value is outside the allowable range, an execution time error results. Typically the program terminates with an error message and perhaps a listing of information which the programmer may use to help find the statement which caused the problem. Frequently the programmer has to rerun the program with some diagnostic output to determine the values of appropriate variables. Diagnostic output need consist only of the values of variables and perhaps labels to help in evaluating the output produced. For example, suppose the cause of an execution time error has been traced to a statement such as:

```
.
.
.
COMPUTE TABL (X, Y) = ...
.
.
.
```

It would be useful to know the values of X and Y prior to the error. By inserting code such as the following, the programmer can determine these values:

```
.
.
.
PERFORM DIAGNOSTIC-OUTPUT.
COMPUTE TABL (X, Y) = ...
.
.
.
DIAGNOSTIC-OUTPUT.
    MOVE X TO X-OUT.
    MOVE Y TO Y-OUT.
    WRITE PRINT-LINE FROM DIAGNOSTIC-LINE AFTER 1.
```

Once the cause of the problem has been found and eliminated, it is necessary to remove all executions of diagnostic output. It is not necessary to remove code from the DATA DIVISION or the diagnostic routine itself unless you want to optimize use of memory. Leaving these elements in a program may make the program easier to debug for some future programmer required to perform maintenance on the program.

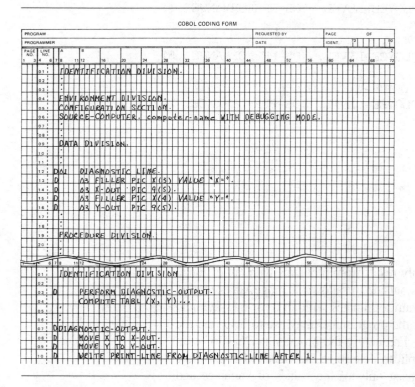

Figure 8.11   Debug example

The Debug Facility

Some COBOL compilers permit the use of a standard debugging facility which can be of considerable value in providing diagnostic output. When the debug facility is available the programmer places a D in position of 7 of any program line which is a part of the diagnostic procedure. In the above example, the code in the DATA DIVISION which defined the output record DIAGNOSTIC-LINE and all references to the paragraph DIAGNOSTIC-OUTPUT would include a D in position 7 (Fig. 8-11). The compiler ordinarily will omit any line coded with a D in position 7; in order to include such lines in the compiled program, the clause WITH DEBUGGING MODE must be included in the SOURCE COMPUTER paragraph of the ENVIRONMENT DIVISION (Fig. 8-11). If this clause is omitted, lines of the program which contain a D in position 7 are treated as comments; they are included in the program listing but not translated into the object program. If the clause is included, debug lines are translated as a part of the object program. Without the debug facility it is necessary to remove references to diagnostic output from a program after the program is debugged. Using the debug facility enables the programmer to include or omit diagnostic output from a program by changing only the SOURCE COMPUTER paragraph.

8.15 SELF TEST EXERCISES

1. Draw a structure diagram for Program 8.1.
2. The following partial program contains a table for the description, part number and price for the inventory of a small retail store. (Only a few items are listed, but the same principles would apply to a complete table or file on a mass storage device.)

```
01    TABLE.
      03   FILLER PIC X(13)  VALUE "AUDIO CABLE".
      03   FILLER PIC X(4)   VALUE "1258".
      03   FILLER PIC 99V99  VALUE 04.00.
      03   FILLER PIC X(13)  VALUE "EARPHONE".
      03   FILLER PIC X(4)   VALUE "1296".
      03   FILLER PIC 99V99  VALUE 37.50.
      03   FILLER PIC X(13)  VALUE "MICROPHONE".
      03   FILLER PIC X(4)   VALUE "1459".
      03   FILLER PIC 99V99  VALUE 29.75.
      03   FILLER PIC X(13)  VALUE "BATTERIES".
      03   FILLER PIC X(4)   VALUE "1678".
      03   FILLER PIC 99V99  VALUE 02.35.
      03   FILLER PIC X(13)  VALUE "CARRYING CASE".
      03   FILLER PIC X(4)   VALUE "1789".
      03   FILLER PIC 99V99  VALUE 13.92.
      03   FILLER PIC X(13)  VALUE "**NO MATCH**".
      03   FILLER PIC X(4)   VALUE "9999".
      03   FILLER PIC 99V99  VALUE ZERO.
01    PARTS-TABLE REDEFINES TABLE.
   02    PART OCCURS 6 TIMES.
         03    PART-DESCRIPTION PIC X(13).
         03    PAR-NUMBER        PIC X(4).
         03    PART-PRICE        PIC 99V99.
```

   a. Write the PROCEDURE DIVISION for a program that could be used to change a price if the part number is known.

b. Given a file with records containing part numbers and quantity ordered, write the PROCEDURE DIVISION for a program that will print billing invoices.

3. Draw a flowchart showing the execution of each of the following:
   a. PERFORM PARA-X
      VARYING J FROM 1 BY 1 UNTIL J > N.

   b. PERFORM PARA-Y
      VARYING L FROM 10 BY -1 UNTIL L = O.

   c. PERFORM PARA-2
      VARYING K FROM 1 BY 1 UNTIL K = N
      AFTER M FROM 1 BY 1 UNTIL M = N.

   d. PERFORM PARA-W
      VARYING P FROM 2 BY 2 UNTIL P > N
      AFTER Q FROM 1 BY 3 UNTIL Q > N
      AFTER R FROM 1 BY 1 UNTIL R > N.

4. How many times will the specified paragraph be executed in each part of Exercise 3 if N has value 7? Show the values generated for the variables.

5. a. Consider the program example in section 8.11 (Widget production data storage). Suppose that an output record is defined as:

```
01   DAILY-OUTPUT.
     03   DAY-DO   PIC 999.
     03   DAILY-PRODUCTION-DO OCCURS 5 TIMES.
          05   FILLER PIC X(5).
          05   DAY-PRODUCTION-DO PIC Z(5).
```

Write PROCEDURE DIVISION code to write out the content of the table PRODUCTION-DATA.
   b. Write PROCEDURE DIVISION code to compute the average production by line for the table PRODUCTION-DATA.
   c. On some days the production lines must be closed due to malfunction of equipment. On these days production is zero. Write PROCEDURE DIVISION code required to compute the number of days in which production is zero for each line.

6. Write PROCEDURE DIVISION code to compute the total of the elements of BONUS-TABLE defined in section 8.12.

7. Given the array GRADE-TABLE-EXTENDED defined in section 8.12, write PROCEDURE DIVISION code to compute the class average for each test and class.

8. True/False
   a. Standard COBOL permits use of expressions as subscripts.
   b. The VALUE clause may be used with the OCCURS clause in a DATA DIVISION entry.
   c. The use of the DEPENDING ON clause saves space since only the required amount of storage is allocated.
   d. When used, the EXIT statement must be the only statement in a paragraph.
   e. The REDEFINES clause may be used only on an entry with the same level number as the data-name being redefined.
   f. In the PERFORM/VARYING statement it is possible that the specified paragraph may never be executed.
   g. The maximum number of subscripts allowed in COBOL is three.
   h. Debug lines are coded by placing a D in position 7.

8.16 PROGRAMMING EXERCISES

1. Records in a file consist of student names and one test grade per student. Load a table with this data. Compute the average grade. Count the number of grades above the average and number of grades below the average.

2. Write a program that will list the daily sales of soft drinks to retail dealers under the major headings: DEALER, ITEM, QUANTITY, UNIT PRICE and TOTAL. The QUANTITY and TOTAL columns should be summed for all dealers serviced that day. An input record includes the dealer's name, type of drink and the number of cases. Using the OCCURS clause, set up a table of unit costs (constants) in storage for each type of drink. Use these values to compute the total sales for each transaction as it is read. Types of drinks and unit costs are as follows:

Regulars	4.00 per case
Kings	5.00 per case
Cans	4.50 per case

3. Rewrite the program written for Chapter 5, Exercise 6 (page 110) using a table to store the digits of the account number.

4. Sales employees of ABC Furniture, Inc. are paid on a commission basis. The commission rate varies from item to item. A commission rate code, which is the last digit in the item stock number, is used to determine the percentage of the wholesale price to be paid as a commission. The following table shows the association between rate codes and commission rate:

Rate-code	Commission-rate
1	1.0%
2	3.5%
3	7.0%
4	10.5%
5	12.0%
6	15.75%

Data records containing the following fields are to be processed to produce an employee earnings report:

Employee number
Date of sale
Retail price
Wholesale price
Stock number

Assume that the records are sorted into sequence by employee number and date. Your program should list each item sold and the associated commission. Subtotals should be written for daily sales and commissions and each salesperson's total sales and commissions. Final totals of sales and commissions also should be written.
Use the following sample data:

Employee Number	Date of Sale	Retail Price	Wholesale Price	Stock Number
100	1/1/82	5.00	4.00	103
100	1/1/82	6.00	3.00	205
100	1/2/82	7.00	5.00	131
101	1/1/82	18.00	15.00	322
101	1/1/82	6.00	3.00	325
101	1/2/82	7.00	4.00	444
101	1/3/82	7.00	5.00	106
102	1/1/82	12.00	10.00	133

5. Modify the program for Exercise 4 above to calculate the average commission rate earned by each salesperson. Average commission rate is calculated by finding the sum of the commission rates and dividing by the number of sales.

6. Modify the program for Exercise 4 above to calculate the profit from each sale, total profit by salesperson, and total profits for the period. Profit is computed by subtracting the commission from the markup. Markup is the difference between retail price and wholesale price.

7. The Julian date is a number associated with each date based on its position in the total number of days in a year. Thus, since January 1 is the first day of the year, its Julian date is 1. The Julian date for January 31 is 31; the Julian date for February 1 is 32. The Julian date for December 31 is either 365 or, in a leap year, 366. Write a program to compute Julian dates based on input records containing month, day and year. (Hint: A table showing the number of days in each month may help in this program.)

8. Modify the program written for Exercise 4 above to produce a report summarizing each salesperson's earnings. Print the report after the body of the existing output. Use tables to store each employee number and appropriate summary data. Assume that no more than 25 salespersons are employed.

9. Modify the program written for Exercise 4 above to produce a report summarizing sales by date. Print the report after the existing output. Use a table to accumulate sales for each date. Assume that no more than 31 different dates will be processed by the program.

10. Each record in a data file contains the following fields:

> Department number (1 to 9)
> Salesman number (1 to 25)
> Amount of sales

Write a program to compute the total sales for each salesperson and each department. The data is *not* sorted into sequence by department or salesperson. Assume that employee numbers are not uniquely assigned (e.g., Department 1 may have a Salesperson 1 and Department 2 may have a Salesperson 1, and so forth).

11. Each record in a data file contains the following fields:

> Department number (1 to 9)
> Salesperson number (1 to 25)
> Amount of sales for Monday
> Amount of sales for Tuesday
> Amount of sales for Wednesday
> Amount of sales for Thursday
> Amount of sales for Friday

Write a program to determine which salespersons have total weekly sales more than ten percent above the average weekly sales for all salespersons. Make the same assumptions regarding salesperson numbers as in Exercise 10 above.

12. Records in a data file contain a date and number of sales for that date. Write a program to produce a bar graph to represent this data. For example:

Date	Sales	
1/1/81	3	***
		***
1/2/81	4	****
		****
1/3/81	0	
1/4/81	7	*******
		*******

13. Same as Exercise 12 above, except produce a vertical bar graph. Assume that the data file contains seven records. For example:

```
                                        **
                                        **
                                        **
                                        **
                       **               **
        **             **               **
        **             **               **
        **             **               **
      1/1/81         1/2/81   1/3/81   1/4/81   ...
```

14. A file contains the results of a survey conducted by the marketing department of XYZ Corp. Each record contains the following fields:

   age of respondent (1 to 99)
   brand preference (1, 2, 3, or 4)

   Write a program to summarize brand preference by age group. Your output should contain the number of respondents in each age group and the percentage of each age group which preferred each brand. The output should be similar to

Age	Number	Brand			
		1	2	3	4
1-10	17	20%	10%	5%	65%
11-20	80	30%	10%	0%	60%
.	.	.	.	.	.
.	.	.	.	.	.
91-100	1	100%	0%	0%	0%

15. Management at XYZ Burger Corporation would like a report showing the average daily sales at each of its 25 branch stores. Each store has an identifying number 1, 2, ... 25. Input into your program consists of sales records containing the following data:

   store-id-number
   date
   total sales

   You may not assume that the data is sorted into any particular order.

16. Compute the overall average daily sales amount and the standard deviation of the average for the program in Exercise 15 above. Flag those stores with average sales which deviate by more than two standard deviations from the overall average. The standard deviation is computed as

$$\sqrt{\frac{\sum\limits_{i=1}^{n} (x_i - \overline{x})^2}{n \cdot (n-1)}}$$

where x_i represents the data items; $\overline{x}$ represents the average for the data items; and n represents the number of items. In this problem, x represents the average daily sales for each store, $\overline{x}$ represents the overall average daily sales amount and n represents the number of stores.

SEQUENTIAL FILE PROCESSING 9

Up to this point we have used data files with little regard to the characteristics of the device used or to the various options available to enable the optimization of the operation of programs which access the data. We also have neglected procedures by which data files can be changed to reflect the current status of the subject of the file. This chapter presents a detailed discussion of these very important topics as they relate to the most commonly used types of mass storage: magnetic tape and magnetic disk.

9.1   TAPE CONCEPTS

Data records stored on magnetic tape are separated by an *inter-record-gap* (IRG) as shown in Figure 9.1. The IRG is an unused block of tape which is typically six-tenths of an inch long. When a magnetic tape drive is started, some tape (about three tenths of an inch) will move past the read/write head before operating speed is reached. When a tape drive is stopped, approximately three-tenths of an inch of tape will move past the read/write head before the tape comes to a stop. The IRG is an allowance for the tape required in both starting and stopping the drive in order to minimize errors in reading and writing data.

It is often convenient to create on the tape physical data records which contain more than one logical data record. This arrangement is called *blocking*. Two or more logical data records may make up a physical record on the tape. For example, if the blocking factor is three, the data would appear on the tape as shown in Figure 9.2.

The use of blocked records serves to utilize as much tape as possible and also to minimize access time. The programmer must know the size of the blocking factor when he or she is writing a program to process a file. If a file is being created by a program, the programmer should choose as large a blocking factor as possible. The maximum size for a blocking factor is limited by the amount of main memory available. When a physical record is read, all of the data contained on it must be stored in memory.

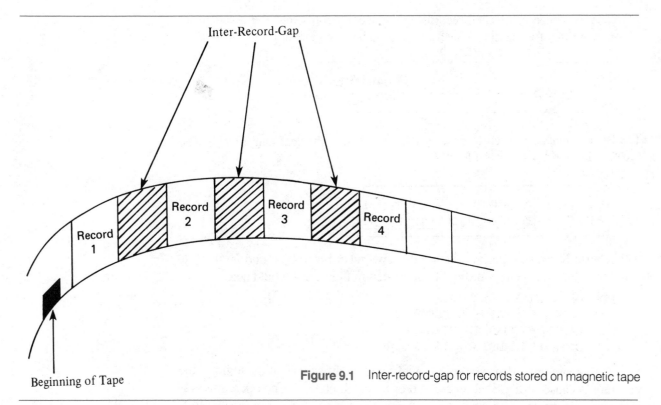

Figure 9.1   Inter-record-gap for records stored on magnetic tape

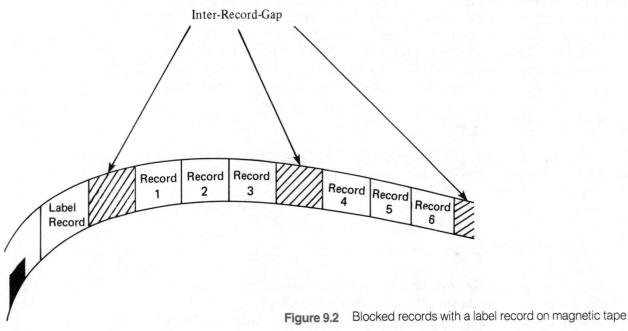

Figure 9.2   Blocked records with a label record on magnetic tape

There is a provision for creating a record at the beginning of the tape which will contain identifying data about the file. This record is called a *label record* (Fig. 9.2). The label record is created by the operating system when the file is opened as an output file. When the data file is used as an input file, the operating system will check the content of the label record to verify that the correct tape has been mounted.

The existence of blocked records and/or label records must be noted in the FD entry written for the file. The BLOCK clause has the general form:

$$\underline{\text{BLOCK}} \text{ CONTAINS integer } \left\{ \begin{array}{l} \text{CHARACTERS} \\ \underline{\text{RECORDS}} \end{array} \right\}$$

The BLOCK clause is used to specify the size of the physical data block. The LABEL clause has the general form:

$$\underline{\text{LABEL}} \left\{ \begin{array}{l} \underline{\text{RECORD}} \text{ IS} \\ \underline{\text{RECORDS}} \text{ ARE} \end{array} \right\} \left\{ \begin{array}{l} \underline{\text{OMITTED}} \\ \underline{\text{STANDARD}} \end{array} \right\}$$

This clause is used to specify whether the label record is to be found on the file. For example, the FD entry for the file illustrated in Figure 9.2 would be:

```
FD   DATA-FILE
     BLOCK CONTAINS 3 RECORDS
     LABEL RECORD IS STANDARD
     DATA RECORD IS DATA-RECORD.
```

The programmer does not need to make any modifications to the logic of the program because of the label record and/or blocked records. The operating system performs the required label record creation/checking, and deblocks the physical data record into logical records (as described in the DATA DIVISION FDs) which are made available to the program for processing one at a time.

The computer requires that you tell it not only which file to use but also what equipment to use to access the file. The SELECT statement is used to associate the file with a physical device. The general form of a SELECT statement is:

$$\boxed{\underline{\text{SELECT}} \text{ file-name } \underline{\text{ASSIGN}} \text{ TO system-name.}}$$

The form taken by the *system-name* differs widely among different versions of COBOL. The reader must check the system COBOL manual supplied by the manufacturer for specific details.

9.2 DISK CONCEPTS

A disk contains one or more recording surfaces. Each surface is organized into *tracks* on which data is recorded. The tracks on a surface may be thought of as a series of concentric circles (Fig. 9.3). There may be anywhere from 40 to 400 or more tracks per surface depending on the size of the disk. A track may store from 1000 to 8000 or more characters depending on the size of the disk. Data is organized on each track into records. As with data stored on tape, there is typically an IRG between records. A typical track containing records is shown in Figure 9.4. Data is read from and written onto a disk one record at a time. In order to optimize access time and utilization of space on the disk, records may be blocked in much the same fashion as was done on tape files.

A typical sequence of events required to read a record on disk includes the following steps:

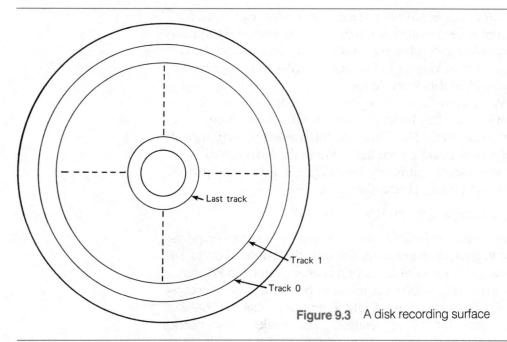

Figure 9.3 A disk recording surface

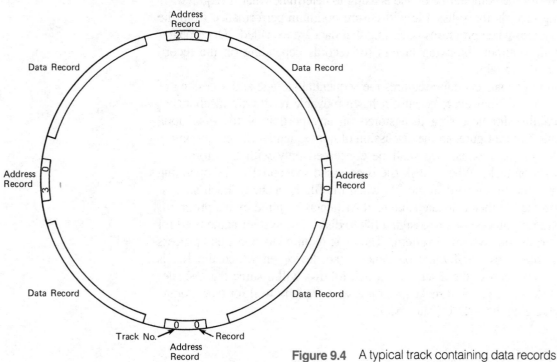

Figure 9.4 A typical track containing data records

1. A program requests a record from a disk file.
2. The operating system (which keeps track of the physical disk address of files and records) instructs the disk drive to read a particular record from a specified surface and track.
3. The disk drive moves its read/write head to the track and when the disk surface has rotated into position for reading the required record, the data is read.

A similar sequence of events occurs when a record is written onto a disk file. One entire physical record is read/written at a time. The operating system handles the details of accumulating a sufficient number of logical records before writing a physical record, and making logical records available to a program one at a time after reading a block of data from the file.

A disk usually contains many files. The operating system maintains a directory of existing files on a disk. This directory contains such information as the location and name of each file. The directory information is the logical equivalent of the label record found on the tape. While the label record is an optional feature for a tape file, the directory information is a required part of creating and accessing a file on disk. Hence, the clause

LABEL RECORD IS STANDARD

usually *must* be included in the FD for a file found on disk. On some compilers (including the one used to prepare programs for this text) the LABEL RECORD IS STANDARD clause is assumed if the LABEL RECORD is omitted from an FD entry. On the other compilers the LABEL RECORD clause must be included in FD entries for all files. The ANSI-74 standard for COBOL indicates that the LABEL RECORD clause is required for all FD entries. The reader must check specifications for the compiler he or she is using to determine what is required.

Blocking records for a disk file will ensure optimum performance from the computing system when programs accessing that data are executed. Documentation specifying optimum blocking factors for records depending on the record length is usually available.

The nature of magnetic tape requires the sequential storage and accessing of the records. A disk, however, because it has a movable read/write mechanism, has the capability for accessing data stored on any portion of the disk upon demand. This feature figures in the discussion of nonsequential file processing in chapter 12. For the moment we shall be concerned only with the storage of sequential files on disk. When a disk file is accessed sequentially, the operating system locates the first record in the file when the file is opened. Each successive record in the file then is located and read/written as required by the program.

The SELECT entry is used to assign a file to disk. The system-name used for a disk file varies from system to system. The logic required to create and process a sequential file is essentially independent of the device on which the file is stored. For convenience, the discussion which follows will assume that the files will be on disk, but you could make programs work equally well for tape storage simply by changing the SELECT statement.

9.3   THE OPEN STATEMENT

The OPEN statement causes the operating system to make a file available for processing. A file must be opened before any input or output operation can be performed on it. A sequential file can be opened in one of four modes: INPUT, OUTPUT, I-O and EXTEND (Fig. 9.5).

When a file is opened in INPUT mode, the records from the file are made available to the program one at a time from first to last. The file must exist on the device specified in the SELECT statement for the file. Two options exist for tape files opened as INPUT mode: WITH NO REWIND and REVERSED.[1] Ordinarily, a tape reel is rewound from the takeup reel onto its original reel and positioned at

$$
\text{OPEN}
\left\{
\begin{array}{l}
\underline{\text{INPUT}}\text{ file-name}\\[2pt]
\underline{\text{OUTPUT}}\text{ file-name}\\
\underline{\text{I-O}}\text{ file-name } \dots\\
\underline{\text{EXTEND}}\text{ file-name } \dots
\end{array}
\right.
\left.
\begin{array}{l}
\left[
\left\{
\begin{array}{l}
\underline{\text{REVERSED}}\\
\text{WITH } \underline{\text{NO}}\ \underline{\text{REWIND}}
\end{array}
\right\}
\right]\\[4pt]
[\text{WITH } \underline{\text{NO}}\ \underline{\text{REWIND}}\,] \ \dots
\end{array}
\ \dots
\right\}
$$

Figure 9.5   General form of the OPEN statement

the first record in the file when the file is opened. The NO REWIND clause can be used when a reel of tape contains multiple files and you want to process each file in succession. When the first file is closed it must not be rewound so that the reel is left in position for the next file to be opened. The WITH NO REWIND clause would then be used to open the second file. The REVERSED option will cause the file to be positioned at its last record and read in reverse order from last to first. The REVERSED and NO REWIND options are not included in all COBOL compilers.

When a file is opened in OUTPUT mode, the file is assumed to have no data records in it. WRITE statements cause records to be placed in the file sequentially from first to last. If records already were present in the file they would be destroyed. The WITH NO REWIND clause has the same effect here as it does for the INPUT mode.

When a file is opened in I-O (Input-Output) mode, it is assumed to exist and may be processed by READ and REWRITE statements. The REWRITE statement will cause the content of a record which has been read (and perhaps changed by the processing program) to be rewritten, thereby destroying the content of the original. This mode can be used for disk files only; it is not valid for tape files. (A complete discussion of use of the I-O mode for file updating is later in this chapter.)

When a file is opened in EXTEND mode, records are written in the file following the last record in the file. When the file is opened the operating system locates the last record in the file; any record written in the file will follow that record. EXTEND mode may not be implemented on all compilers. (See complete discussion of the EXTEND mode in section 9.11.)

9.4   THE CLOSE STATEMENT

The CLOSE statement terminates processing of a file. The file must be open at the time of execution of a CLOSE statement. After a file has been closed no further input or output operations may be executed. A general form of the CLOSE statement is shown in Figure 9.6.

$$
\underline{\text{CLOSE}}\text{ file-name }
\left[
\text{WITH }
\left\{
\begin{array}{l}
\underline{\text{NO}}\ \underline{\text{REWIND}}\\
\underline{\text{LOCK}}
\end{array}
\right\}
\right]
$$

Figure 9.6   General form of the CLOSE statement

---

[1]These options are ignored if the file is assigned to a disk.

When a file is assigned to tape, the NO REWIND clause will prevent the reel of tape from being repositioned to the beginning of the file. Repositioning of the tape reel (rewinding) is performed as part of the CLOSE operation if the NO REWIND clause is omitted.

The LOCK option will prevent the current program (or any subsequent program in the job) from reopening the file. The LOCK option should be invoked if it would be an error for any further processing of the file to take place.[2]

9.5   FILE CREATION

In creating a sequential file, it is usually important that the records be stored in sequence based on one field within the record. This field, designated as the *key field*, is used as the basis for organizing the file. An account number, a product number or a social security number are typical examples of fields used as key fields. The records within a file are organized into ascending or descending

Program 9.1   File creation program

```
1        IDENTIFICATION DIVISION.
2        PROGRAM-ID.  CHAPTER 9 EXAMPLE 1.
3        AUTHOR.  GARY GLEASON.
4        ENVIRONMENT DIVISION.
5        INPUT-OUTPUT SECTION.
6        FILE-CONTROL.
7            SELECT INFD ASSIGN TO READER.
8            SELECT ACCOUNTS-RECEIVABLE-FILE ASSIGN TO DISK.
9            SELECT PRINT ASSIGN TO PRINTER.
10       DATA DIVISION.
11       FILE SECTION.
12       FD   INFD
13            LABEL RECORDS ARE OMITTED
14            DATA RECORD IS INPUT-RECORD.
15       01   INPUT-RECORD.
16            02   ACCOUNT-NUMBER-IR        PIC 9(5).
17            02   NAME-IR                  PIC X(20).
18            02   ADDRESS-IR.
19                 03   STREET-IR           PIC X(15).
20                 03   CITY-IR             PIC X(15).
21                 03   STATE-IR            PIC X(2).
22                 03   ZIP-CODE-IR         PIC X(5).
23            02   AMOUNT-OWED-IR           PIC 9(4)V99.
24            02   CREDIT-MAXIUM-IR         PIC 9(4)V99.
25            02   DATE-OF-LAST-PAYMENT-IR.
26                 03   MONTH-IR            PIC 99.
27                 03   DAY-IR              PIC 99.
28                 03   YEAR-IR             PIC 99.
29       FD   ACCOUNTS-RECEIVABLE-FILE
30            LABEL RECORDS ARE STANDARD
```

(continued)

---

[2] In some operating systems the LOCK phrase has the additional function of causing the file to become permanent, if the file is being created by this program. For these operating systems a file will be purged from the disk at the end of the program unless the LOCK option is used.

Program 9.1   (continued)

```
31              BLOCK CONTAINS 10 RECORDS
32              DATA RECORD IS ACCOUNTS-RECEIVABLE-RECORD.
33       01     ACCOUNTS-RECEIVABLE-RECORD.
34              02   ACCOUNT-NUMBER-ARR        PIC 9(5).
35              02   NAME-ARR                  PIC X(20).
36              02   ADDRESS-ARR.
37                   03   STREET-ARR           PIC X(15).
38                   03   CITY-ARR             PIC X(15).
39                   03   STATE-ARR            PIC X(2).
40                   03   ZIP-CODE-ARR         PIC X(5).
41              02   AMOUNT-OWED-ARR           PIC 9(4)V99.
42              02   CREDIT-MAXIUM-ARR         PIC 9(4)V99.
43              02   DATE-OF-LAST-PAYMENT-ARR.
44                   03   MONTH-ARR            PIC 99.
45                   03   DAY-ARR              PIC 99.
46                   03   YEAR-ARR             PIC 99.
47       FD   PRINT
48              LABEL RECORDS ARE OMITTED
49              DATA RECORD IS PRINT-LINE.
50       01   PRINT-LINE            PIC X(132).
51       WORKING-STORAGE SECTION.
52       01   EOF-FLAG                    PIC 9     VALUE ZERO.
53       01   RECORDS-COUNT               PIC 999   VALUE ZERO.
54       01   ACCOUNT-NUMBER              PIC 9(5)  VALUE ZERO.
55       PROCEDURE DIVISION.
56       1000-MAIN-LOGIC.
57          OPEN INPUT INFD.
58          OPEN OUTPUT ACCOUNTS-RECEIVABLE-FILE.
59          OPEN OUTPUT PRINT.
60          PERFORM 2500-FIRST-RECORD.
61          PERFORM 3000-WRITE-READ UNTIL EOF-FLAG = 1.
62          CLOSE INFD.
63          CLOSE ACCOUNTS-RECEIVABLE-FILE LOCK.
64          CLOSE PRINT.
65          STOP RUN.
66       2500-FIRST-RECORD.
67          READ INFD AT END MOVE 1 TO EOF-FLAG.
68          ADD 1 TO RECORDS-COUNT.
69          MOVE INPUT-RECORD TO ACCOUNTS-RECEIVABLE-RECORD.
70          WRITE ACCOUNTS-RECEIVABLE-RECORD.
71          MOVE ACCOUNT-NUMBER-IR TO ACCOUNT-NUMBER.
72          READ INFD AT END MOVE 1 TO EOF-FLAG.
73       3000-WRITE-READ.
74          IF   ACCOUNT-NUMBER-IR > ACCOUNT-NUMBER
75              ADD 1 TO RECORDS-COUNT
76              MOVE ACCOUNT-NUMBER-IR TO ACCOUNT-NUMBER
77              MOVE INPUT-RECORD TO ACCOUNTS-RECEIVABLE-RECORD
78              WRITE ACCOUNTS-RECEIVABLE-RECORD
79          ELSE
80              PERFORM 7000-ERROR-PARA-1.
81          READ INFD AT END MOVE 1 TO EOF-FLAG.
82       7000-ERROR-PARA-1.
83          EXIT.
```

Program 9.2   File merge program

```
1       IDENTIFICATION DIVISION.
2       PROGRAM-ID. CHAPTER 9 EXAMPLE 2.
3       AUTHOR. GARY GLEASON.
4       ENVIRONMENT DIVISION.
5       INPUT-OUTPUT SECTION.
6       FILE-CONTROL.
7            SELECT TRANSACTION-FILE ASSIGN TO DISK.
8            SELECT  OLD-MASTER-FILE ASSIGN TO DISK.
9            SELECT  NEW-MASTER-FILE ASSIGN TO DISK.
10      DATA DIVISION.
11      FILE SECTION.
12      FD   TRANSACTION-FILE
13           LABEL RECORDS ARE STANDARD
14           DATA RECORD IS TRANSACTION-RECORD.
15      01   TRANSACTION-RECORD.
16           02   ACCOUNT-NUMBER-TR       PIC 9(5).
17           02   NAME-TR                 PIC X(20).
18           02   ADDRESS-TR.
19                03   STREET-TR          PIC X(15).
20                03   CITY-TR            PIC X(15).
21                03   STATE-TR           PIC X(2).
22                03   ZIP-CODE-TR        PIC X(5).
23           02   AMOUNT-OWED-TR          PIC 9(4)V99.
24           02   CREDIT-MAXIUM-TR        PIC 9(4)V99.
25           02   DATE-OF-LAST-PAYMENT-TR.
26                03   MONTH-TR           PIC 99.
27                03   DAY-TR             PIC 99.
28                03   YEAR-TR            PIC 99.
29      FD   OLD-MASTER-FILE
30           BLOCK CONTAINS 10 RECORDS
31           LABEL RECORDS ARE STANDARD
32           DATA RECORD IS OLD-MASTER-RECORD.
33      01   OLD-MASTER-RECORD.
34           02   ACCOUNT-NUMBER-OMR      PIC 9(5).
35           02   NAME-OMR                PIC X(20).
36           02   ADDRESS-OMR.
37                03   STREET-OMR         PIC X(15).
38                03   CITY-OMR           PIC X(15).
39                03   STATE-OMR          PIC X(2).
40                03   ZIP-CODE-OMR       PIC X(5).
41           02   AMOUNT-OWED-OMR         PIC 9(4)V99.
42           02   CREDIT-MAXIUM-OMR       PIC 9(4)V99.
43           02   DATE-OF-LAST-PAYMENT-OMR.
44                03   MONTH-OMR          PIC 99.
45                03   DAY-OMR            PIC 99.
46                03   YEAR-OMR           PIC 99.
47      FD   NEW-MASTER-FILE
48           BLOCK CONTAINS 10 RECORDS
49           LABEL RECORDS ARE STANDARD
50           DATA RECORD IS NEW-MASTER-RECORD.
51      01   NEW-MASTER-RECORD.
52           02   ACCOUNT-NUMBER-NMR      PIC 9(5).
53           02   NAME-NMR                PIC X(20).
```

(continued)

Program 9.2 (continued)

```
54          02  ADDRESS-NMR.
55              03  STREET-NMR          PIC X(15).
56              03  CITY-NMR            PIC X(15).
57              03  STATE-NMR           PIC X(2).
58              03  ZIP-CODE-NMR        PIC X(5).
59          02  AMOUNT-OWED-NMR         PIC 9(4)V99.
60          02  CREDIT-MAXIUM-NMR       PIC 9(4)V99.
61          02  DATE-OF-LAST-PAYMENT-NMR.
62              03  MONTH-NMR           PIC 99.
63              03  DAY-NMR             PIC 99.
64              03  YEAR-NMR            PIC 99.
65      PROCEDURE DIVISION.
66      1000-MAIN-LOGIC.
67          PERFORM 2000-INITIALIZATION.
68          PERFORM 3000-COMPARE   UNTIL ACCOUNT-NUMBER-TR = 99999
69              AND ACCOUNT-NUMBER-OMR = 99999.
70          PERFORM 6000-TERMINATION.
71      2000-INITIALIZATION.
72          OPEN INPUT  TRANSACTION-FILE.
73          OPEN INPUT  OLD-MASTER-FILE.
74          OPEN OUTPUT NEW-MASTER-FILE.
75          READ TRANSACTION-FILE AT END MOVE 99999 TO ACCOUNT-NUMBER-TR.
76          READ OLD-MASTER-FILE AT END MOVE 99999 TO ACCOUNT-NUMBER-OMR.
77      3000-COMPARE.
78          IF ACCOUNT-NUMBER-TR < ACCOUNT-NUMBER-OMR
79              PERFORM 4000-WRITE-TRANSACTION
80          ELSE
81              PERFORM 5000-WRITE-OLD-MASTER.
82      4000-WRITE-TRANSACTION.
83          MOVE TRANSACTION-RECORD TO NEW-MASTER-RECORD.
84          WRITE NEW-MASTER-RECORD.
85          READ TRANSACTION-FILE AT END MOVE 99999 TO ACCOUNT-NUMBER-TR.
86      5000-WRITE-OLD-MASTER.
87          MOVE  OLD-MASTER-RECORD TO NEW-MASTER-RECORD.
88          WRITE NEW-MASTER-RECORD.
89          READ OLD-MASTER-FILE AT END MOVE 99999 TO ACCOUNT-NUMBER-OMR.
90      6000-TERMINATION.
91          CLOSE TRANSACTION-FILE.
92          CLOSE OLD-MASTER-FILE.
93          CLOSE NEW-MASTER-FILE LOCK.
94          STOP RUN.
```

sequence based on the key field.[3] Ascending sequence is most common; it implies that records with smaller key field values precede larger values in the file.

For example, let's create a file containing master accounts-receivable records for the customers of a business. Each record contains the customer's account number, name, address, amount owed, credit maximum and the date of

---

[3]Most systems contain utility programs designed to sort data files into any desired sequence. COBOL has a SORT facility described in detail in Chapter 10.

last payment. The account number will be the key field; the file will be created in ascending sequence. The input file will be on the card reader or the logical equivalent; the output file (the master file) will be on disk. (For users of conversational systems the input file would be assigned to the terminal. See Appendix A for details.)

Program 9.1 could be used for this purpose. This program performs a sequence check of the input records by comparing the account number of the input record (ACCOUNT-NUMBER-IR) with the account number of the previous record (ACCOUNT-NUMBER) (line 74). If ACCOUNT-NUMBER-IR is not greater than ACCOUNT-NUMBER, the record is out of sequence and is not placed onto the output file. The sequence checking necessitates the processing of the first record separately from other records (lines 66 through 72) in order to initialize the value of ACCOUNT-NUMBER, because when the first record is read, there is no previous record number against which to compare.

9.6   SEQUENTIAL FILE MERGING

Often it is necessary to merge two files of similar data to create one file in proper sequence containing all of the data from the original two files. Both files must be sorted into the same sequence based on the same key field. A program to perform this task is illustrated in Program 9.2. Data from TRANSACTION-FILE is to be merged with OLD-MASTER-FILE to create NEW-MASTER-FILE on disk.

In order to maintain sequence in the output file, one record from each of the two input files is read initially (lines 75 and 76) and the record with the smaller key field value is placed on the output file. The routine 3000-COMPARE (lines 77 through 81) makes this comparison and selects either 4000-WRITE-TRANSACTION (if the transaction key field is less than the old master key field) or 5000-WRITE-OLD-MASTER (if the transaction key field is not less than the old master key field). The 4000-WRITE-TRANSACTION routine (lines 82 through 85) moves the TRANSACTION-RECORD to the NEW-MASTER-RECORD, writes the NEW-MASTER-RECORD, and reads the next TRANSACTION-RECORD. The 5000-WRITE-OLD-MASTER routine (lines 86 through 89) performs a similar function, except the OLD-MASTER-RECORD is written onto the NEW-MASTER-FILE and the new record is read from OLD-MASTER-FILE.

This program utilizes the key field for each file to enable the program to continue processing until end-of-file has been reached on both files. When end-of-file is reached on either of the input files, the value 99999 is moved to the key field for that file. Processing continues (lines 68 through 69) until both key fields have value 99999. This method makes it unnecessary to have separate logic within the program to handle the remaining records on one file when end-of-file has been reached on the other. The paragraph 3000-COMPARE (lines 77 through 81) selects the record with the smallest key field value for output. If the key field for the transaction record is less than the key field for the old master record, the transaction record is written onto the new master file and another transaction record is read (lines 82 through 85). When end-of-file is reached on either of the input files, the paragraph 3000-COMPARE continues to function as before. For example, if end-of-file is first reached on the old master file, the value of ACCOUNT-NUMBER-OMR will become 99999. Since this is the largest value that can be contained in a five-digit field, all values of ACCOUNT-NUMBER-IR must be less than ACCOUNT-NUMBER-OMR which will result in the paragraph 4000-WRITE-TRANSACTION being selected on each execution of 3000-COMPARE. When end-of-file is finally reached on the transaction file, the value of ACCOUNT-NUMBER-IR will become 99999 and the procedure will terminate.

Note that it is possible to create a new file with records having key fields with equal values. This condition may or may not be an error depending on the particular application. The following modification to the paragraph 3000-COMPARE in Program 9.2 could check for key fields having equal values:

```
3000-COMPARE.
    IF  ACCOUNT-NUMBER-IR  =  ACCOUNT-NUMBER-OMR
        PERFORM  6000-ERROR-ROUTINE
    ELSE
        IF  ACCOUNT-NUMBER-TR  <  ACCOUNT-NUMBER-OMR
            PERFORM  4000-WRITE-TRANSACTION
        ELSE
            PERFORM  5000-WRITE-OLD-MASTER.
```

9.7   FILE UPDATING

Data records stored on a file will need to be changed (*updated*) from time to time. Any field on a record can be changed for one reason or another. If the file is stored on tape, an entirely new file must be created each time a file is updated. If the file is stored on disk, a new file may be created or records changed in place (see section 9.12). Even if it is possible to update a file in place, it may be necessary to create a new updated file in order to maintain the old file in case errors are made in the updating process which necessitate *rolling back* the file to its previous state. Also it may be necessary to maintain the previous content of the file to establish an *audit trail*, which enables auditors to verify that the steps being taken in the data processing system are valid.

One approach to file updating is to submit change records in essentially the same format as the records to be updated, but having blanks in fields which do not require changes and new data in all fields which require change. It is desirable for the program which performs the update function to accept any number of changes for a given record; the changes all may be placed on the same change record or on different change records.

The logic required to perform the update function can be treated as an extension of Program 9.2. The paragraph 3000-COMPARE (lines 77 through 81) would be rewritten as:

```
3000-COMPARE.
    IF  ACCOUNT-NUMBER-TR  =  ACCOUNT-NUMBER-OMR
        PERFORM  6000-UPDATE
    ELSE
        .
        .
        .
```

The paragraph 6000-UPDATE would cause the computer to scan the transaction record for nonblank fields. The content of each nonblank field would replace the appropriate field in the master record. The paragraph 6000-UPDATE could be coded as follows:

```
6000-UPDATE.
    IF  NAME-TR  NOT  =  SPACES
        MOVE  NAME-TR  TO  NAME-OMR.
    IF  ADDRESS-TR  NOT  =  SPACES
        MOVE  ADDRESS-TR  TO  ADDRESS-OMR.
    IF  AMOUNT-OWED-TR  NOT  =  SPACES
        MOVE  AMOUNT-OWED-TR  TO  AMOUNT-OWED-OMR.
    IF  CREDIT-MAXIMUM-TR  NOT  =  SPACES
        MOVE  CREDIT-MAXIMUM-TR  TO  CREDIT-MAXIMUM-OMR.
    IF  DATE-OF-LAST-PAYMENT-TR  NOT  =  SPACES
        MOVE  DATE-OF-LAST-PAYMENT-TR  TO  DATE-OF-LAST-PAYMENT-OMR.
    READ  TRANSACTION-FILE  AT  END  MOVE  99999  TO  ACCOUNT-NUMBER-TR.
```

The 6000-UPDATE routine must read the next transaction record, but it does not output the master record to the new file, since the master record may be updated by any number of change records. The updated master record will be written onto the new file only when a transaction record containing a larger account number has been read. The logic required for this function is already present in the file merge in Program 9.2.

Another type of file updating is the processing of various types of transactions against the master file. In this example payments on the account would be subtracted from the balance due and the date of the payment would be entered in the field which reflects the date of last payment. Charges would be added to the balance-due field. The logic required for this type of program would be similar to the previous update program with the exception of the UPDATE routine itself. When this type of updating is being done, it is common to define code in the transaction record which will be used by the program to determine what action to take on the transaction. For example, let's define the following transaction codes:

Code	Meaning
C1	Change Name
C2	Change Street
C3	Change City
C4	Change State
C5	Change Zip
C6	Change Address
C7	Change Amount-owed
C8	Change Credit-maximum
C9	Change Date-of-last-payment
P	Payment — Update Amount-owed and change Date-of-last-payment
R	Merchandise return — update Amount-owed
C	Charge purchase — update Amount-owed
A	Add record to master file

The transaction record would now contain the transaction code and a field for transaction amount (payment, charge amount, and so on) as shown below:

```
01   TRANSACTION-RECORD.
     02   ACCOUNT-NUMBER-TR  PIC 9(5).
     02   NAME-TR  PIC X(20).
       .
       .
       .
```

```
02    TRANSACTION-AMOUNT-TR   PIC 9(4)V99.
02    TRANSACTION-CODE   PIC XX.
      88   CHANGE-NAME            VALUE "C1".
      88   CHANGE-STREET          VALUE "C2".
      88   CHANGE-CITY            VALUE "C3".
      88   CHANGE-STATE           VALUE "C4".
      88   CHANGE-ZIP             VALUE "C5".
      88   CHANGE-ADDRESS         VALUE "C6".
      88   CHANGE-AMOUNT-OWED     VALUE "C7".
      88   CHANGE-CREDIT-MAX      VALUE "C8".
      88   CHANGE-DATE            VALUE "C9".
      88   PAYMENT                VALUE "P".
      88   RETURN                 VALUE "R".
      88   CHARGE-PURCHASE        VALUE "C".
      88   ADD-RECORD             VALUE "A".
      88   VALID-UPDATE-TRANSACTION
                VALUES ARE "C1" THRU "C9", "P", "R", "C".
```

The paragraph 6000-UPDATE would now be written as:

```
6000-UPDATE.
    IF PAYMENT
        SUBTRACT TRANSACTION-AMOUNT-TR FROM
                AMOUNT-OWED-OMR
        MOVE DATE-OF-LAST-PAYMENT-TR TO
            DATE-OF-LAST-PAYMENT-OMR.
    IF RETURN
        SUBTRACT TRANSACTION-AMOUNT-TR FROM
            AMOUNT-OWED-OMR.
    IF CHARGE-PURCHACE
        ADD TRANSACTION-AMOUNT-TR TO AMOUNT-OWED-OMR.
    IF CHANGE-NAME
        MOVE NAME-TR TO NAME-OMR.
    IF CHANGE-STREET
        MOVE STREET-TR TO STREET-OMR
    IF CHANGE-CITY
        MOVE CITY-TR TO CITY-OMR.
    IF CHANGE-STATE
        MOVE STATE-TR TO STATE-OMR.
    IF CHANGE-ZIP
        MOVE ZIP-TR TO ZIP-OMR.
    IF CHANGE-ADDRESS
        MOVE ADDRESS-TR TO ADDRESS-OMR.
    IF CHANGE-AMOUNT-OWED
        MOVE AMOUNT-OWED-TR TO AMOUNT-OWED-OMR.
    IF CHANGE-CREDIT-MAX
        MOVE CREDIT-MAXIMUM-TR TO CREDIT-MAXIMUM-OMR.
    IF CHANGE-DATE
        MOVE DATE-OF-LAST-PAYMENT-TR TO
            DATE-OF-LAST-PAYMENT-OMR.
    READ TRANSACTION-FILE
        AT END MOVE 99999 TO ACCOUNT-NUMBER-TR.
```

Note that the transaction code ''A'' is invalid at this point since it represents an attempt to add to the file a record which has the same key field value as an existing record. The paragraph 6000-COMPARE could be rewritten to detect invalid transactions as follows:

```
3002-COMPARE.
    IF ACCOUNT-NUMBER-TR = ACCOUNT-NUMBER-OMR
        AND VALID-UPDATE-TRANSACTION
            PERFORM 6000-UPDATE
    ELSE
        IF ACCOUNT-NUMBER-TR < ACCOUNT-NUMBER-OMR
            AND ADD-RECORD
                PERFORM 4000-WRITE-TRANSACTION
        ELSE
            IF ACCOUNT-NUMBER-TR > ACCOUNT-NUMBER-OMR
                PERFORM 5000-WRITE-OLD-MASTER
            ELSE
                PERFORM 7000-ERROR-IN-TRANSACTION.
```

The paragraph 7000-ERROR-IN-TRANSACTION would write an appropriate error message and read the next record from the transaction file.

9.8   DELETING RECORDS

It is often necessary to delete unneeded records from a file. For a personnel file the employee may have quit or been fired; for an inventory file the item may no longer be stocked. When producing an entirely new updated file, a record is deleted simply by not writing that record onto the new master file. For example, suppose a transaction file consists of records to be deleted from the old master file. The 3000-COMPARE in Program 9.2 could be modified to perform deletion as follows:

```
3003-COMPARE.
    IF ACCOUNT-NUMBER-TR = ACCOUNT-NUMBER-OMR
        PERFORM 8000-READ-OLD-MASTER
        PERFORM 8001-READ-TRANSACTION
    ELSE
        IF ACCOUNT-NUMBER-TR > ACCOUNT-NUMBER-OMR
            PERFORM 5000-WRITE-OLD-MASTER
        ELSE
            PERFORM 7000-ERROR-IN-TRANSACTION.
```

The paragraphs 8000-READ-OLD-MASTER and 8001-READ-TRANSACTION will read one record from their respective files. If the value of the transaction key field is less than the old master key field, the transaction must be an error, since it is impossible to find a record in the old master file which will match the transaction by reading subsequent records from the old master file.

9.9   CHANGE AND DELETE IN ONE PROGRAM

To write a general purpose program to perform all of the required functions on a file, you must use the transaction code scheme described in the previous section. Let's add a transaction code ''D'' to the list of transaction codes to signify the deletion function:

```
02  TRANSACTION-CODE  PIC XX.
        .
        .
        .
        88 DELETE-RECORD   VALUE "D".
```

The paragraph 3002-COMPARE can now be rewritten as

```
3004-COMPARE.
    IF  ACCOUNT-NUMBER-TR  = ACCOUNT-NUMBER-OMR
        AND  VALID-UPDATE-TRANSACTION
            PERFORM  60001-UPDATE
    ELSE
        IF  ACCOUNT-NUMBER-TR  < ACCOUNT-NUMBER-OMR
            AND  ADD-RECORD
                PERFORM  4000-WRITE-TRANSACTION
        ELSE
            IF  ACCOUNT-NUMBER-TR  = ACCOUNT-NUMBER-OMR
                AND  DELETE-RECORD
                    PERFORM  8000-READ-OLD-MASTER
                    PERFORM  8001-READ-TRANSACTION
            ELSE
                IF  ACCOUNT-NUMBER-TR  > ACCOUNT-NUMBER-OMR
                    PERFORM  5000-WRITE-OLD-MASTER
                ELSE
                    PERFORM  7002-ERROR-IN-TRANSACTION.
```

The only difference between this paragraph and 3002-COMPARE is the addition
of the test for a valid deletion when the key field values are equal and the transaction code indicates that the record is to be deleted.

9.10 ADDING RECORDS WITH EXTEND

In order to add records to an existing disk or tape file it is necessary to open the
file in EXTEND mode. For example, to add records to the ACCOUNTS-
RECEIVABLE-FILE in Program 9.1, you would use:

```
OPEN  EXTEND  ACCOUNTS-RECEIVABLE-FILE.
```

EXTEND mode causes the operating system to locate the last record in the file and
place any additional records in the file following that record. The PROCEDURE
DIVISION for a program to add records to the file in Program 9.1 would be:

```
PROCEDURE-DIVISION.
1000-MAIN-LOGIC.
    OPEN  INPUT  INFD
          EXTEND  ACCOUNTS-RECEIVABLE-FILE.
    READ  INFD  AT END  MOVE 1 TO EOF-FLAG.
    PERFORM  2000-WRITE-READ  UNTIL EOF-FLAG = 1.
    CLOSE  INFD  ACCOUNTS-RECEIVABLE-FILE.
    STOP RUN.
2000-WRITE-READ.
    WRITE  ACCOUNTS-RECEIVABLE-RECORD  FROM INPUT-RECORD.
    READ  INFD  AT END  MOVE 1 TO EOF-FLAG.
```

In using EXTEND mode you cannot merge the new records with the existing records in the file. The file ACCOUNTS-RECEIVABLE-FILE will not be in proper sequence as a result of the above program. It would be necessary to sort the file using either a system utility program or the COBOL SORT facility (see Chapter 10) in order to perform any further processing of the file.

9.11   UPDATING A SEQUENTIAL FILE IN PLACE

As noted earlier, a tape file cannot be updated in place; a completely new file must be produced each time an update operation is performed. Files which are stored on disk, however, may be updated in place. New records can be added to the file, and existing records can be changed or even deleted without creating an entirely new file.

Adding records to an existing file is accomplished using EXTEND mode (see Section 9.10). Changing existing records and deleting records is accomplished by opening the file in I-O mode and using the REWRITE verb. When a file is opened in I-O mode, as in

OPEN I-O ACCOUNTS-RECEIVABLE-FILE.

records may be read from the file using the verb READ and written on the file using REWRITE. The REWRITE statement can be used only after a READ operation. It causes the record which was read to be rewritten onto the file; the new copy of the record replaces the old one. The general form of the REWRITE statement is shown in Figure 9.7. For example, in order to rewrite a record onto ACCOUNTS-RECEIVABLE-FILE, the statement

REWRITE ACCOUNTS-RECEIVABLE-RECORD.

can be used. The REWRITE statement may be executed repeatedly for the same record; it will always replace the last record read from the file.

The basic procedure used to change an existing record in a file is to make changes to the record based on transactions. As each transaction regarding a particular record is processed, the changed record is rewritten onto the file using the REWRITE statement. This approach is used in Program 9.3 which will update the ACCOUNTS-RECEIVABLE-FILE created by Program 9.1.

REWRITE record-name [FROM data-name]

Figure 9.7   General form of the REWRITE statement

In order to delete records from a file, you must add a deletion code to the record. When the deletion code has a predetermined value (1 in Program 9.3), the record is considered to have been deleted; If the code has any other value the record is considered to be active. The routine which reads records from the file (4000-READ-ACCOUNTS-RECEIVABLE-FILE, at lines 92-96 in Prog. 9.3) simply bypasses all deleted records. Records from the file are read until either a nondeleted record is found or the end-of-file is reached (lines 95-96). The routine which deletes records from the file (6000-DELETE at lines 131-135) changes the value of the deletion code (line 132) and rewrites the record (line 133).

This method for deleting records has some advantages over physically removing records from a file. The record remains in the file and is therefore accessible by any program processing the file. A report showing all deleted records can be produced at any time. A record can be changed back to active status by changing the value of the deletion code. However, this method does

Program 9.3 In place file update example

```
1       IDENTIFICATION DIVISION.
2       PROGRAM-ID. CHAPTER 9 EXAMPLE 3.
3       AUTHOR. HORN.
4       ENVIRONMENT DIVISION.
5       INPUT-OUTPUT SECTION.
6       FILE-CONTROL.
7           SELECT TRANSACTION-FILE ASSIGN TO DISK.
8           SELECT ACCOUNTS-RECEIVABLE-FILE ASSIGN TO DISK.
9       DATA DIVISION.
10      FILE SECTION.
11      FD  ACCOUNTS-ERECEIVABLE-FILE
12          LABEL RECORDS ARE STANDARD
13          BLOCK CONTAINS 10 RECORDS
14          DATA RECORD IS ACCOUNTS-RECEIVABLE-RECORD.
15      01  ACCOUNTS-RECEIVABLE-RECORD.
16          02  ACCOUNT-NUMBER-ARR          PIC 9(5).
17          02  NAME-ARR                    PIC X(20).
18          02  ADDRESS-ARR.
19              03  STREET-ARR              PIC X(15).
20              03  CITY-ARR                PIC X(15).
21              03  STATE-ARR               PIC X(2).
22              03  ZIP-CODE-ARR            PIC X(5).
23          02  AMOUNT-OWED-ARR             PIC 9(4)V99.
24          02  CREDIT-MAXIMUM-ARR          PIC 9(4)V99.
25          02  DATE-OF-LAST-PAYMENT-ARR.
26              03  MONTH-ARR               PIC 99.
27              03  DAY-ARR                 PIC 99.
28              03  YEAR-ARR                PIC 99.
29          02  DELETION-CODE-ARR           PIC 9.
30              88  DELETED-RECORD          VALUE 1.
31              88  ACTIVE-RECORD           VALUE 0, 2 THRU 9.
32      FD  TRANSACTION-FILE
33          LABEL RECORDS ARE STANDARD
34          DATA RECORD IS TRANSACTION-RECORD.
35      01  TRANSACTION-RECORD.
36          02  ACCOUNT-NUMBER-TR           PIC 9(5).
37          02  NAME-TR                     PIC X(20).
38          02  ADDRESS-TR.
39              03 STREET-TR                PIC X(15).
40              03 CITY-TR                  PIC X(15).
41              03 STATE-TR                 PIC X(2).
```

(continued)

Program 9.3 (continued)

```
42              03  ZIP-CODE-TR                    PIC X(5).
43          02  AMOUNT-OWED-TR                     PIC 9(4)V99.
44          02  CREDIT-MAXIMUM-TR                  PIC 9(4)V99.
45          02  DATE-OF-LAST-PAYMENT-TR.
46              03  MONTH-TR                       PIC 99.
47              03  DAY-TR                         PIC 99.
48              03  YEAR-TR                        PIC 99.
49          02  TRANSACTION-AMOUNT-TR              PIC 9(4)V99.
50          02  TRANSACTION-CODE-TR                PIC XX.
51              88  CHANGE-NAME                    VALUE "C1".
52              88  CHANGE-STREET                  VALUE "C2".
53              88  CHANGE-CITY                    VALUE "C3".
54              88  CHANGE-STATE                   VALUE "C4".
55              88  CHANGE-ZIP                     VALUE "C5".
56              88  CHANGE-ADDRESS                 VALUE "C6".
57              88  CHANGE-AMOUNT-OWED             VALUE "C7".
58              88  CHANGE-CREDIT-MAX              VALUE "C8".
59              88  CHANGE-DATE                    VALUE "C9".
60              88  PAYMENT                        VALUE "P".
61              88  RETURN                         VALUE "R".
62              88  CHARGE-PURCHASE                VALUE "C".
63              88  DELETE-RECORD                  VALUE "D".
64              88  VALID-UPDATE-TRANSACTION VALUES ARE
65                      "C1" THRU "C9", "P", "R", "C".
66  PROCEDURE DIVISION.
67  1000-MAIN-PROCESSING.
68      PERFORM 2000-INITIALIZATION.
69      PERFORM 3000-CONTROL
70          UNTIL
71              ACCOUNT-NUMBER-ARR = 9999 AND
72              ACCOUNT-NUMBER-TR  = 9999.
73      PERFORM 9000-TERMINATION.
74  2000-INITIALIZATION.
75      OPEN INPUT TRANSACTION-FILE
76          I-O   ACCOUNTS-RECEIVABLE-FILE.
77      PERFORM 8000-READ-TRANSACTION-FILE.
78      PERFORM 4000-READ-ACCOUNTS-RECEIVABLE-FILE.
79  3000-CONTROL
80      IF ACCOUNT-NUMBER-TR = ACCOUNT-NUMBER-ARR
81          AND VALID-UPDATE-TRANSACTION
82              PERFORM 5000-UPDATE
83          ELSE
84              IF ACCOUNT-NUMBER-TR = ACCOUNT-NUMBER-ARR
85                  AND DELETE-RECORD
86                      PERFORM 6000-DELETE
87              ELSE
88                  IF ACCOUNT-NUMBER-TR > ACCOUNT-NUMBER-ARR
89                      PERFORM 4000-READ-ACCOUNTS-RECEIVABLE-FILE
90                  ELSE
91                      PERFORM 7000-ERROR-MESSAGE.
92  4000-READ-ACCOUNTS-RECEIVABLE-FILE.
93      PERFORM 4050-READ-ARF-RECORD
```

(continued)

Program 9.3   (continued)

```
94              UNTIL
95                  ACCOUNT-NUMBER-ARR = 99999
96                  OR ACTIVE-RECORD.
97      4050-READ-ARF-RECORD.
98          READ ACCOUNTS-RECEIVABLE-FILE
99              AT END
100                 MOVE 99999 TO ACCOUNT-NUMBER-ARR.
101     5000-UPDATE.
102         IF PAYMENT
103             SUBTRACT TRANSACTION-AMOUNT-TR FROM
104                 AMOUNT-OWED-ARR
105             MOVE DATE-OF-LAST-PAYMENT-TR TO
106                 DATE-OF-LAST-PAYMENT-ARR.
107         IF RETURN
108             SUBTRACT TRANSACTION-AMOUNT-TR FROM
109                 AMOUNT-OWED-ARR.
110         IF CHANGE-NAME
111             MOVE NAME-TR TO NAME-ARR.
112         IF CHANGE-STREET
113             MOVE STREE-TR TO STREET-ARR.
114         IF CHANGE-CITY
115             MOVE CITY-TR TO CITY-ARR.
116         IF CHANGE-STATE
117             MOVE STATE-TR TO STATE-ARR.
118         IF CHANGE-ZIP
119             MOVE ZIP-TR TO ZIP-ARR.
120         IF CHANGE-ADDRESS
121             MOVE ADDRESS-TR TO ADDRESS-ARR.
122         IF CHANGE-AMOUNT-OWED
123             MOVE AMOUNT-OWED-TR TO AMOUNT-OWED-ARR.
124         IF CHANGE-CREDIT-MAX
125             MOVE CREDIT-MAXIMUM-TR TO CREDIT-MAXIMUM-ARR.
126         IF CHANGE-DATE
127             MOVE DATE-OF-LAST-PAYMENT-TR TO
128                 DATE-OF-LAST-PAYMENT-ARR.
129         REWRITE ACCOUNTS-RECEIVABLE-RECORD.
130         PERFORM 8000-READ-TRANSACTION-FILE.
131     6000-DELETE.
132         MOVE 1 TO DELETION-CODE-ARR.
133         REWRITE ACCOUNTS-RECEIVABLE-RECORD.
134         PERFORM 8000-READ-TRANSACTION-FILE.
135         PERFORM 4000-READ-ACCOUNTS-RECEIVABLE-FILE.
136     7000-ERROR-MESSAGE.
137         PERFORM 8000-READ-TRANSACTION-FILE.
138     8000-READ-TRANSACTION-FILE.
139         READ TRANSACTION-FILE
140             AT END
141                 MOVE 99999 TO ACCOUNT-NUMBER-TR.
142     9000-TERMINATION.
143         CLOSE TRANSACTION-FILE
144               ACCOUNTS-RECEIVABLE-FILE.
145         STOP RUN.
```

have some disadvantages. Eventually the file may become full of deleted records which will cause the file to take up too much space on the disk. Since any program processing the file must read (and ignore) deleted records as well as active records, the performance of the computing system for programs processing the file may be degraded. When a file becomes full of deleted records, it is necessary to create a second file which contains only active records and omits those that have been deleted. A backup of the old version of the file can be maintained (usually on tape) should it be necessary to access any of the records in the original version of the file.

9.12 DEBUG CLINIC

When writing programs dealing extensively with files, the programmer may be confronted with system error messages produced during execution of the program if an error is made. Failing to open the file prior to an input or output operation, attempting an input operation on a file opened in output mode; attempting a REWRITE operation when a file is not opened in I-O mode, and so forth, are a few examples of errors which will produce execution time error messages and cause termination of the program.

COBOL provides a way for the programmer to monitor the result of all input/output verbs. To make use of this facility a FILE STATUS clause is added to the SELECT entry as shown in Figure 9.8.

SELECT file-name
     ASSIGN TO system-name
     [FILE STATUS IS data-name.].   **Figure 9.8**   General form of the SELECT entry for sequential files

The data-name declared as a FILE STATUS item is automatically updated to show the result of each input/output operation related to the file. The FILE STATUS item must be two characters in length and must be defined in the DATA DIVISION. For example, to define a FILE STATUS item for ACCOUNTS-RECEIVABLE-FILE in Program 9.1, the SELECT entry (line 8) could be modified as:

```
SELECT ACCOUNTS-RECEIVABLE-FILE
    ASSIGN TO DISK
    FILE STATUS IS ACCOUNTS-RECEIVABLE-STATUS.
```

The field ACCOUNTS-RECEIVABLE-STATUS would be defined in WORKING-STORAGE as:

```
01  ACCOUNTS-RECEIVABLE-STATUS.
    02  AR-STATUS-1  PIC 9.
    02  AR-STATUS-2  PIC 9.
```

Defining the FILE STATUS item as a group item subdivided into two fields, each of length one, is useful because each digit of the FILE STATUS item is a code with a specified meaning (Fig. 9.9).

status key 1	status-key 2	Meaning
0	0	Successful completion
1	0	At end
3	0	Permanent error
3	4	Boundary Violation
9	—	Differs among compilers

Figure 9.12 Meaning of FILE STATUS codes for sequential files

For example, if the value of ACCOUNTS-RECEIVABLE-STATUS was ''00''
after an OPEN, READ or WRITE statement, the file was opened or a record was
read or written without incident. If the value of ACCOUNTS-RECEIVABLE-
STATUS was ''10'' after a READ, the end-of-file was encountered. The meaning
of other settings of the FILE STATUS item may differ among systems; the reader
should check with a COBOL system manual for his or her system. The FILE
STATUS item can be processed by a program as any other item; for example, it
can be tested as in:

IF ACCOUNTS-RECEIVABLE-STATUS NOT = "00"

The FILE STATUS item can be made a part of diagnostic output, as in:

```
READ ACCOUNTS-RECEIVABLE-FILE
    AT END MOVE 1 TO EOF-FLAG.
MOVE ACCOUNTS-RECEIVABLE-STATUS TO AR-STATUS-OUT
WRITE OUTPUT-LINE FROM DIAG-LINE AFTER 1.
```

The use of the FILE STATUS item in diagnostic output is particularly advantageous in debugging programs when system error messages are not specific
enough to enable determination of the error.

9.13 SELF TEST EXERCISES

1. What input/output statements are valid when a file is opened as INPUT, OUTPUT,
   I/O, and EXTEND?
2. Define each of the following terms
   a. IRG
   b. blocking
   c. label records
   d. track
   e. rewind
   f. key field
   g. audit trail
   h. file status
3. Are there any circumstances in which placement of a large value such as 99999 in a
   key field when end-of-file is reached would be invalid? How would the method be
   modified if the key field was alphanumeric?
4. Write the PROCEDURE DIVISION for a program required to merge three files: FILE-
   A, FILE-B, FILE-C with respective record key fields KEY-A, KEY-B, KEY-C The
   key fields are defined as PIC 9 (5) . The output file is NEW-FILE.

5. Consider the paragraph 6002-UPDATE of Program 9.8. What would happen if the value of AMOUNT-OWED-OMR became negative (i.e., the customer had a credit balance)? What could be done to avoid this problem?

6. Write code for the paragraph 7000-ERROR-IN-TRANSACTION in Program 9.2.

7. Modify Program 9.2 to allow records to be added, changed and deleted by the same program. What restrictions would be placed on the order of the transaction records?

8. Rewrite the paragraph 3000-CONTROL of Program 9.3 without using a nested IF statement.

9. Write the PROCEDURE DIVISION for a program to purge the file ACCOUNTS-

9.14 PROGRAMMING EXERCISES

1. Write a program to create a master file for the employees of the PCI Company, including name, social security number, hourly pay rate, number of dependents and year-to-date figures for gross salary. Use the following sample data:

Name	SS-Number	Rate	Dependents	YTD Gross
JAMES JONES	111-22-3333	7.00	3	$3500.00
John Smith	222-33-4444	9.50	2	$3800.00
Mary Doe	333-44-5555	8.00	1	$3200.00
Ed Black	444-55-6666	4.50	2	$1800.00
Susan Anthony	555-66-7777	10.00	0	$4000.00

Include a one-digit deletion code on each record with initial value zero.

2. Write a program to process data records containing social security number and number of hours worked. Using the file created above in Exercise 1, compute the gross pay (including time and one-half for overtime). Update the year-to-date gross pay field in the master file record. Produce a report showing action taken for each record including error messages where appropriate. Use the following sample data:

SS-Number	Hours Worked
222-33-4444	40
333-44-5555	50
444-44-4444	20
555-66-7777	10
666-77-8888	2

3. For the file of Exercise 1, write a program to update the file allowing changes or deletion. Use the codes shown below:

Code	Meaning
CN	change name
CR	change rate
CD	change number dependents
CY	change YTD Gross
D	Delete record

Use the following data:

Name	SS-Number	Rate	Dependents	YTD Gross	Code
	222-33-4444	10.00			CR
	222-33-4444		1		CD
Mary Smith	333-44-5555				CN
	333-44-5555			3400.00	CY
	444-44-4444	16.00			CR
	444-55-5555				D
	555-66-7777				D
	666-77-8888		2		CD
	777-88-9999				D

4. For the file of Exercise 1, write a program to merge new records into the file, creating a new master file. Use the following sample data:

Name	SS-Number	Rate	Dependents	YTD-Gross
Sam Spade	222-22-2222	17.00	0	$3500.00
Jim Jones	333-33-3333	8.00	1	$3800.00
Mary Alice	444-44-4444	9.00	3	$3200.00
Karen Oak	444-55-4444	8.00	1	$1800.00
Nancy Martin	666-77-8888	8.50	3	$4000.00

5. The XYZ Bank maintains a master accounts file with each record containing the following fields:

   Account number
   Name
   Address
   Balance at end of previous month
   Current balance

   Write a program to create this file.

6. The XYZ Bank processes each day's transactions by creating a sequential file and sorting it into order by account number. Records in the transaction file contain the following fields:

   Account number
   Transaction amount
   Date of transaction
   Type of transaction
   1 = Deposit
   2 = Other credit
   3 = Other debit
   4 = Check

   Write a program to process the transaction file and the master file described in Exercise 5 above to produce a new master file. Note that the previous month's balance is not changed by this program. If a check or debit causes the account to be overdrawn, write a message on the printer containing specifics of the account and the transaction causing the problem.

7. At the end of the month, all daily transaction files described in Exercise 6 are merged into one file and sorted by account number. The master file and the monthly transaction file are processed to produce statements showing specifics of the account, the previous balance, all transactions and the current balance. Write a program to perform this task. Your program should also produce a new master file showing a revised end-of-month balance. If the balance computed by this program does not equal the current balance contained on the old master file, write an appropriate error message.

8. Modify the program written for Exercise 7 above to institute a service charge for checks. If the lowest balance in the month is less than $100, there is a $.10 charge per check. If the balance is above $100 at all times, there is no charge for checks.

9. Create an inventory control system for use by ABC Furniture, Inc. Include in your design a master file and facilities for updating the master file. Management wishes to know the following facts about each item stocked:

Stock number	Supplier name
Description	Supplier address
Wholesale price	Reorder point
Retail price	Reorder amount
Number on hand	Date of last order
Number of order	Date of last sale

When the number on hand plus number on order falls below the reorder point, your system should automatically generate an order to replenish the stock. (Reorder amount refers to the number of items to be ordered at any one time.)

10. Create an accounts-receivable system for ABC Furniture, Inc. The master file should contain records having the following fields:

> Account number
> Name
> Address
> Balance due
> Date of last payment
> Date of last purchase

Transactions to be processed include payments and purchases. Your system should create monthly billings with a $1\frac{1}{2}\%$ service charge added to accounts which have a positive balance due and on which no payment or only a partial payment has been received in the last month.

11. The student academic records for XYZ College are to be processed to produce a dean's list (grade point average ≥ 3.7) and an honor roll ($3.7 >$ grade point average ≥ 3.5). Each record contains the following relevant data items:

> Student number
> Name
> Address
> Grade point average

Write one program to produce both reports.

12. For some purposes (e.g., for critical data in which completeness is a crucial factor), pages must be numbered in the following fashion:

Total number of pages in the report

PAGE XX OF XX PAGES

Current page number

The basic problem in producing this type of output is that the total number of pages must be known before the first page can be written. One approach to this problem is to process the input file(s) once to determine the number of pages and then to process the file(s) again to produce the final report. Try out this technique on any previously written program.

SORT AND PROCEDURE DIVISION SECTIONS 10

10.1 INTRODUCTION TO SORTING

A set of data items in either ascending sequence or descending sequence are said to be in *sorted* order. *Sorting* refers to the process of transforming unsorted data items into sorted order. For example, consider the data items:

$$16, 25, 90, 42, 70$$

They are neither in ascending sequence (each item smaller than its successor) nor in descending sequence (each item larger than its successor). If the data items were rearranged as

$$16, 25, 42, 70, 90$$

they would be sorted into ascending sequence. If the data items were rearranged as

$$90, 70, 42, 25, 16$$

they would be sorted into descending sequence.

In a data processing situation it is often desirable to have data records in some sequence based on one or more fields within the record. The field used for this sequencing is called the *key* field. For example, consider the following set of data records:

Employee Number	Name		Age	Department
123	DOE	JOHN	32	3
492	SMITH	MARY	40	4
479	JAMES	JOHN	19	4
333	QUE	SUSY	40	2
695	BROWN	JAMES	25	2

This data could be sorted into sequence in a number of different ways. Each of the four fields could be used individually as a key field. If the employee number is chosen as the key field and descending sequence is desired, the resulting set of data would be:

	Employee Number	Name		Age	Department
	695	BROWN	JAMES	25	2
Descending	492	SMITH	MARY	40	4
sequence	479	JAMES	JOHN	19	4
	333	QUE	SUSY	40	2
	123	DOE	JOHN	32	3

Using the name as the key field and sorting for ascending sequence would result in:

Employee Number		Name		Age	Department
695		BROWN	JAMES	25	2
123	Ascending	DOE	JOHN	32	3
479	sequence	JAMES	JOHN	19	4
333		QUE	SUSY	40	2
492		SMITH	MARY	40	4

It is possible to sort a file using more than one key field. For example, we might want a listing of the above data to be grouped by department number. Also, within each department, the data should be listed in ascending sequence based on employee name. In this case, the department number is called the *primary key* (or *major key*) and the name field is the *secondary key* (or *minor key*). The resulting data would be:

Employee Number		Name		Age	Department	
695		BROWN	JAMES	25	2	
333	Ascending	QUE	SUSY	40	2	Ascending
123	sequences	DOE	JOHN	32	3	sequence
479	(three)	JAMES	JOHN	19	4	
492		SMITH	MARY	40	4	

Many other combinations using two or more key fields could conceivably be of value depending on the logical requirements of the problem being solved.

The COBOL programmer may make use of the COBOL SORT feature in order to sort a file on one or more key fields into any desired sequence. The SORT statement is used in the PROCEDURE division. It specifies the source of the records to be sorted, the key field(s), the sequencing desired (ascending or descending), the destination for the sorted records and the name of a *sort work-file* which will be used by the computing system in the performance of the sort. Setting up the sort work-file must be done in the ENVIRONMENT and DATA division in preparation for utilization of the SORT statement in the PROCEDURE division.

10.2   THE SORT WORK-FILE

A sequential disk file is required as a sort work-file for utilization of the COBOL SORT command. First, the SORT statement causes records to be read from some source file and copied into the sort work-file. Second, the records are sorted and then, third, copied from the sort work-file into some specified destination. Setting up the sort work-file requires a SELECT sentence in the ENVIRONMENT divi-

```
SD    file-name
      [RECORD  CONTAINS [integer-1 TO] integer-2 CHARACTERS

      ┌           ⎧ RECORD  IS   ⎫                      ┐
      │ DATA      ⎨              ⎬   data-name . . .    │  .
      ⎣           ⎩ RECORDS  ARE ⎭                      ⎦
```

Figure 10.1   General form of the SD entry

sion for the file in exactly the same manner as for any other file. The description
of the file in the DATA division requires the use of an SD (Sort Description) rather
than an FD entry. The general form for an SD entry is shown in Figure 10.1.

The file description used in an SD entry is much the same as an FD entry.
The record described for the sort work-file must contain data-names for any
desired key fields. For example, the required files for sorting the data in the
preceding example could be as follows:

```
ENVIRONMENT DIVISION
        .
        .
        .
        SELECT DATA-FILE ASSING TO DISK.
        SELECT SORT-WORK-FILE ASSIGN TO SORT DISK.
        SELECT SORTED-EMPLOYEE-FILE ASSIGN TO DISK.
        .
        .
        .
DATA DIVISION.
FILE SECTION.
FD   DATA-FILE.
        DATA RECORD IS DATA-RECORD.
01   DATA-RECORD.
        02   EMP-NUM-DR     PIC 999.
        02   EMP-NAME-DR    PIC X(20).
        02   EMP-AGE-DR     PIC 99.
        02   EMP-DEPT-DR    PIC 9.
        02   FILLER         PIC X(54).
SD   SORT-WORK-FILE
        DATA-RECORD IS SORT-WORK-RECORD.
01   SORT-WORK-RECORD.
        02   EMP-NUM-SWR    PIC 999.
        02   EMP-NAME-SWR   PIC X(20).
        02   EMP-AGE-SWR    PIC 99.
        02   EMP-DEPT-SWR   PIC 9.
        02   FILLER         PIC X(54).
FD   SORTED-EMPLOYEE-FILE
        DATA-RECORD IS SORTED-EMPLOYEE-RECORD.
01   SORTED-EMPLOYEE-RECORD.
        02   EMP-NUM-SER    PIC 999.
        02   EMP-NAME-SER   PIC X(20).
        02   EMP-AGE-SER    PIC 99.
        02   EMP-DEPT-SER   PIC 9.
        02   FILLER         PIC X(54).
```

10.3   THE SORT STATEMENT

The SORT statement is used in the PROCEDURE division to activate the sort procedure. A general form for the SORT statement is shown in Figure 10.2.

```
SORT    sort-work-file-name

     {      { ASCENDING  }                          }
     { ON   { DESCENDING } KEY key-field-name . . . }  . . .

              USING input-file-name . . .
              GIVING output-file-name.
```

Figure 10.2   General form of SORT with USING and GIVING

The *sort-work-file-name* must be specified in an SD entry in the DATA DIVISION. The ON. . .KEY clause gives the programmer the choice of specifying ASCENDING sequence or DESCENDING sequence for the records. The *key-field-name(s)* must be defined within the record associated with the sort work-file. If more than one key field is specified, the first field is the primary key and the following fields are secondary keys. The USING clause specifies the destination of the sorted data records. In execution, the SORT command performs the following three functions in sequential order:

1) Read the file or files specified in the USING clause and place the records in the sort work-file.
2) Sort the sort work-file on the specified key field(s).
3) Copy the sorted records from the sort work-file into the file specified in the GIVING clause.

For example, the following code could be used to sort the data defined above into alphabetic sequence by name:

```
SORT    SORT-WORK-FILE
        ON ASCENDING KEY EMP-NAME-SWR
        USING DATA-FILE
        GIVING SORTED-EMPLOYEE-FILE.
```

To sort the records into ascending alphabetic sequence within departments, the following code could be used:

```
SORT    SORT-WORK-FILE
        ON ASCENDING KEY EMP-NAME-SWR   EMP-NAME-SWR
        USING SORTED-EMPLOYEE-FILE
        GIVING SORTED-EMPLOYEE-FILE.
```

In this example the department number is declared to be the primary key and the employee's name is a secondary key. As many secondary keys as desired may be specified. Furthermore, it is possible to include as many ON. . .KEY clauses as desired. For example, suppose we want to sort the data into descending sequence by age within ascending department number sequence. In this example the arrangement of the data desired is:

Employee Number	Name	Age		Department	
333	QUE SUSY	40	Descending	2	Ascending
695	BROWN JAMES	25	sequence	2	sequence
123	DOE JOHN	53		3	
492	SMITH MARY	40	Descending	4	
497	JAMES JOHN	19	sequence	4	

The required code is:

```
SORT    SORT-WORK-FILE
        ON ASCENDING KEY EMP-DEPT-SWR
        ON DESCENDING KEY EMP-AGE-SWR
        USING SORTED-EMPLOYEE-FILE
        GIVING SORTED-EMPLOYEE-FILE.
```

The sequence of clauses governs the sequence of keys — primary to secondary.

It is possible to sort more than one file with the same SORT statement. For example, to sort DATA-FILE and NEW-DATA-FILE into ascending sequence by employee number, the following statement could be used:

```
SORT    SORT-WORK-FILE
        ON ASCENDING KEY EMPLOYEE-NUM-SWR
        USING DATA-FILE NEW-DATE-FILE
        GIVING SORTED-EMPLOYEE-FILE.
```

This statement would have the effect of merging the records from the two input files into one output file. This facility can be used to add records to an existing file while preserving the sequencing of the records.

For example, to add the records contained in NEW-DATA-FILE to those contained in SORTED-EMPLOYEE-FILE, the following statement could be used:

```
SORT    SORT-WORK-FILE
        ON ASCENDING KEY EMPLOYEE-NUM-SWR
        USING SORTED-EMPLOYEE-FILE NEW-DATE-FILE
        GIVING SORTED-EMPLOYEE-FILE.
```

The new version of SORTED-EMPLOYEE-FILE will contain all of the records from the old version plus all of the records from NEW-DATA-FILE and will be in sequence by employee number.

10.4   A COMPLETE EXAMPLE

The library of XYZ College throws away outdated and mutilated books at the end of each semester. Two lists of the discarded books are required. One list, for use by the catalog department of the library, must be in ascending sequence based on LCC (Library of Congress Card Catalog) call number. Another list, for the auditor, should be in ascending sequence based on the item number. Program 10.1 could be used to produce both reports.

The input file INFD is read and copied onto the file BOOK-FILE (lines 123 through 127). The paragraph 6000-SORT-BY-LCC-NUMBER (lines 128 through 132) is then performed (line 100) to sort BOOK-FILE by call number. When this is completed, the paragraph 7000-WRITE (lines 138 through 153) is performed to produce the first required report. The file BOOK-FILE is then sorted into

Program 10.1 SORT program with USING and GIVING

```
Line
1         IDENTIFICATION DIVISION.
2         PROGRAM-ID.  CHAPTER 10 EXAMPLE 1.
3         AUTHOR.  GARY GLEASON.
4         ENVIRONMENT DIVISION.
5         INPUT-OUTPUT SECTION.
6         FILE-CONTROL.
7             SELECT INFD ASSIGN TO READER.
8             SELECT BOOK-FILE ASSIGN TO DISK.
9             SELECT SORT-FILE ASSIGN TO SORT DISK.
10            SELECT PRINT ASSIGN TO PRINTER.
11        DATA DIVISION.
12        FILE SECTION.
13        FD  INFD
14            DATA RECORD IS INPUT-RECORD.
15        01   INPUT-RECORD.
16             02   CALL-NUMBER-IR    PIC 9(20).
17             02   AUTHOR-IR         PIC X(15).
18             02   TITLE-IR          PIC X(28).
19             02   DATE-IR           PIC X(2).
20             02   ITEM-NUMBER-IR    PIC X(8).
21             02   PRICE-IR          PIC X(6).
22             02   DISCARD-CODE-IR   PIC X.
23        FD  BOOK-FILE
24            DATA RECORD IS BOOK-RECORD.
25        01  BOOK-RECORD.
26             02   CALL-NUMBER-BR    PIC 9(20).
27             02   AUTHOR-BR         PIC X(15).
28             02   TITLE-BR          PIC X(28).
29             02   DATE-BR           PIC X(2).
30             02   ITEM-NUMBER-BR    PIC X(8).
31             02   PRICE-BR          PIC X(6).
32             02   DISCARD-CODE-BR   PIC X.
33        SD  SORT-FILE
34            DATA RECORD IS SORT-RECORD.
35        01  SORT-RECORD.
36             02   CALL-NUMBER-SR    PIC 9(20).
37             02   AUTHOR-SR         PIC X(15).
38             02   TITLE-SR          PIC X(28).
39             02   DATE-SR           PIC X(2).
40             02   ITEM-NUMBER-SR    PIC X(8).
41             02   PRICE-SR          PIC X(6).
42             02   DISCARD-CODE-SR   PIC X.
43        FD  PRINT
44            DATA RECORD IS PRINT-LINE.
45        01  PRINT-LINE              PIC X(132).
46        WORKING-STORAGE SECTION.
47        01  EOF-FLAG               PIC 9      VALUE ZERO.
48        01  KOUNT                  PIC 9(4)   VALUE ZERO.
49        01  N                      PIC 9(4)   VALUE ZERO.
50        01  MY-LINE-COUNTER        PIC 99     VALUE ZERO.
51        01  CALL-NUMBER-HEADING.
```

(continued)

Program 10.1   (continued)

```
52              02  FILLER              PIC X(40) VALUE SPACES.
53              02  FILLER              PIC X(19) VALUE "LIST BY CALL NUMBER".
54              02  FILLER              PIC X(85) VALUE SPACES.
55          01  ITEM-NUMBER-HEADING.
56              02  FILLER              PIC X(40) VALUE SPACES.
57              02  FILLER              PIC X(19) VALUE "LIST BY ITEM NUMBER".
58              02  FILLER              PIC X(85) VALUE SPACES.
59          01  SUBHEADING.
60              02  FILLER              PIC X(5)  VALUE SPACES.
61              02  FILLER              PIC X(11) VALUE "CALL NUMBER".
62              02  FILLER              PIC X(10) VALUE SPACES.
63              02  FILLER              PIC X(6)  VALUE "AUTHOR".
64              02  FILLER              PIC X(10) VALUE SPACES.
65              02  FILLER              PIC X(5)  VALUE "TITLE".
66              02  FILLER              PIC X(20) VALUE SPACES.
67              02  FILLER              PIC X(4)  VALUE "DATE".
68              02  FILLER              PIC X(5)  VALUE SPACES.
69              02  FILLER              PIC X(11) VALUE "ITEM NUMBER".
70              02  FILLER              PIC X(10) VALUE SPACES.
71              02  FILLER              PIC X(5)  VALUE "PRICE".
72              02  FILLER              PIC X(5)  VALUE SPACES.
73              02  FILLER              PIC X(12) VALUE "DISCARD CODE".
74          01  DETAIL-LINE.
75              02  CALL-NUMBER-DL   PIC X(20).
76              02  AUTHOR-DL        PIC X(15).
77              02  TITLE-DL         PIC X(28).
78              02  FILLER           PIC X(5)  VALUE SPACES.
79              02  DATE-DL          PIC X(2).
80              02  FILLER           PIC X(10) VALUE SPACES.
81              02  ITEM-NUMBER-DL   PIC X(8).
82              02  FILLER           PIC X(10) VALUE SPACES.
83              02  PRICE-DL         PIC X(6).
84              02  FILLER           PIC X(10) VALUE SPACES.
85              02  DISCARD-CODE-DL  PIC X.
86      PROCEDURE DIVISION.
87      1000-MAIN-LOGIC.
88          PERFORM 1200-CREATE-BATCH-FILE.
89          PERFORM 1400-REPORT-BY-LCC-NUMBER.
90          PERFORM 1600-REPORT-BY-ITEM-NUMBER.
91          PERFORM 9000-TERMINATION.
92      1200-CREATE-BATCH-FILE.
93          OPEN INPUT INFD.
94          OPEN OUTPUT BOOK-FILE.
95          READ INFD AT END MOVE 1 TO EOF-FLAG.
96          PERFORM 5000-BUILD-BOOK-FILE UNTIL EOF-FLAG = 1.
97          CLOSE INFD.
98          CLOSE BOOK-FILE.
99      1400-REPORT-BY-LCC-NUMBER.
100         PERFORM 6000-SORT-BY-LCC-NUMBER.
101         OPEN INPUT BOOK-FILE.
102         OPEN OUTPUT PRINT.
103         MOVE CALL-NUMBER-HEADING TO PRINT-LINE.
```

(continued)

```
104        WRITE PRINT-LINE AFTER PAGE.
105        MOVE 5 TO MY-LINE-COUNTER.
106        MOVE SUBHEADING TO PRINT-LINE.
107        WRITE PRINT-LINE AFTER 3.
108        READ BOOK-FILE AT END MOVE 1 TO EOF-FLAG.
109        PERFORM 7000-WRITE VARYING N FROM 1 BY 1 UNTIL N > KOUNT.
110        CLOSE BOOK-FILE.
111    1600-REPORT-BY-ITEM-NUMBER.
112        PERFORM 6200-SORT-BY-ITEM-NUMBER.
113        OPEN INPUT BOOK-FILE.
114        MOVE ITEM-NUMBER-HEADING TO PRINT-LINE.
115        WRITE PRINT-LINE AFTER PAGE.
116        MOVE 5 TO MY-LINE-COUNTER.
117        MOVE SUBHEADING TO PRINT-LINE.
118        WRITE PRINT-LINE AFTER 3.
119        READ BOOK-FILE AT END MOVE 1 TO EOF-FLAG.
120        PERFORM 7000-WRITE VARYING N FROM 1 BY 1 UNTIL N > KOUNT.
121        CLOSE BOOK-FILE.
122        CLOSE PRINT.
123    5000-BUILD-BOOK-FILE.
124        ADD 1 TO KOUNT.
125        MOVE INPUT-RECORD TO BOOK-RECORD.
126        WRITE BOOK-RECORD.
127        READ INFD AT END MOVE 1 TO EOF-FLAG.
128    6000-SORT-BY-LCC-NUMBER.
129        SORT SORT-FILE
130            ON ASCENDING KEY CALL-NUMBER-SR
131            USING BOOK-FILE
132            GIVING BOOK-FILE.
133    6200-SORT-BY-ITEM-NUMBER.
134        SORT SORT-FILE
135            ON ASCENDING KEY ITEM-NUMBER-SR
136            USING BOOK-FILE.
137            GIVING BOOK-FILE.
138    7000-WRITE.
139        MOVE CALL-NUMBER-BR   TO CALL-NUMBER-DL.
140        MOVE AUTHOR-BR        TO AUTHOR-DL.
141        MOVE TITLE-BR         TO TITLE-DL.
142        MOVE DATE-BR          TO DATE-DL.
143        MOVE ITEM-NUMBER-BR   TO ITEM-NUMBER-DL.
144        MOVE PRICE-BR         TO PRICE-DL.
145        MOVE DISCARD-CODE-BR TO DISCARD-CODE-DL.
146        MOVE DETAIL-LINE TO PRINT-LINE.
147        WRITE PRINT-LINE AFTER 2.
148        ADD 2 TO MY-LINE-COUNTER.
149        IF MY-LINE-COUNTER > 56
150            MOVE SUBHEADING TO PRINT-LINE
151            WRITE PRINT-LINE AFTER PAGE
152            MOVE 2 TO MY-LINE-COUNTER.
153        READ BOOK-FILE AT END MOVE 1 TO EOF-FLAG.
154    9000-TERMINATION.
155        STOP RUN.
```

LIST BY ITEM NUMBER

CALL NUMBER	AUTHOR	TITLE	DATE	ITEM NUMBER	PRICE	DISCARD CODE
HF5721.S251949	SAUNDERS, A.	EFFECTIVE BUSINESS ENGLISH	49	0000,930	6.95	1
HG16019K581949	KNIFFIN, W.H.	HOW TO USE YOUR BANK	49	0000,956		1
HF5721.S571957	SMART, W.	BUSINESS LETTERS	57	0001,009	4.95	1
HF5547.T251949	TAINTOR, S.	SECRETARY'S HANDBOOK	49	0002,029	GIFT	1
HB171.G15	GAMBS, J.S.	MAN, MONEY AND GOODS	52	0004,436	5.00	1
HF5549.G551952	GLOVER, J.	THE ADMINISTRATOR	52	0008,011		1
HE2751.F3	FARRINGTON, S.	RAILROADING THE MODERN WAY	51	0009,690	1.98	1
HG289.J58	JOESTEN, J.	GOLD TODAY	54	0009,743	1.00	1
HB171.635	SHOERMAN, H	PROMISES MEN LIVE BY	38	0013,087	2.00	1
HB171.P25	PATON, W.A.	SHIRTSLEEVE ECONOMICS	52	0013,265	4.50	1
E 188.B26	BARCK, O.T.	COLONIAL AMERICA	58	0014,294	7.50	1
RM216.P821950	PROUDFIT, F.T.	NUTRITION AND DIET THERAPY	50	0016,873		1
RM216.P82195OC.2	PROUDFIT, F.T.	NUTRITION AND DIET THERAPY	50	0016,879		1
HG161.C67	COOKE, H.J..	ROLE OF DEBT IN THE ECONOMY	61	0025,526	3.25	1
RD41	HARLOW, F.	AN ATLAS OF SURGERY	58	0028,538	10.00	1
RJ499.W44C.2	WEXLER, S.S.	STORY OF SANDY	55	0092,381		3
RT62.J41962	JENSEN, D.	PRACTICAL NURSING	62	0097,315		2

Figure 10.3 Sample output from Sort program

sequence by item number in the paragraph SORT-BY-ITEM-NUMBER (lines 133 through 137). When this is complete, 7000-WRITE again is performed to produce the second required report. Figure 10.3 shows sample output from this program.

10.5 PROCEDURE DIVISION **SECTIONS**

The SORT feature also provides a means by which a programmer can construct his/her own routines for storing the records to be sorted on the sort work-file (an INPUT PROCEDURE) and copying the sort records from the sort work-file (an OUTPUT PROCEDURE). The routine to be used in this fashion must be place in a separate PROCEDURE DIVISION section.

Up to this point the PROCEDURE DIVISION of a program has consisted only of a sequence of paragraphs and no mention has been made of sections in the PROCEDURE DIVISION. It is possible to segment a PROCEDURE DIVISION into named sections, each of which consists of one or more paragraphs. The paragraphs in a section usually are related in some way. For example, they all may be update routines for a particular file, or they may perform related computations, or they may constitute an input or output routine. It is the latter usage which is important when writing an INPUT PROCEDURE or OUTPUT PROCEDURE for a SORT verb. In order to segment paragraphs of a PROCEDURE DIVISION, each group of paragraphs must be preceded by a section header which has the general form:

section-name SECTION.

For example, suppose a PROCEDURE DIVISION is made up of the paragraphs 1100-MAIN-LOGIC, 2100-INITIALIZATION, 2200-CONTROL, 2300-TERMINATION, 3100-READFILE-A, and 3200-READ-FILE-B. The following code divides these paragraphs into three sections: 1000-MAIN, 2000-SECONDARY and 3000-INPUT-OUTPUT:

```
PROCEDURE DIVISION.
1000-MAIN SECTION.
1100-MAIN-LOGIC.
        .
        .
        .

2000-SECONDARY SECTION.
2100-INITIALIZATION.
        .
        .
        .

2200-CONTROL.
        .
        .
        .

2300-TERMINATION.
        .
        .
        .

3000-INPUT-OUTPUT SECTION.
3100-READ-FILE-A.
        .
        .
        .

3200-READ-FILE-B.
        .
        .
        .
```

Dividing a PROCEDURE DIVISION into sections in no way affects the logic of a program or the way in which statements within a program are executed. For example, a statement in one section may PERFORM a paragraph in another section; after execution of the last statement in the paragraph, control passes back to the PERFORM statement.

If a section is referenced in a PERFORM statement, the paragraphs of that section will be executed in succession and the program will return to the PER-FORM statement only after the last statement in the last paragraph of the section has been completed. For example, if the statement

PERFORM 3000-INPUT-OUTPUT

were executed in the above example, all of the statements in 3100-READ-FILE-A and 3200-READ-FILE-B would be executed in sequence. Only after both paragraphs have been completed will the program return to the statement following the PERFORM.

In the theory of structured programming, a *module* is defined to be a procedure which carries out a well-defined task and has a single entry point and a single exit. All of our programs thus far have been composed of single paragraph modules. Each paragraph carried out a (hopefully) well-defined function; execution of each paragraph began at its first statement and continued through its last. Dividing a PROCEDURE DIVISION into sections enables us to construct modules consisting of more than one paragraph; the module begins with the first statement of the first paragraph and concludes with the last statement of the last paragraph. It is often advantageous to build multiparagraph modules because each individual paragraph still is usable as a single paragraph module. For example, in the above program it is still possible to use statements such as PERFORM 3100-READ-FILE-A or PERFORM 3200-READ-FILE-B; in either case control returns to the PERFORM statement when the paragraph has been completed.

The programmer must exercise caution when writing sections containing several paragraphs. If the entire section is performed when the first paragraph of the section is complete control passes to the next paragraph, and so on. Only by branching to the last paragraph in the section can the module return control to the performing statement. This usually necessitates use of the GO TO statement.

10.6   THE GO TO STATEMENT

The general form of the GO TO statement is shown in Figure 10.4.

$$\underline{GO\ TO}\quad \begin{Bmatrix} \text{paragraph-name} \\ \text{section-name} \end{Bmatrix}$$

Figure 10.4   General form of the GO TO statement

When the GO TO statement is executed, an immediate branch is made to the specified paragraph/section. Control does not return automatically at the end of the execution of the paragraph/section as it does when branching takes place via the PERFORM statement. The GO TO statement causes an unconditional branch with *no* provision for return; the PERFORM statement causes an unconditional branch *with* provision for return.

Unstructured programs frequently use GO TO statements. Structured programs also use the GO TO statement in a more restricted and disciplined fashion. A primary usage of the GO TO statement in structured COBOL programming is to transfer control to the last paragraph in a multiparagraph section which has been performed. Typically the last paragraph contains the single statement EXIT and serves only to return control to the PERFORM statement. A typical situation is shown below:

```
        PERFORM 1000-ABC.◄──────   Return mechanism is inserted at the end
           .                       of section 1000-ABC by the PERFORM statement.
           .
           .
    1000-ABC SECTION.
    1010-PARA-A.
           .                       The first paragraph in the section controls
           .                       execution of the other paragraphs. At the
           .                       end of the control paragraph, branch to
        GO TO 1040-PARA-ABC-EXIT.  the last paragraph in the section.
    1020-PARA-B.
           .
           .
           .
    1030-PARA-C.
```

(continued)

```
            .
            .
            .
  1040-PARA-ABC-EXIT.              Return mechanism has been inserted here.
      EXIT.                        Branching to this paragraph causes
                                   control to return to PERFORM statement.
```

Other uses of the GO TO statement are discussed in chapter 11.

10.7   INPUT/OUTPUT **PROCEDURES**

A complete form of the SORT statement is shown in Figure 10.5.

```
SORT    sort-file-name

        {       { ASCENDING  }                        }
        { ON    {────────── } KEY  key-field-name ... }
        {       { DESCENDING }                        }


        { USING  input-file-name ...                 }
        { INPUT  PROCEDURE   IS  section-name=1       }


        { GIVING  output-file-name                    }
        { OUTPUT  PROCEDURE   IS  section-name=2       }
```

Figure 10.5   General form of the SORT verb

When the INPUT PROCEDURE option is used, the SORT procedure performs the specified INPUT PROCEDURE section prior to sorting the records in the sort work-file. It is the task of the section to store the desired records on the sort work-file. When the OUTPUT PROCEDURE option is used, the SORT procedure performs the specified OUTPUT PROCEDURE section after sorting the records in the sort work-file. The records in the sort work-file are available to the program for further processing in any desired fashion.

The RELEASE and RETURN statements are used, instead of ordinary WRITE and READ statements. The RELEASE statement has the general form shown in Figure 10.6.

```
RELEASE  sort-record-name [ FROM  data-name ] .
```

Figure 10.6   General form of the RELEASE statement

The RELEASE statement is used instead of a WRITE statement, and causes a record to be written onto the sort work-file.

The RETURN statement has the general form shown below (Fig. 10.7).

```
RETURN  sort-file-name [ INTO  data-name ]
        AT END  statement ...
```

Figure 10.7   General form of the RETURN statement

It is used instead of a READ statement. The RETURN statement causes a record to be read from a sort work-file. The statements in the AT END clause are executed when the end of the sort work-file is reached.

For example, the following code could be used to sort the employee data of section 10.1, on page 229, by employee number:

```
SORT    SORT-WORK-FILE
        ON ASCENDING KEY EMP-NUM-SWR
        INPUT PROCEDURE IS 2000-READ-AND-STORE-RECORDS
        GIVING SORTED-EMPLOYEE-FILE.
        .
        .
        .

2000-READ-AND-STORE-RECORDS SECTION.
2010-READ-STORE-CONTROL.
        OPEN INPUT DATA-FILE.
        READ DATA-FILE AT END MOVE 1 TO EOF.
        PERFORM 2020-RELEASE-AND-READ UNTIL EOF = 1.
        CLOSE DATA-FILE.
        GO TO 2030-READ-STORE-EXIT.
2020-RELEASE-AND-READ.
        RELEASE SORT-WORK-RECORD FROM DATA-RECORD.
        READ DATA-FILE AT END MOVE 1 TO EOF.
2030-READ-STORE-EXIT.
        EXIT.
```

Note that the INPUT PROCEDURE above is completely self-contained (i.e., it does not perform any paragraph outside the section). This conforms to a restriction on INPUT/OUTPUT PROCEDURES: An INPUT or OUTPUT PROCEDURE must not transfer control (via GO TO or PERFORM) to a point outside the procedure.

For the example above, the SORT verb causes the following sequence of tasks to be executed:

1) The section 2000-READ-AND-STORE-RECORDS is PERFORMed. At the end of the procedure control returns to the SORT verb.
2) The file SORT-WORK-FILE is sorted.
3) The content of SORT-WORK-FILE is copied onto SORTED-EMPLOYEE-FILE.

In this example, there seems to be no advantage to using the INPUT PROCEDURE option, since the USING option would have an identical effect. However, note that the logic contained in 2000-READ-AND-STORE-RECORDS could process the data contained on DATA-RECORD in any desired way. For example, a listing of the data could be produced, or fields within the data record could be verified, or any desired computations could be performed.

Suppose you want to print a listing of the records and to sort the records alphabetically by name within descending age sequence. Assuming that an appropriate PRINT file has been defined previously, the following code could be used:

```
SORT    SORT-WORK-FILE
        ON DESCENDING KEY EMP-AGE-SWR
        ON ASCENDING KEY EMP-NAM-SWR
        USING SORTED-EMPLOYEE-FILE
        OUTPUT PROCEDURE IS 4000-PRINT-FILE-LISTING.
        .
        .
        .
```

(continued)

```
4000-PRINT-FILE-LISTING SECTION.
4010-PRINT-LISTING-CONTROL.
    OPEN OUTPUT PRINT.
    RETURN SORT-WORK-FILE AT END MOVE 1 TO EOF-SWF.
    PERFORM 4020-WRITE-RETURN UNTIL EOF-SWF = 1.
    CLOSE PRINT.
    GO TO 4030-PRINT-LIST-EXIT.
4020-WRITE-RETURN.
    MOVE EMP-NUM-SWR TO EMP-NUM-PRINT.
    MOVE EMP-NAME-SWR TO EMP-NAME-PRINT.
    MOVE EMP-AGE-SWR TO EMP-AGE-PRINT.
    MOVE EMP-DEPT-SWR TO EMP-DEPT-PRINT.
    WRITE PRINT AFTER 1.
    RETURN SORT-WORK-FILE AT END MOVE 1 TO EOF-SWF.
4030-PRINT-LIST-EXIT.
    EXIT.
```

This code will cause the following sequence of events:

1) The content of SORTED-EMPLOYEE-FILE will be copied onto SORT-WORK-FILE.

2) The SORT-WORK-FILE will be sorted into prescribed sequence.

3) The section 4000-PRINT-FILE-LISTING will be executed. At the termination of this procedure, control passes to the statement following the SORT statement.

Of course, it is possible to specify both an INPUT PROCEDURE and an OUTPUT PROCEDURE in a SORT statement. An example of this code would be:

```
SORT    SORT-WORK-FILE
        ON ASCENDING KEY EMP-NAME-SWR
        INPUT PROCEDURE 2000-READ-AND-STORE-RECORD
        OUTPUT PROCEDURE 4000-PRINT-FILE-LISTING.
```

Note that in an INPUT/OUTPUT PROCEDURE it is necessary to OPEN the files from which data is to be read or onto which data is to be written, but it is *not* necessary to OPEN the sort work-file. The sort work-file *must not* be opened or closed. The operations are a built-in part of the SORT verb.

Example

Program 10.1 makes extensive use of the USING and GIVING options of the SORT verb. The program could be made somewhat more efficient by using the INPUT PROCEDURE and OUTPUT PROCEDURE options. Program 10.2 illustrates the revised approach to the problem. The two SORT statements in 1000-MAIN-LOGIC (lines 3 through 12) not only sort the data into the required sequence but also create the file BOOK-FILE (in the INPUT PROCEDURE 2000-BUILD-FILE, lines 13 through 26) and produce the required report (in the OUTPUT PROCEDURE 3000-REPORT, lines 27 through 52). Note that the OUTPUT PROCEDURE 3000-REPORT is utilized by both SORT statements. The procedure is self-contained; it opens the required files (line 33), takes care of page headings (lines 38 through 40) and processing the sort work-file until all data from it has been read (line 36); and when processing has been completed, it closes files it has used (line 52).

Program 10.2   Sort program with INPUT/OUTPUT PROCEDURE

```
1       PROCEDURE DIVISION.
2       1000-MAIN-CONTROL SECTION.
3       1010-MAIN-LOGIC.
4           SORT SORT-FILE
5                   ON ASCENDING KEY CALL-NUMBER-SR
6                   INPUT PROCEDURE IS 2000-BUILD-FILE
7                   OUTPUT PROCEDURE IS 3000-REPORT
8           SORT SORT-FILE
9                   ON ASCENDING KEY ITEM-NUMBER-SR
10                  USING BOOK-FILE
11                  OUTPUT PROCEDURE IS 3000-REPORT.
12          STOP RUN.
13      2000-BUILD-FILE SECTION.
14      2010-BUILD-CONTROL.
15          OPEN INPUT INFD
16                  OUTPUT BOOK-FILE.
17          READ INFD AT END MOVE 1 TO EOF-FLAG.
18          PERFORM 2020-RELEASE-READ UNTIL EOF-FLAG = 1.
19          CLOSE INFD BOOK-FILE.
20          GO TO 2030-BUILD-EXIT.
21      2020-RELEASE-READ.
22          RELEASE SORT-RECORD FROM INPUT-RECORD.
23          WRITE BOOK-RECORD FROM INPUT-RECORD.
24          READ INFD AT END MOVE 1 TO EOF-FLAG.
25      2030-BUILD-EXIT.
26          EXIT.
27      3000-REPORT SECTION.
28      3010-REPORT-CONTROL.
29          PERFORM 3020-INITIALIZATION.
30          PERFORM 3030-REPORT-BODY.
31          GOTO 3040-REPORT-TERMINATION.
32      3020-INITIALIZATION.
33          OPEN OUTPUT PRINT.
34          MOVE 0 TO EOF-FLAG.
35          MOVE 57 TO MY-LINE-COUNTER.
36          RETURN SORT-FILE AT END MOVE 1 TO EOF-FLAG.
37      3030-REPORT-BODY.
38          IF MY-LINE-COUNTER > 56
39              WRITE PRINT-LINE FROM SUBHEADING AFTER PAGE
40              MOVE 1 TO MY-LINE-COUNTER.
41          MOVE CALL-NUMBER-SR   TO CALL-NUMBER-DL.
42          MOVE AUTHOR-SR        TO AUTHOR-DL.
43          MOVE TITLE-SR         TO TITLE-DL.
44          MOVE DATE-SR          TO DATE-DL.
45          MOVE ITEM-NUMBER-SR   TO ITEM-NUMBER-DL.
46          MOVE PRICE-SR         TO PRICE-DL.
47          MOVE DISCARD-CODE-SR TO DISCARD-CODE-DL.
48          WRITE PRINT-LINE FROM DETAIL-LINE AFTER 2.
49          ADD 2 TO MY-LINE-COUNTER.
50          RETURN SORT-FILE AT END MOVE 1 TO EOF-FLAG.
51      3040-REPORT-TERMINATION.
52          CLOSE PRINT.
```

10.8   DEBUG CLINIC

The SORT verb and multiparagraph sections are very powerful features; however, there are a number of restrictions on their use. Failure to observe these restrictions will result in debugging problems. Some of the most common errors result from failure to observe the following rules:

1) *Sort work-files must not be opened or closed.* The SORT verb takes care of opening and closing the sort work-file. The OPEN and CLOSE statements are invalid for sort work-files.

2) *Use* RETURN *and* RELEASE *rather than* READ *and* WRITE *for a sort work-file.* Use of READ and WRITE verbs for a sort work-file is invalid. Use of RETURN and RELEASE for ordinary files is also invalid.

3) *Define the sort work-file with an* SD *rather than an* FD *entry.* A file defined with an FD entry cannot be used as a sort work-file.

4) *An* INPUT/OUTPUT PROCEDURE *cannot contain a* SORT *statement.* The SORT verb causes the execution of a specific routine; this routine cannot be asked to execute itself.

5) *A file used in* USING *or* GIVING *clause must not be open.* A file to be used in USING or GIVING must be closed at the time the SORT statement is executed. Of course, these files may be opened and processed in other parts of the program.

6) *A sort work-file must be assigned to disk.* There may be a special designation used in the system name used in the ASSIGN entry for a sort work-file. The reader must check local documentation for specific details.

7) *An* INPUT/OUTPUT PROCEDURE *may not reference a paragraph or section outside of the procedure.* INPUT/OUTPUT PROCEDUREs must be wholly self-contained sections; there must not be any PERFORM or GO TO statements which address paragraphs or sections external to the section being used to specify the INPUT/OUTPUT PROCEDURE.

8) *In order to exit a multiparagraph section branch to its last paragraph.* When a section is executed either with a PERFORM statement or SORT statement, the return mechanism is inserted following the last statement of the last paragraph of the section. The GO TO statement is used to branch from the controlling paragraph to the last paragraph to effect a return; omission of the GO TO statement will result in the sequential execution of the paragraphs in the section. Omission of the GO TO statement almost always will be an error, since the paragraphs which will be executed have already been performed under control of the first paragraph of the section.

9) *Use the* GO TO *statement only to branch to the last paragraph of a multiparagraph section.* Unrestricted use of the GO TO statement results in unstructured program modules. This usage of the GO TO is necessary to create a single entry/single exit module from a section which is composed of more than one paragraph.

10.9   SELF TEST EXERCISES

1. Draw structure diagrams for Programs 10.1 and 10.2. How will you handle multiparagraph sections? (Structure diagrams should reflect the relationships among program modules rather than paragraphs.)

2. List the actions taken by the paragraph 600-SORT-BY-LCC-NUMBER (lines 128 through 132) of Program 10.1.

3. List the actions taken by the SORT statements in lines 4 through 11 of Program 10.2.

4. Fill in the blanks:
   a. A sort work-file is defined in the FILE SECTION by a(n) _____.
   b. A field used to govern the sequence of records in a file is called a(n) _____.
   c. A primary difference between the GO TO and PERFORM statements is _____.
   d. A PROCEDURE DIVISION section is declared by _____.
   e. In structured programming a procedure which carries out a well defined task and has a single entry and a single exit is called a(n) _____.
   f. One permitted use to the GO TO statement is to _____.
   g. The equivalent of READ for a sort work-file is _____.
   h. The equivalent of WRITE for a sort work-file is _____.
   i. The EXIT statement is used as _____.
   j. Two statements which cannot be used in an INPUT/OUTPUT PROCEDURE are _____ and _____.
   k. In order to exit a multiparagraph section a program must _____.
   l. A sort work-file must be assigned to a(n) _____.

5. Modify Program 10.2 to include the major headings for each report.

6. Consider the following file descriptions:
```
   FILE SECTION.
   FD   DATA-FILE
        DATA RECORD IS DATA-RECORD.
   01   DATA-RECORD.
        03   SS-NUM-DR    PIC 9(9).
        03   NAME-DR      PIC X(20).
        03   ST-ADDR-DR   PIC X(S0).
        03   CITY-DR      PIC X(10).
        03   STATE-DR     PIC XX.
        03   ZIP-DR       PIC 9(5).
   SD   SORT-FILE
        DATA RECORD IS SORT-RECORD.
   01   SORT-RECORD.
        03   SS-NUM-SR    PIC 9(9).
        03   NAME-SR      PIC X(20).
        03   ST-ADDR-SR   PIC X(S0).
        03   CITY-SR      PIC X(10).
        03   STATE-SR     PIC XX.
        03   ZIP-SR       PIC 9(5).
```
Assume that DATA-FILE is assigned to DISK.
   a. Write a SORT statement to sort DATA-FILE into ascending sequence by social security number.
   b. Write a SORT statement to sort DATA-FILE into sequence by zip code, and within each zip code order the records alphabetically by name.

7. Add the following file description to those given in Exercise 6:
```
   FD   NEW-DATA-FILE
        DATA RECORD IS NEW-DATA-RECORD.
   01   NEW-DATA-RECORD.
        03   NAME-NDR      PIC X(20).
        03   SS-NUM-NDR    PIC X(20).
        03   ZIP-NDR       PIC 9(5).
        03   ST-ADDR-NDR   PIC X(20).
        03   CITY-NDR      PIC X(10).
        03   STATE-NDR     PIC XX.
```

Write a SORT statement to sort NEW-DATA-FILE into ascending sequence by state. *Place the sorted data in* DATA-FILE.

8. Write a SORT statement using the files defined in Exercises 6 and 7 to merge the content of DATA-FILE and NEW-DATA-FILE, placing the resulting file into DATA-FILE in descending sequence by zip code.

10.10 PROGRAMMING EXERCISES

1. The records in an employee file contain (among other items) the employee name, sex, date of birth and date of hire by a company. Write COBOL programs to produce these required reports:
    a. A list sorted by seniority.
    b. An alphabetic list of all employees over 60 years old.
    c. Separate list of men and women sorted in alphabetic order.
    d. A list of employees sorted into descending order by seniority (highest seniority first).
    e. Separate lists of men and women sorted into descending order by seniority.

2. The records of an inventory file contain the following items: product code, description, selling price, cost, number on hand. Write COBOL programs to:
    a. List the items sorted by product code.
    b. List the items which have a markup in excess of 20 percent, sorted by product code.
    c. List the "big ticket" items (selling price greater than $200) sorted by description.

3. Revise the program written for Section 9.15, Exercise 1 to create the master file sequenced by social security number. Use the following sample data:

Name	SS-Number	Rate	Dependents	YTD Gross
Ed Black	444-55-6666	4.50	2	1800.00
John Smith	222-33-4444	9.50	2	3300.00
Mary Doe	333-44-5555	8.00	1	3200.00
James Jones	111-22-3333	7.00	3	3500.00
Susan Anthony	555-66-7777	10.00	0	4000.00

4. Revise the program written for Section 9.15, Exercise 2, to sort the input file into sequence by social security number. Update the master file and produce the required report with an OUTPUT PROCEDURE. Use the following sample data:

SS-Number	Hours-worked
555-66-7777	10
333-44-5555	50
666-77-8888	2
444-44-4444	20
222-33-4444	40

5. Modify the program written for Section 9.15, Exercise 3, to sort the transactions into sequence before performing the update. Use the following sample data:

Name	SS-Number	Rate	Dependents	YTD-Gross	Code
	555-66-7777				D
	777-88-9999				D
	666-77-8888		2		CD
	222-33-4444	10.00			CR
Mary Smith	333-44-5555				CN
	222-33-4444		1		CD
	333-44-5555			3400.00	CY
	444-44-4444	16.00			CR
	444-55-5555				D

6. Modify the program written for Section 9.15, Exercise 4, to use the SORT to merge the two files. Use the following sample data:

Name	SS-Number	Rate	Dependents	YTD-Gross
Sam Spade	222-22-2222	17.00	0	0
Nancy Martin	666-77-8888	8.50	3	0
Karen Oak	444-55-4444	8.00	1	0
Jim Jones	333-44-5555	8.00	1	0
Mary Alice	444-44-4444	8.00	3	0

7. Revise the program written for Section 9.15, Exercise 3 to allow a code "A" for *add record to master file* in addition to the existing transaction codes. Use sample data from Exercises 5 and 6 above to test your program.

ADDITIONAL COBOL FEATURES 11

11.1 MULTIPLE TYPES OF INPUT RECORDS

In many instances there will be more than one type of data record format in a file to be processed. For example, suppose you wish to process a file containing records in the following two formats:

Name and Address Record

Positions	
1-9	Identifying number
10-25	Name
26-40	Street address
41-50	City
51-52	State
53-57	Zip Code
58	Record identification code (1)

Time Record

Positions	
1-9	Identifying number
10-15	Hours worked
16-21	Date
22-57	Blank
58	Record identification code (2)

When a file contains records having different formats, there must be some way for the program to determine which type of record has been read after a READ operation takes place. One way to accomplish this is to place a specific code in a field common to the two records. In the example above, position 58 is used as a record identification code field. This field has the value 1 on a name-and-address record and the value 2 on the time record.

It is possible to define the different types of input records in either the FILE section of the DATA division or in the WORKING-STORAGE section of the DATA division. Description of the records in the FILE section requires that all record descriptions be placed following the FD entry for the file, and that the names of the records be included in the DATA RECORDS clause of the FD entry. For example, the following code could be used for the preceding data file:

```
FD   DATA-FILE
     DATA RECORDS ARE NAME-ADDRESS-RECORD, TIME-RECORD.
01   NAME-ADDRESS-RECORD.
       03   ID-NUM-NAR        PIC 9(9).
       03   NAME-NAR          PIC X(16).
       03   STREET-ADR-NAR    PIC X(15).
       03   CITY-NAR          PIC X(10).
       03   STATE-NAR         PIC X(2).
       03   ZIP-NAR           PIC 9(5).
       03   REC-ID-NAR        PIC 9.
01   TIME-RECORD.
       03   ID-NUM-TR         PIC 9(9).
       03   HOURS-TR          PIC 9(4)V99.
       03   DATE-TR           PIC 9(6).
       03   FILLER            PIC X(37).
       03   REC-ID-TR         PIC 9.
```

Note that there is only one area in memory allocated for the data record for a given file regardless of the number of data records declared for the file. The data record area for this file may be visualized as:

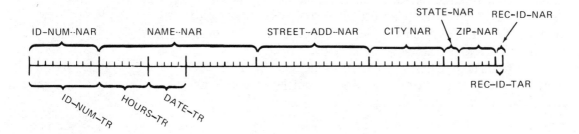

When a file is read, the content of a data record is placed in the memory locations allocated as the data record area for that file. The program may then choose to use any of the descriptions of that record which have been specified. For example, if the record is a name-and-address record, then the fields NAME-NAR, STREET-ADR-NAR, CITY-NAR and so on would be processed. However, if the record is a time record, the fields HOURS-TR and DATE-TR would be processed.

The program must decide which of the data descriptions is appropriate for this record. In our example, the decision can be made based on the content of REC-ID-NAR or REC-ID-TR, since these names describe the same field on the record. The following code could be used to make this decision:

```
PROCESS-DATA-READ.
    IF REC-ID-NAR = 1
        PERFORM PROCESS-NAME-ADDRESS-RECORD
    ELSE
        PERFORM DATA-RECORD-ERROR.
    READ DATA-FILE AT END MOVE 1 TO EOF-FLAG.
```

Since there is only one memory area allocated to the data record, the content of all of the fields will change each time a new record is read, since data from the new record replaces the data from the previous record. Suppose, for example, that the first record is a name-and-address record and the second record is a time record. The content of the fields NAME-NAR, STREET-ADD-NAR, CITY-NAR, and so forth will change when the second record is read, since characters from the second record now occupy the locations in the data record as read. This will cause no inconvenience if the data from the name-and-address record is moved immediately to another location when the program determines that name-and-address record has been read. In the above example, the content of the paragraph PROCESS-NAME-ADDRESS-RECORD could be as follows:

```
PROCESS-NAME-ADDRESS-RECORD.
    MOVE  ID-NUM-NAR TO ID-NUM-HOLD.
    MOVE  NAME-NAR TO NAME-HOLD.
    MOVE  STREET-ADR-NAR TO STREET-ADR-HOLD.
    MOVE  CITY-NAR TO CITY-HOLD.
    MOVE  STATE-NAR TO STATE-HOLD.
    MOVE  ZIP-NAR TO ZIP-HOLD.
    .
    .
    .
```

The fields with suffix ''HOLD'' would, of course, be defined in the WORKING STORAGE section.

When there are a great many record types, moving fields to different locations can become a nuisance. As an alternative, multiple records may be described in the WORKING STORAGE section. Using this technique, a minimal description of the record is made in the FILE section; the only field which needs to be specified is the record identification field. Detailed description of the records is given in the WORKING-STORAGE section.

When a record is read, the contents are moved to the appropriate location based on the record identification. For the previous example, this technique could be implemented by the following code:

```
DATA DIVISION.
FILE SECTION.
FD DATA-FILE
    DATA RECORD ID DATA-RECORD.
01  DATA-RECORD.
    03  FILLER       PIC X(79).
    03  RECORD-ID    PIC 9.
WORKING-STORAGE SECTION.

    .
    .
    .

01  NAME-ADDRESS-RECORD.
    03  ID-NUM-NAR        PIC 9(9).
    03  NAME-NAR          PIC X(16).
    03  STREET-ADR-NAR    PIC X(15).
    03  CITY-NAR          PIC X(10).
    03  STATE-NAR         PIC X(2).
    03  ZIP-NAR           PIC 9(9).
01  TIME-RECORD.
    03  ID-NUM-TR         PIC 9(9).
    03  HOURS-TR          PIC 9(4)V99.
    03  DATE-TR           PIC 9(6).
PROCEDURE DIVISION.
1000-MAIN-ROUTINE.
    .
    .
```

```
        .
     READ DATA-FILE AT END MOVE 1 TO EOF-FLAG
     PERFORM 2010-PROCESS-DATA-READ UNTIL EOF-FLAG = 1.
        .

        .

        .
  2010-PROCESS-DATA-READ.
     IF RECORD-ID = 1
        MOVE DATA-RECORD TO NAME-ADDRESS-RECORD
        PERFORM PROCESS-NAME-ADDRESS-RECORD
     ELSE
        IF RECORD-ID = 2
           MOVE DATA-RECORD TO TIME-RECORD
           PERFORM PROCESS-TIME-RECORD
        ELSE
           PERFORM DATA-RECORD-ERROR.
     READ DATA-FILE AT END MOVE 1 TO EOF-FLAG.
```

One advantage to the preceding method is that the contents of NAME-ADDRESS-RECORD are changed only when a new record of the same type is read; a disadvantage is the necessity of allocating memory locations in addition to the record area required for the file. If records are lengthy and/or there are many different types of records in the file, this excess memory requirement may be a significant factor, particularly in systems with limited memory available.

11.2   ADDITIONAL OUTPUT TECHNIQUES

The WRITE statement for the printer has some powerful options which were not discussed in the earlier chapter. A general form of the WRITE statement is shown in Figure 11.1.

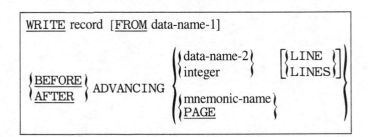

Figure 11.1   General form of the WRITE statement for the printer

We already have discussed and illustrated the use of the *integer* and PAGE options. The use of a *data-name-2* in the BEFORE/AFTER clause will cause the system to advance a number of lines equal to the value of *data-name-2*. For example, the code

```
MOVE 3 TO SPACING-COUNT.
WRITE PRINT-REC AFTER ADVANCING SPACING-COUNT.
```

is equivalent to:

```
        WRITE PRINT-REC AFTER ADVANCING 3.
```

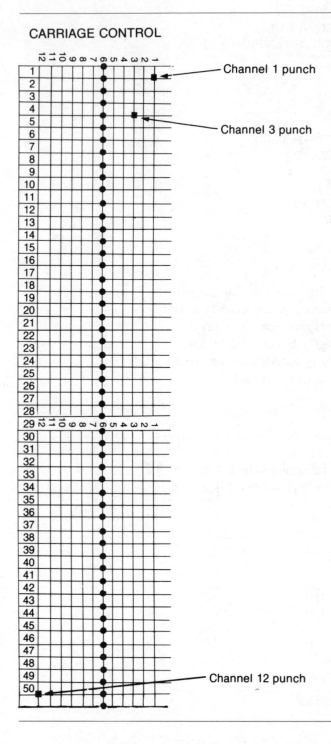

CARRIAGE CONTROL

Channel 1 punch

Channel 3 punch

Channel 12 punch

Figure 11.2 Carriage control tape

The use of a variable in the BEFORE/AFTER clause gives the program considerable flexibility in the spacing of output lines without requiring extra output statements.

The flow of paper through a printer is controlled by a carriage control tape (Fig. 11.2). A carriage control tape is glued into a continuous loop and placed inside the printer mechanism, where a special device senses holes punched in various positions of the tape. A carriage control tape is divided into twelve channels. A hole punched in channel 1 typically denotes the top of a page of print; a hole punched in channel 12 denotes the bottom of a page. Typically, other channels are punched to correspond to positions on special preprinted forms (such as checks, invoices or statements) that will be used for output operations. When the PAGE option is used, the printer begins spacing paper forward until the first channel punch is sensed on the carriage control tape.

Using the mnemonic option in the BEFORE/AFTER clause, the program can execute an advance to any desired channel punch. The mnemonic must be declared in the SPECIAL NAMES paragraph of the ENVIRONMENT division. The general form of this paragraph is shown in Figure 11.3.

SPECIAL-NAMES.
     function-name IS mnemonic-name ...

Figure 11.3 General form of the SPECIAL NAMES entry

The purpose of the *mnemonic-name* is to assign a meaningful name to the technical function to be performed. Mnemonic-names are governed by the same rules as other COBOL data-names; however, mnemonic-names should be as descriptive as possible of the function to be performed. Typical mnemonic-names would be:

```
TOP-OF-PAGE
BOTTOM-OF-PAGE
BEGINNING-OF-INVOICE-ITEMS
```

The exact form taken by function names varies somewhat from one system to another. The following form is quite common:

Function-name	Meaning
C01	channel 1
C02	channel 2
C03	channel 3
.	.
.	.
.	.
C12	channel 12

For example, in order to associate the mnemonic TO-TOP-OF-PAGE with a channel 1 punch, TO-BEGINNING-OF-ADDRESS with channel 3, and TO-BOTTOM-OF-PAGE with channel 12, the following SPECIAL-NAMES entry would be used:

```
SPECIAL-NAMES.
    C01  IS TO-TOP-OF-PAGE.
    C03  IS TO-BEGINNING-OF-ADDRESS.
    C12  IS TO-BOTTOM-OF-PAGE.
```

The following WRITE statement then could be used to write a record at the top of a page:

```
WRITE PRINT-REC AFTER ADVANCING TO-TOP-OF-PAGE.
```

A skip to channel 1 will be executed by the above sentence before writing commences. In order to place a record in the portion of the page designated by the channel 3 punch, the following `WRITE` statement would be used:

```
WRITE PRINT-REC AFTER ADVANCING TO-BEGINNING-OF-ADDRESS.
```

A skip to channel 3 will be executed by the above sentence before writing commences.

WARNING! Don't rush to your computer center to try out this useful output feature. Find out first if your printer has a carriage control tape, and if so what is on that tape. If a programmer executes a skip to a channel which has no corresponding punch on whatever carriage control tape happens to be mounted when the program is executed, the result may be "run away" paper. That is, paper will be ejected continuously while the printer is searching the specific carriage control tape for the control punch. For this reason the use of this feature is not encouraged in most student oriented computing environments, though it can be quite valuable to the professional programmer.

11.3 QUALIFICATION AND THE MOVE CORRESPONDING STATEMENTS

In most COBOL programs, essentially identical data items are defined in a number of different places. For example, data items may be defined on both an input record and an output record. Data must be moved from the input record to the output record one item at a time. Names for data items are uniquely defined by using prefixes or suffixes. The following coding illustrates the usual procedure for handling this situation:

```
DATA DIVISION.
FILE SECTION.
FD   DATA-FILE
     DATA RECORD IS DATA-RECORD.
01   DATA-RECORD.
     03   NAME-DR      PIC X(20).
     03   ADDRESS-DR   PIC X(25).
FD   REPORT-FILE
     DATA RECORD IS PRINT-LINE.
01   PRINT-LINE.
     03   FILLER       PIC X.
     03   NAME-PL      PIC X(20).
     03   FILLER       PIC X(4).
     03   ADDRESS-PL   PIC X(25).
     03   FILLER       PIC X(83).
PROCEDURE DIVISION.
          .
          .
          .
MOVE-AND-WRITE-ROUTINE.
     MOVE SPACES TO PRINT-LINE.
     MOVE NAME-DR TO NAME-PL.
     MOVE ADDRESS-DR TO ADDRESS-PL.
     WRITE PRINT-LINE AFTER 1.
```

It is possible, however, to use the same data-name in more than one data definition specification in the DATA division. For example, the following code is valid:

```
DATA DIVISION.
FILE SECTION.
FD   DATA-FILE
     DATA RECORD IS DATA-RECORD.
01   DATA-RECORD.
     03   NAME          PIC X(20).
     03   ADDRESS       PIC X(25).
FD   REPORT-FILE
     DATA RECORD IS PRINT-LINE.
01   PRINT-LINE.
     03   FILLER        PIC X.
     03   NAME          PIC X(20).
     03   FILLER        PIC X(4).
     03   ADDRESS       PIC X(25).
```

To process a data item which has been defined in more than one place, it is necessary to use qualification (i.e., to specify the group item in which the specific item occurs). The general form for qualification of a data-name is given in Figure 11.4.

$$\text{data-name-1} \left[\left\{ \begin{matrix} \underline{\text{IN}} \\ \underline{\text{OF}} \end{matrix} \right\} \text{data-name-2} \right]$$

Figure 11.4   General form of qualification

The use of IN or OF for qualification is purely a matter of personal taste. For example, the data movement operation in our preceding example could be accomplished with:

```
MOVE NAME IN DATA-RECORD TO NAME IN PRINT-LINE.
MOVE ADDRESS OF DATA-RECORD TO ADDRESS OF PRINT-LINE.
```

When several data items with like names must be moved, the MOVE CORRESPONDING statement is useful (Fig. 11.5).

MOVE [CORRESPONDING] data -name-1 TO data-name-2 ...

Figure 11.5   General form of the MOVE

Data items with like names in both records will be moved from *data-name-1* to *data-name-2*. For example, NAME and ADDRESS both could be moved by the coding

```
MOVE CORRESPONDING DATA-RECORD TO PRINT-LINE.
```

which is equivalent to the following:

```
MOVE NAME IN DATA-RECORD TO NAME IN PRINT-LINE.
MOVE ADDRESS IN DATA-RECORD TO ADDRESS IN PRINT-LINE.
```

There is one possible disadvantage to using like names in more than one record. When like names are used, it is necessary to use the qualification statement any time these data names are used in the program. Thus, the statement

MOVE NAME TO NAME-TR.

would have to be rewritten as

MOVE NAME IN DATA-RECORD TO NAME-TR.

or as

MOVE NAME IN PRINT-LINE TO NAME-TR.

11.4 PERFORM/THRU STATEMENT

Any version of the PERFORM statement may use a THRU clause to specify that a number of paragraphs are to be executed. This statement allows the programmer to construct program *modules* made up of two or more paragraphs. Without the THRU option, a program module is equivalent to a single paragraph or section. The general form of the PERFORM/THRU is shown in Figure 11.6.

PERFORM paragraph-1 [THRU paragraph-2].

Figure 11.6   General form of the PERFORM/THRU statement

All of the paragraphs from *paragraph-1* thru *paragraph-2* will be executed. Return to the PERFORM statement will be made only at the conclusion of *paragraph-2*. The THRU option may be used on any format of the PERFORM statement.

Example

```
PERFORM 4000-INPUT PROCEDURE
    THRU 5000-OUTPUT-PROCEDURE UNTIL END-OF-FILE.

PERFORM 2000-COMP THRU 2010-COMP-EXIT
    VARYING K FROM 10 BY 1 UNTIL K > 17.
```

A group of paragraphs used in this fashion is the logical equivalent of a PROCEDURE DIVISION section described in Chapter 10. Since control does not return automatically to the PERFORM statement at the end of the first paragraph in the series, it usually is necessary to use the GO TO statement to branch to the last paragraph in the module in order to terminate execution of the module.

11.5 ADDITIONAL USES OF THE GO TO STATEMENT

When the GO TO statement is executed, an immediate branch is made to the specified paragraph/section. Control does not automatically return at the end of the paragraph/section, but goes to where the paragraph/section directs. The GO TO statement can handle error conditions as they are encountered. Note the following illustration of a branch to an ERROR-EXIT paragraph:

```
        IF  ACCOUNT-NUM < ACCOUNT-NUM-HOLD
            GO  TO  9000-ERROR-EXIT.
        .
        .
        .
    9000-ERROR-EXIT.
        WRITE PRINT-LINE FROM ERROR-LINE AFTER 1.
        CLOSE DATA-FILE PRINT-FILE.
        STOP RUN.
```

In this case, the GO TO signals a branch to 9000-ERROR-EXIT and no return to the following statement will take place. The statement PERFORM 9000-ERROR-EXIT could be used in place of GO TO 9000-ERROR-EXIT. In general, the PERFORM statement implies that after the 9000-ERROR-EXIT paragraph is executed, the program will return to the statement following the PERFORM statement. Since this implication does not apply in this case (because 9000-ERROR-EXIT contains STOP RUN), the GO TO statement may be preferred over the PERFORM statement.

The GO TO statement also is allowed by some practitioners for tightly controlled loops. Most specifications for use of GO TO for this purpose state that the target of the GO TO must be "close" to the statement, and may require other restrictions on its use. For example, one might allow use of the GO TO but require that the target must be within the same program module. This would allow the following structure:

```
        PERFORM 4000-PARA THRU 4010-PARA-EXIT.
        .
        .
        .
    4000-PARA.
        .
        .
        .
        IF  CONDITION
            GO  TO  4000-PARA
        ELSE
            NEXT SENTENCE.
    4010-PARA-EXIT.
        EXIT.
```

4000-PARA will be executed repeatedly as long as CONDITION remains true. Note that 4000-PARA will be executed at least once. This logical sequence may closely represent the logic of a programming task, and thus may be a desirable structure.

At the present time, computer scientists disagree on the proper role for the GO TO statement in a structured programming environment. There are as yet no universally adopted standards. Some have prescribed the total nonuse of the GO TO, while others have adopted a position of allowing the GO TO for implementing selected structures in a disciplined fashion.

11.6 THE GO TO/DEPENDING STATEMENT

The GO TO/DEPENDING statement is useful for selecting among a number of actions, the execution of which depend upon the value of a variable. The general form of the statement is shown in Figure 11.7.

```
GO TO para-1, para-2, para-3,...,para-n DEPENDING ON data-name
```

Figure 11.7   General form of the GO TO/DEPENDING ON statement

If the value of the *data-name* is 1, the program will branch to *para-1*; if the value of *data-name* is 2, the program will branch to *para-2*; and so forth. If the value of *data-name* is outside the range 1 through n, the statement following the GO TO/DEPENDING statement will be executed.

Example

```
GO TO PARA-S, PARA-B, PARA-C
   DEPENDING ON CODE-X.
```

If CODE-X = 1, the program will branch to PARA-S. If CODE-X = 2, the program will branch to PARA-B. If CODE-X = 3, the program will branch to PARA-C. If CODE-X is any other value, the statement following the GO TO/DEPENDING will be executed. The logic is equivalent to the following IF statements:

```
IF CODE-X = 1
   GO TO PARA-S
ELSE
   IF CODE-X = 2
      GO TO PARA-B
   ELSE
      IF CODE-X = 3
         GO TO PARA-C
      ELSE
         NEXT SENTENCE.
```

The GO TO/DEPENDING statement may be preferred over the nested IF statement when there are a number of test values, and because it documents well the correspondence between the value of the variable and the action taken.

The following program segment will assign a bonus based on the value of   *Example*
BONUS-CODE as follows:

Value of BONUS-CODE	Bonus amount
1	$10
2	$30
3	$40

```
PERFORM 4000-BONUS-ROUTINE
   THRU 4050-BONUS-ROUTINE-EXIT.
   .
   .
   .

4000-BONUS-ROUTINE.
   GO TO 4020-BONUS-1, 4030-BONUS-2, 4040-BONUS-3
      DEPENDING ON BONUS-CODE.
4010-ERROR-IN-BONUS-CODE.
   MOVE 0 TO BONUS-AMOUNT.
   GO TO 4050-BONUS-ROUTINE-EXIT.
4020-BONUS-1.
   MOVE 10 TO BONUS-AMOUNT.
   GO TO 4050-BONUS-ROUTINE-EXIT.
```

```
4030-BONUS-2
    MOVE 30 TO BONUS-AMOUNT.
    GO TO 4050-BONUS-ROUTINE-EXIT.
4040-BONUS-3
    MOVE 40 TO BONUS-AMOUNT.
    GO TO 4050-BONUS-ROUTINE-EXIT.
4050-BONUS-ROUTINE-EXIT.
    EXIT.
```

The preceding coding illustrates a program module consisting of paragraphs from 4000-BONUS-ROUTINE through 4050-BONUS-ROUTINE-EXIT. Note that 4010-ERROR-IN-BONUS-CODE will be executed if the value of BONUS-CODE is not 1, 2 or 3. Use of the GO TO/DEPENDING statement generally requires the use of the GO TO for local branching (i.e., branching to points within the program module). Note that the paragraphs 4020-BONUS-1 and 4030-BONUS-2 require a GO TO statement as the last statement to avoid "falling through" and executing unwanted statements. The GO TO statement in 4040-BONUS-3 really is not necessary, since the next statement is in 4050-BONUS-ROUTINE-EXIT. However, it would be necessary if additional paragraphs representing actions to be taken for additional values of BONUS-CODE were inserted between 4040-BONUS-3 and 4050-BONUS-ROUTINE-EXIT.

11.7   DATA REPRESENTATION ON IBM SYSTEMS

In most computing systems more than one method for representing numeric data internally is used, and methods vary somewhat from system to system. In the discussion which follows, we shall restrict ourselves to a description of data representation used on IBM Systems 360/370/43xx/30xx.

Although it is usually not absolutely necessary for the COBOL programmer to be aware of the different forms of data representation, there are some instances in which this knowledge enables the programmer to write programs which either are more efficient or use less memory, or both. This knowledge also may be required to process files output by programs written in languages other than COBOL. On the IBM systems the following types of data representation are available:

Zoned decimal
Packed decimal
Binary
Single precision floating point
Double precision floating point

Zoned decimal data representation uses one byte (eight bits) to store each decimal digit. The first four bits for each byte are called the *zone* for the digit. The codes used are shown in Figure 11.8. Thus, a field containing three digits having value 370 would be represented as:

F3 | F7 | F0

The zone in the rightmost digit in the field is used to represent the sign. The fol-

Digit	Binary representation	Hexadecimal representation
	Zone ↓	Zone ↓
1	1111 0001	F1
2	1111 0010	F2
3	1111 0011	F3
4	1111 0100	F4
5	1111 0101	F5
6	1111 0110	F6
7	1111 0111	F7
8	1111 1000	F8
9	1111 1001	F9
0	1111 0000	F0

Figure 11.8   Representation of the zoned decimal data

lowing correspondence is used:

Zone	Meaning
F	unsigned (positive value)
C	signed positive
D	signed negative

For example, the value –23 would be represented as:

|F2|D3|

Packed decimal data representation uses each byte except the rightmost byte in the field to store *two* decimal digits. The rightmost four bits of the rightmost byte are used to store the sign using the codes described above. For example, the value 370 would be represented as:

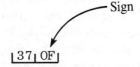

Note that the value 370, which requires three bytes when represented in zoned decimal, may be represented in just two bytes in packed decimal. The value of –23 would be represented as:

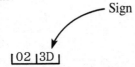

In general, values larger than two digits in length occupy fewer bytes when represented in packed decimal than in zoned decimal. When computation is performed on zoned decimal data, the data must be transformed into packed decimal form. This transformation, of course, takes a certain amount of time, a consideration which could become significant if a large volume of computations are to be performed.

Binary data representation utilizes straight binary numeration to represent values. Either 16, 32 or 64 bits may be used for the data item. For example, the value 370 would be represented in 16 bits as:

$$\lfloor 00000001 \mid 01110010 \rfloor$$

Binary data is used for data items such as indices, which are not used for input or output and which can benefit from the very efficient manner in which the computer hardware performs computations with binary data.

Floating point data representation is similar in many respects to scientific notation. A data item is represented in memory by storing a sequence of significant digits and an exponent representing a power of the base. The following scheme is used:

$$\lfloor \text{exponent} \mid \text{fraction} \rfloor$$

↑
Assumed position of the decimal point

The value represented is then:

$$\text{fraction} \times \text{base}^{\text{exponent}}$$

For example, assuming a base 10 system, the number 37000000 might be represented as

$$\lfloor 08 \mid 37\ 00\ 00 \rfloor$$

which would stand for

$$.370000 \times 10^8 = 37000000$$

On IBM Systems, the actual base used is 16. Floating point data may be represented utilizing 32 bits (single precision). A single precision item utilizes the first 8 bits to represent the exponent and the remaining 24 bits to represent the fraction. A double precision item utilizes the first 8 bits for the exponent, just as for a single precision item, but the fraction is now longer (56 bits). The basic advantage to utilizing floating point data is that values with very large and very small magnitudes may be represented in a fixed space. The primary disadvantage is that only a limited number of significant digits can be represented. A COBOL programmer might wish to use floating point data when evaluating certain formulas which are primarily scientific in nature, or when processing a file which contains data items stored in this format.

11.8 THE USAGE CLAUSE

The USAGE clause used in the definition of an elementary data item in the DATA division specifies the type of data representation to be assumed for this data item. The general form for the USAGE clause is shown in Figure 11.9.

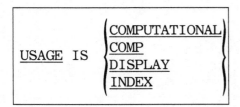

Figure 11.9 General form of the USAGE clause

The details of internal representation of all data types are compiler dependent. DISPLAY is the default type for all numeric fields. Thus the definition

         03   FLDA PIC 99V9 USAGE IS DISPLAY.

is equivalent to

             03   FLDA PIC 99V9.

The type DISPLAY is used primarily for fields contained on input/output records.

A data item which has a USAGE of COMPUTATIONAL (or the equivalent COMP) is a numeric field typically used to store results of computations. Usually a field will be transformed from DISPLAY into COMPUTATIONAL any time an arithmetic operation is performed on the field. (The compiler inserts the code required to perform these transformations.) Defining fields used as counters, accumulators, and so on as USAGE COMPUTATIONAL makes the transformation unnecessary, thereby increasing the efficiency of the computer in executing the program.

USAGE type INDEX is used for data items which are to be used as subscripts for table references. The primary value of specifying a data item to have USAGE INDEX is to make table references more efficient. Data items specified as USAGE INDEX may be manipulated only by the PERFORM/VARYING statement (see Section 8.5) and the SET statement (see Section 12.10).

IBM compilers provide additional types of data in the USAGE clause as illustrated in Figure 11.10.

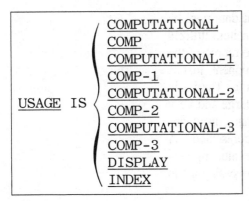

Figure 11.10   USAGE clause for IBM systems

The correspondence between the data types defined in the USAGE clause and the internal types defined in section 11.7 above is shown in Figure 11.11 below.

USAGE description	Data representation
DISPLAY	Zoned decimal
COMPUTATIONAL	Binary (no restrictions on manipulation)
COMPUTATIONAL-1	Single precision floating point
COMPUTATIONAL-2	Double precision floating point
COMPUTATIONAL-3	Packed decimal
INDEX	Binary (restrictions on manipulation)

Figure 11.11   Correspondence between USAGE and data representation for IBM systems

COMPUTATIONAL-3 data may be specified for fields which are going to be used for computational purposes to reduce the amount of time required to convert from DISPLAY to COMPUTATIONAL-3 and back. For example, counters and accumulators which are used repeatedly in computation may be specified as COMPUTATION-3.

Example

```
01 SUM PIC 9999V99 USAGE COMPUTATIONAL-3.

01 KOUNT PIC 9(5) USAGE COMPUTATIONAL-3.
```

Binary data is required in a COBOL program for subscript values. For example, the value of IND must be represented in binary when the statement MOVE DATA (IND) TO DATA-OUT is executed. If a data item used as a subscript is not a binary type item, the COBOL compiler generates code required to make the transformation, but this transformation takes time to perform. COMPUTATIONAL or INDEX data may be specified for fields which will be used as subscripts to reduce the time required to convert from DISPLAY to COMPUTATIONAL for each table reference.

Example

```
01   I PIC 99 USAGE COMPUTATIONAL.
     .
     .
     .
PROCEDURE DIVISION.
     .
     .
     .
     MOVE TABLE (I) TO AMOUNT-OUT.
```

The USAGE clause also may be required for describing records in files produced by other programs. For example, suppose we are given the following record description:

Record position	Description
1-16	Name
17-21	Year to date salary (packed decimal)
22-26	Year to date FICA (packed decimal)
27-35	Social security number

The record description which would be coded into the COBOL program would be:

```
01   INPUT-RECORD.
     02   NAME PIC X(16).
     02   YTD-SAL PIC 9999999V99 USAGE COMPUTATIONAL-3.
     02   YTD-FICA PIC 9999999V99 USAGE COMPUTATIONAL-3.
     02   SS-NUM PIC 9(9) USAGE DISPLAY.
```

Note that the field YTD-SAL occupies five bytes in the input record but is given a picture allowing for nine digits. When you use packed decimal data representation, a five-byte field can accommodate a number of this size. The use of USAGE DISPLAY to describe SS-NUM in the above example is for documentation purposes only; the record description would be used also by the program which first created the records in the file.

11.9   THE SEARCH ALL STATEMENT

It is often necessary to search a table to locate specific items required by a program. For example, consider the table in Figure 11.12 showing the course number and description of courses offered at a college. In preparing grade reports, a program might search the table to locate the description for each course a student has completed. One method of accomplishing this task is to compare each element of the course table with the course number to be located, as follows:

```
PERFORM SEARCH-EXIT
    VARYING INDX FROM 1 BY 1 UNTIL
        INDX = 50 OR COURSE-NUM = TABLE-COURSE-NUM (INDX).
IF COURSE-NUM NOT = TABLE-COURSE-NUM (INDX)
    MOVE "INVALID COURSE" TO COURSE-DESC
ELSE
    MOVE TABLE-DESC (INDX) TO COURSE-DESC.
    .
    .
    .

SEARCH-EXIT.
    EXIT.
```

```
01   TABLE-CONSTANTS.
     02 FILLER          PIC        X(6)     VALUE "COC 130".
     02 FILLER    PIC X(20) VALUE "INTRODUCTION TO COMPUTERS".
     02 FILLER          PIC        X(6)     VALUE "COC 200".
     02 FILLER    PIC X(20)        VALUE  "COMPUTER MATHEMATICS".
     02 FILLER          PIC        X(6)     VALUE "COP 100".
     02 FILLER          PIC        X(20)    VALUE "COBOL".
         .
         .
         .
01   COURSE-TABLE REDEFINES TABLE-CONSTANTS.
     02 COURSE-TABLE-ENTRY OCCURS 50 TIMES.
        03   TABLE-COURSE-NUM    PIC X(6).
        03   TABLE-DESC          PIC X(20).
```

Figure 11.12   Definition of COURSE-TABLE

Many versions of COBOL include the SEARCH ALL and SEARCH statements to perform this operation. In order to use these statements, you must include the INDEXED and KEY clauses in the OCCURS clause which is used to define the table. The general form of the OCCURS clause with these options is shown in Figure 11.13.

The data-names specified in the KEY clause must be data fields within the table itself. The table must be organized into ASCENDING or DESCENDING sequence based on the key field(s). The index-name used in the INDEXED clause will be used by the SEARCH statement in its search of the table. The index-name must not be defined elsewhere in the program, since further definition of this

```
OCCURS    integer TIMES
            [ {ASCENDING }                    KEY IS data-name . . . ]
            [ {DESCENDING}
            [ INDEXED BY index-name]
```

Figure 11.13   General form of the OCCURS clause

variable will be handled by the compiler automatically. For example, the table shown in Figure 11.12 could be defined in the DATA division by the following statements:

```
01   TABLE-CONSTANTS.
        .
        .
        .

01   COURSE-TABLE REDEFINES TABLE-CONSTANTS.
     02   COURSE-TABLE-ENTRY OCCURS 50 TIMES
             ASCENDING KEY IS TABLE-COURSE-NUM
             INDEXED BY TAB-INDEX.
        03   TABLE-COURSE-NUM PIC X(6).
        03   TABLE-DESC       PIC X(20).
```

The SEARCH ALL statement is used to perform a search of all of the table entries until a desired condition has been satisfied (Fig. 11.14).

```
SEARCH ALL    data-name-1 [AT END statement-1]

   WHEN       {data-name-2  {IS EQUAL TO}  value-1}
              {             {IS =       }         }
              {condition-name-1                   }


              [     {data-name-3  {IS EQUAL TO}value-2}]  ...
              [AND  {            {IS =       }       }]
              [     {condition-name-2                }]


              {statement-2   }
              {NEXT SENTENCE } .
```

Figure 11.14   General form of the SEARCH ALL statement

The conditions specified in the WHEN clause are tested for successive values of the table index.[1] When the condition is satisfied the statement following the condition is executed. The condition must not be a compound or named condition; it must test for equality of key field (index) to some value. If the system searches the entire table without finding the condition to be satisfied, the statement in the AT END clause is executed. The programmer need not initialize or modify the

---

[1]Some systems perform a sequential search of all table elements, while others perform a binary search. In general the binary search which involves successively dividing the table into halves is more efficient.

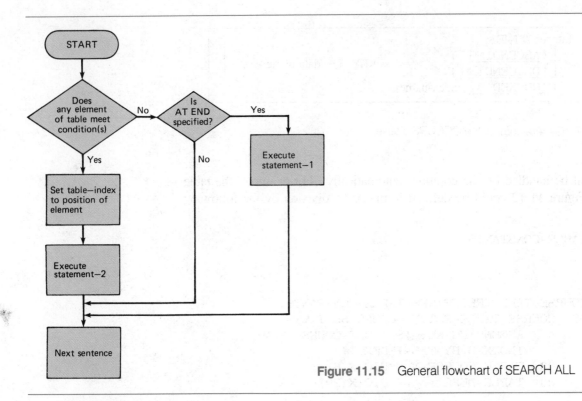

Figure 11.15   General flowchart of SEARCH ALL

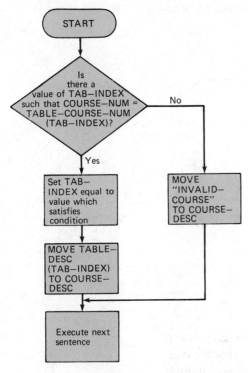

Figure 11.16   Flowchart of SEARCH ALL example

table index variable; the SEARCH ALL statement performs these tasks automatically. For example, the search procedure above could now be coded as follows:

```
SEARCH ALL COURSE-TABLE-ENTRY
     AT END MOVE "INVALID COURSE" TO COURSE-DESC
     WHEN COURSE-NUM = TABLE-COURSE-NUM (TAB-INDEX)
          MOVE TABLE-DESC (TAB-INDEX) TO COURSE-DESC.
```

A flowchart showing how the general SEARCH ALL statement is executed is shown in Figure 11.15 and the SEARCH ALL statement is illustrated in Figure 11.16.

11.10   THE SET STATEMENT

It is convenient to use the table index when referencing elements of the table for purposes of placing data in the table or modifying data in the table. However, the index variable cannot be modified by the usual arithmetic operation statements used for other COBOL variables. An index variable may be initialized only by the SET statement which has the general form shown in Figure 11.17.[2]

SET index-name. . . TO value.

Figure 11.17   General form of the SET TO statement

The value may be an integer constant, another index name or a variable having an integer value. For example, the index variable TAB-INDEX in the previous example could be initialized to value 1 by the statement:

SET TAB-INDEX TO 1.

An index variable may be incremented (or decremented) by the SET statement, the general form of which is shown in Figure 11.18.

SET index-name. . . $\left\{ \dfrac{\text{UP BY}}{\text{DOWN BY}} \right\}$ value.

Figure 11.18   General form of SET UP/DOWN statement

For example, the statement

SET TAB-INDEX UP BY 1.

would cause the value 1 to be added to TAB-INDEX. The statement

SET TAB-INDEX DOWN BY 2.

would cause 2 to be subtracted from TAB-INDEX.

Example

Suppose that the 50 course numbers and descriptions described at the beginning of Section 11.9 are to be loaded into the table from a file, rather than being coded as constants into the DATA division of the program. The following program segment will perform this task:

```
3000-LOAD-TABLE SECTION.
3010-LOAD-CONTROL.
    SET TAB-INDEX TO 0.
    OPEN INPUT COURSE-TABLE-FILE.
```

---

[2]An index variable is defined in an INDEXED BY clause or by specifying USAGE IS INDEX.

```
READ COURSE-TABLE-FILE
    AT END MOVE 1 TO EOF-FLAG.
PERFORM 3010-LOAD-READ UNTIL
    EOF-FLAG = 1 OR TAB-INDEX = 50.
IF EOF-FLAG NOT = 1 OR TAB-INDEX < 50
    PERFORM 3020-LOAD-ERROR.
GO TO 3020 LOAD-EXIT.
3010-LOAD-READ.
    SET TAB-INDEX UP BY 1.
    MOVE COURSE-TABLE-RECORD
        TO COURSE-TABLE-ENTRY (TAB-INDEX).
    READ COURSE-TABLE-FILE
        AT END MOVE 1 TO EOF-FLAG.
3020-LOAD-ERROR.
    EXIT.
3020-LOAD-EXIT.
    EXIT.
```

It is improbable, however, that this table would contain such a precisely defined number of entries, since courses are added and deleted regularly. It would be unfortunate to have to recompile a program because the number of courses changed, and indeed this is not necessary. As noted earlier in Section 8.4, it is possible to set up the table to contain a variable number of entries using the DEPENDING ON clause. The table in the preceding example could now be defined by:

```
01   NUMBER-OF-COURSES PIC 999 VALUE 0.
01   COURSE-TABLE.
     02   COURSE-TABLE-ENTRY
          OCCURS 1 TO 999 TIMES
          DEPENDING ON NUMBER-OF-COURSES
          ASCENDING KEY IS TABLE-COURSE-NUM
          INDEXED BY TAB-INDEX.
          03   TABLE-COURSE-NUM PIC X(6).
          03   TABLE-DESC PIC X(20).
```

The routine to load the data into the table will appear as:

```
3010-LOAD-TABLE SECTION.
3110-LOAD-CONTROL.
    SET TAB-INDEX TO 0.
    OPEN INPUT COURSE-TABLE-FILE.
    READ COURSE-TABLE-FILE AT END MOVE 1 TO EOF-FLAG.
    PERFORM 3120-LOAD-READ UNTIL
        EOF-FLAG = 1 OR NUMBER-OF-COURSES = 999.
    IF EOF-FLAG NOT = 1
        PERFORM 3130-LOAD-ERROR.
    GO TO 3140-LOAD-EXIT.
3120-LOAD-TABLE.
    SET TAB-INDEX UP BY 1.
    ADD 1 TO NUMBER-OF-COURSES.
    MOVE COURSE-TABLE-RECORD TO COURSE-TABLE-ENTRY (TAB-INDEX).
    READ COURSE-TABLE-FILE AT END MOVE 1 TO EOF-FLAG.
3130-LOAD-ERROR.
    EXIT.
3140-LOAD-EXIT.
    EXIT.
```

11.11 THE SEARCH STATEMENT

The general form of the SEARCH statement is shown below in Figure 11.19.

SEARCH data-name [AT END statement-1]

$\left\{ \underline{\text{WHEN}} \text{ condition-1 } \left\{ \begin{array}{l} \text{statement-2} \\ \underline{\text{NEXT SENTENCE}} \end{array} \right\} \right\} \ldots$

Figure 11.19 General form of the SEARCH statement

The SEARCH statement is similar in many respects to the SEARCH ALL statement; however, there is one essential difference. The SEARCH ALL statement includes a provision to initialize the index automatically, while the SEARCH statement does not include this feature. When using the SEARCH verb, the programmer must initialize the index prior to execution of the SEARCH statement. Another difference between the SEARCH ALL and SEARCH statements is that conditions may be simple or compound and may involve inequalities as well as equality. As with the SEARCH ALL statement, the SEARCH statement provides for automatic incrementing of the index and performance of the statements in the AT END clause if the value of the index exceeds the number of elements in the table. Figure 11.20 illustrates a flowchart of the execution of the SEARCH statement.

For example, let's use the SEARCH statement to look up the tax deduction permitted by the IRS for gasoline tax at five cents per gallon (Fig. 11.21). The

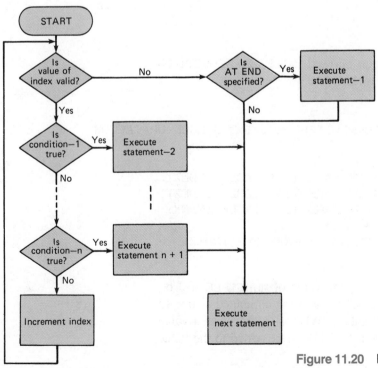

Figure 11.20 Flowchart of the SEARCH statement

Miles Driven	Deduction Amount
Under 3,000	$8
3,000 under 4,000 ..	14
4,000 under 5,000 ..	19
5,000 under 6,000 ..	23
6,000 under 7,000 ..	27
7,000 under 8,000 ..	31
8,000 under 9,000 ..	35
9,000 under 10,000 ..	39
10,000 under 11,000 ..	43
11,000 under 12,000 ..	48
12,000 under 13,000 ..	51
13,000 under 14,000 ..	56
14,000 under 15,000 ..	60
15,000 under 16,000 ..	64
16,000 under 17,000 ..	68
17,000 under 18,000 ..	72
18,000 under 19,000 ..	76
19,000 under 20,000 ..	81
20,000*	83

*For over 20,000 miles, use table amounts for total miles driven. For example, for 25,000 miles, add the deduction for 5,000 to the deduction for 20,000 miles.

Figure 11.21   Deduction table

code required to set up the table is shown below:

```
01   TAX-TABLE.
     02  TAX-ENTRY OCCURS 18 TIMES
         ASCENDING KEY IS BREAK-MILEAGE
         INDEXED BY TAX-TABLE-INDEX.
         03  LOW-MILEAGE PIC 9(5).
         03  BREAK-MILEAGE PIC 9(5).
         03  DEDUCTION-AMT PIC 9(3).
```

The code required to compute the deduction allowed (MILEAGE-DEDUCTION)
for the number of miles driven (MILEAGE) is shown below:

```
DIVIDE MILEAGE BY 20000 GIVING MULTIPLE REMAINDER LOOK-UP-FACTOR.
SET TAX-TABLE-INDEX TO 1.
SEARCH TAX-ENTRY
    WHEN (LOOK-UP-FACTOR > LOW-MILEAGE (TAX-TABLE-INDEX)
       OR LOOK-UP-FACTOR = LOW-MILEAGE (TAX-TABLE-INDEX))
    AND LOOK-UP-FACTOR < BREAK-MILEAGE (TAX-TABLE-INDEX)
    COMPUTE MILEAGE-DEDUCTION =
        MULTIPLE * 83 + DEDUCTION-AMT (TAX-TABLE-INDEX).
```

Note that when MILEAGE is less than 20,000, the value of MULTIPLE will be
zero, resulting in the value of MILEAGE-DEDUCTION being computed as 0 * 83
plus the appropriate value from the TAX-TABLE. When MILEAGE has a value
greater than 20,000, an appropriate MULTIPLE of 83 will be added to the value
from the TAX-TABLE.

11.12   INTERNATIONAL APPLICATIONS FEATURES

The SPECIAL-NAMES entry of the CONFIGURATION SECTION of the ENVIRONMENT DIVISION can be used to modify the usual symbols used to denote the decimal point and the currency symbol. This feature is useful in data processing applications involving European and other currencies which do not use the symbol "$" for a currency symbol and/or the period for the decimal point. The general form of these entries is shown in Figure 11.22.

```
SPECIAL-NAMES.
    [CURRENCY SIGN IS literal]
    [DECIMAL-POINT IS COMMA].
```

Figure 11.22   General form of SPECIAL-NAMES entries for international applications

The DECIMAL-POINT IS COMMA clause causes the role of the comma and the period to be interchanged in specifying PICTUREs in the DATA DIVISION. This is required for certain European countries in which a value such as 12,345,678.90 would be written as 12.345.678,90. If the DECIMAL-POINT IS COMMA clause is used, PICTUREs such as 99.999.999,99 will cause the period to be used to denote groups of digits and the comma to be inserted as a decimal point.

The CURRENCY SIGN IS clause enables the use of the specified literal in the DATA DIVISION instead of the dollar sign. For example, to enable use of the pound sign " $\pounds\pounds\pounds$ " as a currency symbol the entry

CURRENCY SIGN IS " $\pounds\pounds\pounds$ ".

would be used. With this entry PICTURE codes such as

$\pounds\pounds\pounds,\pounds\pounds\pounds.99$ and $\pounds\pounds\pounds$ZZ,ZZZ.99

may be used in the DATA DIVISION. The system will use the specified symbol in exactly the same way as dollar sign for editing data. The literal used in the CURRENCY SIGN clause may be any single character except 0 through 9, A, B, C, D, L, P, R, S, V, X, Z, *, +, (, −,), /, =, comma, period, quotation mark or space.

11.13   THE COPY STATEMENT

Program segments can be stored in a library and made available to COBOL programs. This facility is particularly useful for record descriptions, table definitions and PROCEDURE DIVISION modules. Thus, if a data file will be processed by many programs, it is more efficient to store the record description for the file in a library and allow each programmer to insert the record description into the program than to force each programmer to write out the complete record description for each program requiring access to the file. Not only does this technique save coding effort but also it forces all programs to use the same data-names for each field in the record. This can be a distinct advantage in debugging and updating programs in the system.

Another advantage to using this library facility is that if the record layout for the file is changed, it is only necessary to change the record description in the library and then recompile all programs which access the file. Similar advantages accrue from placing other portions of COBOL programs in libraries.

The COPY statement is used to insert code from a library into a program. A general form of the COPY statement is shown in Figure 11.23.

COPY text-name $\quad \left[\left\{ \begin{array}{c} \underline{\text{IN}} \\ \underline{\text{OF}} \end{array} \right\} \text{library-name} \right]$.

Figure 11.23 General form of the COPY statement

The COPY statement may be used at any point in a COBOL program, and causes the compiler to copy the specified text from the library into the program. The copied text is then compiled as though the programmer had included the code in the usual fashion. Procedures for establishing libraries and storing text within libraries vary from one system to another.

For example, suppose the following code has been placed in a library called RECORD-DESCRIPTIONS under the text name DATA-RECORD-DESCRIPTION:

```
02   DATA RECORD.
     03   FIELD-A  PIC X.
     03   FIELD-B  PIC 9(9).
```

Placing the statement

```
COPY DATA-RECORD-DESCRIPTION OF RECORD-DESCRIPTION.
```

into the DATA DIVISION of a COBOL program would cause the three statements stored in this entry to be ''copied'' into the body of the program.

11.14   ABBREVIATIONS IN RELATION CONDITIONS

Relation conditions are made up of three parts:

1) subject
2) relation-operator
3) object

For example, in the relation condition

$$A + B < 32$$

the subject is ''A + B'', the relation-operator is ''<'' and the object is ''32''. When relation conditions are linked by AND or OR to form compound conditions, it is possible to abbreviate the condition when the subject, or the subject and the relation, are the same. Abbreviation is accomplished by omitting the common subject or subject and relation in subsequent relations. Figure 11.24 gives the general form of an abbreviated compound condition.

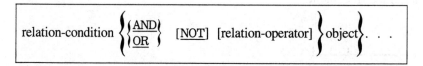

Figure 11.24   General form of the abbreviated compound condition

Non-Abbreviated Form	Abbreviated Form	Comment	*Example*
A < B AND A < C	A < B AND C	Both the subject and relational operator omitted in abbreviated form	
A > B OR A NOT < C	A > B OR NOT < C	Subject is omitted in abbreviated form	
A < B AND A < C OR A > D	A < B AND C OR > D	Subject and is omitted for the first abbreviation; only the subject is omitted in the second abbreviation.	

It is *not* possible to omit objects in forming abbreviations. For example, the correct abbreviation for A < B OR A =B is A < B OR =B, not the common mistake A < OR =B.

11.15   THE STRING STATEMENT

There are many instances when a program has to bring data items which have been defined separately together into one field. An example would be to convert the contents of the two data items defined as

```
03   FIRST-NAME   PIC X(20).
03   LAST-NAME    PIC X(20).
```

into a single string of characters to be contained in a field called NAME with the first and last names separated by a single space. Suppose the content of the data items FIRST-NAME and LAST-NAME are as shown below:

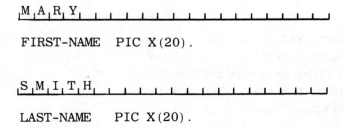

FIRST-NAME   PIC X(20).

LAST-NAME   PIC X(20).

The desired transformation would be a field with content:

```
 M A R Y   S M I T H
```

NAME   PIC X(17).

The STRING statement offers the COBOL programmer a very convenient means for performing such transformations. A general form of the STRING statement is shown in Figure 11.25.

```
STRING      {{data-name-1}...  DELIMITED BY  {data-name-2}}...
            {{literal-1   }                  {literal-2  }}
                                             {SIZE       }
            INTO data-name-3
            [ON OVERFLOW statement]
```

Figure 11.25   General form of the STRING statement

The items specified before the DELIMITED phrase are sending fields; the item specified by *data-name-3* is the receiving field. Data is transferred from the sending fields to the receiving field as with the alphanumeric MOVE, except that filling the receiving field with blanks is not performed. The DELIMITED BY clause specifies the condition for termination of transfer of characters from the sending field. The content of *data-name-2* or *literal-2* must be a single character. Transfer of data terminates when that character is found in the sending field. Specification of SIZE in the DELIMITED BY clause will cause transfer of all characters of the sending item.

Example

```
STRING FLD-A FLD-B DELIMITED BY SPACE
       INTO FLD-C.
```

```
 A B C D
```

FLD-A PIC X(8).

```
 1 2 3   4 5 6 7 8
```

FLD-B PIC X(10).

From FLD-A From FLD-B   These characters not replaced

```
 A B C D 1 2 3
```

FLD-C PIC X(10).

First the characters "ABCD" are moved from FLD-A into FLD-C. When the space is encountered in FLD-A, characters from FLD-B are transferred into FLD-C. Transfer of characters from FLD-B terminates after the first three characters because the fourth character is a space. Note that the remaining characters of FLD-C retain their former content.

Example

```
STRING ITEM-1 DELIMITED BY SIZE
       ITEM-2 DELIMITED BY "-"
       INTO ITEM-3.
```

|_A_|_B_|_C_|___|___| |_1_|_2_|_-_|_3_|_4_|

ITEM-1 PIC X(5)   ITEM-2 PIC X(5)

From ITEM-1   From ITEM-2   This character
                                 not replaced

|_A_|_B_|_C_|___|___|_1_|_2_|___|

ITEM-3 PIC X(8)

All of the characters from ITEM-1 are moved to ITEM-3 because ITEM-1
is delimited by SIZE. The first two characters from ITEM-2 are moved into
ITEM-3. Transfer of characters terminates when the delimiting character
"−" is encountered in ITEM-2.

Example

```
STRING FIRST-NAME DELIMITED BY SPACE
       " "        DELIMITED BY SIZE
       LAST-NAME  DELIMITED BY SPACE
       INTO NAME.
```

|_M_|_A_|_R_|_Y_|___|___|___|___|___|___|___|___|___|___|___|___|___|___|___|___|

FIRST-NAME   PIC X(20).

|_S_|_M_|_I_|_T_|_H_|___|___|___|___|___|___|___|___|___|___|___|___|___|___|___|

LAST-NAME   PIC X(20).

From   From   From   These characters
FIRST-NAME   Literal   LAST-NAME   not changed.

|_M_|_A_|_R_|_Y_|___|_S_|_M_|_I_|_T_|_H_|___|___|___|___|___|___|___|

NAME   PIC X(17).

Note that it is necessary to ensure that the receiving field contains spaces
before execution of the STRING statement because the trailing characters are
not modified.

If the delimiting character is not found in a sending field, all of the characters in the field are transferred to the receiving field.

```
STRING FLD-X, "-", FLD-Y DELIMITED BY CHAR
       INTO FLD-Z.
```

⌞*⌟

```
CHAR  PIC X.
```

⌞A⌞B⌞C⌞D⌞⌟

```
FLD-X  PIC X(5).
```

⌞1⌞2⌞*⌞3⌞⌟

```
FLD-Y  PIC X(5).
```

From FLD-X From Literal From FLD-Y These characters not changed.

⌞A⌞B⌞C⌞D⌞-⌞1⌞2⌞⌟

```
FLD-Z   PIC X(10).
```

The content of CHAR is used as the delimiting character for FLD-X, FLD-Y and the literal "−". All characters of FLD-X and the literal are transferred to FLD-Z since neither contains the delimiting character.

Transfer of characters terminates either when all of the characters in the sending fileds have been transferred or when there is no more room in the receiving field. The ON OVERFLOW clause can be used to take action in the latter case—when the receiving field is full and there are more characters in the sending fields to be transferred.

```
STRING FLD-Q FLD-R DELIMITED BY SIZE
       INTO FLD-S
       ON OVERFLOW PERFORM ERROR-MSG.
```

⌞1⌞2⌞3⌟   ⌞A⌞B⌞C⌟

```
FLD-Q PIC 999      FLD-R PIC XXX
```

From   From
FLD-Q   FLD-R

⌞1⌞2⌞3⌞A⌟

```
FLD-S  PIC X(4).
```

In this case FLD-S is too short to contain all characters from the receiving fields, resulting in an overflow situation. The paragraph ERROR-MSG would be executed. If the ON OVERFLOW clause had been omitted, the content of FLD-S would be as shown and the program would continue with the next statement.

11.16   THE UNSTRING STATEMENT

The UNSTRING statement performs the inverse function of the STRING statement. The STRING statement brings many separate items together into one field;
the UNSTRING statement enables the program to separate the content of one field
into many different items. For example, suppose you want to separate the characters in a field such as

```
M A R Y   S M I T H
```

NAME   PIC X(17).

into two items such as

```
M A R Y
```

FIRST-NAME   PIC X(20).

```
S M I T H
```

LAST-NAME   PIC X(20).

The UNSTRING statement will enable the program to make this transformation.
A general form for the UNSTRING statement is shown in Figure 11.26.

UNSTRING data-name-1

$$\left[\underline{\text{DELIMITED}} \text{ BY } [\underline{\text{ALL}}] \quad \left\{ \begin{array}{l} \text{data-name-2} \\ \text{literal} \end{array} \right\} \right]$$

INTO data-name-3 . . .
[ON OVERFLOW statement]

Figure 11.26   A general form of the UNSTRING
statement

Data-name-1 is the sending field; *data-name-3* and those following are receiving
fields. Characters are transferred from the sending field to the receiving fields
from left to right. If the DELIMITED BY clause is omitted, characters are moved
into the first receiving field until the field is filled, then characters are moved into
the second receiving field and so forth. Transfer of characters terminates when
all of the characters in the sending field have been transferred or when all of the
receiving fields have been filled.

Example

UNSTRING FLD-A INTO FLD-B FLD-C.

```
A B C D E F G H
```

FLD-A PIC X(8)

```
A B C
```

FLD-B PIC X(3)

```
D E F G
```

FLD-C PIC X(4)

The DELIMITED BY clause enables the programmer to specify a character or characters to be used to terminate transfer of characters into a receiving field. When the delimiter is found in the sending field, transfer of characters to the receiving field ceases. If other receiving fields are present, transfer of characters resumes with the leftmost character following the delimiter.

Example

```
UNSTRING FLD-E
      DELIMITED BY "-"
      INTO FLD-F, FLD-G, FLD-H.
```

```
1 2 3 - 4 5 - 6 7 8 9
```

FLD-E PIC X(11).

```
1 2 3
```

FLD-F PIC 999.

```
4 5
```

FLD-G PIC 99.

```
6 7 8 9
```

FLD-H PIC 9999.

Transfer of data into FLD-F ceases when the first "−" is encountered in FLD-E. In like fashion, transfer into FLD-G is terminated by the second "−".

Example

```
UNSTRING NAME
      DELIMITED BY SPACE
      INTO FIRST-NAME LAST-NAME.
```

```
M A R Y   S M I T H
```

NAME PIC X(17).

```
M A R Y
```

FIRST-NAME PIC X(20)

```
S M I T H
```

LAST-NAME PIC X(20)

Note that receiving fields are padded on the right with blanks if the number of characters received is less than the field width.

If two or more delimiters appear in adjacent positions of the sending field, the affected receiving field will be either blank filled (if an alphanumeric item) or zero filled (if a numeric item).

Example

```
UNSTRING INPUT-STRING
    DELIMITED BY ","
    INTO NUM-1, NUM-2, NUM-3.
```

```
 1 2 3 , , 4 5
```

INPUT-STRING PIC X(10).

```
 1 2 3
```

NUM-1 PIC 999.

```
 0 0 0
```

NUM-2 PIC 999.

```
 4 5
```

NUM-3 PIC 999.

The first occurrence of the comma terminates transfer of characters into NUM-1. The second occurrence of a comma terminates transfer of data into NUM-2; since no data was transferred and the field is numeric, it is zeroed out. Note that NUM-3 receives data as an alphanumeric data item rather than a numeric item; the program should ensure that each item has valid data in it before any further processing takes place. If the ALL option is used in the DELIMITED BY clause, all adjacent delimiters are treated as one delimiter.

Example

```
UNSTRING NAME
    DELIMITED BY ALL SPACES
    INTO FIRST-NAME LAST-NAME.
```

```
 J O H N   D O E
```

NAME PIC X(17).

```
 J O H N
```

FIRST-NAME PIC X(20).

```
 D O E
```

LAST-NAME PIC X(20).

The three adjacent spaces in positions 5 through 7 of NAME are treated as one delimiter. Transfer of data into LAST-NAME begins at position 8.

The ON OVERFLOW clause can be used to take action when there are additional characters in the sending field, when all receiving fields have been filled, or when all characters in the sending field have been used and additional receiving fields have not been filled.

```
UNSTRING FLD-A INTO FLD-B FLD-C
    ON OVERFLOW PERFORM ERROR-MSG.
```

A B C   A   B
└─┴─┴─┘   └─┘   └─┘

FLD-A PIC X(3)   FLD-B PIC X   FLD-C PIC X

Since FLD-A has an additional character which is not examined, an overflow
condition results in the execution of ERROR-MSG.

```
UNSTRING FLD-D
    DELIMITED BY SPACE
    INTO FLD-E, FLD-F
    ON OVERFLOW MOVE "YES" TO ERROR-FLAG.
```

┌A┬B┬C┬D┐
└─┴─┴─┴─┘

FLD-D PIC X(4)

┌A┬B┬C┐
└─┴─┴─┘

FLD-E PIC X(3)

└─┴─┴─┴─┴─┘

FLD-F PIC X(5)

Since the sending field does not contain an instance of the delimiter, transfer
of data into FLD-F cannot begin, hence an overflow condition occurs.

11.17   THE INSPECT STATEMENT

The INSPECT statement allows a program to process individual characters in a
data item by replacing some certain characters with other characters. A general
form for the INSPECT statement is shown in Figure 11.27.

The INSPECT statement will cause some (or all) of the characters in *data-
name-1* to be replaced. *Literal-1* or *data-name-2* specifies the character(s) to be
replaced. *Literal-2* or *data-name-3* specifies the replacement character(s).

The LEADING option will cause leftmost occurrences of specified characters
to be replaced.

Suppose you wish to insert asterisks in place of leading zeros in a field. The   *Example*
following code could be used:

```
INSPECT DATA-FIELD REPLACING LEADING "0" BY "*".
```

```
INSPECT  data-name-1 REPLACING  ⎰ ALL   ⎱ ⎰literal-1     ⎱ BY ⎰literal-2   ⎱
                                ⎱ LEADING⎰ ⎱data-name-2⎰     ⎱data-name-3⎰
                                  FIRST
```

Figure 11.27   A general form for INSPECT

Before execution

0	0	0	4	3	0	5	7

DATA-FIELD

After execution

*	*	*	4	3	0	5	7

DATA-FIELD

The second zero is not replaced because it is not a leading zero. If no characters satisfying the condition LEADING ''0'' had been found, content of the field would not be changed.

The ALL option will cause all occurrences of specified characters to be replaced.

Example

EXAMINE FLD-OUT REPLACING ALL " " BY ","

Before execution

1	2	3		4	5		6	7	8	9

FLD-OUT

After execution

1	2	3	,	4	5	,	6	7	8	9

FLD-OUT

The FIRST option will replace the first (leftmost) occurrence of a specified character by another character. All other occurrences of the character will be unaffected.

Example

EXAMINE ITEM-A REPLACING FIRST " $" BY "A$"

Before execution

					$	1	2	.	3	0

ITEM-A

After execution

				A	$	1	2	.	3	0

ITEM-A

The INSPECT statement actually has many more options than shown in Figure 11.27. The following section contains a complete description of the INSPECT statement.

11.18 COMPLETE DESCRIPTION OF INSPECT

Function

The INSPECT statement provides the ability to tally (Format 1), replace (Format 2), or tally and replace (Format 3) occurrences of single characters or groups of characters in a data item.

General Format

Format 1

INSPECT identifier-1 TALLYING

$$
\left\{ \text{, identifier-2 } \underline{\text{FOR}} \left\{ \left\{ \begin{matrix} \underline{\text{ALL}} \\ \underline{\text{LEADING}} \\ \underline{\text{CHARACTERS}} \end{matrix} \right\} \begin{Bmatrix} \text{identifier-3} \\ \text{literal-1} \end{Bmatrix} \left[\begin{Bmatrix} \underline{\text{BEFORE}} \\ \underline{\text{AFTER}} \end{Bmatrix} \text{INITIAL} \begin{Bmatrix} \text{identifier-4} \\ \text{literal-2} \end{Bmatrix} \right] \right\} \cdots \right\} \cdots
$$

Format 2

INSPECT identifier-1 REPLACING

$$
\left\{ \begin{matrix} \underline{\text{CHARACTERS}} \ \underline{\text{BY}} \begin{Bmatrix} \text{identifier-6} \\ \text{literal-4} \end{Bmatrix} \left[\begin{Bmatrix} \underline{\text{BEFORE}} \\ \underline{\text{AFTER}} \end{Bmatrix} \text{INITIAL} \begin{Bmatrix} \text{identifier-7} \\ \text{literal-5} \end{Bmatrix} \right] \\ \left\{ \begin{matrix} \underline{\text{ALL}} \\ \underline{\text{LEADING}} \\ \underline{\text{FIRST}} \end{matrix} \right\} \left\{ \begin{Bmatrix} \text{identifier-5} \\ \text{literal-3} \end{Bmatrix} \underline{\text{BY}} \begin{Bmatrix} \text{identifier-6} \\ \text{literal-4} \end{Bmatrix} \left[\begin{Bmatrix} \underline{\text{BEFORE}} \\ \underline{\text{AFTER}} \end{Bmatrix} \text{INITIAL} \begin{Bmatrix} \text{identifier-4} \\ \text{literal-5} \end{Bmatrix} \right] \right\} \cdots \end{matrix} \right\} \cdots
$$

Format 3

INSPECT identifier-1 TALLYING

$$
\left\{ \text{, identifier-2 } \underline{\text{FOR}} \left\{ \left\{ \begin{matrix} \underline{\text{ALL}} \\ \underline{\text{LEADING}} \\ \underline{\text{CHARACTERS}} \end{matrix} \right\} \begin{Bmatrix} \text{identifier-6} \\ \text{literal-1} \end{Bmatrix} \left[\begin{Bmatrix} \underline{\text{BEFORE}} \\ \underline{\text{AFTER}} \end{Bmatrix} \text{INITIAL} \begin{Bmatrix} \text{identifier-4} \\ \text{literal-2} \end{Bmatrix} \right] \right\} \cdots \right\} \cdots
$$

REPLACING

$$
\left\{ \begin{matrix} \underline{\text{CHARACTERS}} \ \underline{\text{BY}} \begin{Bmatrix} \text{identifier-6} \\ \text{literal-4} \end{Bmatrix} \left[\begin{Bmatrix} \underline{\text{BEFORE}} \\ \underline{\text{AFTER}} \end{Bmatrix} \text{INITIAL} \begin{Bmatrix} \text{identifier-7} \\ \text{literal-5} \end{Bmatrix} \right] \\ \left\{ \begin{matrix} \underline{\text{ALL}} \\ \underline{\text{LEADING}} \\ \underline{\text{FIRST}} \end{matrix} \right\} \left\{ \begin{Bmatrix} \text{identifier-5} \\ \text{literal-3} \end{Bmatrix} \underline{\text{BY}} \begin{Bmatrix} \text{identifier-6} \\ \text{literal-4} \end{Bmatrix} \left[\begin{Bmatrix} \underline{\text{BEFORE}} \\ \underline{\text{AFTER}} \end{Bmatrix} \text{INITIAL} \begin{Bmatrix} \text{identifier-7} \\ \text{literal-5} \end{Bmatrix} \right] \right\} \cdots \end{matrix} \right\} \cdots
$$

Syntax Rules

All Formats

1) Identifier-1 must reference either a group item or any category of elementary item, described (either implicitly or explicitly) as usage is DISPLAY.

2) Identifier-3...identifier-n must reference either an elementary alphabetic, alphanumeric or numeric item described (either implicitly or explicitly) as usage in DISPLAY.

3) Each literal must be nonnumeric an may be any figurative constant, except ALL.

4) In Level 1, literal-1, literal-2, literal-3, literal-4, and literal-5 and the data items referenced by identifier-3, identifier-4, identifier-5, identifier-6 and identifier-7 must be one character in length. Except as specifically noted in syntax and general rules, this restriction on length does not apply to Level 2.

Formats 1 and 3 Only

5) Identifier-2 must reference an elementary numeric data item.

6) If either literal-1 or literal-2 is a figurative constant, the figurative constant refers to an implicit one-character data item.

Formats 2 and 3 Only

7) The size of the data referenced by literal-4 or identifier-6 must be equal to the size of the data referenced by literal-3 or identifier-5. When a figurative constant is used as literal-4, the size of the figurative constant is equal to the size of literal-3 or the size of the data item referenced by identifier-5.

8) When the CHARACTERS phrase is used, literal-4, literal-5, or the size of the data item referenced by identifier-6, identifier-7 must be one character in length.

9) When a figurative constant is used as literal-3, the data referenced by literal-4 or identifier-6 must be one character in length.

General Rules

1) Inspection (which includes the comparison cycle, the establishment of boundaries for the BEFORE or AFTER phrase, and the mechanism for tallying and/or replacing) begins at the leftmost character position of the data item referenced by identifier-1, regardless of its class, and proceeds from left to right to the rightmost character position as described in general rules 4 through 6.

2) For use in the INSPECT statement, the contents of the data item referenced by identifier-1, identifier-3, identifier-4, identifier-5, identifier-6 or identifier-7 will be treated as follows:

   a) If any of identifier-1, identifier-3, identifier-4, identifier-5, identifier-6 or identifier-7 are described as alphanumeric, the INSPECT statement treats the contents of each such identifier as a character-string.

   b) If any of identifier-1, identifier-3, identifier-4, identifier-5, identifier-6 or identifier-7 are described as alphanumeric edited, numeric edited or unsigned numeric, the data item is inspected as though it had been redefined as alphanumeric (see general rule 2a) and the INSPECT statement had been written to reference the redefined data item.

   c) If any of identifier-1, identifier-3, identifier-4, identifier-5, identifier-6 or identifier-7 are described as signed numeric, the data item is inspected as though it had been moved to an unsigned numeric data item of the same length and then the rules in general rule 2b had been applied.

3) In general rules 4 through 11 all references to literal-1, literal-2, literal-3, literal-4, and literal-5 apply equally to the contents of the data item referenced by identifier-3, identifier-4, identifier-5, identifier-6, and identifier-7, respectively.

4) During inspection of the contents of the data item referenced by identifier-1, each properly matched occurrence of literal-1 is tallied (Formats 1 and 3) and/or each properly matched occurrence of literal-3 is replaced by literal-4 (Formats 2 and 3).

5) The comparison operation to determine the occurrences of literal-1 to be tallied and/or occurrences of literal-3 to be replaced, occurs as follows:

   a) The operands of the TALLYING and REPLACING phrases are considered in the order they are specified in the INSPECT statement from left to right. The first literal-1, literal-3 is compared to an equal number of contiguous characters, starting with the leftmost character position in the data item referenced by identifier-1. Literal-1, literal-3 and that portion of the contents of the data item referenced by identifier-1 match, if and only if, they are equal, character for character.

   b) If no match occurs in the comparison of the first literal-1, literal-3, the comparison is repeated with each successive literal-1, literal-3, if any, until either a match is found or there is no next next successive literal-1, literal-3. When there is no next successive literal-1, literal-3, the character position in the data item referenced by identifier-1 immediately to the right of the leftmost character position considered in the last comparison cycle is considered as the leftmost character position, and the comparison cycle begins again with the first literal-1, literal-3.

   c) Whenever a match occurs, tallying and/or replacing takes place as described in general rules 8 through 10 below. The character position in the data item referenced by identifier-1 immediately to the right of the rightmost character position that participated in the match is now considered to be the leftmost character position of the data item referenced by identifier-1, and the comparison cycle starts again with the first literal-1, literal-3.

   d) The comparison operation continues until the rightmost character position of the data item referenced by identifier-1 has participated in a match or has been considered as the leftmost character position. When this occurs, inspection is terminated.

   e) If the CHARACTERS phrase is specified, an implied one-character operand participates in the cycle described in general rules 5a through 5d above, except that no comparison to the contents of the data item referenced by identifier-1 takes place. This implied character is considered always to match the leftmost character of the contents of the data item referenced by identifier-1 participating in the current comparison cycle.

6) The comparison operation defined in general rule 5 is affected by the BEFORE and AFTER phrases as follows:

   a) If the BEFORE or AFTER phrase is not specified, literal-1, literal-3 or the implied operand of the CHARACTERS phrase participates in the comparison operation as described in general rule 5.

b) If the BEFORE phrase is specified, the associated literal-1, literal-3 or the implied operand of the CHARACTERS phrase participates only in those comparison cycles which involve that portion of the contents of the data item referenced by identifier-1 from its leftmost character position up to, but not including, the first occurrence of literal-2, literal-5 within the contents of the data item referenced by identifier-1. The position of this first occurrence is determined before the first cycle of the comparison operation described in general rule 5 is begun. If, on any comparison cycle, literal-1, literal-3 or the implied operand of the CHARACTERS phrase is not eligible to participate, it is considered not to match the contents of the data item referenced by identifier-1. If there is no occurrence of literal-2, literal-5 within the contents of the data item referenced by identifier-1, its associated literal-1, literal-3, or the implied operand of the CHARACTERS phrase participates in the comparison operation as though the BEFORE phrase had not been specified.

c) If the AFTER phrase is specified, the associated literal-1, literal-3 or the implied operand of the CHARACTERS phrase may participate only in those comparison cycles which involve that portion of the contents of the data item referenced by identifier-1 from the character position immediately to the right of the rightmost character position of the first occurrence of literal-2, literal-5 within the contents of the data item referenced by identifier-1, and the rightmost character position of the data item referenced by identifier-1. The position of this first occurrence is determined before the first cycle of the comparison operation described in general rule 5 is begun. If, on any comparison cycle, literal-1, literal-3 or the implied operand of the CHARACTERS phrase is not eligible to participate, it is considered not to match the contents of the data item referenced by identifier-1. If there is no occurrence of literal-2, literal-5 within the contents of the data item referenced by identifier-1, its associated literal-1, literal-3 or the implied operand of the CHARACTERS phrase never is eligible to participate in the comparison operation.

Format 1

7) The content of the data item referenced by identifier-2 is not initialized by the execution of the INSPECT statement.

8) The rules for tallying are as follows:

a) If the ALL phrase is specified, the contents of the data item referenced by identifier-2 is incremented by one (1) for each occurrence of literal-1 matched within the contents of the data item referenced by identifier-1.

b) If the LEADING phrase is specified, the contents of the data item referenced by identifier-2 is incremented by one (1) for each contiguous occurrence of literal-1 matched within the contents of the data item referenced by identifier-1, provided that the leftmost such occurrence is at the point where comparison began in the first comparison cycle in which literal-1 was eligible to participate.

c) If the CHARACTERS phrase is specified, the contents of the data item referenced by identifier-2 is incremented by one (1) for each character matched—in the sense of general rule 5e—within the contents of the data item referenced by identifier-1.

Format 2

9) The required words ALL, LEADING and FIRST are adjectives that apply to each succeeding BY phrase until the next adjective appears.

10) The rules for replacement are as follows:

a) When the CHARACTERS phrase is specified, each character matched (in the sense of general rule 5e) in the contents of the data item referenced by identifier-1 is replaced by literal-4.

b) When the adjective ALL is specified, each occurrence of literal-3 matched in the contents of the data item referenced by identifier-1 is replaced by literal-4.

c) When the adjective LEADING is specified, each contiguous occurrence of literal-3 matched in the contents of the data item reference by identifier-1 is replaced by literal-4, provided that the leftmost occurrence is at the point where comparison began in the first comparison cycle in which literal-3 was eligible to participate.

d) When the adjective FIRST is specified, the leftmost occurrence of literal-3 matched within the contents of the data item refenced by identifier-1 is replaced by literal-4.

Format 3

11) A Format 3 INSPECT statement is interpreted and executed as though two successive INSPECT statements specifying the same identifier-1 had been written, with one statement being a Format 1 statement with TALLYING phrases identical to those specified in the Format 3 statement and the other statement being a Format 2 statement with REPLACING phrases identical to those specified in the Format 3 statement. The general rules given for matching and counting apply to the Format 1 statement; the general rules given for matching and replacing apply to the Format 2 statement. Below are six examples of the INSPECT statement.

INSPECT word TALLYING count FOR LEADING ''L'' BEFORE INITIAL ''A'', count-1 FOR LEADING ''A'' BEFORE INITIAL ''L''. *Example*

Where word = LARGE, count = 1, count-1 = 0.
Where word = ANALYST, count = 0, count-1 = 1.

INSPECT word TALLYING count FOR ALL ''L'', REPLACING LEADING ''A'' BY ''E'' AFTER INITIAL ''L''.

Where word = CALLAR, count = 2, word = CALLAR.
Where word = SALAMI, count = 1, word = SALEMI.
Where word = LATTER, count = 1, word = LETTER.

INSPECT word REPLACING ALL ''A'' BY ''G'' BEFORE INITIAL ''X''.

Where word = ARXAX, word = GRXAX.
Where word = HANDAX, word = HGNDGX.

INSPECT word TALLYING count FOR CHARACTERS AFTER INITIAL ''J'' REPLACING ALL ''A'' BY ''B''.

Where word = ADJECTIVE, count = 6, word = BDJECTIVE.
Where word = JACK, count = 3, word = JBCK.
Where word = JUJMAB, count = 5, word = JUJMBB.

INSPECT word REPLACING ALL "X" BY "Y", "B" BY "Z", "W" BY "Q" AFTER INITIAL "R".

Where word = RXXBOWY, word = RYYZOOY.
Where word = YZACDWBR, word = YZACDWZR.
Where word = RAWRXEB, word = RAORYEZ.

INSPECT word REPLACING CHARACTERS BY "B" BEFORE INITIAL "A".

word before : 1 2 X Z A B C D
word after   B B B B B A B C D

11.18 SELF TEST EXERCISES

1. Write DATA DIVISION entries required to define the following file and its records:

File name: DATA-FILE
Record names: DATA-REC-A, DATA-REC-B

Record type A:

1-10	Bid-number
11-20	Project Description
21-30	Bid amount
31	Record identification code ("A")

Record type B:

1-10	Bid-number
11-20	Dispersement amount
21-30	Dispersement description
31	Record identification code ("" B"")

2. Write PROCEDURE DIVISION entries required to read DATA-FILE defined in Exercise 1 above.

3. Using the GO TO/DEPENDING statement, write a PROCEDURE DIVISION module to compute SHIFT-DIFFERENTIAL based on SHIFT-CODE as follows:

Shift code	Differential
1	1.00
2	1.25
3	1.35

4. Write DATA DIVISION code required to define the following table:

Order amount	Cost
1 - 100	.04 each
101 - 300	$4.00 + .03 for each unit over 100
301 - 500	$10.00 + .025 for each unit over 300
501 - 700	$15.00 + .02 for each unit over 500
701 -9999	$19.00 + .015 for each unit over 700

5. Using the SEARCH statement, write a procedure to compute ORDER-COST for AMOUNT-OF-ORDER given the table defined in Exercise 4.

6. Write DATA DIVISION code required to define the following table:

Item number	Item Description
100	NUTS
125	BOLTS
130	SCREWS
155	WASHERS
460	GASKETS

7. Using the SEARCH ALL statement, write a procedure to move an appropriate item description to an output field based on ITM-NUM.

8. When possible, write an abbreviated version of each of the following conditions:
   a. A < B AND A EQUAL C
   b. A < B OR C AND A > D
   c. A < B AND C < B
   d. A IS GREATER THAN B OR A < D
   e. A LESS THAN B AND A < C
   f. A NOT > B AND A < C AND A NOT = C

9. Given the fields shown below, show the result of each STRING statement.

```
 A  B  -  C
└──┴──┴──┴──┘
ITM-A  PIC X(4).
```

```
 1  2  *  3  4
└──┴──┴──┴──┴──┘
ITM-B  PIC X(5).
```

```
 A  -  1  2  *
└──┴──┴──┴──┴──┘
ITM-C  PIC X(5).
```

```
ITM-R  PIC X(10) VALUE SPACES.
```

   a. STRING ITM-A, ITM-B, ITM-C
           DELIMITED BY "-"
           INTO ITM-R.
   b. STRING ITM-B DELIMITED BY "*"
               ITM-C, ITM-A DELIMITED BY "-"
               INTO ITM-R.
   c. STRING ITM-C DELIMITED BY SIZE
               ITM-A DELIMITED BY "C"
               ITM-B DELIMITED BY "*"
               INTO ITM-R.
   d. STRING ITM-A DELIMITED BY "*"
               ITM-B DELIMITED BY "-"
               INTO ITM-R.

10. Given the fields shown below, show the result of each UNSTRING statement

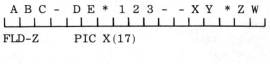

```
 A  B  C  -  D  E  *  1  2  3  -  -  X  Y  *  Z  W
└──┴──┴──┴──┴──┴──┴──┴──┴──┴──┴──┴──┴──┴──┴──┴──┴──┘
FLD-Z      PIC X(17)
```

```
└──┴──┴──┴──┘
FLD-A      PIC X(4).
```

```
└──┴──┴──┴──┴──┘
FLD-B      PIC X(5).
```

```
└──┴──┴──┴──┴──┴──┘
FLD-C      PIC X(6).
```

a. UNSTRING FLD-Z
    INTO FLD-A, FLD-B, FLD-C.
b. UNSTRING FLD-Z
    DELIMITED BY "*"
    INTO FLD-A, FLD-B, FLD-C.
c. UNSTRING FLD-Z
    DELIMITED BY "-"
    INTO FLD-A, FLD-B, FLD-C.
d. UNSTRING FLD-Z
    DELIMITED BY ALL "-"
    INTO FLD-A, FLD-B, FLD-C.
e. UNSTRING FLD-Z
    DELIMITED BY "--"
    INTO FLD-A, FLD-B.

11. A field NAME-IN contains a name in the form

        first-name   middle-initial   last-name

where one or more spaces separates each group of characters. The output required is a field NAME-OUT in the form:

        last-name,   first-name   middle-initial.

Write PROCEDURE DIVISION code to transform NAME-IN into NAME-OUT. For example:

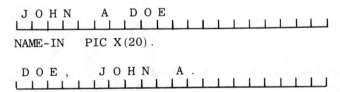

JOHN   A   DOE

NAME-IN   PIC X(20).

DOE,   JOHN   A.

NAME-OUT PIC X(20).

12. Write PROCEDURE DIVISION code to transform a nine-digit social security number into the form:

                  ddd-dd-dddd.

13. For an IBM system show the internal hexadecimal representation of a field with value +298 defined as:
a. USAGE DISPLAY
b. USAGE COMP
c. USAGE COMP-3
d. USAGE INDEX

14. Write SPECIAL names entries required to substitute the symbol ''Q'' for the dollar sign. Write a PICTURE code to edit a field defined as 9(6)V99.

15. Show the result of each INSPECT statement

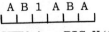

AB1ABA

ITEM-A   PIC X(6)

a. INSPECT ITEM-A REPLACING ALL ''A'' BY ''B''.
b. INSPECT ITEM-A REPLACING LEADING ''A'' BY '' ''.
c. INSPECT ITEM-A REPLACING FIRST ''B'' BY '' ''.

11.20   PROGRAMMING EXERCISES

1. The first record in a file contains the current date, and subsequent records each contain a name and a birthday. The output is to include the number of people contained in the file, the name of the oldest person and his or her date of birth, and the name of the youngest person and his or her date of birth.

2. The first record in a file contains the current date. Each succeeding record contains (among other items) the date of the last time an item was sold, the number of items on hand, the cost per item and the regular selling price. A store plans to have a sale on slow moving items. The purpose of the program is to produce a report showing recommended sale prices as follows:

> If the item has not been sold in the last 30 days, discount is 10%.
> If the item has not been sold in the last 60 days, discount is 20%.
> If the item has not been sold in the last 90 days, discount is 40%.

Any item which has sold in the last 30 days is not to be placed on sale. If there is only one of any item left in stock, it is to be discounted only five percent. Sale prices may not be lower than cost.

6. Revise the program in Section 6.11, Exercise 6 on pages 145-146 to use a date record for the current date.

4. Write a program to calculate the depreciation expense and book value for an asset. Depreciation should be calculated using the following three methods:

   a. *Straight Line Method*
      The amount of depreciation per year is:

      $$\frac{\text{cost - salvage value}}{\text{number of years}}$$

   For example, for an asset which cost $22,000 and has a salvage value of $2,000 and a life expectancy of five years, the depreciation amount is:

   $(22,000 - 2,000) / 5 = 4,000$

   The new book value is computed by subtracting the depreciation amount from the current book value. The resulting table would be:

Year	Depreciation expense	Book value
1	4,000	18,000
2	4,000	14,000
3	4,000	10,000
4	4,000	6,000
5	4,000	2,000

   b. *Sum of Years Digits Method*
      The amount of depreciation for the *i*th year is:

      $(\text{cost} - \text{salvage value}) * P_i$

      where P_i is a factor computed in the following way:
      1) Compute the sum:
         $S = 1 + 2 + 3 + ... + n$ where n represents the number of years
      2) Compute $P_i = (n + 1 - i) / S$ for i = 1, 2, 3 ... n.
      For example, if cost = 22,000, salvage value = $2,000 and n = 5, we find

      $S = 1 + 2 + 3 + 4 + 5 = 15$

      and

      $P_1 = (5 + 1 - 1) / 15 = 1/3$
      $P_2 = (5 + 1 - 2) / 15 = 4/15$

Thus the depreciation amount for the first year is

$(22,000 - 2,000) * 1/3 = 6,666$

For the second year the amount is

$(22,000 - 2,000) * 4/15 = 5,333$

The resulting table would be

Year	Depreciation expense	Book value
1	6,666	15,333
2	5,333	10,000
3	4,000	6,000
4	2,666	3,333
5	1,333	2,000

c. *Declining Balance Method*

The depreciation value is computed by multiplying the old book value by a constant fraction M. The value of M is defined by

$M = P / n$

where P is a proportion chosen by the accountant and n represents the number of years. For example, suppose cost = \$22,000, n = 5 and P = 150 (there is no allowance for salvage value using this method). Then,

$M = 150\% / 5 = 30\%$
depreciation $= 22,000 * .30 = 6,600$
new book value $= 22,000 - 6,600 = 15,400$

The resulting table would be

Year	Depreciation expense	Book value
1	6,600	15,400
2	4,620	10,780
3	3,234	7,546
4	2,263	5,282
5	1,584	3,697

5. A file contains records pertaining to the amount and analysis of the milk given by cows at a dairy. Each record contains the following items:

Cow i.d. number
Date
Amount of milk
Butterfat content of milk (percentage)

Write a program to compute the mean and standard deviation for the butterfat content of the milk. The mean is computed by finding the sum of all the observations and dividing by the number of observations:

$$m = \frac{\Sigma x_i}{n}$$

The standard deviation (represented by σ) is computed using the formula:

$$\sigma = \sqrt{\frac{\Sigma(x_i - m)^2}{n}}$$

Your program should flag the output for each cow which has an average butterfat content greater than $m + 2\sigma$ or less than $m - 2\sigma$.

6. XYZ Pharmacy, Inc. maintains a system designed to give their customers a statement at the end of each year showing all medicines purchased during the year. Design such a system, making appropriate assumptions regarding what data will be collected and what files will be maintained.

7. An insurance company maintains a file which has records containing (among other things):

> Policy number
> Amount of claim
> Date of accident
> Sex of driver
> Age of driver

Write a program to compute the frequency of claims and average claim amount for each cell of the following table:

```
           Sex
    AGE    M    F
   18-21
   22-25
   26-30
   31-35
   36-50
   51-65
   Over 65
```

8. Modify the program written for Exercise 8 above to print the proportion of claims computed by dividing the number claims for drivers in a particular age/sex group by the total number of policyholders in this age/sex group. Assume that your program has access to the master policy file to calculate the required totals for all policy-holders.

9. Write a program to produce personalized form letters for use in a promotional scheme for Widgets Inc. The company is sponsoring a contest which requires that the contestant return his or her letter to be eligible to win. The format of the letter can be discerned from the following sample letter addressed to John K. Doe, 123 MAPLE ST., ANYWHERE, FL, 32534. (Underlined portions of the letter must be changed for each recipient.)

> Widgets, Inc.
> 1000 Boulevard
> Somewhere, FL 10000

> John K. Doe
> 123 Maple Street
> Anywhere, FL   32534

> Dear John:

> How would you like to add $10,000 to the Doe bank account? You could make this deposit to an Anywhere bank by returning this letter to Widgets, Inc. in the enclosed envelope.

> Imagine the envy of your neighbors on Maple Street when they learn of your good fortune! Nothing to buy. Enter today.

> Yours truly,
> Widgets, Inc.

Record Layout

Positions	Description
1-10	Last name
11-20	First name
21-21	Middle initial
22-35	Street address
36-45	City
46-47	State
48-52	Zip

Use the following sample data:

Name	Address			
DOE JOHN K	123 MAPLE STREET	ANYWHERE	FL	32555
SMITH MARY A	1000 OAK AVE	SOMEWHERE	FL	32544
BROWN SUSAN S	14 MAIN RD	OVERTHERE	AL	52055
JONES JIM	1421 BROADWAY	NEW YORK	NY	10000

INDEXED FILES 12

12.1 SEQUENTIAL VS. RANDOM ACCESS

The only way to access records stored in a sequential file is one after another—that is, sequentially. Sequential access always means the processing of each record in a file from first to last, one after the other. While this step-by-step process may be suitable for many purposes, there are some applications in which the computer must access records randomly. For example, it may be desirable to update a file without having the transactions sorted into sequential order. As each transaction is processed, the associated master file record must be read (i.e., the master file must be accessed randomly). *Random access* is the ability to access any record regardless of its position in the file and without accessing previous records. A type of file organization technique which permits random access is *indexed* organization, available to COBOL programmers in most computer systems.

12.2 WHAT IS AN INDEXED FILE?

An indexed file is a sequential file similar in many ways to those discussed in Chapter 9. In fact, an indexed file can be used in place of any sequential file if desired. However, indexed files give us a very powerful added capability—the ability to process records from the file randomly. In random processing, the program specifies a value and the READ statement immediately returns the record from the file that has a key field with that value. Records not only may be read from the file but also may be changed and placed directly back into the file. Unlike the technique used in sequential processing, with random processing records also may be deleted from or added to the file without the program having to create an entirely new file.

In a sense, storing records in an indexed file is like storing pages in a looseleaf notebook with external tabs on each page showing page numbers. The user can retrieve any page from the notebook at will by using the appropriate tab.

In a similar way, a program can retrieve any desired record from an indexed file by specifying the key field value. The user of the looseleaf notebook can retrieve any desired record, make changes and reinsert it into the notebook. In much the same way, a program can perform similar operations on data records contained in an indexed file. The notebook user has the option of throwing pages away at will; in a similar way, records can be deleted from an indexed file.

The implementation of indexed files differs in many details among various computing systems. Typically, however, the system maintains at least one *index*, a table of pointers to records within the file. To access a record, the system looks up the key field value in the index and uses the pointer (which may be the actual physical address of the record) to read the desired record from the file. In some systems more than one index is maintained, which requires the look-up operation to proceed from a master index through one or more subindices to find the record in the file. These indices may be stored in the computer's memory or as part of the disk file itself. Using the looseleaf notebook analogy, the index corresponds roughly to the tabs on each page; it gives the system the ability to access records on demand.

Records within an indexed file generally are stored in sequential order to permit rapid and efficient sequential retrieval of the records. Thus, when the file is created initially, the records stored in the file must be in sequential order. All required indices are built by the operating system at the time the file is created. Adding records to and deleting records from the file are done in ways which do not destroy the sequential ordering of the records in the file. This is because typically there will be associated with the file an *overflow area*, a disk area into which added records are placed. In order to maintain the sequential nature of the file, appropriate pointers are constructed to indicate the sequential position within the file for added records. Deleted records generally are removed from the file by setting a code rather than by physically removing the data.

If a great many records have been added to or deleted from an indexed file, the overflow area may be filled up entirely with new records, while the deleted records still are occupying physical space within the file. At this point it becomes necessary to reorganize the file by physically removing the deleted records and inserting the added records into their appropriate physical position. This operation typically is provided for by an operating system *utility* program designed for this task. Utility programs are provided for the user as a part of the operating system.

12.3   FILE CREATION

To create an indexed file, the SELECT sentence for that file must contain entries shown in Figure 12.1.

```
SELECT    file-name ASSIGN TO system-name
          ACCESS IS SEQUENTIAL
          ORGANIZATION IS INDEXED
          RECORD KEY IS data-name.
```

Figure 12.1   SELECT entries for creation of an indexed file

The ACCESS clause specifies SEQUENTIAL, since the records placed in the file will be in sequential order. The ORGANIZATION clause specifies the type of file organization—in this case INDEXED. If the ORGANIZATION clause were omitted, the file would be assumed to have standard sequential organization. The RECORD KEY clause specifies the name of the field within the record defined for the file which will be used for creating and accessing the file. The records must be in ascending sequence based on the value contained in the field. There must not be any records with the same key field value. For example, note the SELECT entry for the file INVENTORY-FILE defined in Program 12.1 (lines 8 through 11).

Program 12.1   Indexed file creation/listing program

```
Line
1        IDENTIFICATION DIVISION.
2        PROGRAM-ID.   PROGRAM 12.1.
3        AUTHOR.   GARY GLEASON.
4        ENVIRONMENT DIVISION.
5        INPUT-OUTPUT SECTION.
6        FILE-CONTROL.
7            SELECT INFD ASSIGN TO DISK.
8            SELECT INVENTORY-FILE ASSIGN TO DISK
9                    ACCESS IS SEQUENTIAL
10                   ORGANIZATION IS INDEXED
11                   RECORD KEY IS INVENTORY-NUMBER-IRR.
12           SELECT PRINT ASSIGN TO PRINTER.
13       DATA DIVISION.
14       FILE SECTION.
15       FD   INFD.
16           DATA RECORD IS INPUT-RECORD.
17       01   INPUT-RECORD.
18           02   INVENTORY-NUMBER-IR      PIC X(5).
19           02   DESCRIPTION-IR           PIC X(20).
20           02   QUANTITY-ON-HAND-IR      PIC 9(5).
21           02   REORDER-POINT-IR         PIC 9(5).
22           02   REORDER-AMOUNT-IR        PIC 9(5).
23           02   UNIT-SELLING-PRICE-IR    PIC 9(4)V99.
24           02   UNIT-COST-PRICE-IR       PIC 9(4)V99.
25       FD   INVENTORY-FILE
26           DATA RECORD IS INVENTORY-RECORD.
27       01   INVENTORY-RECORD.
28           02   INVENTORY-NUMBER-IRR     PIC X(5).
29           02   DESCRIPTION-IRR          PIC X(20).
30           02   QUANTITY-ON-HAND-IRR     PIC 9(5).
31           02   REORDER-POINT-IRR        PIC 9(5).
32           02   REORDER-AMOUNT-IRR       PIC 9(5).
33           02   UNIT-SELLING-PRICE-IRR   PIC 9(4)V99.
34           02   UNIT-COST-PRICE-IRR      PIC 9(4)V99.
35       FD   PRINT
36           DATA RECORD IS PRINT-LINE.
37       01   PRINT-LINE      PIC X(132).
38       WORKING-STORAGE SECTION.
39       01   EOF-FLAG        PIC 9 VALUE ZERO.
```

(continued)

Program 12.1 (continued)

```
40      PROCEDURE DIVISION.
41      1000-MAJOR-LOGIC.
42          PERFORM 2000-INITIALIZATION.
43          PERFORM 3000-CONTROL UNTIL EOF-FLAG = 1.
44          PERFORM 5000-RE-INITIALIZE.
45          PERFORM 6000-LIST-READ UNTIL EOF-FLAG = 1
46          PERFORM 9000-TERMINATION.
47      2000-INITIALIZATION.
48          OPEN INPUT INFD.
49          OPEN OUTPUT INVENTORY-FILE.
50          READ INFD AT END MOVE 1 TO EOF-FLAG.
51      3000-CONTROL.
52          MOVE INPUT-RECORD TO INVENTORY-DATA-IRR.
53          WRITE INVENTORY-RECORD
54              INVALID KEY
55                  PERFORM 8000-ERROR.
56          READ INFD AT END MOVE 1 TO EOF-FLAG.
57      5000-RE-INITIALIZE.
58          CLOSE INFD.
59          CLOSE INVENTORY-FILE.
60          OPEN INPUT INVENTORY-FILE.
61          OPEN OUTPUT PRINT.
62          MOVE ZERO TO EOF-FLAG.
63          READ INVENTORY-FILE
64              AT END
65                  MOVE 1 TO EOF-FLAG.
66      6000-LIST-READ.
67          MOVE INVENTORY-DATA-IRR TO PRINT-LINE.
68          WRITE PRINT-LINE AFTER 2.
69          READ INVENTORY-FILE
70              AT END MOVE 1 TO EOF-FLAG.
71      8000-ERROR.
72          EXIT.
73      8200-ERROR.
74          EXIT.
75      9000-TERMINATION.
76          CLOSE INVENTORY-FILE LOCK.
77          CLOSE PRINT.
78          STOP RUN.
```

The WRITE statement for an indexed file must be of the form shown in Figure 12.2.

```
WRITE record-name [FROM data-name]
    INVALID KEY statement
```

Figure 12.2 WRITE statement for indexed file

The statement in the INVALID KEY clause is executed when an attempt is made to write a record which has an invalid key field value into the file. When creating an indexed file, the INVALID KEY condition will be encountered when the key fields of the records are not in ascending sequence or when an attempt is made to place two records with the same key field value into the file. In Program 12.1, the WRITE statement (lines 53 through 55)

```
WRITE INVENTORY-RECORD
    INVALID KEY
        PERFORM 8000-ERROR.
```

will cause the paragraph 8000-ERROR to be executed if the record keys are duplicated or out of sequence. For the sake of simplicity, this paragraph has been left empty in Program 12.1. However, in any real application appropriate error messages (such as KEY IS DUPLICATED) would be placed in this paragraph.

Program 12.1 creates an indexed file. Note the entries required in the SELECT sentence (lines 8 through 11), and the format of the WRITE statement for the indexed file (lines 53 through 55). Creation of the file requires only that the data records be read and written into the file (lines 51 through 56) in sequential order with unique key field records. The program also creates a listing of the file after it has been created. When accessed sequentially an indexed file is read in the same way as any other sequential file (lines 63 through 65).

12.4   ACCESSING DATA RECORDS

When an indexed file is used as an input file in a program, the records subsequently may be accessed either sequentially or randomly. Sequential accessing of records in an indexed file is like processing a sequential file. Records are read from the beginning to the end of the file. The READ statement must include an AT END clause to specify the action to be taken when end-of-file is found. The SELECT entry used for sequential processing of an indexed file is the same as that used for creation of the file. For example, the following COBOL statements could be used to list the records contained in INVENTORY-FILE created by Program 12.1:

```
PROCEDURE DIVISION.
1000-MAIN-LOGIC.
    OPEN INPUT INVENTORY-FILE
        OUTPUT PRINT.
    READ INVENTORY-FILE AT END MOVE 1 TO EOF-SWITCH.
    PERFORM 2000-WRITE-READ UNTIL EOF-SWITH = 1.
    CLOSE INVENTORY-FILE PRINT.
    STOP RUN.
2000-WRITE-READ.
    WRITE PRINT-LINE FROM INVENTORY-RECORD AFTER 1.
    READ INVENTORY-FILE AT END MOVE 1 TO EOF-SWITCH.
```

To get the computer to read records from an indexed file in random sequence you must to use the SELECT entry shown in Figure 12.3.

The ACCESS clause specifies RANDOM, since the records will be read only on demand rather than sequentially. As with sequential processing, the RECORD KEY clause specifies the field which has been used as the basis for organizing the

---

```
SELECT     file-name ASSIGN TO system-name
           ACCESS IS RANDOM
           ORGANIZATION IS INDEXED
           RECORD KEY IS data-name.
```

Figure 12.3   SELECT entry for random access to an indexed file

file. In order to access a record from the file, the program must place a value in
the field specified as the RECORD key. If such a record exists, the data is
returned to the program and processing continues normally. If such a record
does not exist or if the record has been deleted, an INVALID KEY condition will
be detected and reported.

The general form for a READ statement for randomly accessing a file is
shown in Figure 12.4. If an INVALID KEY condition is detected, the statement in
the INVALID KEY clause will be executed.

```
READ file-name [INTO data-name]
    INVALID KEY statement
```

Figure 12.4   General form of READ statement for random access to an indexed file

Consider Program 12.2 in the next section. The INVENTORY-FILE is being
processed randomly. Reading a record from the file with a key field value equal
to INVENTORY-NUMBER-IR is accomplished by the following statements (lines
46 through 49):

```
MOVE INVENTORY-NUMBER-IR TO INVENTORY-NUMBER-IRR.
READ INVENTORY-FILE
    INVALID KEY
        PERFORM 7000-ERROR.
```

If the INVENTORY-FILE does not contain an active record with the desired key
field value, the statements of the INVALID KEY clause will be executed.

12.5   UPDATING AN INDEXED FILE

When a complete update is performed on a sequential file, it is necessary to
create an entirely new file with the changes inserted at appropriate points.
Indexed files may be updated in place; records may be added, changed or deleted
in an existing file without having to create a new file. Moreover, since an
indexed file can be accessed randomly, the transaction records do not have to be
in any particular sequence; as each transaction record is read, the appropriate
master file record will be read, the changes will be made to it, and the record will
be rewritten onto the master file.

The SELECT sentence for an indexed file to be updated randomly will be the
same as for a file to be processed randomly. A file to be updated will be proc-

---

```
REWRITE file-name [FROM data-name]
    INVALID KEY statement
```

Figure 12.5   General form of the REWRITE statement or an indexed file

---

essed as both an input file (when a record is read from the file) and an output file (when the updated record is written onto the file). For this reason, the file must be opened in I-O mode. The format of the READ statement required to access a data record from a file is the same as when the file simply is being processed randomly. The INVALID KEY clause must be present. The statement required to rewrite the changed record into the file has the form shown in Figure 12.5.

In order to use the REWRITE statement, a record first must have been accessed via a READ statement. The INVALID KEY condition for the REWRITE statement will be found when the key field value is not equal to the key field of the last record read from the file. Therefore, it is important that the program does not modify this value between the point at which the record is read and when it is rewritten onto the file.

Program 12.2 illustrates the updating process. The inventory master file constructed by Program 12.1 is to be updated to reflect the number of items sold. As each transaction record is read (line 54), the corresponding master file record is read (line 47) and the number of items sold is subtracted from the number of items on hand (line 50). The changed record then is rewritten onto the inventory file using the REWRITE statement (lines 51 through 53). This process is repeated until all of the transactions have been processed.

Two error detection/recovery routines—7000-ERROR (lines 55 and 56) and 7200-ERROR-RECOVERY (lines 57 and 58)—are required in this program. 7000-ERROR is executed if an attempt is made to read a record which is not present from INVENTORY FILE. 7200-ERROR-RECOVERY is executed if the content of the key field is not equal to the key field of the last record read from the file when the REWRITE statement is executed (lines 51 through 53). For the sake of simplicity, these routines have not been completely coded. In practice, the programmer would want to pay careful attention to handling of errors of these types.

Program 12.2   Indexed file update program

```
Line
1         IDENTIFICATION DIVISION.
2         PROGRAM-ID.   PROGRAM 12.2.
3         AUTHOR.   GARY GLEASON.
4         ENVIRONMENT DIVISION.
5         INPUT-OUTPUT SECTION.
6         FILE-CONTROL.
7            SELECT INFD ASSIGN TO DISK.
8            SELECT INVENTORY-FILE ASSIGN TO DISK
9                   ACCESS IS RANDOM
10                  ORGANIZATION IS INDEXED
11                  RECORD KEY IS INVENTORY-NUMBER-IRR.
```

(continued)

Program 12.2   (continued)

```
12            SELECT PRINT ASSIGN TO PRINTER.
13       DATA DIVISION.
14       FILE SECTION.
15       FD   INFD.
16            DATA RECORD IS INPUT-RECORD.
17       01   INPUT-RECORD.
18            02   INVENTORY-NUMBER-IR      PIC X(5).
19            02   NUMBER-SOLD-IR           PIC 999.
20       FD   INVENTORY-FILE
21            DATA RECORD IS INVENTORY-RECORD.
22       01   INVENTORY-RECORD.
23            02   INVENTORY-NUMBER-IRR     PIC X(5).
24            02   DESCRIPTION-IRR          PIC X(20).
25            02   QUANTITY-ON-HAND-IRR     PIC 9(5).
26            02   REORDER-POINT-IRR        PIC 9(5).
27            02   REORDER-AMOUNT-IRR       PIC 9(5).
28            02   UNIT-SELLING-PRICE-IRR   PIC 9(4)V99.
29            02   UNIT-COST-PRICE-IRR      PIC 9(4)V99.
30       FD   PRINT
31            DATA RECORD IS PRINT-LINE.
32       01   PRINT-LINE     PIC X(132).
33       WORKING-STORAGE SECTION.
34       01   EOF-FLAG       PIC 9 VALUE ZERO.
35       PROCEDURE DIVISION.
36       1000-MAIN-LOGIC.
37            PERFORM 2000-INITIALIZATION.
38            PERFORM 3000-UPDATE UNTIL EOF-FLAG = 1.
39            PERFORM 9000-TERMINATION.
40       2000-INITIALIZATION.
41            OPEN INPUT INFD.
42            OPEN I-O INVENTORY-FILE.
43            OPEN OUTPUT PRINT.
44            READ INFD AT END MOVE 1 TO EOF-FLAG.
45       3000-UPDATE.
46            MOVE INVENTORY-NUMBER-IR TO INVENTORY-NUMBER-IRR.
47            READ INVENTORY-FILE
48               INVALID KEY
49                   PERFORM 7000-ERROR.
50            SUBTRACT NUMBER-SOLD-IR FROM QUANTITY-ON-HAND-IRR.
51            REWRITE INVENTORY-RECORD
52               INVALID KEY
53                   PERFORM 7200-ERROR-RECOVERY.
54            READ INFD AT END MOVE 1 TO EOF-FLAG.
55       7000-ERROR.
56            EXIT.
57       7200-ERROR-RECOVERY.
58            EXIT.
59       9000-TERMINATION.
60            CLOSE INVENTORY-FILE LOCK.
61            CLOSE PRINT.
62            STOP RUN.
```

12.6 ADDING AND DELETING RECORDS

In order to add records to an indexed file it is necessary to use the SELECT clause shown in Figure 12.3 (Access must be RANDOM) and open the file in I-O mode. The WRITE statement shown in Figure 12.2 is used to write new records in the file. The INVALID KEY condition occurs when an attempt is made to write a record with a key field value which duplicates the key field of a record already present in the file. The DELETE statement, which has the general form shown in Figure 12.6 is used to delete records from an indexed file.

```
DELETE file-name RECORD
    INVALID KEY statement
```

Figure 12.6   General form of the DELETE statement

If the file is being processed in sequential access mode, the DELETE statement will cause deletion of the last record read from the file. The INVALID KEY clause cannot be specified in this case.

If the file is being processed in random access mode, the content of the record key is used to determine the record to be deleted from the file. The INVALID KEY condition occurs if the file does not contain a record with a record key equal to that contained in the record key field.

In order for the records to be deleted from a file, the file must be opened in I-O mode since deletion actually causes the system to read the file (to determine if a record exists) and write a new value into a code field to indicate that the record is deleted.

12.7 A COMPLETE FILE UPDATE EXAMPLE

The Program 12.3 illustrates the transaction code approach to file maintenance which was applied to sequential files in Section 9.12. The transaction file contains records in essentially the same format as the records in the file to be updated, with the addition of a transaction code. The update program processes each transaction, taking appropriate action on records in the file to be updated. Program 12.3 provides a complete update procedure for the file INVENTORY-FILE created by Program 12.1. The following transaction codes are used:

code	meaning
CD	change description
CQ	change quantity on hand
CP	change reorder point
CA	change reorder amount
CS	change unit selling price
CC	change unit cost
AQ	add to quantity on hand
SQ	subtract from quantity on hand
AR	add record to file
DR	delete record from file

Program 12.3 Indexed file update program

```
Line
1         IDENTIFICATION DIVISION.
2         PROGRAM-ID.   PROGRAM 12.3.
3         AUTHOR.   HORN.
4         ENVIRONMENT DIVISION.
5         CONFIGURATION SECTION.
6             SOURCE-COMPUTER.
7             OBJECT-COMPUTER.
8         INPUT-OUTPUT SECTION.
9         FILE-CONTROL.
10            SELECT TRANSACTION ASSIGN TO DISK.
11            SELECT INVENTORY-FILE ASSIGN TO DISK
12                ACCESS IS RANDOM
13                ORGANIZATION IS INDEXED
14                RECORD KEY IS INVENTORY-NUMBER-IRR.
15            SELECT PRINT ASSING TO PRINTER.
16        DATA DIVISION.
17        FILE SECTION.
18        FD   TRANSACTIONS
19             DATA RECORD IS TRANSACTION-RECORD.
20        01   TRANSACTION-RECORD.
21             03    INVENTORY-NUMBER-TR           PIC X(5).
22             03    DESCRIPTION-TR                PIC X(20).
23             03    QUANTITY-ON-HAND-TR           PIC 9(5).
24             03    REORDER-POINT-TR              PIC 9(5).
25             03    REORDER-AMOUNT-TR             PIC 9(5).
26             03    UNIT-SELLING-PRICE-TR         PIC 9(4)V99.
27             03    UNIT-COST-PRICE-TR            PIC 9(4)V99.
28             03    TRANSACTION-CODE-TR           PIC XX.
29                 88    CHANGE-DESCRIPTION           VALUE "CD".
30                 88    CHANGE-QUANTITY-ON-HAND      VALUE "CQ".
31                 88    CHANGE-REORDER-POINT         VALUE "CP".
32                 88    CHANGE-REORDER-AMOUNT        VALUE "CA".
33                 88    CHANGE-UNIT-SELLING-PRICE    VALUE "CS".
34                 88    CHANGE-UNIT-COST             VALUE "CC".
35                 88    ADD-TO-QTY-ON-HAND           VALUE "AQ".
36                 88    SUBTRACT-FROM-QTY-ON-HAND    VALUE "SQ".
37                 88    ADD-RECORD                   VALUE "AR".
38                 88    DELETE-RECORD                VALUE "DR".
39                 88    VALID-TRANSACTION-CODE       VALUE
40                     "CD",  "CQ",  "CP",  "CA",  "CS",
41                     "CC",  "AQ",  "SQ",  "AR",  "DR".
42        FD   INVENTORY-FILE
43             DATA RECORD IS INVENTORY-RECORD.
44        01   INVENTORY-RECORD.
45             03    INVENTORY-NUMBER-IR           PIC X(5).
46             03    DESCRIPTION-IR                PIC X(20).
47             03    QUANTITY-ON-HAND-IR           PIC 9(5).
48             03    REORDER-POINT-IR              PIC 9(5).
49             03    UNIT-SELLING-PRICE-IR         PIC 9(4)V99.
50             03    UNIT-COST-PRICE-IR            PIC 9(4)V99.
51        FD   PRINT
```

(continued)

Program 12.3   (continued)

```
52            DATA RECORD IS PRINT-RECORD.
53      01    PRINT-RECORD  PIC X(132).
54      WORKING-STORAGE-SECTION.
55      01    EOF-FLAG  PIC X(3)  VALUE "NO".
56            88  END-OF-TRANSACTION  VALUE "YES".
57      01    RECORD-FOUND-FLAG  PIC X(3)  VALUE "YES".
58            88  RECORD-FOUND  VALUE "YES".
59      PROCEDURE DIVISION.
60      1000-MAIN-LOGIC.
61          PERFORM 2000-INITIALIZATION.
62          PERFORM 3000-UPDATE-READ UNTIL END-OF-TRANSACTIONS.
63          PERFORM 4000-TERMINATION.
64      2000-INITIALIZATION.
65          OPEN INPUT TRANSACTIONS
66                  I-O INVENTORY-FILE
67                  OUTPUT PRINT.
68          READ TRANSACTIONS
69            AT END
70                MOVE "YES" TO EOF-FLAG.
71      3000-UPDATE-READ.
72          IF NOT VALID-TRANSACTION-CODE
73                PERFORM 5000-ERROR-IN-TRANS-CODE
74          ELSE
75            IF ADD-RECORD
76                PERFORM 6000-ADD-RECORD-TO-FILE
77            ELSE
78              IF DELETE-RECORD
79                  PERFORM 7000-DELETE-RECORD-FROM-FILE
80              ELSE
81                  PERFORM 8000-UPDATE-RECORD.
82          READ TRANSACTIONS
83            AT END
84                MOVE "YES" TO EOF-FLAG.
85      4000-TERMINATION.
86          CLOSE TRANSACTIONS
87                  INVENTORY-FILE
88                  PRINT.
89          STOP RUN.
90      5000-ERROR-IN-TRANS-CODE.
91          EXIT.
92      6000-ADD-RECORD-TO-FILE.
93          MOVE TRANSACTION-RECORD TO INVENTORY-RECORD.
94          WRITE INVENTORY-RECORD
95            INVALID KEY
96                PERFORM 6100-ERROR-IN-ADD.
97      6100-ERROR-IN-ADD.
98          EXIT.
99      7000-DELETE-RECORD-FROM-FILE.
100         MOVE INVENTORY-NUMBER-TR TO INVENTORY-NUMBER-IR.
101         DELETE INVENTORY-RECORD
102           INVALID KEY
103               PERFORM 7100-ERROR-IN-DELETE.
104     7100-ERROR-IN-DELETE.
```

(continued)

Program 12.3   (continued)

```
105            EXIT.
106        8000-UPDATE-RECORD.
107            MOVE INVENTORY-NUMBER-ID TO INVENTORY-NUMBER-IR.
108            MOVE "YES" TO RECORD-FOUND-FLAG.
109            READ INVENTORY-FILE
110                INVALID KEY
111                    MOVE "NO" TO RECORD-FOUND-FLAG.
112            IF RECORD-FOUND
113                PERFORM 9000-CHANGE-FIELD
114            ELSE
115                PERFORM 8100-ERROR-IN-UPDATE.
116        8100-ERROR-IN-UPDATE.
117            EXIT.
118        9000-CHANGE-FIELD.
119            IF CHANGE-DESCRIPTION
120                MOVE DESCRIPTION-TR TO DESCRIPTION-IR.
121            IF CHANGE-QUANTITY-ON-HAND
122                MOVE QUANTITY-ON-HAND-TR TO QUANTITY-ON-HAND-IR.
123            IF CHANGE-REORDER-POINT
124                MOVE REORDER-POINT-TR TO REORDER-POINT-IR.
125            IF CHANGE-REORDER-AMOUNT
126                MOVE REORDER-AMOUNT-TR TO REORDER-AMOUNT-TR.
127            IF CHANGE-UNIT-SELLING-PRICE
128                MOVE UNIT-SELLING-PRICE-TR TO
129                    UNIT-SELLING-PRICE-IR.
130            IF CHANGE-UNIT-COST
131                MOVE UNIT-COST-PRICE-TR TO UNIT-COST-PRICE-IR.
132            IF ADD-TO-QTY-ON-HAND
133                ADD QUANTITY-ON-HAND-TR TO QUANTITY-ON-HAND-IR.
134            IF SUBTRACT-FROM-QTY-ON-HAND
135                SUBTRACT QUANTITY-ON-HAND-TR FROM
136                    QUANTITY-ON-HAND-IR.
137            REWRITE INVENTORY-RECORD
138                INVALID KEY
139                    PERFORM 9100-ERROR-IN-PROGRAM.
140        9100-ERROR-IN-PROGRAM.
141            EXIT.
```

In Program 12.3, access to the file is random (line 12) since the transaction records are not in sequence by inventory number. As each transaction is read (lines 82 through 84) an appropriate paragraph is selected (lines 72 through 81) to take action on the transaction as specified by the transaction code. Note the extensive use of error detection procedures in the program. The following errors can occur and would be handled by the program:

Invalid transaction code (lines 72 and 73).
Attempt to add a duplicate record to the file (lines 95 and 96).
Attempt to delete a record not present in the file (lines 102 and 103).
Attempt to change a record not present in the file (lines 110 and 111).
Key field value has changed between the point at which a record is read and the point at which the updated record is written onto the file (lines 138 and 139).

Specific coding of the procedures executed when an error is detected is covered in section 12.11, Exercise 2.

12.8 DYNAMIC ACCESS

In addition to sequential and random access methods discussed previously, COBOL permits dynamic access to an indexed file. Dynamic access permits both sequential access and random access to the same file in the same program. The general form of the SELECT entry for dynamic access is shown in Figure 12.7.

```
SELECT    file-name ASSIGN TO system-name
          ORGANIZATION IS INDEXED
          ACCESS MODE IS DYNAMIC
          RECORD KEY IS data-name.
```

Figure 12.7   General form of SELECT entry for dynamic access to an indexed file

When an indexed file is accessed dynamically and opened in either INPUT or I-O mode, records are read sequentially from the file using the Format-1 READ statement with the NEXT RECORD option as shown in Figure 12.8; in order to read records randomly from a file a Format-2 READ statement is required.

```
Format-1    (for sequential access)
   READ     file-name [NEXT] RECORD
            [INTO data-name]
            [AT END statement]
Format-2    (for random access)
   READ     file-name RECORD
            [INTO data-name]
            [INVALID KEY statement]
```

Figure 12.8   General form of READ statements

When a Format-1 READ statement is executed, the next available record is read from the file; if the file has just been opened, then the first record is read. When a Format-2 READ statement is executed, the value contained in the key field specified for the file is used to determine the record to be read. If a Format-1 READ statement is executed after a Format-2 statement, the record immediately following the record by the Format-2 statement will be read. This feature can be used to continue the processing of an indexed file in a sequential manner after reading a specified record. For example, suppose we want to process all of the

records of the file INVENTORY-FILE of Program 12.1 which follow the record
with key field value 5000. The following program segment could be used:

```
        .
        .
        .

SELECT INVENTORY-FILE ASSIGN TO DISK
    ACCESS IS DYNAMIC
    ORGANIZATION IS INDEXED
    RECORD KEY IS INVENTORY-NUMBER-IRR.
        .

        .

        .

PROCEDURE DIVISION.
1000-MAIN-LOGIC.
    OPEN INPUT INVENTORY-FILE.
    MOVE "5000" TO INVENTORY-NUMBER-IRR.
    READ INVENTORY-FILE
        INVALID-KEY PERFORM 3000-ERROR.
    READ INVENTORY-FILE NEXT RECORD
        AT END MOVE 1 TO EOF-FLAG.
    PERFORM 2000-PROCESS-READ
        UNTIL EOF-FLAG = 1.
    CLOSE INVENTORY-FILE.
    STOP RUN.
2000-PROCESS-READ.

        .

        .

    READ INVENTORY-FILE NEXT RECORD
        AT END MOVE 1 TO EOF-FLAG.
3000-ERROR.
    EXIT.
```

Of course, the above code assumes that a record with a key field value of 5000
exist in the file. If such a record does not exist the Format-1 READ statement
results in an INVALID KEY condition and the subsequent Format-2 READ statment will cause the first record in the file to be read.

Some versions of COBOL support the START statement which can be used
to begin processing of an indexed file accessed in dynamic mode at a specified
record. The general form of the START statement is shown in Figure 12.9.

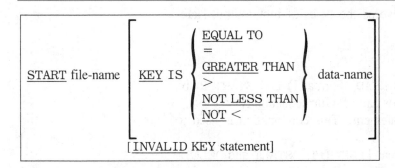

Figure 12.9 General form of the START statement

The START statement will cause subsequent access to the file to begin with a record whose key field value satisfies the relation specified in the KEY IS clause. The data-name specified in the KEY IS clause will normally be the RECORD KEY field specified for the file. For example, in order to begin processing the file INVENTORY-FILE with a record following the record with inventory number equal to 5000, the following could be used:

```
MOVE "5000" TO INVENTORY-NUMBER-IR.
START INVENTORY-FILE KEY > INVENTORY-NUMBER-IR
    INVALID KEY PERFORM 3000-ERROR.
```

The INVALID KEY condition will result if there is no record in the file satisfying the condition (i.e., no record with key field value greater than 5000). If the KEY IS clause is omitted, the current content of the RECORD KEY field is used for comparison and the "equal to" relation is assumed. For example, to begin processing of the file with record "5000", either of the following two coding sequences could be used:

```
MOVE "5000" TO INVENTORY-NUMBER-IR.
START INVENTORY-FILE
    KEY IS EQUAL TO INVENTORY-NUMBER-IR
    INVALID PERFORM 3000-ERROR.
```
or
```
MOVE "5000" TO INVENTORY-NUMBER-IR.
START INVENTORY-FILE
    INVALID KEY PERFORM 3000-ERROR.
```

The NOT LESS THAN option is useful to begin processing of a file at a specified record if it exists or, if it does not, at the next record. For example, to begin the processing of INVENTORY-FILE at record 5000 or if record 5000 is not in the file with the first record with key field greater than 5000, the following code could be used:

```
MOVE "5000" TO INVENTORY-NUMBER-IR.
START INVENTORY-FILE
    KEY NOT LESS THAN INVENTORY-NUMBER-IR
    INVALID KEY PERFORM 3000-ERROR.
```

12.9   ACCESS METHOD AND OPEN MODES

An indexed file may be accessed by three methods (SEQUENTIAL, RANDOM and (DYNAMIC) and opened in three modes (INPUT, OUTPUT, I-O). The combination of access method and open mode governs the types of input/output statements which may be used.

Sequential Access

INPUT mode permits the statements READ (Format-1) and START to be used. This combination is used to read all or part of a file sequentially.

OUTPUT mode permits the WRITE statement. This combination is used to create an indexed file.

I-O mode permits use of READ (Format-1) REWRITE, START and DELETE statements. This combination is used for sequentially updating an indexed file. Note that new records cannot be added since the WRITE statement cannot be used.

Random Access

INPUT mode permits the Format-2 READ statement only. This combination is used to access data records in the file randomly; no changes to the file can be made.

OUTPUT mode permits the WRITE statement only. This combination is used to add records to a file randomly.

I-O mode permits the use of the READ (Format-2), WRITE, REWRITE and DELETE statements. This combination is used to perform random updating of an indexed file; it permits addition, deletion and changing of records.

Dynamic Access

INPUT mode permits the Format-1 READ for sequential access, the Format-2 READ for random access, and the START statement. This combination is used to process sequential segments of an indexed file.

OUTPUT mode permits the WRITE statement only. This combination can be used only to add records to an indexed file; dynamic access always implies that the file is in existence.

I-O mode permits use of the Format-1 READ (for sequential access), Format-2 READ (for random access), WRITE, REWRITE, START and DELETE statements. This combination allows the program greatest possible flexibility in processing an indexed file.

Choosing the Best Combination

In general a programmer should choose that combination of access method and open mode which permits only the type of operation on a file required by the particular program. This practice will result in fewer potential errors in the long run, and it is in keeping with a widely held belief that restricting operations on a file to the minimum required to perform a given task enhances the overall security of the data processing system.

12.10   DEBUG CLINIC

The use of a FILE STATUS item can help ease the task of debugging a program which processes an indexed file. The FILE STATUS item is updated automatically after each input/output operation. The value contained in the item shows the status of the input/output operation. In order to make use of a FILE STATUS item, you must include a FILE STATUS entry in the SELECT sentence for the file, as shown in Figure 12.10.

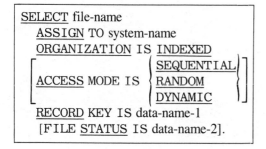

Figure 12.10   General form of SELECT for indexed files

First Character	Second Character	Meaning
0	0	Successful Completion
0	2	Successful Completion, Duplicate Key
1	0	At End
2	1	Sequence Error
2	2	Duplicate Key
2	3	No Record Found
2	4	Boundary Violation
3	4	Permanent Error
9	—	Implementor Defined

Figure 12.11   Meaning of FILE STATUS item for indexed input/output

A FILE STATUS item must be defined as a two-character field in WORKING-STORAGE as described in Section 9.13. The meaning ascribed to each possible setting of the FILE STATUS item is shown in Figure 12.11.

12.11 SELF TEST EXERCISES

1. Complete the following table by entering valid input/output statements for each combination of file access method and open mode:

	OPEN MODE		
	INPUT	OUTPUT	I/O
SEQUENTIAL			
RANDOM			
DYNAMIC			

(FILE ACCESS METHOD)

2. Write appropriate error messages for each of the error routines in Program 12.3.

3. What combination of Access method and open mode would be best for the indexed file described in each of the following operations:
   a. creating an indexed file.
   b. making a sequential listing of an indexed file.
   c. processing a sequentially organized file of transactions to update an indexed file.
   d. deleting records randomly from an indexed file.
   e. reading data randomly contained in an indexed file (no updating).

   f. adding records randomly to an indexed file.

   g. sequentially listing a portion of the records in an indexed file.

   h. updating (add/delete/change) records in an indexed file randomly and creating a sequential listing of the indexed file with the same program.

4. Distinguish between the WRITE and REWRITE statements. What purpose is served by each?

5. Distinguish between Format-1 READ and Format-2 READ. What purpose is served by each?

6. Can an indexed file be created under dynamic access? Explain.

7. Write code required to begin sequential processing of an indexed file, beginning with the record with key field value 200 or the next available record.

8. A Format-2 READ statement for an indexed file has resulted in a FILE STATUS item value "23". Were the statements in the INVALID KEY clause of the statement executed? Why or why not?

12.12 PROGRAMMING EXERCISES

1. Write a program to create an indexed file for the payroll master file described in Section 9.14, Exercise 1 on page 226. Use the sample data provided in Section 9.13, Exercise 2.

2. Write a program to update the file created in Exercise 1 above allowing additions, changes, and deletions. Use the codes shown below:

```
code |        meaning
 CN  | change name
 CR  | change rate
 CD  | change number dependents
 CY  | change YTD gross
  D  | delete record
  A  | add record
```

Use the sample data provided for Section 9.14, Exercises 3 and 4.

3. Rewrite the program for Section 9.14, Exercise 6 using an indexed master file. Is it necessary to sort the transaction file using this revised approach?

4. Revise the system designed for Section 9.14, Exercise 9 using an indexed master file. What changes does this type of file organization enable you to make in your system?

Appendix A

REPORT WRITER

The report writer module allows the programmer to specify report features including headings, subtotals, and final totals without writing the detailed PRO-CEDURE DIVISION logic required to produce these elements. The required PRO-CEDURE DIVISION logic is generated by the COBOL compiler; the programmer is freed from the tedious task of coding and debugging routines for line counting, page numbering, data movement, and control breaks. The report writer is not available on all COBOL compilers; the reader should check locally available documentation before attempting to write programs using report writer.

The report writer contains facilities to automatically generate the following report elements:

1. Report heading—produced automatically once at the beginning of the report
2. Page heading—produced automatically at the beginning of each page
3. Detail line—as many different types of detail lines as may be required may be specified; production is under the control of the programmer
4. Control heading—produced automatically once at the beginning of processing of each control group
5. Control footing—produced automatically at the end of processing of each control group
6. Page footing—produced automatically at the end of each page
7. Report footing—produced automatically at the end of the report

Additionally, the report writer contains facilities for generating subtotals, line and page counting, generating output lines without MOVE or WRITE statements and a variety of other features to facilitate the programmer's task in writing report type programs. The report writer does not assume the complete task of controlling the program; the programmer must still open files, control the proc-

essing of records and close files upon completion of processing. The report writer does include three additional and very powerful PROCEDURE DIVISION
verbs:

1. INITIATE—used to begin the production of the report
2. GENERATE—used to produce detail, control break and page related lines
3. TERMINATE—used to end the production of the report

Use of these verbs causes the "automatic" features of the report writer module to
be carried out during execution of the program.

A.1 PROGRAM EXAMPLE

Program 7.1 of Chapter 7 is rewritten using the report writer and shown as Program A.1. The report produced by this program makes use of the following elements:

- Report heading
- Page heading
- Detail line
- Page footing (page totals)
- Control footing (final totals)

Let us examine the program required to produce this report.

Program A.1 Alphabetic employee report using report writer

```
1        IDENTIFICATION DIVISION.
2        PROGRAM-ID. BASIC REPORT.
3        ENVIRONMENT DIVISION.
4        INPUT-OUTPUT SECTION.
5        FILE-CONTROL.
6            SELECT IN-FILE ASSIGN TO DISK.
7            SELECT OUT-FILE ASSIGN TO PRINTER.
8        DATA DIVISION.
9         FILE SECTION.
10      FD IN-FILE
11           DATA RECORD IS IN-REC.
12       01 IN-REC.
13           02 IR-NAME                 PIC X(16).
14           02 IR-INITIAL              PIC X.
15           02 IR-EMPLOYEE-NUMBER       PIC X(9).
16           02 IR-DEPARTMENT            PIC X(3).
17           02 IR-SALARY               PIC 9(6).
```

(continued)

Program A.1   (continued)

```
18          02 FILLER                    PIC X(45).
19     FD OUT-FILE
20          REPORT IS EMPLOYEE-REPORT.
21     WORKING-STORAGE SECTION.
22     01  EOF-FLAG                      PIC 9           VALUE ZERO.
23          88 NOT-END-OF-FILE                           VALUE ZERO.
24          88 END-OF-FILE                               VALUE 1.
25     01  PAGE-TOTAL                    PIC  9(6)V99.
26     01  NUMBER-OF-EMPLOYEES           PIC 9(4)        VALUE 0.
27     REPORT SECTION.
28     RD  EMPLOYEE-REPORT
29          CONTROL IS FINAL
30          PAGE LIMIT IS 45 LINES
31          HEADING 1
32          FIRST DETAIL 5
33          LAST DETAIL 43
34          FOOTING     45.
35     01  TYPE IS REPORT HEADING
36          LINE NUMBER IS 1.
37          02   COLUMN NUMBER IS 48
38               PICTURE IS X(11)
39               VALUE IS "ABC COMPANY".
40          02   COLUMN NUMBER IS 61
41               PICTURE X(10)
42               VALUE "ALPHABETIC".
43          02   COLUMN 72
44               PICTURE X(8)
45               VALUE "EMPLOYEE".
46          02   COLUMN 81 PIC X(6) VALUE "REPORT".
47     01  COLUMN-HEAD
48          TYPE IS PAGE HEADING
49          LINE NUMBER IS 3.
50          02   COLUMN 27 PIC X(9) VALUE "LAST NAME".
51          02   COLUMN 44 PIC X(7) VALUE "INITIAL".
52          02   COLUMN 59 PIC X(15) VALUE "EMPLOYEE NUMBER".
53          02   COLUMN 82 PIC X(10) VALUE "DEPARTMENT".
54          02   COLUMN 100 PIC X(6) VALUE "SALARY".
55          02   COLUMN 103 PIC X(4) VALUE "PAGE".
56          02   COLUMN 108 PIC ZZ SOURCE IS PAGE-COUNTER.
57     01  DETAIL-LINE
58          TYPE IS DETAIL
59          LINE NUMBER IS PLUS 2.
60          02   COLUMN 27 PIC X(16) SOURCE IS IR-NAME.
61          02   COLUMN 44 PIC X SOURCE IS IR-INITIAL.
62          02   COLUMN 59 PIC X(9) SOURCE IS IR-EMPLOYEE-NUMBER.
63          02   COLUMN 84 PIC X(3) SOURCE IS IR-DEPARTMENT.
64          02   COLUMN 97 PIC $ZZZ,ZZZ SOURCE IS IR-SALARY.
65     01  TYPE IS PAGE FOOTING
66          LINE IS PLUS 2.
67          02   PF-PAGE-TOTAL
68                  COLUMN 89 PIC $ZZZ,ZZZ.99
69                  SOURCE IS PAGE-TOTAL.
```

(continued)

Program A.1   (continued)

```
70     01   TYPE IS CONTROL FOOTING FINAL
71          LINE IS PLUS 2.
72          02   COLUMN 71 PIC ZZZ9
73               SOURCE IS NUMBER-OF-EMPLOYEES.
74          02   COLUMN 80 PIC X(9) VALUE "EMPLOYEES".
75          02   COLUMN 96 PIC $**,***,999
76               SUM IR-SALARY.
77     PROCEDURE DIVISION.
78     DECLARATIVES.
79     100-END-OF-PAGE SECTION.
80          USE BEFORE REPORTING COLUMN-HEAD.
81     110-INITIALIZE-PAGE-TOTAL.
82          MOVE 0 TO PAGE-TOTAL.
83     END DECLARATIVES.
84     200-MAIN SECTION.
85     210-MAIN-LOGIC.
86          PERFORM 300-INITIALIZATION.
87          PERFORM 400-CONTROL UNTIL END-OF-FILE.
88          PERFORM 500-TERMINATION.
89     300-INITIALIZATION.
90          OPEN     INPUT IN-FILE
91                   OUTPUT OUT-FILE.
92          INITIATE EMPLOYEE-REPORT.
93          PERFORM 600-READ.
94     400-CONTROL.
95          ADD 1 TO NUMBER-OF-EMPLOYEES.
96          ADD IR-SALARY TO PAGE-TOTAL.
97          GENERATE DETAIL-LINE.
98          PERFORM 600-READ.
99     500-TERMINATION.
100         TERMINATE EMPLOYEE-REPORT.
101         CLOSE IN-FILE
102              OUT-FILE.
103         STOP RUN.
104    600-READ.
105         READ IN-FILE AT END MOVE 1 TO EOF-FLAG.
```

(continued)

Comparison of programs 7.1 and A.1 will reveal major differences in the DATA and PROCEDURE Divisions.

The program involves two files—IN-FILE and OUT-FILE—defined in SELECT statements (lines 6-7) and in FD entries (lines 10-20). The FD entry for OUT-FILE (lines 19-20) makes use of the REPORT clause:

```
FD OUT-FILE
   REPORT IS EMPLOYEE-REPORT.
```

The REPORT clause specifies the report name and serves to link the file to the RD entry of the REPORT SECTION which follows.

The WORKING-STORAGE SECTION of the DATA DIVISION (lines 21-26) contains far fewer entries in Program A.1 compared to Program 7.1. The specifi-

Program A.1   (continued)

		ABC COMPANY ALPHABETIC EMPLOYEE REPORT			
LAST NAME	INITIAL	EMPLOYEE NUMBER	DEPARTMENT	SALARY	PAGE 1
ABNER	L	987654321	654	$ 90,000	
ACHER	W	011907260	001	$ 57,000	
ADAMS	S	123456789	234	$ 75,300	
ALDRIDGE	M	159763548	222	$ 14,000	
ALSIP	J	762158345	222	$ 10,000	
AMORE	M	562160536	042	$ 17,000	
ANDERSON	J	123456789	123	$ 10,000	
ARD	S	745213214	298	$ 13,000	
BROXTON	D	987987987	042	$ 30,000	
BUTTER	B	036028036	203	$125,000	
CADENHEAD	J	142753869	241	$ 50,000	
CALDWELL	W	654654654	072	$ 10,000	
CANDY	D	320220290	542	$ 24,000	
CANTRELL	S	980250026	555	$ 14,000	
CARTER	T	345678901	456	$ 85,000	
CARTOLER	V	028099812	021	$ 75,000	
CHRISTOPHER	B	024631205	216	$ 19,000	
CHRISTY	C	421360380	777	$ 35,000	
COOPER	R	019876536	438	$ 15,000	
CUNNINGHAM	C	439726158	555	$ 12,000	
				$704,300.00	
LAST NAME	INITIAL	EMPLOYEE NUMBER	DEPARTMENT	SALARY	PAGE 4
PARKER	L	147147147	062	$ 20,000	
POWELL	D	785452113	235	$ 12,000	
QUEST	H	365245362	666	$ 35,000	
RASSMUSEN	J	081000001	721	$ 20,000	
RHODES	D	962385174	243	$ 10,000	
ROBERTSON	M	326985412	021	$ 30,000	
RUSHING	R	901125544	998	$ 14,000	
SELLERS	P	312312312	052	$ 30,000	
SIMPSON	D	412578525	652	$ 10,000	
SMITH	R	320120354	012	$ 7,000	
SPRINGER	S	452831429	701	$ 16,000	
THOMPSON	S	262373155	215	$ 10,000	
VINCENT	W	212345226	217	$ 12,000	
WARD	T	321321321	032	$ 11,000	
WATKINS	S	545116355	544	$ 12,000	
WESTINGHOUSE	M	456253255	215	$ 12,000	
WILSON	A	632547328	777	$ 10,000	
		77	EMPLOYEES	$*2,291,300	
				$251,000.00	

cation of an end of file flag is still required (lines 22-24). (Recall that the reading and processing of files is still controlled by the programmer in the usual way.) Also required are accumulators that are not under automatic control of the report writer logic. In this case accumulators PAGE-TOTAL and NUMBER-OF-EMPLOYEES must be defined (lines 25-26). (Note that is not necessary to initialize PAGE-TOTAL to zero since this task will be accomplished within the PROCEDURE DIVISION.) The accumulator for the final total is defined later and will be handled as part of the automatic functions provided by report writer.

The REPORT SECTION of the DATA DIVISION is used to give an overall description of the report (the RD entry at lines 28-34) and to describe the different types of lines to be included in the report (as 01 entries following the RD entry at lines 35-76). The overall syntax of the REPORT SECTION is similar to that of the FILE SECTION with the RD entry taking the place of the FD entry and line descriptions taking the place of record descriptions.

The RD entry (at lines 28-34) contains the report name and numerous clauses specifying information pertaining to the entire report as shown below:

```
RD   EMPLOYEE-REPORT
     CONTROL IS FINAL
     PAGE LIMIT IS 45 LINES
     HEADING 1
     FIRST DETAIL 5
     LAST DETAIL 43
     FOOTING 45.
```

The report name (EMPLOYEE-REPORT) must match the name specified in the REPORT clause of the FD entry of the associated file. The CONTROL IS clause specifies the level(s) of control breaks to be recognized in the report. CONTROL IS FINAL specifies that the only control break desired is to be the end of the report. If other levels of subtotals had been desired, the names of the control files would be specified here. (A more complete discussion of this feature is presented in Section A.3.) The PAGE LIMIT clause specifies the total number of lines on a report page. The HEADING clause specifies the line number for the page headings. The FIRST DETAIL and LAST DETAIL clauses specify the line number for the first and last detail lines respectively. The FOOTING clause specifies the line number for page footing output.

The 01 entries following the RD entry specify the lines of the report and differentiate them by type. The first 01 entry (lines 35-36) specifies the report heading as follows:

```
01   TYPE IS REPORT HEADING
     LINE NUMBER IS 1.
```

The 02 entries which follow (lines 37-46) specify the content of the report heading:

```
02   COLUMN NUMBER IS 48
     PICTURE IS X(11)
     VALUE IS "ABC COMPANY".
02   COLUMN NUMBER IS 61
     PICTURE X(10)
     VALUE "ALPHABETIC".
02   COLUMN 62
     PICTURE X(8)
     VALUE "EMPLOYEE".
02   COLUMN 81 PIC X(6) VALUE "REPORT".
```

Note that most entries in the REPORT SECTION do not have to have a data-name associated with them; even the data-name FILLER is not required. Note also the use of the LINE NUMBER and COLUMN NUMBER clauses. The LINE NUMBER clause specifies the line number on the page for the placement of the line; the COLUMN NUMBER clause specifies the column number in the line for the placement of the item being described. Compare the above specifications for the heading line to the specification of essentially the same line of output in Program 7.1 (lines 38-47). In Program 7.1 this heading also includes the page number and was reproduced on each page of the report. In Program A.1 this heading is produced only once—at the beginning of the report—and hence page numbers have been included in the column heading line which will be produced at the top of each page.

The page headings are defined in the next series of entries (lines 47-56):

```
01   COLUMN-HEAD
     TYPE IS PAGE HEADING
     LINE NUMBER IS 3.
     02      COLUMN 27 PIC X(9) VALUE "LAST NAME".
     02      COLUMN 44 PIC X(7) VALUE "INITIAL".
     02      COLUMN 59 PIC X(15) VALUE "EMPLOYEE NUMBER".
     02      COLUMN 82 PIC X(10) VALUE "DEPARTMENT".
     02      COLUMN 100 PIC X(6) VALUE "SALARY".
     02      COLUMN 103 PIC X(4) VALUE "PAGE".
     02      COLUMN 105 PIC ZZ SOURCE IS PAGE-COUNTER.
```

In the above 01 entry the data-name COLUMN-HEAD is required because it will be referenced later in the PROCEDURE DIVISION. Note the use of the SOURCE IS clause in the last 02 entry above. The SOURCE IS clause takes the place of a MOVE instruction. When this line of output is generated the content of the field designated in a SOURCE IS clause is moved to the specified field on the output record automatically. Note that it is not even necessary to designate a data-name for the receiving field. In this case the field designated in the SOURCE IS clause is PAGE-COUNTER which is a field automatically defined and incremented by the report writer.

The next series of entries specify the detail line of the report (lines 57-64):

```
01   DETAIL-LINE
     TYPE IS DETAIL
     LINE NUMBER IS PLUS 2.
     02   COLUMN 27 PIC X(16) SOURCE IS IR-NAME.
     02   COLUMN 44 PIC X SOURCE IS IR-INITIAL.
     02   COLUMN 59 PIC X(9) SOURCE IS IR-EMPLOYEE-NUMBER.
     02   COLUMN 84 PIC X(3) SOURCE IS IR-DEPARTMENT.
     02   COLUMN 97 PIC $ZZZ,ZZZ SOURCE IS IR-SALARY.
```

The data-name for a type DETAIL line is not optional as with other lines because it is necessary to reference this line by name from the PROCEDURE DIVISION. (The GENERATE statement must include a data-name.) Note the use of the clause

LINE NUMBER IS PLUS 2

in the definition of the detail line. This entry specifies where the next detail line is to be placed (in this case double spacing is specified). Recall that the position of the first detail line is specified in the RD entry.

The next series of entries specify the page footing (lines 65-69):

```
01   TYPE IS PAGE FOOTING
     LINE IS PLUS 2.
     02   PF-PAGE-TOTAL
          COLUMN 89 PIC $ZZZ,ZZZ.99
          SOURCE IS PAGE-TOTAL.
```

This line will automatically be produced when a page is full and before page headings on the next page.

The last series of entries in the REPORT SECTION define the line containing final totals (lines 70-76):

```
01    TYPE IS CONTROL FOOTING FINAL
      LINE IS PLUS 2.
      02   COLUMN 71 PIC ZZZ9
           SOURCE IS NUMBER-OF-EMPLOYEES.
      02   COLUMN 80 PIC X(9) VALUE "EMPLOYEES".
      02   COLUMN 96 PIC $**,***,999
           SUM IR-SALARY.
```

Note the use of the SUM clause in the last entry for this line. This clause causes the sum of the values of the specified field to be computed automatically and, when the line is generated, the value of the sum is moved to the designated receiving field in the output record. Only lines of type CONTROL FOOTING can contain an element specified with the SUM clause. (One might inquire why this line is declared to be type CONTROL FOOTING rather than type REPORT FOOT-ING since both are produced one time at the end of the report. The necessity of including a SUM clause governed the choice of line types.)

Comparison of the PROCEDURE DIVISION of Programs 7.1 and A.1 will reveal the extent of the programming effort saved by use of the report writer features. Note the absence of routine MOVE statements, manipulation of the PAGE-COUNTER and LINE-COUNTER, and WRITE statements. All of this logic will be generated by report writer.

In Program A.1 it is necessary to include DECLARATIVES prior to the description of the program logic. DECLARATIVES generally are used to specify actions that are to be performed automatically by the program when certain conditions are encountered. In this case a DECLARATIVES procedure is required to zero out the field PAGE-TOTAL for each new page. The DECLARATIVES specifications from lines 78-83 are shown below:

```
DECLARATIVES.
100-END-OF-PAGE SECTION.
     USE BEFORE REPORTING COLUMN-HEAD.
110-INITIALIZE-PAGE-TOTAL.
     MOVE 0 TO PAGE-TOTAL.
END DECLARATIVES.
```

DECLARATIVES are terminated by the sentence END DECLARATIVES. and are composed of any number of SECTION's. The SECTION header describes when the procedure described in that SECTION is to be executed. The USE statement describes the relevant condition. In this case,

```
          USE BEFORE REPORTING COLUMN-HEAD.
```

means that the procedure is to be executed automatically prior to producing the line COLUMN-HEAD. (Any named line from the report could be included in a USE specification.) Note that if the DECLARATIVES procedure had been omitted, the page total would have become a running total. There is no other way in the program to zero out this field because production of the line is controlled "automatically" by report writer.

The main portion of the PROCEDURE DIVISION logic resembles that of any other COBOL program (lines 84-105) as shown below:

```
200-MAIN SECTION.
210-MAIN-LOGIC.
```

```
        PERFORM 300-INITIALIZATION.
        PERFORM 400-CONTROL UNTIL END-OF-FILE.
        PERFORM 500-TERMINATION.
    300-INITIALIZATION.
        OPEN    INPUT IN-FILE
                OUTPUT OUT-FILE.
        INITIATE EMPLOYEE-REPORT.
        PERFORM 600-READ.
    400-CONTROL.
        ADD 1 TO NUMBER-OF-EMPLOYEES.
        ADD IR-SALARY TO PAGE-TOTAL.
        GENERATE DETAIL-LINE.
        PERFORM 600-READ.
    500-TERMINATION.
        TERMINATE EMPLOYEE-REPORT.
        CLOSE IN-FILE
              OUT-FILE.
        STOP RUN.
    600-READ.
        READ IN-FILE AT END MOVE 1 TO EOF-FLAG.
```

The section header is required following DECLARATIVES. The paragraph 210-MAIN-LOGIC controls execution of other paragraphs as in any structured program. The paragraph 300-INITIALIZATION serves to OPEN the required files, INITIATE the report and cause the first record to be read. As a result of the INITIATE verb

1. all accumulators automatically controlled by report writer are set to zero (in this program the field used to accumulate the sum of the values is IR-SALARY)
2. PAGE-COUNTER is set to 1
3. LINE-COUNTER is set to 0 (LINE-COUNTER is an automatically allocated and controlled data-name similar to PAGE-COUNTER).

The paragraph 400-CONTROL causes processing of the data record just read, the production of the relevant report lines (via the GENERATE statement) and the reading of the next record. In this case, processing the data record entails incrementing the accumulator NUMBER-OF-EMPLOYEES and adding IR-SALARY to PAGE-TOTAL. (Recall that the SUM clause can only be used in conjunction with CONTROL FOOTING lines, hence accumulating PAGE-TOTAL must be accomplished "manually".) The effect of the GENERATE statement is dependent on the current stage of program execution. If this is the first execution of the GENERATE statement the following actions take place.

1. produce report heading
2. execute DELCARATIVES procedure
3. produce COLUMN-HEADING
4. produce DETAIL-LINE
5. increment LINE-COUNTER

On subsequent executions of the GENERATE statement the following actions take place:

1. if LINE-COUNTER > last detail line number
   produce page footing
   execute DECLARATIVES procedure

       increment PAGE-COUNTER
       produce COLUMN-HEADING
       initialize LINE-COUNTER
  2. produce DETAIL-LINE
  3. increment LINE-COUNTER

The paragraph 500-TERMINATION is executed after all records from the file IN-FILE have been processed. The paragraph terminates production of the report (via the TERMINATE statement) closes the files and stops execution of the program. The TERMINATE statement causes CONTROL FOOTING FINAL type lines to be produced followed by production of REPORT FOOTING lines (if any—in this example there were none).

A.2   GENERAL FORMS

Complete explanation of all facets of report writer is beyond the scope of this appendix. General forms of all elements of ANSI-74 COBOL including report writer are shown in Appendix C. Following is a description of some of the more useful features of report writer.

REPORT SECTION.
RD   report name

$$\left[\left\{\begin{matrix}\underline{CONTROL}\ IS \\ \underline{CONTROLS}\ ARE\ \underline{FINAL}\end{matrix}\right\}\left\{\begin{matrix}\text{data-name-1}\dots \\ [\text{data-name-1}]\dots\end{matrix}\right\}\right]$$

$$\underline{PAGE}\ \left[\left[\left\{\begin{matrix}\text{LIMIT IS} \\ \text{LIMITS ARE}\end{matrix}\right\}[\text{integer-1}]\left\{\begin{matrix}\text{LINE} \\ \text{LINES}\end{matrix}\right\}\right]\right]$$

    [HEADING integer-2]
    [FIRST DETAIL integer-3]
    [LAST DETAIL integer-4]
    [FOOTING integer-5].
report-group-description-entry. . . .

Figure A.1   General form of the REPORT SECTION entry

The REPORT SECTION

The general form of the REPORT SECTION is shown in Figure A.1. Of particular importance is the CONTROL clause of the RD entry. In this entry a list of data-names is specified which form the basis for detection of control breaks and the generation of subtotals. For example, in order to produce subtotals for departments in Program A.1, the RD entry would be

    RD   DEPARTMENT-REPORT
          CONTROL IS IR-DEPARTMENT
          .
          .
          .

In order to produce both department subtotals and final totals, the RD entry would be (see Program A.2)

```
RD   DEPARTMENT-REPORT
        CONTROLS ARE FINAL
                      IR-DEPARTMENT
                 .
                 .
                 .
```

The order of listing of data-names in the CONTROL IS clause determines the relative ordering of control breaks from highest to lowest level. Lower level breaks occur more frequently than higher level breaks. For example, in order to produce both department and division subtotals as in Program 7.3 the following RD entry would be used:

```
RD   DIVISION-REPORT
        CONTROLS ARE FINAL
                      IR-DIVISION
                      IR-DEPARTMENT
                 .
                 .
                 .
```

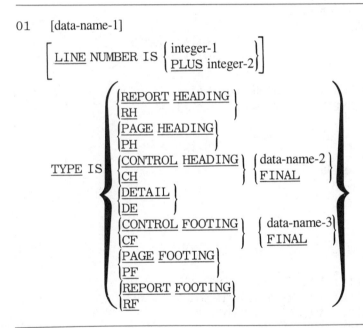

```
01    [data-name-1]
```

Figure A.2

The Report Group Description

The general form of the 01 level report group description is shown in Figure A.1. Following the RD entry, 01 level descriptors are required to specify the various elements of the report. Of particular importance is the CONTROL FOOTING entry which is used to generate control breaks for each of the control fields specified in the CONTROL clause of the RD entry. For example, to generate department subtotals for the report of Program A.1 an 01 entry such as the following would be required:

```
01   LINE NUMBER IS PLUS 2
        TYPE IS CONTROL FOOTING IR-DEPARTMENT.
```

Program A.2   Department employee report using report writer

```
1          IDENTIFICATION DIVISION.
2          PROGRAM-ID. CONTROL BREAK REPORT.
3          ENVIRONMENT DIVISION.
4          INPUT-OUTPUT SECTION.
5          FILE-CONTROL.
6              SELECT IN-FILE ASSIGN TO READER.
7              SELECT OUT-FILE ASSIGN TO PRINTER.
8          DATA DIVISION.
9          FILE SECTION.
10         FD IN-FILE
11             DATA RECORD IS IN-REC.
12             01 IN-REC.
13                  02 IR-NAME             PIC X(16).
14                  02 IR-INITIAL          PIC X.
15                  02 IR-EMPLOYEE-NUMBER   PIC X(9).
16                  02 IR-DEPARTMENT        PIC X(3).
17                  02 IR-SALARY            PIC 9(6).
18                  02 FILLER               PIC X(45).
19             FD OUT-FILE
20                 REPORT IS EMPLOYEE-REPORT.
21         WORKING-STORAGE SECTION.
22         01   EOF-FLAG                    PIC 9      VALUE ZERO.
23              88 NOT-END-OF-FILE                     VALUE ZERO.
24              88 END-OF-FILE                         VALUE 1.
25         01   TOTAL-NUMBER-OF-EMPLOYEES  PIC 9(4)   VALUE O.
26         01   DEPT-NUMBER-OF-EMPLOYEES   PIC 9(4)   VALUE O.
27         REPORT SECTION.
28         RD   EMPLOYEE REPORT
29              CONTROLS ARE FINAL
30                           IR-DEPARTMENT
31              PAGE LIMIT IS 45 LINES
32              HEADING 1
33              FIRST DETAIL 5.
34              LAST DETAIL 45.
35         01   TYPE IS PAGE HEADING.
36            02 LINE NUMBER IS 1.
37               03 COLUMN 48 PIC X(11) VALUE  "ABC COMPANY".
38               03 COLUMN 61 PIC X(10) VALUE  "DEPARTMENT".
39               03 COLUMN 72 PIC X(8)  VALUE  "EMPLOYEE".
40               03 COLUMN 81 PIC X(6)  VALUE  "REPORT".
41               03 COLUMN 103 PIC X(4) VALUE  "PAGE "
42               03 COLUMN 108 PIC ZZ SOURCE IS PAGE-COUNTER.
43            02 LINE NUMBER IS PLUS 2.
44               03 COLUMN 27 PIC X(9)  VALUE  "LAST NAME".
45               03 COLUMN 44 PIC X(7)  VALUE  "INITIAL".
46               03 COLUMN 59 PIC X(15) VALUE  "EMPLOYEE NUMBER".
47               03 COLUMN 82 PIC X(10) VALUE  "DEPARTMENT".
48               03 COLUMN 100 PIC X(6) VALUE  "SALARY".
49         01 DETAIL-LINE
50             TYPE IS DETAIL
51             LINE NUMBER IS PLUS 2.
52            02 COLUMN 27 PIC X(16) SOURCE IS IR-NAME.
53            02 COLUMN 44 PIC X SOURCE IS IR-INITIAL.
```

(continued)

Program A.2   (continued)

```
54                02 COLUMN 59 PIC X(9) SOURCE IS IR-EMPLOYEE-NUMBER.
55                02 COLUMN 84 PIC X(3) SOURCE IS IR-DEPARTMENT GROUP INDICATE.
56                02 COLUMN 97 PIC ZZZZ,ZZZ SOURCE IS IR-SALARY.
57            01  DEPARTMENT-HEADING-LINE
58                TYPE IS CONTROL HEADING IR-DEPARTMENT
59                LINE IS PLUS 1.
60                02 COLUMN 1 PIC X VALUE SPACES.
61            01  DEPARTMENT-SUMMARY-LINE
62                TYPE IS CONTROL FOORINT IR-DEPARTMENT
63                LINE IS PLUS 2.
64                02 COLUMN 71 PIC Z9 SOURCE IS DEPT-NUMBER-OF-EMPLOYEES.
65                02 COLUMN 77
66                    PIC X(9)
67                    VALUE "EMPLOYEES".
68                02 COLUMN 94
69                    PIC $**,***,***
70                    SUM IR-SALARY.
71            01  TYPE IS CONTROL FOOTING FINAL
72                      LINE IS PLUS 2.
73                02 COLUMN 71 PIC ZZZ9
74                    SOURCE IS TOTAL-NUMBER-OF-EMPLOYEES.
75                02 COLUMN 80 PIC X(9) VALUE "EMPLOYEES".
76                02 COLUMN 96 PIC $**,***,***
77                    SUM IR-SALARY.
78            PROCEDURE DIVISION.
79            DECLARATIVES.
80            100-INITIALIZE SECTION.
81                    USE BEFORE REPORTING DEPARTMENT-HEADING-LINE.
82            110-INIT-DEPT-NUMBER-EMPLOYEES.
83                    MOVE 0 TO DEPT-NUMBER-OF-EMPLOYEES.
84            END DECLARATIVES.
85            200-MAIN SECTION.
86            300-MAIN-LOGIC.
87                    PERFORM 400-INITIALIZATION.
88                    PERFORM 500-CONTROL UNTIL END-OF-FILE.
89                    PERFORM 600-TERMINATION.
90            400-INITIALIZATION.
91                    OPEN INPUT IN-FILE.
92                        OUTPUT OUT-FILE.
93                    INITIATE EMPLOYEE-REPORT.
94                    PERFORM 700-READ.
95            500-CONTROL.
96                    GENERATE DETAIL-LINE.
97                    ADD 1 TO TOTAL-NUMBER-OF-EMPLOYEES.
98                    ADD 1 TO DEPT-NUMBER-OF-EMPLOYEES.
99                    PERFORM 700-READ.
100           600-TERMINATION.
101                   TERMINATE EMPLOYEE-REPORT.
102                   CLOSE IN-FILE.
103                         OUT-FILE.
104                   STOP RUN.
105           700-READ.
106                   READ IN-FILE AT END MOVE 1 TO EOF-FLAG.
```

Format 1
level-number   [data-name-1]

$$\left[\underline{\text{LINE}} \text{ NUMBER IS } \left\{ \begin{array}{l} \text{integer-1} \\ \underline{\text{PLUS}} \text{ integer-2} \end{array} \right\} \right]$$

Format 2
level-number   [data-name-1]
                      [<u>GROUP</u> INDICATE]
                      [<u>COLUMN</u> NUMBER IS integer-1]

$$\left\{ \begin{array}{l} \underline{\text{PICTURE}} \\ \underline{\text{PIC}} \end{array} \right\} \text{ IS picture-codes}$$

$$\left\{ \begin{array}{l} \underline{\text{SOURCE}} \text{ IS data-name-2} \\ \underline{\text{VALUE}} \text{ IS literal} \\ \underline{\text{SUM}} \text{ data-name-3 . . .} \end{array} \right\}$$ **Figure A.3**

Each level of control break required a separate 01 report group description entry. The content of the line is produced when a change in the control field is encountered.

The general forms of subordinate report group descriptions are shown in Figure A.3. Format 1 type descriptions may be used to create multiple report lines of a particular type. Format 2 type descriptions are used to specify elementary data items for a line. For example, suppose we wish to create two lines of output per page heading so that the output from the Program A.1 would more closely resemble that of Program 7.1. The following code could be used:

```
01   TYPE IS PAGE HEADING.
     02   LINE NUMBER IS 1.
          03   COLUMN 48  PIC X(11)  VALUE "ABC COMPANY".
          03   COLUMN 61  PIC X(10)  VALUE "ALPHABETIC".
          03   COLUMN 72  PIC X(8)   VALUE "EMPLOYEE".
          03   COLUMN 81  PIC X(6)   VALUE "REPORT".
          03   COLUMN 95  PIC X(4)   VALUE "PAGE".
          03   COLUMN 100 PIC ZZZ SOURCE IS PAGE-NUMBER.
     02   LINE NUMBER IS PLUS 2.
          03   COLUMN 27 PIC X(9)  VALUE "LAST NAME".
          03   COLUMN 44 PIC X(7)  VALUE "INITIAL".
          03   COLUMN 59 PIC X(15) VALUE "EMPLOYEE NUMBER".
          03   COLUMN 82 PIC X(10) VALUE "DEPARTMENT".
          03   COLUMN 100 PIC X(6) VALUE "SALARY".
```

With the above code page headings would consist of two lines at line numbers 1 and 3 on each page.

The GROUP INDICATE clause can be used only on specification of lines of type DETAIL. When the clause is present the content of the field is printed for the first record of each control group and for the first record at the top of a new page. See, for example, line 55 of Program A.2. Without this clause the department number would be printed with each record producing output similar to that of Program 7.2.

The SUM clause causes the automatic accumulation of the sum of specified data items. The clause can only be used in the specification of lines of type CONTROL FOOTING. The value of the accumulator is reset to zero each time the content is printed hence this feature is well suited to the automatic generation of subtotals as shown in Program A.2.

A.3 CONTROL BREAK EXAMPLE

Program A.2 uses report writer to produce essentially the same report as that of Program 7.2. The output consists of a detailed listing of the input file with totals for each department as well as final totals. Report writer elements found in Program A.2 include

- multiple line page heading
- detail line
- control heading based on department number
- control footing based on department number
- control footing final

As with Program A.1, most of the desired output can be handled "automatically" by features of report writer. However, the process of counting elements of each control group makes the use of DECLARATIVES necessary to zero out the counter DEPT-NUMBER-OF-EMPLOYEES. The appropriate time to perform this task would normally be after the value of the field has been printed and before processing the next record. Unfortunately the USE statement contains only the option BEFORE REPORTING; there is no direct way to cause the desired action after the control footing line has been produced. The problem is solved in the following fashion: We introduce a line of type CONTROL HEADING into the report. Lines of this type are produced automatically at the beginning of processing of each control group. In our case the timing of the production of the line is more important than its content (which is merely a sequence of spaces). We use DELARATIVES to execute a procedure prior to production of this line. In the procedure we zero out the counter thus forcing the counter to be reset to zero at the beginning of processing of each control group. When the GENERATE statement (line 96) is executed the following actions take place:

1. if LINE-COUNTER > last detail line number
   increment PAGE-COUNTER
   produce page headings
   initialize LINE-COUNTER
2. if control break has occured
   produce DEPARTMENT-SUMMARY-LINE
   zero out salary accumulator on this line
   execute DECLARATIVES procedure
   produce DEPARTMENT-HEADING-LINE
   increment LINE-COUNTER
3. produce DETAIL-LINE
4. add IR-SALARY to appropriate accumulators
5. increment LINE-COUNTER

Because to the timing of the production of DEPARTMENT-HEADING-LINE we are able to use the BEFORE REPORTING feature of the USE statement to cause the desired actions to be taken at the appropriate time—after the totals have been produced and before processing of the next record.

Careful analysis of the examples and explanations in this appendix should enable the reader to get started using report writer. A useful exercise would be to rewrite any program from Chapter 7 using report writer. Report writer has a great many restrictions which the programmer may inadvertently violate in his/her initial programming efforts. If problems are encountered, the COBOL reference manual for the user's system should be consulted.

Appendix B

COBOL FOR INTERACTIVE SYSTEMS

In many computing systems the user's primary means of communication with the system is a computer terminal. The user enters data at the terminal and the computer responds with appropriate messages. Such systems are referred to as *interactive* systems since the user and computer system engage in a very immediate form of interaction.

When using an interactive system for program development the user's primary tool is an operating system program called an *editor*. An editor allows the user to create and update files. The first step in developing a COBOL program is to build a file containing the COBOL program statements. The editor usually contains provisions for listing files, adding records to files, changing all or part of existing records and deleting records from files. The COBOL programmer makes use of this facility to list the program, and add, change or delete portions of the program. When the programmer is satisfied with the program, he/she then enters appropriate operating system instructions to compile the program. If the compilation is successful, the output produced by the program is generally directed either to the terminal or an auxiliary printer associated with the terminal. If the compilation is not successful because of syntax errors, the programmer may display the error messages produced by the compiler at his/her terminal. It is then necessary to use the editor to make necessary revisions to the program. Specific details on use of terminals, operating system instructions, and editor instructions vary greatly from one computing system to another; the reader must secure detailed information appropriate to the system available for his/her use before attempting to enter a COBOL program.

B.1 THE ACCEPT STATEMENT

Users of interactive systems may choose to enter data to be processed by a program at the terminal itself. The ACCEPT statement is used for this purpose. The general form of the ACCEPT statement is shown in Figure B.1.

```
ACCEPT data-name FROM {hardware-name }
                      {mnemonic-name }
```

Figure B.1   General form of the ACCEPT statement

Depending on the system in use, the ACCEPT statement without the FROM option may automatically cause the system to input data from the terminal being used to execute the program. On other systems it is necessary to define a mnemonic-name in the SPECIAL-NAMES paragraph of the IDENTIFICATION DIVISION to identify the specific device to be used in the operation. For example, an appropriate SPECIAL-NAMES entry would be:

```
SPECIAL-NAMES.
    CONSOLE IS OPERATORS-INPUT-DEVICE.
```

With this mnemonic declared, an appropriate ACCEPT statement would be:

```
ACCEPT DATA FROM OPERATORS-INPUT-DEVICE.
```

When an ACCEPT statement is executed, a message is displayed at the console alerting the user that the program is waiting for him/her to enter some data. Execution of the program is suspended until the user completes the input operation.

Suppose the data-item NUMBER is defined as   *Example*

```
03 NUMBER PIC 9(4).
```

and the program statement

```
ACCEPT NUMBER.
```

is executed. After displaying an appropriate message the system will wait until the user enters data at the terminal. The characters entered by the user will be stored in NUMBER and execution will proceed with the next statement.

It is important that the user enter the data expected by the program. The characters entered by the user are stored in the designated memory location in order from left to right. If too few characters are entered the remaining right most characters may be padded with blanks or zeroes or the system may respond with a message requesting more data. If too many characters are entered excess characters on the right are ignored.

Example

```
03 NUMBER PIC 9(4)
   .
   .
   .
ACCEPT NUMBER.
```

If the user enters 1234, the value store in NUMBER will be

```
1 2 3 4
L_L_L_L_J
```

If the user enters 12345, the value stored in NUMBER will be

$$\underline{1 \quad 2 \quad 3 \quad 4}$$

because excess digits on the right are truncated. If the user enters 123 the value stored in NUMBER will be

$$\underline{1 \quad 2 \quad 3}$$

The right most position in NUMBER will then be filled by a zero (because the field is numeric) on some systems or the system will request that the user enter more data which will be used to fill out the remaining position in NUMBER.

Example

```
01 DATA-REC.
   03 NAME-DR PIC X(10).
   03 SS-NUM-DR PIC 9(9).
      .
      .
      .
ACCEPT DATA-REC.
```

The expected number of characters is 19—the length of the group item DATA-REC. The first 10 characters entered will be stored in NAME-DR; the next 9 characters will be stored in SS-NUM-DR.

The ACCEPT statement may also be used in a batch oriented computing system to allow the system operator to enter small amounts of data.

This statement is used only for small amounts of data because of the low speed which is typical of an operator's console and because it takes up the operator's time. It can, however, be useful to allow the operator to enter a data item such as the current date for a report or to allow the operator to select among various functions which a program might perform. Also, a program might, for security reasons, ask the operator to enter his or her name and the time of the run.

B.2   THE DISPLAY STATEMENT

Corresponding to the input statement ACCEPT which allows the user to enter data at a terminal is the output statement DISPLAY which causes output at the terminal. The general form of the DISPLAY statement is shown in Figure B.2.

```
DISPLAY  { literal   }  UPON  { hardware-name }
         { data-name }        { mnemonic-name }
```

Figure B.2   General form of the DISPLAY statement

The preceding comments about MNEMONIC-NAMES apply to both the DISPLAY and ACCEPT statements. Any sequence of literals or data items may be written on the terminal using the DISPLAY statement. For example:

DISPLAY DATA.

would cause the contents of DATA to be written. The statement

DISPLAY "ENTER CURRENT DATE".

could be followed by

ACCEPT DATE-IN.

The written message serves to guide the operator's response to that item required by the ACCEPT statement.

Example

```
DISPLAY "ENTER NAME AND SOCIAL SECURITY NUMBER".
ACCEPT DATA-REC.
DISPLAY "NAME", NAME-DR, "SS-NO.", SS-NUM-DR.
```

This example illustrates use of the DISPLAY statement to prompt the user as to what data he/she is expected to enter and to "echo" the input received by writing it immediately after it is received. Suppose INPUT-REC is defined as in the Example above and the user enters the following data:

JOHN JONES, 123456789

The expected output from the second DISPLAY statement is

NAME JOHN JONES   SS-NO. 123456789

The use of an echo such as this is important to ensure that the data entered by the user is correct, and if not to give the user a change to correct the data.

Example

The program shown in Program B.1 illustrates the general logic required to build a disk file from data entered by the program user. The program creates a file DATA-FILE assigned to disk. The user enters records one at a time at the terminal (line 28). The program echos the data (line 29) and give the user the opportunity to reject the data or accept it for entry onto the file (lines 30-31). Note the use of a special value contained in the field NAME-DR used to end the data entry/file building process. When the user enters the characters "END" as the content of NAME-DR, the program closes the output file thereby making the data permanent (see lines 21-22). The general approach used in this program is useful for building data files required for most programming exercises in this text.

In batch oriented systems, the DISPLAY statement may be used to direct messages to the system operator's console. It may be used to prompt the operator regarding data requested by an ACCEPT statement. It may also be used to write messages regarding errors or exceptional conditions encountered during the execution of the program.

Typically, error messages regarding data being processed are displayed on the operator's console only on small scale computing systems which run one program at a time. On larger systems which may execute many programs at one time, error messages are usually written on the printer or are written on a disk file which is examined after the completion of the program.

Program B.1 File creation program

```
1        IDENTIFICATION DIVISION.
2        PROGRAM-ID. FILE-BUILDER.
3        AUTHOR. HORN.
4        ENVIRONMENT DIVISION.
5        INPUT-OUTPUT SECTION.
6        FILE-CONTROL.
7            SELECT-DATA FILE ASSIGN TO DISK.
8        DATA DIVISION.
9        FILE SECTION.
10       FD  DATA-FILE
11           DATA RECORD IS DATA-REC.
12       01  DATA-REC.
13           03  NAME-DR      PIC X(10).
14           03  SS-NUM-DR    PIC 9(9).
15       WORKING-STORAGE SECTION.
16       01  ANSWER           PIC X VALUE "N".
17       PROCEDURE DIVISION.
18       1000-MAIN-LOGIC.
19           PERFORM 2000-INITIALIZATION.
20           PERFORM 3000-GET-DATA UNTIL ANSWER = "Y".
21           PERFORM 4000-BUILD-FILE UNTIL NAME-DR = "END".
22           PERFORM 5000-TERMINATION.
23       2000-INITIALIZATION.
24           OPEN OUTPUT DATA-FILE.
25           DISPLAY "ENTER END IN NAME FIELD TO TERMINATE PROGRAM.
26       3000-GET-DATA.
27           DISPLAY "ENTER NAME AND SOCIAL SECURITY NUMTER".
28           ACCEPT DATA-REC.
29           DISPLAY "NAME", NAME-DR, "SS-NO.", SS-NUM-DR.
30           DISPLAY "IS DATA CORRECT?".
31           ACCEPT ANSWER.
32       4000-BUILD-FILE.
33           WRITE DATA-REC.
34           MOVE "N" TO ANSWER.
35           PERFORM 3000-GET-DATA UNTIL ANSWER = "Y".
36       5000-TERMINATION.
37           CLOSE DATA-FILE.
38           STOP RUN.
```

GENERAL FORM OF COBOL ELEMENTS

GENERAL FORMAT FOR IDENTIFICATION DIVISION

IDENTIFICATION DIVISION.

PROGRAM-ID. program-name.

[AUTHOR. [comment-entry] ...]

[INSTALLATION. [comment-entry] ...]

[DATE-WRITTEN. [comment-entry] ...]

[DATE-COMPILED. [comment-entry] ...]

[SECURITY. [comment-entry] ...]

GENERAL FORMAT FOR ENVIRONMENT DIVISION

ENVIRONMENT DIVISION.

CONFIGURATION SECTION.

SOURCE-COMPUTER. computer-name [WITH DEBUGGING MODE] .

OBJECT-COMPUTER. computer-name

$$\left[, \underline{\text{MEMORY}} \text{ SIZE integer } \left\{ \begin{array}{l} \underline{\text{WORDS}} \\ \underline{\text{CHARACTERS}} \\ \underline{\text{MODULES}} \end{array} \right\} \right]$$

[, PROGRAM COLLATING SEQUENCE IS alphabet-name]

$$\left[, \underline{\text{SEGMENT-LIMIT}}\ \underline{\text{IS}}\ \text{segment-number} \right]\ .$$

$$\left[\underline{\text{SPECIAL-NAMES}}.\ \left[, \text{implementor-name} \right. \right.$$

$$\left\{ \begin{array}{l} \underline{\text{IS}}\ \text{mnemonic-name}\ \left[, \underline{\text{ON}}\ \text{STATUS}\ \underline{\text{IS}}\ \text{condition-name-1}\ \left[, \underline{\text{OFF}}\ \text{STATUS}\ \underline{\text{IS}}\ \text{condition-name-2} \right] \right] \\ \underline{\text{IS}}\ \text{mnemonic-name}\ \left[, \underline{\text{OFF}}\ \text{STATUS}\ \underline{\text{IS}}\ \text{condition-name-2}\ \left[, \underline{\text{ON}}\ \text{STATUS}\ \underline{\text{IS}}\ \text{condition-name-1} \right] \right] \\ \underline{\text{ON}}\ \text{STATUS}\ \underline{\text{IS}}\ \text{condition-name-1}\ \left[, \underline{\text{OFF}}\ \text{STATUS}\ \underline{\text{IS}}\ \text{condition-name-2} \right] \\ \underline{\text{OFF}}\ \text{STATUS}\ \underline{\text{IS}}\ \text{condition-name-2}\ \left[, \underline{\text{ON}}\ \text{STATUS}\ \underline{\text{IS}}\ \text{condition-name-1} \right] \end{array} \right\} \right] \ldots$$

$$\left[, \text{alphabet-name IS} \left\{ \begin{array}{l} \underline{\text{STANDARD-1}} \\ \underline{\text{NATIVE}} \\ \text{implementor-name} \\ \text{literal-1}\ \left[\left\{ \begin{array}{l} \underline{\text{THROUGH}} \\ \underline{\text{THRU}} \end{array} \right\}\ \text{literal-2} \\ \underline{\text{ALSO}}\ \text{literal-3}\ \left[, \underline{\text{ALSO}}\ \text{literal-4} \right] \ldots \right] \\ \qquad \left[\text{literal-5}\ \left[\left\{ \begin{array}{l} \underline{\text{THROUGH}} \\ \underline{\text{THRU}} \end{array} \right\}\ \text{literal-6} \\ \underline{\text{ALSO}}\ \text{literal-7}\ \left[, \underline{\text{ALSO}}\ \text{literal-8} \right] \ldots \right] \right] \ldots \end{array} \right\} \right] \ldots$$

$$\left[, \underline{\text{CURRENCY}}\ \text{SIGN}\ \underline{\text{IS}}\ \text{literal-9} \right]$$

$$\left. \left[, \underline{\text{DECIMAL-POINT}}\ \text{IS}\ \underline{\text{COMMA}} \right]\ . \right]$$

GENERAL FORMAT FOR ENVIRONMENT DIVISION

$$\left[\underline{\text{INPUT-OUTPUT}}\ \underline{\text{SECTION}}. \right.$$

$$\underline{\text{FILE-CONTROL}}.$$

$$\left\{ \text{file-control-entry} \right\}\ \ldots$$

$$\left[\underline{\text{I-O-CONTROL}}. \right.$$

$$\left[;\ \underline{\text{RERUN}}\ \left[\underline{\text{ON}}\ \left\{ \begin{array}{l} \text{file-name-1} \\ \text{implementor-name} \end{array} \right\} \right] \right.$$

$$\underline{\text{EVERY}}\ \left\{ \begin{array}{l} \left\{ \left[\underline{\text{END}}\ \text{OF} \right]\ \left\{ \begin{array}{l} \underline{\text{REEL}} \\ \underline{\text{UNIT}} \end{array} \right\} \right\}\ \text{OF file-name-2} \\ \text{integer-1}\ \underline{\text{RECORDS}} \\ \text{integer-2}\ \underline{\text{CLOCK-UNITS}} \\ \text{condition-name} \end{array} \right\} \right]\ \ldots$$

$$\left[;\ \underline{\text{SAME}}\ \left[\begin{array}{l} \underline{\text{RECORD}} \\ \underline{\text{SORT}} \\ \underline{\text{SORT-MERGE}} \end{array} \right]\ \text{AREA FOR file-name-3}\ \left\{ , \text{file-name-4} \right\}\ \ldots \right]\ \ldots$$

$$\left[;\ \underline{\text{MULTIPLE}}\ \underline{\text{FILE}}\ \text{TAPE CONTAINS file-name-5}\ \left[\underline{\text{POSITION}}\ \text{integer-3} \right] \right.$$

$$\left. \left[, \text{file-name-6}\ \left[\underline{\text{POSITION}}\ \text{integer-4} \right] \right] \ldots \right]\ \ldots\ \left. . \right] \right]$$

GENERAL FORMAT FOR FILE CONTROL ENTRY

FORMAT 1:

SELECT [OPTIONAL] file-name

    ASSIGN TO implementor-name-1 [, implementor-name-2] ...

    $\left[; \underline{\text{RESERVE}} \text{ integer-1} \begin{bmatrix} \text{AREA} \\ \text{AREAS} \end{bmatrix} \right]$

    [; ORGANIZATION IS SEQUENTIAL]

    [; ACCESS MODE IS SEQUENTIAL]

    [; FILE STATUS IS data-name-1] .

FORMAT 2:

SELECT file-name

    ASSIGN TO implementor-name-1 [, implementor-name-2] ...

    $\left[; \underline{\text{RESERVE}} \text{ integer-1} \begin{bmatrix} \text{AREA} \\ \text{AREAS} \end{bmatrix} \right]$

    ; ORGANIZATION IS RELATIVE

    $\left[; \underline{\text{ACCESS}} \text{ MODE IS} \left\{ \begin{array}{l} \underline{\text{SEQUENTIAL}} \quad [, \underline{\text{RELATIVE}} \text{ KEY IS data-name-1}] \\ \left\{ \begin{array}{l} \underline{\text{RANDOM}} \\ \underline{\text{DYNAMIC}} \end{array} \right\} \quad , \underline{\text{RELATIVE}} \text{ KEY IS data-name-1} \end{array} \right\} \right]$

    [; FILE STATUS IS data-name-2] .

FORMAT 3:

SELECT file-name

    ASSIGN TO implementor-name-1 [, implementor-name-2] ...

    $\left[; \underline{\text{RESERVE}} \text{ integer-1} \begin{bmatrix} \text{AREA} \\ \text{AREAS} \end{bmatrix} \right]$

    ; ORGANIZATION IS INDEXED

    $\left[; \underline{\text{ACCESS}} \text{ MODE IS} \left\{ \begin{array}{l} \underline{\text{SEQUENTIAL}} \\ \underline{\text{RANDOM}} \\ \underline{\text{DYNAMIC}} \end{array} \right\} \right]$

    ; RECORD KEY IS data-name-1

    [; ALTERNATE RECORD KEY IS data-name-2 [WITH DUPLICATES]] ...

    [; FILE STATUS IS data-name-3] .

FORMAT 4:

<u>SELECT</u> file-name <u>ASSIGN</u> TO implementor-name-1 [, implementor-name-2] ...

GENERAL FORMAT FOR DATA DIVISION

<u>DATA</u> DIVISION.

[<u>FILE</u> <u>SECTION</u>.

[<u>FD</u> file-name

    [; <u>BLOCK</u> CONTAINS [integer-1 <u>TO</u>] integer-2 $\left\{ \begin{array}{c} \underline{\text{RECORDS}} \\ \text{CHARACTERS} \end{array} \right\}$]

    [; <u>RECORD</u> CONTAINS [integer-3 <u>TO</u>] integer-4 CHARACTERS]

    ; <u>LABEL</u> $\left\{ \begin{array}{c} \underline{\text{RECORD}} \text{ IS} \\ \underline{\text{RECORDS}} \text{ ARE} \end{array} \right\}$ $\left\{ \begin{array}{c} \underline{\text{STANDARD}} \\ \underline{\text{OMITTED}} \end{array} \right\}$

    [; <u>VALUE</u> <u>OF</u> implementor-name-1 IS $\left\{ \begin{array}{c} \text{data-name-1} \\ \text{literal-1} \end{array} \right\}$

        [, implementor-name-2 IS $\left\{ \begin{array}{c} \text{data-name-2} \\ \text{literal-2} \end{array} \right\}$] ...]

    [; <u>DATA</u> $\left\{ \begin{array}{c} \underline{\text{RECORD}} \text{ IS} \\ \underline{\text{RECORDS}} \text{ ARE} \end{array} \right\}$ data-name-3 [, data-name-4] ...]

    [; <u>LINAGE</u> IS $\left\{ \begin{array}{c} \text{data-name-5} \\ \text{integer-5} \end{array} \right\}$ LINES [, WITH <u>FOOTING</u> AT $\left\{ \begin{array}{c} \text{data-name-6} \\ \text{integer-6} \end{array} \right\}$]

        [, LINES AT <u>TOP</u> $\left\{ \begin{array}{c} \text{data-name-7} \\ \text{integer-7} \end{array} \right\}$] [, LINES AT <u>BOTTOM</u> $\left\{ \begin{array}{c} \text{data-name-8} \\ \text{integer-8} \end{array} \right\}$]]

    [; <u>CODE-SET</u> IS alphabet-name]

    [; $\left\{ \begin{array}{c} \underline{\text{REPORT}} \text{ IS} \\ \underline{\text{REPORTS}} \text{ ARE} \end{array} \right\}$ report-name-1 [, report-name-2] ...] .

[record-description-entry] ...] ...

[<u>SD</u> file-name

    [; <u>RECORD</u> CONTAINS [integer-1 <u>TO</u>] integer-2 CHARACTERS]

    [; <u>DATA</u> $\left\{ \begin{array}{c} \underline{\text{RECORD}} \text{ IS} \\ \underline{\text{RECORDS}} \text{ ARE} \end{array} \right\}$ data-name-1 [, data-name-2] ...] .

{record-description-entry} ...]]

$$\left[\begin{array}{l} \underline{\text{WORKING-STORAGE}} \ \underline{\text{SECTION}}. \\ \left[\begin{array}{l} \text{77-level-description-entry} \\ \text{record-description-entry} \end{array} \right] \ \cdots \end{array} \right]$$

$$\left[\begin{array}{l} \underline{\text{LINKAGE}} \ \underline{\text{SECTION}}. \\ \left[\begin{array}{l} \text{77-level-description-entry} \\ \text{record-description-entry} \end{array} \right] \ \cdots \end{array} \right]$$

$$\left[\begin{array}{l} \underline{\text{COMMUNICATION}} \ \underline{\text{SECTION}}. \\ \text{[communication-description-entry} \\ \text{[record-description-entry} \ ] \ \cdots \ ] \ \cdots \end{array} \right]$$

[REPORT SECTION.

[RD   report-name

    [; CODE literal-1]

$$\left[; \ \left\{ \begin{array}{l} \underline{\text{CONTROL}} \ \text{IS} \\ \underline{\text{CONTROLS}} \ \text{ARE} \end{array} \right\} \ \left\{ \begin{array}{l} \text{data-name-1} \ [, \ \text{data-name-2}] \ \cdots \\ \underline{\text{FINAL}} \ [, \ \text{data-name-1} \ [, \ \text{data-name-2}] \ \cdots] \end{array} \right\} \right]$$

$$\left[; \ \underline{\text{PAGE}} \ \left[\begin{array}{l} \text{LIMIT IS} \\ \text{LIMITS ARE} \end{array} \right] \ \text{integer-1} \ \left[\begin{array}{l} \text{LINE} \\ \text{LINES} \end{array} \right] \ [, \ \underline{\text{HEADING}} \ \text{integer-2} \right.$$

        $[, \ \underline{\text{FIRST}} \ \underline{\text{DETAIL}} \ \text{integer-3}] \ [, \ \underline{\text{LAST}} \ \underline{\text{DETAIL}} \ \text{integer-4}]$

        $[, \ \underline{\text{FOOTING}} \ \text{integer-5} \ ] \ ] \ .$

$\{\text{report-group-description-entry}\} \ \cdots \ ] \ \cdots]$

GENERAL FORMAT FOR DATA DESCRIPTION ENTRY

FORMAT 1:

level-number $\left\{\begin{array}{l}\text{data-name-1}\\ \underline{\text{FILLER}}\end{array}\right\}$

$\left[\text{; } \underline{\text{REDEFINES}} \text{ data-name-2}\right]$

$\left[\text{; } \left\{\begin{array}{l}\underline{\text{PICTURE}}\\ \underline{\text{PIC}}\end{array}\right\} \text{ IS character-string}\right]$

$\left[\text{; } \left[\underline{\text{USAGE}} \text{ IS}\right] \left\{\begin{array}{l}\underline{\text{COMPUTATIONAL}}\\ \underline{\text{COMP}}\\ \underline{\text{DISPLAY}}\\ \underline{\text{INDEX}}\end{array}\right\}\right]$

$\left[\text{; } \left[\underline{\text{SIGN}} \text{ IS}\right] \left\{\begin{array}{l}\underline{\text{LEADING}}\\ \underline{\text{TRAILING}}\end{array}\right\} \left[\underline{\text{SEPARATE}} \text{ CHARACTER}\right]\right]$

$\left[\text{; } \underline{\text{OCCURS}} \left\{\begin{array}{l}\text{integer-1 } \underline{\text{TO}} \text{ integer-2 TIMES } \underline{\text{DEPENDING}} \text{ ON data-name-3}\\ \text{integer-2 TIMES}\end{array}\right\}\right.$

$\left[\left\{\begin{array}{l}\underline{\text{ASCENDING}}\\ \underline{\text{DESCENDING}}\end{array}\right\} \text{ KEY IS data-name-4 } \left[\text{, data-name-5}\right] \text{ ... }\right] \text{ ...}$

$\left.\left[\underline{\text{INDEXED}} \text{ BY index-name-1 } \left[\text{, index-name-2}\right] \text{ ... }\right]\right]$

$\left[\text{; } \left\{\begin{array}{l}\underline{\text{SYNCHRONIZED}}\\ \underline{\text{SYNC}}\end{array}\right\} \left[\begin{array}{l}\underline{\text{LEFT}}\\ \underline{\text{RIGHT}}\end{array}\right]\right]$

$\left[\text{; } \left\{\begin{array}{l}\underline{\text{JUSTIFIED}}\\ \underline{\text{JUST}}\end{array}\right\} \text{ RIGHT}\right]$

$\left[\text{; } \underline{\text{BLANK}} \text{ WHEN } \underline{\text{ZERO}}\right]$

$\left[\text{; } \underline{\text{VALUE}} \text{ IS literal}\right] \text{ .}$

FORMAT 2:

66 data-name-1; $\underline{\text{RENAMES}}$ data-name-2 $\left[\left\{\begin{array}{l}\underline{\text{THROUGH}}\\ \underline{\text{THRU}}\end{array}\right\} \text{ data-name-3}\right]$.

FORMAT 3:

88 condition-name; $\left\{\begin{array}{l}\underline{\text{VALUE}} \text{ IS}\\ \underline{\text{VALUES}} \text{ ARE}\end{array}\right\}$ literal-1 $\left[\left\{\begin{array}{l}\underline{\text{THROUGH}}\\ \underline{\text{THRU}}\end{array}\right\} \text{ literal-2}\right]$

$\left[\text{, literal-3 } \left[\left\{\begin{array}{l}\underline{\text{THROUGH}}\\ \underline{\text{THRU}}\end{array}\right\} \text{ literal-4}\right]\right] \text{ ... } \text{ .}$

GENERAL FORMAT FOR COMMUNICATION DESCRIPTION ENTRY

FORMAT 1:

CD cd-name;

```
FOR [INITIAL] INPUT

[
  [; SYMBOLIC QUEUE IS data-name-1]
        [; SYMBOLIC SUB-QUEUE-1 IS data-name-2]
        [; SYMBOLIC SUB-QUEUE-2 IS data-name-3]
        [; SYMBOLIC SUB-QUEUE-3 IS data-name-4]
        [; MESSAGE DATE IS data-name-5]
        [; MESSAGE TIME IS data-name-6]
        [; SYMBOLIC SOURCE IS data-name-7]
        [; TEXT LENGTH IS data-name-8]
        [; END KEY IS data-name-9]
        [; STATUS KEY IS data-name-10]
        [; MESSAGE COUNT IS data-name-11]]
  [data-name-1, data-name-2, ..., data-name-11]
]
```

FORMAT 2:

CD cd-name; FOR OUTPUT

```
[; DESTINATION COUNT IS data-name-1]

[; TEXT LENGTH IS data-name-2]

[; STATUS KEY IS data-name-3]

[; DESTINATION TABLE OCCURS integer-2 TIMES
      [; INDEXED BY index-name-1 [, index-name-2]... ] ]

[; ERROR KEY IS data-name-4]

[; SYMBOLIC DESTINATION IS data-name-5] .
```

GENERAL FORMAT FOR REPORT GROUP DESCRIPTION ENTRY

FORMAT 1:

01 [data-name-1]

    $\left[\text{; } \underline{\text{LINE}} \text{ NUMBER IS } \left\{ \begin{array}{l} \text{integer-1 } [\text{ON } \underline{\text{NEXT PAGE}}] \\ \underline{\text{PLUS}} \text{ integer-2} \end{array} \right\} \right]$

    $\left[\text{; } \underline{\text{NEXT GROUP}} \text{ IS } \left\{ \begin{array}{l} \text{integer-3} \\ \underline{\text{PLUS}} \text{ integer-4} \\ \underline{\text{NEXT PAGE}} \end{array} \right\} \right]$

    $\text{; } \underline{\text{TYPE}} \text{ IS } \left\{ \begin{array}{l} \left\{ \begin{array}{l} \underline{\text{REPORT HEADING}} \\ \underline{\text{RH}} \end{array} \right\} \\ \left\{ \begin{array}{l} \underline{\text{PAGE HEADING}} \\ \underline{\text{PH}} \end{array} \right\} \\ \left\{ \begin{array}{l} \underline{\text{CONTROL HEADING}} \\ \underline{\text{CH}} \end{array} \right\} \left\{ \begin{array}{l} \text{data-name-2} \\ \underline{\text{FINAL}} \end{array} \right\} \\ \left\{ \begin{array}{l} \underline{\text{DETAIL}} \\ \underline{\text{DE}} \end{array} \right\} \\ \left\{ \begin{array}{l} \underline{\text{CONTROL FOOTING}} \\ \underline{\text{CF}} \end{array} \right\} \left\{ \begin{array}{l} \text{data-name-3} \\ \underline{\text{FINAL}} \end{array} \right\} \\ \left\{ \begin{array}{l} \underline{\text{PAGE FOOTING}} \\ \underline{\text{PF}} \end{array} \right\} \\ \left\{ \begin{array}{l} \underline{\text{REPORT FOOTING}} \\ \underline{\text{RF}} \end{array} \right\} \end{array} \right\}$

    $\left[\text{; } [\underline{\text{USAGE}} \text{ IS}] \ \underline{\text{DISPLAY}} \right] .$

FORMAT 2:

level-number [data-name-1]

    $\left[\text{; } \underline{\text{LINE}} \text{ NUMBER IS } \left\{ \begin{array}{l} \text{integer-1 } [\text{ON } \underline{\text{NEXT PAGE}}] \\ \underline{\text{PLUS}} \text{ integer-2} \end{array} \right\} \right]$

    $\left[\text{; } [\underline{\text{USAGE}} \text{ IS}] \ \underline{\text{DISPLAY}} \right] .$

FORMAT 3:

level-number [data-name-1]

    $\left[\text{; } \underline{\text{BLANK}} \text{ WHEN } \underline{\text{ZERO}} \right]$

    $\left[\text{; } \underline{\text{GROUP}} \text{ INDICATE} \right]$

    $\left[\text{; } \left\{ \begin{array}{l} \underline{\text{JUSTIFIED}} \\ \underline{\text{JUST}} \end{array} \right\} \text{ RIGHT} \right]$

    $\left[\text{; } \underline{\text{LINE}} \text{ NUMBER IS } \left\{ \begin{array}{l} \text{integer-1 } [\text{ON } \underline{\text{NEXT PAGE}}] \\ \underline{\text{PLUS}} \text{ integer-2} \end{array} \right\} \right]$

$$\left[; \underline{\text{COLUMN}} \text{ NUMBER IS integer-3}\right]$$

$$; \left\{ \begin{array}{c} \underline{\text{PICTURE}} \\ \underline{\text{PIC}} \end{array} \right\} \text{ IS character-string}$$

$$\left\{ \begin{array}{l} ; \underline{\text{SOURCE}} \text{ IS identifier-1} \\ ; \underline{\text{VALUE}} \text{ IS literal} \\ \left\{; \underline{\text{SUM}} \text{ identifier-2 } \left[, \text{ identifier-3}\right] \dots \right. \\ \qquad \left[\underline{\text{UPON}} \text{ data-name-2 } \left[, \text{ data-name-3}\right] \dots \right]\right\} \dots \\ \qquad \left[\underline{\text{RESET}} \text{ ON } \left\{ \begin{array}{c} \text{data-name-4} \\ \underline{\text{FINAL}} \end{array} \right\}\right] \end{array} \right\}$$

$$\left[; \left[\underline{\text{USAGE}} \text{ IS}\right] \underline{\text{DISPLAY}}\right].$$

GENERAL FORMAT FOR PROCEDURE DIVISION

FORMAT 1:

$\underline{\text{PROCEDURE}}$ $\underline{\text{DIVISION}}$ $\left[\underline{\text{USING}} \text{ data-name-1 } \left[, \text{ data-name-2}\right] \dots \right]$.

$\left[\underline{\text{DECLARATIVES}}\right.$.

$\left\{\text{section-name } \underline{\text{SECTION}} \left[\text{segment-number}\right].$ declarative-sentence

$\left[\text{paragraph-name. } \left[\text{sentence}\right] \dots \right] \dots \right\} \dots$

$\underline{\text{END}}$ $\underline{\text{DECLARATIVES}}.\right]$

$\left\{\text{section-name } \underline{\text{SECTION}} \left[\text{segment-number}\right].$

$\left[\text{paragraph-name. } \left[\text{sentence}\right] \dots \right] \dots \right\} \dots$

FORMAT 2:

$\underline{\text{PROCEDURE}}$ $\underline{\text{DIVISION}}$ $\left[\underline{\text{USING}} \text{ data-name-1 } \left[, \text{ data-name-2}\right] \dots \right]$.

$\left\{\text{paragraph-name. } \left[\text{sentence}\right] \dots \right\} \dots$

GENERAL FORMAT FOR VERBS

ACCEPT identifier [FROM mnemonic-name]

ACCEPT identifier FROM $\begin{Bmatrix} \text{DATE} \\ \text{DAY} \\ \text{TIME} \end{Bmatrix}$

ACCEPT cd-name MESSAGE COUNT

ADD $\begin{Bmatrix} \text{identifier-1} \\ \text{literal-1} \end{Bmatrix}$ $\begin{bmatrix} \text{, identifier-2} \\ \text{, literal-2} \end{bmatrix}$ ... TO identifier-m [ROUNDED]

   [, identifier-n [ROUNDED]] ... [; ON SIZE ERROR imperative-statement]

ADD $\begin{Bmatrix} \text{identifier-1} \\ \text{literal-1} \end{Bmatrix}$, $\begin{Bmatrix} \text{identifier-2} \\ \text{literal-2} \end{Bmatrix}$ $\begin{bmatrix} \text{, identifier-3} \\ \text{, literal-3} \end{bmatrix}$ ...

    GIVING identifier-m [ROUNDED] [, identifier-n [ROUNDED]] ...

   [; ON SIZE ERROR imperative-statement]

ADD $\begin{Bmatrix} \underline{\text{CORRESPONDING}} \\ \underline{\text{CORR}} \end{Bmatrix}$ identifier-1 TO identifier-2 [ROUNDED]

   [; ON SIZE ERROR imperative-statement]

ALTER procedure-name-1 TO [PROCEED TO] procedure-name-2

   [, procedure-name-3 TO [PROCEED TO] procedure-name-4] ...

CALL $\begin{Bmatrix} \text{identifier-1} \\ \text{literal-1} \end{Bmatrix}$ [USING data-name-1 [, data-name-2] ...]

   [; ON OVERFLOW imperative-statement]

CANCEL $\begin{Bmatrix} \text{identifier-1} \\ \text{literal-1} \end{Bmatrix}$ $\begin{bmatrix} \text{, identifier-2} \\ \text{, literal-2} \end{bmatrix}$ ...

CLOSE file-name-1 $\begin{bmatrix} \begin{Bmatrix} \text{REEL} \\ \text{UNIT} \end{Bmatrix} \begin{bmatrix} \text{WITH NO REWIND} \\ \text{FOR REMOVAL} \end{bmatrix} \\ \text{WITH} \begin{Bmatrix} \text{NO REWIND} \\ \text{LOCK} \end{Bmatrix} \end{bmatrix}$

$\begin{bmatrix} \text{, file-name-2} \begin{bmatrix} \begin{Bmatrix} \text{REEL} \\ \text{UNIT} \end{Bmatrix} \begin{bmatrix} \text{WITH NO REWIND} \\ \text{FOR REMOVAL} \end{bmatrix} \\ \text{WITH} \begin{Bmatrix} \text{NO REWIND} \\ \text{LOCK} \end{Bmatrix} \end{bmatrix} \end{bmatrix}$ ...

CLOSE file-name-1 [WITH LOCK] [, file-name-2 [WITH LOCK]] ...

COMPUTE identifier-1 $\left[\underline{ROUNDED}\right]$ $\left[,\ identifier-2\ \left[\underline{ROUNDED}\right]\right]$ ...

   = arithmetic-expression $\left[;\ ON\ \underline{SIZE}\ \underline{ERROR}\ imperative-statement\right]$

DELETE file-name RECORD $\left[;\ \underline{INVALID}\ KEY\ imperative-statement\right]$

DISABLE $\left\{\begin{array}{l}\underline{INPUT}\\\underline{OUTPUT}\end{array}\left[\underline{TERMINAL}\right]\right\}$ cd-name WITH $\underline{KEY}$ $\left\{\begin{array}{l}identifier-1\\literal-1\end{array}\right\}$

DISPLAY $\left\{\begin{array}{l}identifier-1\\literal-1\end{array}\right\}$ $\left[\begin{array}{l},\ identifier-2\\,\ literal-2\end{array}\right]$ ... $\left[\underline{UPON}\ mnemonic-name\right]$

DIVIDE $\left\{\begin{array}{l}identifier-1\\literal-1\end{array}\right\}$ $\underline{INTO}$ identifier-2 $\left[\underline{ROUNDED}\right]$

   $\left[,\ identifier-3\ \left[\underline{ROUNDED}\right]\right]$ ... $\left[;\ ON\ \underline{SIZE}\ \underline{ERROR}\ imperative-statement\right]$

DIVIDE $\left\{\begin{array}{l}identifier-1\\literal-1\end{array}\right\}$ $\underline{INTO}$ $\left\{\begin{array}{l}identifier-2\\literal-2\end{array}\right\}$ $\underline{GIVING}$ identifier-3 $\left[\underline{ROUNDED}\right]$

   $\left[,\ identifier-4\ \left[\underline{ROUNDED}\right]\right]$ ... $\left[;\ ON\ \underline{SIZE}\ \underline{ERROR}\ imperative-statement\right]$

DIVIDE $\left\{\begin{array}{l}identifier-1\\literal-1\end{array}\right\}$ $\underline{BY}$ $\left\{\begin{array}{l}identifier-2\\literal-2\end{array}\right\}$ $\underline{GIVING}$ identifier-3 $\left[\underline{ROUNDED}\right]$

   $\left[,\ identifier-4\ \left[\underline{ROUNDED}\right]\right]$ ... $\left[;\ ON\ \underline{SIZE}\ \underline{ERROR}\ imperative-statement\right]$

DIVIDE $\left\{\begin{array}{l}identifier-1\\literal-1\end{array}\right\}$ $\underline{INTO}$ $\left\{\begin{array}{l}identifier-2\\literal-2\end{array}\right\}$ $\underline{GIVING}$ identifier-3 $\left[\underline{ROUNDED}\right]$

   $\underline{REMAINDER}$ identifier-4 $\left[;\ ON\ \underline{SIZE}\ \underline{ERROR}\ imperative-statement\right]$

DIVIDE $\left\{\begin{array}{l}identifier-1\\literal-1\end{array}\right\}$ $\underline{BY}$ $\left\{\begin{array}{l}identifier-2\\literal-2\end{array}\right\}$ $\underline{GIVING}$ identifier-3 $\left[\underline{ROUNDED}\right]$

   $\underline{REMAINDER}$ identifier-4 $\left[;\ ON\ \underline{SIZE}\ \underline{ERROR}\ imperative-statement\right]$

ENABLE $\left\{\begin{array}{l}\underline{INPUT}\\\underline{OUTPUT}\end{array}\left[\underline{TERMINAL}\right]\right\}$ cd-name WITH $\underline{KEY}$ $\left\{\begin{array}{l}identifier-1\\literal-1\end{array}\right\}$

ENTER language-name $\left[routine-name\right]$.

EXIT $\left[\underline{PROGRAM}\right]$.

GENERATE $\left\{\begin{array}{l}data-name\\report-name\end{array}\right\}$

$\underline{GO}$ TO $\left[procedure-name-1\right]$

$\underline{GO}$ TO procedure-name-1 $\left[,\ procedure-name-2\right]$ ... , procedure-name-n

   $\underline{DEPENDING}$ ON identifier

$\underline{IF}$ condition; $\left\{\begin{array}{l}statement-1\\\underline{NEXT}\ \underline{SENTENCE}\end{array}\right\}$ $\left\{\begin{array}{l};\ \underline{ELSE}\ statement-2\\;\ \underline{ELSE}\ \underline{NEXT}\ \underline{SENTENCE}\end{array}\right\}$

INITIATE report-name-1 $\left[,\ report-name-2\right]$ ...

<u>INSPECT</u> identifier-1 <u>TALLYING</u>

$$\left\{ , \text{ identifier-2 } \underline{\text{FOR}} \left\{ , \left\{ \begin{matrix} \underline{\text{ALL}} \\ \underline{\text{LEADING}} \\ \underline{\text{CHARACTERS}} \end{matrix} \right\} \left\{ \begin{matrix} \text{identifier-3} \\ \text{literal-1} \end{matrix} \right\} \left[\left\{ \begin{matrix} \underline{\text{BEFORE}} \\ \underline{\text{AFTER}} \end{matrix} \right\} \text{ INITIAL } \left\{ \begin{matrix} \text{identifier-4} \\ \text{literal-2} \end{matrix} \right\} \right] \right\} \dots \right\} \dots$$

<u>INSPECT</u> identifier-1 <u>REPLACING</u>

$$\left\{ \begin{matrix} \underline{\text{CHARACTERS}} \ \underline{\text{BY}} \ \left\{ \begin{matrix} \text{identifier-6} \\ \text{literal-4} \end{matrix} \right\} \left[\left\{ \begin{matrix} \underline{\text{BEFORE}} \\ \underline{\text{AFTER}} \end{matrix} \right\} \text{ INITIAL } \left\{ \begin{matrix} \text{identifier-7} \\ \text{literal-5} \end{matrix} \right\} \right] \\ \left\{ , \left\{ \begin{matrix} \underline{\text{ALL}} \\ \underline{\text{LEADING}} \\ \underline{\text{FIRST}} \end{matrix} \right\} \left\{ , \left\{ \begin{matrix} \text{identifier-5} \\ \text{literal-3} \end{matrix} \right\} \ \underline{\text{BY}} \ \left\{ \begin{matrix} \text{identifier-6} \\ \text{literal-4} \end{matrix} \right\} \left[\left\{ \begin{matrix} \underline{\text{BEFORE}} \\ \underline{\text{AFTER}} \end{matrix} \right\} \text{ INITIAL } \left\{ \begin{matrix} \text{identifier-7} \\ \text{literal-5} \end{matrix} \right\} \right] \right\} \dots \right\} \dots \end{matrix} \right\}$$

<u>INSPECT</u> identifier-1 <u>TALLYING</u>

$$\left\{ , \text{ identifier-2 } \underline{\text{FOR}} \left\{ , \left\{ \begin{matrix} \underline{\text{ALL}} \\ \underline{\text{LEADING}} \\ \underline{\text{CHARACTERS}} \end{matrix} \right\} \left\{ \begin{matrix} \text{identifier-3} \\ \text{literal-1} \end{matrix} \right\} \left[\left\{ \begin{matrix} \underline{\text{BEFORE}} \\ \underline{\text{AFTER}} \end{matrix} \right\} \text{ INITIAL } \left\{ \begin{matrix} \text{identifier-4} \\ \text{literal-2} \end{matrix} \right\} \right] \right\} \dots \right\} \dots$$

<u>REPLACING</u>

$$\left\{ \begin{matrix} \underline{\text{CHARACTERS}} \ \underline{\text{BY}} \ \left\{ \begin{matrix} \text{identifier-6} \\ \text{literal-4} \end{matrix} \right\} \left[\left\{ \begin{matrix} \underline{\text{BEFORE}} \\ \underline{\text{AFTER}} \end{matrix} \right\} \text{ INITIAL } \left\{ \begin{matrix} \text{identifier-7} \\ \text{literal-5} \end{matrix} \right\} \right] \\ \left\{ , \left\{ \begin{matrix} \underline{\text{ALL}} \\ \underline{\text{LEADING}} \\ \underline{\text{FIRST}} \end{matrix} \right\} \left\{ , \left\{ \begin{matrix} \text{identifier-5} \\ \text{literal-3} \end{matrix} \right\} \ \underline{\text{BY}} \ \left\{ \begin{matrix} \text{identifier-6} \\ \text{literal-4} \end{matrix} \right\} \left[\left\{ \begin{matrix} \underline{\text{BEFORE}} \\ \underline{\text{AFTER}} \end{matrix} \right\} \text{ INITIAL } \left\{ \begin{matrix} \text{identifier-7} \\ \text{literal-5} \end{matrix} \right\} \right] \right\} \dots \right\} \dots \end{matrix} \right\}$$

<u>MERGE</u> file-name-1 ON $\left\{ \begin{matrix} \underline{\text{ASCENDING}} \\ \underline{\text{DESCENDING}} \end{matrix} \right\}$ KEY data-name-1 [, data-name-2] ...

$$\left[\text{ON} \left\{ \begin{matrix} \underline{\text{ASCENDING}} \\ \underline{\text{DESCENDING}} \end{matrix} \right\} \text{ KEY data-name-3 } [, \text{ data-name-4}] \dots \right] \dots$$

[COLLATING <u>SEQUENCE</u> IS alphabet-name]

<u>USING</u> file-name-2, file-name-3 [, file-name-4] ...

$$\left\{ \begin{matrix} \underline{\text{OUTPUT}} \ \underline{\text{PROCEDURE}} \text{ IS section-name-1 } \left[\left\{ \begin{matrix} \underline{\text{THROUGH}} \\ \underline{\text{THRU}} \end{matrix} \right\} \text{ section-name-2} \right] \\ \underline{\text{GIVING}} \text{ file-name-5} \end{matrix} \right\}$$

<u>MOVE</u> $\left\{ \begin{matrix} \text{identifier-1} \\ \text{literal} \end{matrix} \right\}$ <u>TO</u> identifier-2 [, identifier-3] ...

<u>MOVE</u> $\left\{ \begin{matrix} \underline{\text{CORRESPONDING}} \\ \underline{\text{CORR}} \end{matrix} \right\}$ identifier-1 <u>TO</u> identifier-2

<u>MULTIPLY</u> $\left\{ \begin{matrix} \text{identifier-1} \\ \text{literal-1} \end{matrix} \right\}$ <u>BY</u> identifier-2 [<u>ROUNDED</u>]

[, identifier-3 [<u>ROUNDED</u>]] ... [; ON <u>SIZE</u> <u>ERROR</u> imperative-statement]

$$\underline{\text{MULTIPLY}} \quad \begin{Bmatrix} \text{identifier-1} \\ \text{literal-1} \end{Bmatrix} \quad \underline{\text{BY}} \quad \begin{Bmatrix} \text{identifier-2} \\ \text{literal-2} \end{Bmatrix} \quad \underline{\text{GIVING}} \text{ identifier-3 } \left[\, \underline{\text{ROUNDED}} \,\right]$$

$$\left[\, , \text{ identifier-4 } \left[\underline{\text{ROUNDED}} \right] \right] \, \ldots \, \left[\, ; \text{ ON } \underline{\text{SIZE}} \ \underline{\text{ERROR}} \text{ imperative-statement} \right]$$

$$\underline{\text{OPEN}} \left\{ \begin{array}{l} \underline{\text{INPUT}} \text{ file-name-1 } \left[\begin{array}{l} \underline{\text{REVERSED}} \\ \underline{\text{WITH}} \ \underline{\text{NO}} \ \underline{\text{REWIND}} \end{array} \right] \left[, \text{ file-name-2 } \left[\begin{array}{l} \underline{\text{REVERSED}} \\ \underline{\text{WITH}} \ \underline{\text{NO}} \ \underline{\text{REWIND}} \end{array} \right] \right] \ldots \\ \underline{\text{OUTPUT}} \text{ file-name-3 } \left[\underline{\text{WITH}} \ \underline{\text{NO}} \ \underline{\text{REWIND}} \right] \left[, \text{ file-name-4 } \left[\underline{\text{WITH}} \ \underline{\text{NO}} \ \underline{\text{REWIND}} \right] \right] \ldots \\ \underline{\text{I-O}} \text{ file-name-5 } \left[, \text{ file-name-6 } \right] \ldots \\ \underline{\text{EXTEND}} \text{ file-name-7 } \left[, \text{ file-name-8 } \right] \ldots \end{array} \right\} \ldots$$

$$\underline{\text{OPEN}} \left\{ \begin{array}{l} \underline{\text{INPUT}} \text{ file-name-1 } \left[, \text{ file-name-2 } \right] \ldots \\ \underline{\text{OUTPUT}} \text{ file-name-3 } \left[, \text{ file-name-4 } \right] \ldots \\ \underline{\text{I-O}} \text{ file-name-5 } \left[, \text{ file-name-6 } \right] \ldots \end{array} \right\} \ldots$$

$$\underline{\text{PERFORM}} \text{ procedure-name-1 } \left[\begin{Bmatrix} \underline{\text{THROUGH}} \\ \underline{\text{THRU}} \end{Bmatrix} \text{ procedure-name-2} \right]$$

$$\underline{\text{PERFORM}} \text{ procedure-name-1 } \left[\begin{Bmatrix} \underline{\text{THROUGH}} \\ \underline{\text{THRU}} \end{Bmatrix} \text{ procedure-name-2} \right] \begin{Bmatrix} \text{identifier-1} \\ \text{integer-1} \end{Bmatrix} \ \underline{\text{TIMES}}$$

$$\underline{\text{PERFORM}} \text{ procedure-name-1 } \left[\begin{Bmatrix} \underline{\text{THROUGH}} \\ \underline{\text{THRU}} \end{Bmatrix} \text{ procedure-name-2} \right] \underline{\text{UNTIL}} \text{ condition-1}$$

$$\underline{\text{PERFORM}} \text{ procedure-name-1 } \left[\begin{Bmatrix} \underline{\text{THROUGH}} \\ \underline{\text{THRU}} \end{Bmatrix} \text{ procedure-name-2} \right]$$

$$\underline{\text{VARYING}} \begin{Bmatrix} \text{identifier-2} \\ \text{index-name-1} \end{Bmatrix} \ \underline{\text{FROM}} \begin{Bmatrix} \text{identifier-3} \\ \text{index-name-2} \\ \text{literal-1} \end{Bmatrix}$$

$$\underline{\text{BY}} \begin{Bmatrix} \text{identifier-4} \\ \text{literal-3} \end{Bmatrix} \ \underline{\text{UNTIL}} \text{ condition-1}$$

$$\left[\underline{\text{AFTER}} \begin{Bmatrix} \text{identifier-5} \\ \text{index-name-3} \end{Bmatrix} \ \underline{\text{FROM}} \begin{Bmatrix} \text{identifier-6} \\ \text{index-name-4} \\ \text{literal-3} \end{Bmatrix} \right.$$

$$\underline{\text{BY}} \begin{Bmatrix} \text{identifier-7} \\ \text{literal-4} \end{Bmatrix} \ \underline{\text{UNTIL}} \text{ condition-2}$$

$$\left[\underline{\text{AFTER}} \begin{Bmatrix} \text{identifier-8} \\ \text{index-name-5} \end{Bmatrix} \ \underline{\text{FROM}} \begin{Bmatrix} \text{identifier-9} \\ \text{index-name-6} \\ \text{literal-5} \end{Bmatrix} \right.$$

$$\left. \left. \underline{\text{BY}} \begin{Bmatrix} \text{identifier-10} \\ \text{literal-6} \end{Bmatrix} \ \underline{\text{UNTIL}} \text{ condition-3} \right] \right]$$

$$\underline{\text{READ}} \text{ file-name RECORD } \left[\underline{\text{INTO}} \text{ identifier} \right] \left[\, ; \text{ AT } \underline{\text{END}} \text{ imperative-statement} \right]$$

$$\underline{\text{READ}} \text{ file-name } \left[\underline{\text{NEXT}} \right] \text{ RECORD } \left[\underline{\text{INTO}} \text{ identifier} \right]$$

$$\left[\, ; \text{ AT } \underline{\text{END}} \text{ imperative-statement} \right]$$

<u>READ</u> file-name RECORD $\left[\underline{INTO}\ identifier\right]$ $\left[;\ \underline{INVALID}\ KEY\ imperative\text{-}statement\right]$

<u>READ</u> file-name RECORD $\left[\underline{INTO}\ identifier\right]$

  $\left[;\ \underline{KEY}\ IS\ data\text{-}name\right]$

  $\left[;\ \underline{INVALID}\ KEY\ imperative\text{-}statement\right]$

<u>RECEIVE</u> cd-name $\left\{\begin{array}{l}\underline{MESSAGE}\\\underline{SEGMENT}\end{array}\right\}$ <u>INTO</u> identifier-1 $\left[;\ \underline{NO}\ \underline{DATA}\ imperative\text{-}statement\right]$

<u>RELEASE</u> record-name $\left[\underline{FROM}\ identifier\right]$

<u>RETURN</u> file-name RECORD $\left[\underline{INTO}\ identifier\right]$; AT <u>END</u> imperative-statement

<u>REWRITE</u> record-name $\left[\underline{FROM}\ identifier\right]$

<u>REWRITE</u> record-name $\left[\underline{FROM}\ identifier\right]$ $\left[;\ \underline{INVALID}\ KEY\ imperative\text{-}statement\right]$

<u>SEARCH</u> identifier-1 $\left[\underline{VARYING}\ \left\{\begin{array}{l}identifier\text{-}2\\index\text{-}name\text{-}1\end{array}\right\}\right]$ $\left[;\ AT\ \underline{END}\ imperative\text{-}statement\text{-}1\right]$

  ; <u>WHEN</u> condition-1 $\left\{\begin{array}{l}imperative\text{-}statement\text{-}2\\\underline{NEXT}\ \underline{SENTENCE}\end{array}\right\}$

  $\left[;\ \underline{WHEN}\ condition\text{-}2\ \left\{\begin{array}{l}imperative\text{-}statement\text{-}3\\\underline{NEXT}\ \underline{SENTENCE}\end{array}\right\}\right]$ ...

<u>SEARCH</u> <u>ALL</u> identifier-1 $\left[;\ AT\ \underline{END}\ imperative\text{-}statement\text{-}1\right]$

  ; <u>WHEN</u> $\left\{\begin{array}{l}data\text{-}name\text{-}1\ \left\{\begin{array}{l}IS\ \underline{EQUAL}\ TO\\IS\ =\end{array}\right\}\ \left\{\begin{array}{l}identifier\text{-}3\\literal\text{-}1\\arithmetic\text{-}expression\text{-}1\end{array}\right\}\\condition\text{-}name\text{-}1\end{array}\right\}$

  $\left[\underline{AND}\ \left\{\begin{array}{l}data\text{-}name\text{-}2\ \left\{\begin{array}{l}IS\ \underline{EQUAL}\ TO\\IS\ =\end{array}\right\}\ \left\{\begin{array}{l}identifier\text{-}4\\literal\text{-}2\\arithmetic\text{-}expression\text{-}2\end{array}\right\}\\condition\text{-}name\text{-}2\end{array}\right\}\right]$ ...

  $\left\{\begin{array}{l}imperative\text{-}statement\text{-}2\\\underline{NEXT}\ \underline{SENTENCE}\end{array}\right\}$

<u>SEND</u> cd-name <u>FROM</u> identifier-1

<u>SEND</u> cd-name $\left[\underline{FROM}\ identifier\text{-}1\right]$ $\left\{\begin{array}{l}WITH\ identifier\text{-}2\\WITH\ \underline{ESI}\\WITH\ \underline{EMI}\\WITH\ \underline{EGI}\end{array}\right\}$

  $\left[\left\{\begin{array}{l}\underline{BEFORE}\\\underline{AFTER}\end{array}\right\}\ ADVANCING\ \left\{\begin{array}{l}\left\{\begin{array}{l}identifier\text{-}3\\integer\end{array}\right\}\ \left[\begin{array}{l}LINE\\LINES\end{array}\right]\\\left\{\begin{array}{l}mnemonic\text{-}name\\PAGE\end{array}\right\}\end{array}\right\}\right]$

$$\underline{\text{SET}} \quad \begin{Bmatrix} \text{identifier-1} & [\text{, identifier-2}] & \dots \\ \text{index-name-1} & [\text{, index-name-2}] & \dots \end{Bmatrix} \quad \underline{\text{TO}} \quad \begin{Bmatrix} \text{identifier-3} \\ \text{index-name-3} \\ \text{integer-1} \end{Bmatrix}$$

$$\underline{\text{SET}} \quad \text{index-name-4} \quad [\text{, index-name-5}] \quad \dots \quad \begin{Bmatrix} \underline{\text{UP}} \ \underline{\text{BY}} \\ \underline{\text{DOWN}} \ \underline{\text{BY}} \end{Bmatrix} \quad \begin{Bmatrix} \text{identifier-4} \\ \text{integer-2} \end{Bmatrix}$$

$$\underline{\text{SORT}} \quad \text{file-name-1 ON} \quad \begin{Bmatrix} \underline{\text{ASCENDING}} \\ \underline{\text{DESCENDING}} \end{Bmatrix} \quad \text{KEY data-name-1} \quad [\text{, data-name-2}] \quad \dots$$

$$\left[\text{ON} \quad \begin{Bmatrix} \underline{\text{ASCENDING}} \\ \underline{\text{DESCENDING}} \end{Bmatrix} \quad \text{KEY data-name-3} \quad [\text{, data-name-4}] \quad \dots \right] \quad \dots$$

$$\left[\text{COLLATING} \ \underline{\text{SEQUENCE}} \ \text{IS alphabet-name} \right]$$

$$\begin{Bmatrix} \underline{\text{INPUT}} \ \underline{\text{PROCEDURE}} \ \text{IS section-name-1} \left[\begin{Bmatrix} \underline{\text{THROUGH}} \\ \underline{\text{THRU}} \end{Bmatrix} \ \text{section-name-2} \right] \\ \underline{\text{USING}} \ \text{file-name-2} \quad [\text{, file-name-3}] \quad \dots \end{Bmatrix}$$

$$\begin{Bmatrix} \underline{\text{OUTPUT}} \ \underline{\text{PROCEDURE}} \ \text{IS section-name-3} \left[\begin{Bmatrix} \underline{\text{THROUGH}} \\ \underline{\text{THRU}} \end{Bmatrix} \ \text{section-name-4} \right] \\ \underline{\text{GIVING}} \ \text{file-name-4} \end{Bmatrix}$$

$$\underline{\text{START}} \ \text{file-name} \left[\underline{\text{KEY}} \begin{Bmatrix} \text{IS} \ \underline{\text{EQUAL}} \ \text{TO} \\ \text{IS} \ = \\ \text{IS} \ \underline{\text{GREATER}} \ \text{THAN} \\ \text{IS} \ > \\ \text{IS} \ \underline{\text{NOT}} \ \underline{\text{LESS}} \ \text{THAN} \\ \text{IS} \ \underline{\text{NOT}} \ < \end{Bmatrix} \text{data-name} \right]$$

$$\left[\text{; } \underline{\text{INVALID}} \ \text{KEY imperative-statement} \right]$$

$$\underline{\text{STOP}} \quad \begin{Bmatrix} \underline{\text{RUN}} \\ \text{literal} \end{Bmatrix}$$

$$\underline{\text{STRING}} \quad \begin{Bmatrix} \text{identifier-1} \\ \text{literal-1} \end{Bmatrix} \quad \begin{bmatrix} \text{, identifier-2} \\ \text{, literal-2} \end{bmatrix} \quad \dots \quad \underline{\text{DELIMITED}} \ \text{BY} \quad \begin{Bmatrix} \text{identifier-3} \\ \text{literal-3} \\ \underline{\text{SIZE}} \end{Bmatrix}$$

$$\left[\text{,} \begin{Bmatrix} \text{identifier-4} \\ \text{literal-4} \end{Bmatrix} \begin{bmatrix} \text{, identifier-5} \\ \text{, literal-5} \end{bmatrix} \dots \underline{\text{DELIMITED}} \ \text{BY} \begin{Bmatrix} \text{identifier-6} \\ \text{literal-6} \\ \underline{\text{SIZE}} \end{Bmatrix} \right] \dots$$

$$\underline{\text{INTO}} \ \text{identifier-7} \left[\text{WITH} \ \underline{\text{POINTER}} \ \text{identifier-8} \right]$$

$$\left[\text{; ON} \ \underline{\text{OVERFLOW}} \ \text{imperative-statement} \right]$$

$$\underline{\text{SUBTRACT}} \quad \begin{Bmatrix} \text{identifier-1} \\ \text{literal-1} \end{Bmatrix} \quad \begin{bmatrix} \text{, identifier-2} \\ \text{, literal-2} \end{bmatrix} \quad \dots \quad \underline{\text{FROM}} \ \text{identifier-m} \quad \left[\underline{\text{ROUNDED}} \right]$$

$$\left[\text{, identifier-n} \ \left[\underline{\text{ROUNDED}} \right] \right] \quad \dots \quad \left[\text{; ON} \ \underline{\text{SIZE}} \ \underline{\text{ERROR}} \ \text{imperative-statement} \right]$$

SUBTRACT $\left\{\begin{matrix} \text{identifier-1} \\ \text{literal-1} \end{matrix}\right\}$ $\left[\begin{matrix} \text{, identifier-2} \\ \text{, literal-2} \end{matrix}\right]$ ... <u>FROM</u> $\left\{\begin{matrix} \text{identifier-m} \\ \text{literal-m} \end{matrix}\right\}$

     <u>GIVING</u> identifier-n $\left[\underline{\text{ROUNDED}}\right]$ $\left[\text{, identifier-o} \left[\underline{\text{ROUNDED}}\right]\right]$ ...

     $\left[\text{; ON } \underline{\text{SIZE}} \; \underline{\text{ERROR}} \text{ imperative-statement}\right]$

<u>SUBTRACT</u> $\left\{\begin{matrix} \underline{\text{CORRESPONDING}} \\ \underline{\text{CORR}} \end{matrix}\right\}$ identifier-1 <u>FROM</u> identifier-2 $\left[\underline{\text{ROUNDED}}\right]$

     $\left[\text{; ON } \underline{\text{SIZE}} \; \underline{\text{ERROR}} \text{ imperative-statement}\right]$

<u>SUPPRESS</u> PRINTING

<u>TERMINATE</u> report-name-1 $\left[\text{, report-name-2}\right]$ ...

<u>UNSTRING</u> identifier-1

     $\left[\underline{\text{DELIMITED}} \text{ BY } \left[\underline{\text{ALL}}\right] \left\{\begin{matrix} \text{identifier-2} \\ \text{literal-1} \end{matrix}\right\} \left[\text{, } \underline{\text{OR}} \left[\underline{\text{ALL}}\right] \left\{\begin{matrix} \text{identifier-3} \\ \text{literal-2} \end{matrix}\right\}\right] \cdots \right]$

       <u>INTO</u> identifier-4 $\left[\text{, } \underline{\text{DELIMITER}} \text{ IN identifier-5}\right]$ $\left[\text{, } \underline{\text{COUNT}} \text{ IN identifier-6}\right]$

         $\left[\text{, identifier-7 } \left[\text{, } \underline{\text{DELIMITER}} \text{ IN identifier-8}\right] \left[\text{, } \underline{\text{COUNT}} \text{ IN identifier-9}\right]\right]$ ...

     $\left[\text{WITH } \underline{\text{POINTER}} \text{ identifier-10}\right]$ $\left[\underline{\text{TALLYING}} \text{ IN identifier-11}\right]$

     $\left[\text{; ON } \underline{\text{OVERFLOW}} \text{ imperative-statement}\right]$

<u>USE</u> AFTER STANDARD $\left\{\begin{matrix} \underline{\text{EXCEPTION}} \\ \underline{\text{ERROR}} \end{matrix}\right\}$ <u>PROCEDURE</u> ON $\left\{\begin{matrix} \text{file-name-1} \left[\text{, file-name-2}\right] \cdots \\ \underline{\text{INPUT}} \\ \underline{\text{OUTPUT}} \\ \underline{\text{I-O}} \\ \underline{\text{EXTEND}} \end{matrix}\right\}$.

<u>USE</u> AFTER STANDARD $\left\{\begin{matrix} \underline{\text{EXCEPTION}} \\ \underline{\text{ERROR}} \end{matrix}\right\}$ <u>PROCEDURE</u> ON $\left\{\begin{matrix} \text{file-name-1} \left[\text{, file-name-2}\right] \cdots \\ \underline{\text{INPUT}} \\ \underline{\text{OUTPUT}} \\ \underline{\text{I-O}} \end{matrix}\right\}$.

<u>USE</u> <u>BEFORE</u> <u>REPORTING</u> identifier.

<u>USE</u> FOR <u>DEBUGGING</u> ON $\left\{\begin{matrix} \text{cd-name-1} \\ \text{[}\underline{\text{ALL}}\text{ REFERENCES OF] identifier-1} \\ \text{file-name-1} \\ \text{procedure-name-1} \\ \underline{\text{ALL}}\text{ PROCEDURES} \end{matrix}\right\}$

$\left[\text{, } \begin{matrix} \text{cd-name-2} \\ \text{[}\underline{\text{ALL}}\text{ REFERENCES OF] identifier-2} \\ \text{file-name-2} \\ \text{procedure-name-2} \\ \underline{\text{ALL}}\text{ PROCEDURES} \end{matrix}\right]$ ... .

```
WRITE record-name [FROM identifier-1]

  ⎡                                  ⎧⎧⎧identifier-2⎫ ⎡LINE ⎤⎫⎫⎤
  ⎢ ⎧BEFORE⎫                         ⎪⎪⎨            ⎬ ⎢     ⎥⎪⎪⎥
  ⎢ ⎨      ⎬   ADVANCING             ⎨⎪⎩integer    ⎭ ⎣LINES⎦⎪⎬⎥
  ⎢ ⎩AFTER ⎭                         ⎪⎧mnemonic-name⎫        ⎪⎥
  ⎢                                  ⎪⎨            ⎬         ⎪⎥
  ⎣                                  ⎩⎩PAGE        ⎭         ⎭⎦

  ⎡      ⎧END-OF-PAGE⎫                      ⎤
  ⎢ ; AT ⎨          ⎬   imperative-statement⎥
  ⎣      ⎩EOP        ⎭                      ⎦

WRITE record-name [FROM identifier] [; INVALID KEY imperative-statement]
```

GENERAL FORMAT FOR CONDITIONS

RELATION CONDITION:

```
⎧identifier-1             ⎫ ⎧IS [NOT] GREATER THAN⎫ ⎧identifier-2            ⎫
⎪literal-1               ⎪ ⎪IS [NOT] LESS THAN   ⎪ ⎪literal-2              ⎪
⎨arithmetic-expression-1 ⎬ ⎨IS [NOT] EQUAL TO    ⎬ ⎨arithmetic-expression-2⎬
⎪index-name-1            ⎪ ⎪IS [NOT] >           ⎪ ⎪index-name-2           ⎪
⎩                        ⎭ ⎪IS [NOT] <           ⎪ ⎩                       ⎭
                           ⎩IS [NOT] =           ⎭
```

CLASS CONDITION:

```
identifier IS [NOT] ⎧NUMERIC   ⎫
                    ⎨          ⎬
                    ⎩ALPHABETIC⎭
```

SIGN CONDITION:

```
                             ⎧POSITIVE⎫
arithmetic-expression IS [NOT] ⎨NEGATIVE⎬
                             ⎩ZERO    ⎭
```

CONDITION-NAME CONDITION:

condition-name

SWITCH-STATUS CONDITION:

condition-name

NEGATED SIMPLE CONDITION:

NOT simple-condition

COMBINED CONDITION:

$$\text{condition} \ \left\{ \left\{ \frac{\text{AND}}{\text{OR}} \right\} \ \text{condition} \right\} \ \dots$$

ABBREVIATED COMBINED RELATION CONDITION:

$$\text{relation-condition} \ \left\{ \left\{ \frac{\text{AND}}{\text{OR}} \right\} \ [\underline{\text{NOT}}] \ [\text{relational-operator}] \ \text{object} \right\} \ \dots$$

MISCELLANEOUS FORMATS

QUALIFICATION:

$$\left\{ \begin{matrix} \text{data-name-1} \\ \text{condition-name} \end{matrix} \right\} \ \left[\left\{ \frac{\text{OF}}{\text{IN}} \right\} \ \text{data-name-2} \right] \ \dots$$

$$\text{paragraph-name} \ \left[\left\{ \frac{\text{OF}}{\text{IN}} \right\} \ \text{section-name} \right]$$

$$\text{text-name} \ \left[\left\{ \frac{\text{OF}}{\text{IN}} \right\} \ \text{library-name} \right]$$

SUBSCRIPTING:

$$\left\{ \begin{matrix} \text{data-name} \\ \text{condition-name} \end{matrix} \right\} \ (\text{subscript-1} \ [, \ \text{subscript-2} \ [, \ \text{subscript-3}]])$$

INDEXING:

$$\left\{ \begin{matrix} \text{data-name} \\ \text{condition-name} \end{matrix} \right\} \ (\ \left\{ \begin{matrix} \text{index-name-1} \ [\{\pm\} \ \text{literal-2}] \\ \text{literal-1} \end{matrix} \right\}$$

$$\left[, \ \left\{ \begin{matrix} \text{index-name-2} \ [\{\pm\} \ \text{literal-4}] \\ \text{literal-3} \end{matrix} \right\} \ \left[, \ \left\{ \begin{matrix} \text{index-name-3} \ [\{\pm\} \ \text{literal-6}] \\ \text{literal-5} \end{matrix} \right\} \right] \right] \ )$$

IDENTIFIER: FORMAT 1

$$\text{data-name-1} \ \left[\left\{ \frac{\text{OF}}{\text{IN}} \right\} \ \text{data-name-2} \right] \ \dots \ \left[(\text{subscript-1} \ [, \ \text{subscript-2} \right.$$

$$\left. [, \ \text{subscript-3}] \ ] \ ) \right]$$

IDENTIFIER: FORMAT 2

$$\text{data-name-1} \left[\left\{ \begin{array}{c} \underline{OF} \\ \underline{IN} \end{array} \right\} \text{data-name-2} \right] \ldots \left[\left(\left\{ \begin{array}{l} \text{index-name-1} \left[\{\pm\} \text{ literal-2} \right] \\ \text{literal-1} \end{array} \right. \right. \right.$$

$$\left[, \left\{ \begin{array}{l} \text{index-name-2} \left[\{\pm\} \text{ literal-4} \right] \\ \text{literal-3} \end{array} \right\} \left[, \left\{ \begin{array}{l} \text{index-name-3} \left[\{\pm\} \text{ literal-6} \right] \\ \text{literal-5} \end{array} \right\} \right] \right] \right)$$

GENERAL FORMAT FOR COPY STATEMENT

$$\underline{COPY} \text{ text-name} \left[\left\{ \begin{array}{c} \underline{OF} \\ \underline{IN} \end{array} \right\} \text{library-name} \right]$$

$$\left[\underline{REPLACING} \left\{ , \left\{ \begin{array}{l} \text{==pseudo-text-1==} \\ \text{identifier-1} \\ \text{literal-1} \\ \text{word-1} \end{array} \right\} \underline{BY} \left\{ \begin{array}{l} \text{==pseudo-text-2==} \\ \text{identifier-2} \\ \text{literal-2} \\ \text{word-2} \end{array} \right\} \right\} \ldots \right]$$

Appendix D

RESERVED WORDS

The following is a list of reserved words:

ACCEPT	CLOSE	DEBUG-SUB-3	EXIT
ACCESS	COBOL	DEBUGGING	EXTEND
ADD	CODE	DECIMAL-POINT	
ADVANCING	CODE-SET	DECLARATIVES	FD
AFTER	COLLATING	DELETE	FILE
ALL	COLUMN	DELIMITED	FILE-CONTROL
ALPHABETIC	COMMA	DELIMITER	FILLER
ALSO	COMMUNICATION	DEPENDING	FINAL
ALTER	COMP	DESCENDING	FIRST
ALTERNATE	COMPUTATIONAL	DESTINATION	FOOTING
AND	COMPUTE	DETAIL	FOR
ARE	CONFIGURATION	DISABLE	FROM
AREA	CONTAINS	DISPLAY	
AREAS	CONTROL	DIVIDE	GENERATE
ASCENDING	CONTROLS	DIVISION	GIVING
ASSIGN	COPY	DOWN	GO
AT	CORR	DUPLICATES	GREATER
AUTHOR	CORRESPONDING	DYNAMIC	GROUP
	COUNT		
BEFORE	CURRENCY	EGI	HEADING
BLANK		ELSE	HIGH-VALUE
BLOCK	DATA	EMI	HIGH-VALUES
BOTTOM	DATE	ENABLE	
BY	DATE-COMPILED	END	I-O
	DATE-WRITTEN	END-OF-PAGE	I-O-CONTROL
CALL	DAY	ENTER	IDENTIFICATION
CANCEL	DE	ENVIRONMENT	IF
CD	DEBUG-CONTENTS	EOP	IN
CF	DEBUG-ITEM	EQUAL	INDEX
CH	DEBUG-LINE	ERROR	INDEXED
CHARACTER	DEBUG-NAME	ESI	INDICATE
CHARACTERS	DEBUG-SUB-1	EVERY	INITIAL
CLOCK-UNITS	DEBUG-SUB-2	EXCEPTION	INITIATE

INPUT	OF	REPORTS	SYNC
INPUT-OUTPUT	OFF	RERUN	SYNCHRONIZED
INSPECT	OMITTED	RESERVE	
INSTALLATION	ON	RESET	TABLE
INTO	OPEN	RETURN	TALLYING
INVALID	OPTIONAL	REVERSED	TAPE
IS	OR	REWIND	TERMINAL
	ORGANIZATION	REWRITE	TERMINATE
JUST	OUTPUT	RF	TEXT
JUSTIFIED	OVERFLOW	RH	THAN
		RIGHT	THROUGH
KEY	PAGE	ROUNDED	THRU
	PAGE-COUNTER	RUN	TIME
LABEL	PERFORM		TIMES
LAST	PF	SAME	TO
LEADING	PH	SD	TOP
LEFT	PIC	SEARCH	TRAILING
LENGTH	PICTURE	SECTION	TYPE
LESS	PLUS	SECURITY	
LIMIT	POINTER	SEGMENT	UNIT
LIMITS	POSITION	SEGMENT-LIMIT	UNSTRING
LINAGE	POSITIVE	SELECT	UNTIL
LINAGE-COUNTER	PRINTING	SEND	UP
LINE	PROCEDURE	SENTENCE	UPON
LINE-COUNTER	PROCEDURES	SEPARATE	USAGE
LINES	PROCEED	SEQUENCE	USE
LINKAGE	PROGRAM	SEQUENTIAL	USING
LOCK	PROGRAM-ID	SET	
LOW-VALUE		SIGN	VALUE
LOW-VALUES	QUEUE	SIZE	VALUES
	QUOTE	SORT	VARYING
MEMORY	QUOTES	SORT-MERGE	
MERGE		SOURCE	WHEN
MESSAGE	RANDOM	SOURCE-COMPUTER	WITH
MODE	RD	SPACE	WORDS
MODULES	READ	SPACES	WORKING-STORAGE
MOVE	RECEIVE	SPECIAL-NAMES	WRITE
MULTIPLE	RECORD	STANDARD	
MULTIPLY	RECORDS	STANDARD-1	ZERO
	REDEFINES	START	ZEROES
NATIVE	REEL	STATUS	ZEROS
NEGATIVE	REFERENCES	STOP	
NEXT	RELATIVE	STRING	+
NO	RELEASE	SUB-QUEUE-1	−
NOT	REMAINDER	SUB-QUEUE-2	*
NUMBER	REMOVAL	SUB-QUEUE-3	/
NUMERIC	RENAMES	SUBTRACT	**
	REPLACING	SUM	>
OBJECT-COMPUTER	REPORT	SUPPRESS	<
OCCURS	REPORTING	SYMBOLIC	=

GLOSSARY

Abbreviated relation condition. The condition that results from the explicit omission of a common subject or a common subject and common relational operator in a consecutive sequence of relation conditions.

ACCEPT. Verb used to initiate input from the operator's console or user's terminal.

Access mode. The manner in which records are to be operated upon within a file.

Actual decimal point. The physical representation, using either of the decimal point characters period (.) or comma (,), of the decimal point position in a data item.

Alphabet-name. A user defined word, in the SPECIAL-NAMES paragraph of the ENVIRONMENT DIVISION, that assigns a name to a specific character set and/or collating sequence.

Alphabetic character. A character that belongs to the following set of letters: A, B, C, D, E, F, G, H, I, J, K, L, M, N, O, P, Q, R, S, T, U, V, W, X, Y, Z, and the space.

Alphanumeric character. Any character in the computer's character set.

ANSI. American National Standards Institute; organization which adopts standards for COBOL.

Arithmetic expression. An arithmetic expression can be an identifier or a numeric elementary item; a numeric literal, such identifiers and literals separated by arithmetic operators; two arithmetic expressions separated by an arithmetic operator; or an arithmetic expression enclosed in parentheses.

Arithmetic /logical unit. Portion of a computer which performs arithmetic operations and logic comparisons.

Arithmetic operator. A single character, or a fixed two-character combinaton, that belongs to the following set:

Character	Meaning
+	addition
−	subtraction
*	multiplication
/	division
**	exponentiation

Ascending key. A key opon the values of which data is ordered, starting with the lowest value of key up to the highest value of key in accordance with the rules for comparing data items.

Ascending sequence. Each item has a value which is greater than or equal to its predecessor.

Assumed decimal point. A decimal point position which does not involve the existence of an actual character in a data item. The assumed decimal point has logical meaning but no physical representation.

At End condition. A condition caused:

1) During the execution of a READ statement for a sequentially accessed file when no more records exist in the file.
2) During the execution of a RETURN statement, when no next logical record exists for the associated sort file.
3) During the execution of a SEARCH statement, when the search operation terminates without satisfying the condition specified in any of the associated WHEN phrases.

AUTHOR. Paragraph in the IDENTIFICATION DIVISION used to show the name of the programmer.

Binary. Base 2; binary digits are 0 and 1.

Bit. A binary 1 or 0.

Block. A physical unit of data normally composed of one or more logical records. For mass storage files, a block may contain a portion of a logical record. The size of a block has no direct relationship to the size of the file within which the block is contained or to the size of the logical record(s) that are either continued within the block or that overlap the block. The term is synonymous with physical record.

Branch. Execute a program instruction other than the next sequential instruction

Bug. Program error.

Byte. A group of eight bits.

Central Processing Unit (CPU). Portion of the computer containing the control and arithmetic/logical units

Carriage control tape. Paper tape used to control the vertical spacing of paper in a line printer.

Character. The basic indivisible unit of the language.

Character position. The amount of physical storage required to store a single standard data format character described as usage in DISPLAY.

Character-string. A sequence of contiguous characters which form a COBOL word, a literal, a PICTURE character-string, or a comment-entry.

Class condition. The proposition, for which a truth value can be determined, that the content of an item is wholly alphabetic or is wholly numeric.

Clause. An ordered set of consecutive COBOL character-strings whose purpose is to specify an attribute of an entry.

CLOSE. Verb used to terminate processing of a file.

COBOL. *CO*mmon *B*usiness *O*riented *L*anguage.

COBOL character set. The complete COBOL character set consists of the 51 characters listed below;

0,1,...,9	digit
A,B,...,Z	letter
	space (blank)
+	plus sign

-	minus sign (hyphen)
*	asterisk
/	stroke (virgule, slash)
=	equal sign
$	currency sign
,	comma (decimal point)
;	semicolon
.	period (decimal point)
"	quotation mark
(	left parenthesis
)	right parenthesis
>	greater than symbol
<	less then symbol

Collating sequence. The sequence in which the characters that are acceptable in a computer are ordered for purposes of sorting, merging and comparing.

Column. A character position within a print line. The columns are numbered from 1, by 1, starting at the leftmost character position of the print line and extending to the rightmost position of the print line.

Combined condition. A condition that is the result of connecting two or more conditions with the AND or the OR logical operator.

Comment-entry. An entry in the IDENTIFICATION DIVISION that may be any combination of characters from the computer character set.

Comment line. A source program line represented by an asterisk in the indicator area of the line (position 7) and any characters from the computer's set in area A and area B of that line. The comment line serves only for character documentation in a program.

Compiler. A program used to translate a source program into an object program.

Complex condition. A condition in which one or more logical operators act upon one or more conditions.

Compound condition. See complex condition.

COMPUTATIONAL. Reserved word used in the USAGE clause to define a data item which is in binary form on IBM systems.

COMPUTATIONAL-1. Reserved word used in the USAGE clause to define a data item which is in single precision floating point form on IBM systems.

COMPUTATIONAL-2. Reserved word used in the USAGE clause to define a data item which is in double precision floating point form in IBM systems.

COMPUTATIONAL-3. Reserved word used in the USAGE clause to define a data item which is in packed decimal form on IBM systems.

COMPUTE. Verb used with arithmetic operations described in symbolic (algebraic) from.

Computer-name. A system-name that identifies the computer upon which the program is to be compiled or run.

Condition. A logical expression which may be true or false.

Condition-name. A user defined word assign to a specific value, set of values or range of values within the complete set of values that a conditional variable may possess.

Conditional expression. A simple condition or a complex condition specified in an IF, PERFORM, or SEARCH statement.

Conditional statement. A conditional statement specifies that the truth value of a condition is to be determined and that the subsequent action of the object program is dependent on this truth value.

CONFIGURATION SECTION.   Subdivision of the ENVIRONMENT DIVI-SION used to describe various characteristics of computing systems used.

Console.   Device used by the computer operator to communicate with the operating system.

Constant.   A value which does not change.

Contiguous items.   Items that are described by consecutive entries in the DATA DIVISION, and that bear a definite hierarchic relationship to each other.

Control break.   A change in the value of a data item that is used to control the hierarchical structure of a report.

Control break level.   The relative position within a control hierarchy at which the most major control break occurred.

Control unit.   Portion of a computer which executes instructions and thereby controls the functions of all other units.

Counter.   A data item used for storing numbers or number representations in a manner that permits these numbers to be increased or decreased by the value of another number, or to be changed or reset to zero or to an arbitrary positive or negative value.

Currency sign.   The character ''$'' of the COBOL character set.

Currency symbol.   The character defined by the CURRENCY SIGN clause in the SPECIAL-NAMES paragraph. If no CURRENCY SIGN clause is present in a COBOL source program, the currency symbol is identical to the currency sign.

Current record.   The record which is available in the record area associated with the file.

Data.   Symbolic representation of observations of the real world.

DATA DIVISION.   Subdivision of a COBOL program used to describe data to be processed by the program.

Data clause.   A clause that appears in a data description entry in the DATA DIVISION and provides information describing a particular attribute of a data item.

Data description entry.   An entry in the DATA DIVISION that is composed of a level-number followed by a data-name if required, and then followed by a set of data clauses as required.

Data item.   A character or a set of contiguous characters (excluding literals in either case) defined as a unit of data by the COBOL program.

Data-name.   A user defined word that names a data item described in a data description entry in the DATA DIVISION. When used in the general formats, data-name represents a word which can not be subscripted, indexed, or qualified unless specifically permitted by the rules for that format.

DATE-COMPILED.   Paragraph in the IDENTIFICATION DIVISION used to show the date of compilation.

DATE-WRITTEN.   Paragraph in the IDENTIFICATION DIVISION used to show the date the program was written.

Debug.   Process of removing errors in programs.

Debugging line.   A debugging line is any line with ''D'' in the indicator area of the line (column 7).

Delimiter.   A character or a sequence of contiguous characters that identifies the end of a string of characters and separates that string of characters from the following string of characters. A delimiter is not part of the string of characters that it delimits.

Descending key.   A key upon the values of which data is ordered starting with the highest value of key down to the lowest value of key, in accordance with the rules for comparing data items.

Descending sequence. Each item has a value which is less than or equal to its predecessor.

Decision structure. Programming technique which results in the execution of one module out of several alternatives.

Disk drive. Device used for storing data on circular disks.

DISPLAY. Reserved word used in the USAGE clause to define a data item which is in character form; verb used to initiate output particularly to the operator's console.

Division. A set of zero, one or more sections of paragraphs, called the *division body*, that are formed and combined in accordance with a specific set of rules. There are four (4) divisions in a COBOL program: IDENTIFICATION, ENVIRONMENT, DATA, and PROCEDURE.

Division header. A combination of words followed by a period and a space that indicates that beginning of a division. The division headers are:

```
IDENTIFICATION DIVISION.
ENVIRONMENT DIVISION.
DATA DIVISION.
PROCEDURE DIVISION.
```

Dynamic access. An access mode in which specific logical records can be obtained from or placed into a mass storage file in a nonsequential manner (see random access) and obtained from a file in a sequential manner (see sequential access), during the scope of the same OPEN statement.

Editing. The insertion of spaces, commas, decimal points, and so forth into output fields to enhance readability.

Editing character. A single character or a fixed two-character combiniation belong to the following set:

Character	Meaning
B	space
0	zero
+	plus
−	minus
CR	credit
DB	debit
Z	zero suppress
*	check protect
$	currency sign
,	comma (decimal point)
.	period (decimal point)
/	stroke (virgule, slash)

Elementary item. A data item described as not being further logically subdivided.

End-of-file. Condition resulting when there are no more records contained in a file (see At End condition).

Entry. Any descriptive set of consecutive clauses terminated by a period and written in the IDENTIFICATION DIVISION, ENVIRONMENT DIVISION, or DATA DIVISION of a COBOL source program.

ENVIRONMENT DIVISION. Subdivision of a COBOL program used to describe the computing "environment"—the computing system in use, files to be processed, and so on.

Extend mode. The state of a file after execution of an OPEN statement with the EXTEND phrase specified for that file and before the execution of a CLOSE statement for that file.

FD *(File Description).* Entry in the FILE SECTION of the DATA DIVI-SION used to describe each file a program will process.

Field. A group of related characters.

Figurative constants. Constants such as ZERO and SPACE which have been assigned a COBOL reserved word.

File clause. A clause that appears as part of any of the following DATA DIVISION entries:

File description (FD)
Sort-merge file description (SD)

FILE-CONTROL. The name of the ENVIRONMENT DIVISION paragraph in which the data files for a given source program are declared.

File description entry. An entry in the file section of the DATA DIVISION that is composed of the level indicator FD, followed by a file name, and then followed by a set of file clauses as required.

File name. A user defined word that names a file described in a file description entry or a sort-merge file description entry within the file section of the DATA DIVISION.

File Organization. The permanent logical file structure established at the tie that a file is created.

File Section. The section of the DATA DIVISION that contains file description entries and sort-merge file description entries together with their associated record descriptions.

FILLER. Reserved word used as a data-name in the DATA DIVISION for fields which need ot have a unique data-name.

Floating point. Type of data representation resembling scientific notation; a value is represented by storing a series of significant digits and an appropriate power of a base.

Flowchart. Schematic representation of the sequence of execution of statements in a program.

Format. A specific arrangement of a set of data.

GO TO. Verb which causes an unconditional branch.

Group item. A named contiguous set of elementary or group items.

Hardware. Physical equipment making up a computing system.

Hexadecimal. Base 16; the hexadecimal digits are 0, 1, 2, 3, 4, 5, 6, 7, 8, 9, A($=10$), B($=11$), C($=12$), D($=13$), E($=14$), F($=15$).

High order end. The leftmost character of a string of characters.

Hollerith Code. Code used to record data on punched cards.

Identifier. A data-name, followed as required by the syntactically correct combination of qualifiers, subscripts and indices necessary to make unique reference to a data item.

IDENTIFICATION DIVISION. Segment of a COBOL program used to define the name of the program and provide information about the program and programmer.

Indicator area. Position 7 in COBOL source statement.

IF. Verb used to test a condition.

Imperative statement. A statement that begins with an imperative verb and specifies an unconditional action to be taken. An imperative statement may consist of a sequence of imperative statements.

Implementor-name. A system-name that refers to a particular feature available on that implementor's computing system.

Index. A computer storage position or register, the contents of which represent the identification of a particular element in a table.

Index-name. A user defined word that names an index associated with a specific table.

Indexed data-name. An identifier that is composed of a data-name, followed by one or more index-names enclosed in parentheses.

Indexed file. A file with indexed organization. The permanent logical file structure in which each record is identified by the value of a key within that record. This type of file organization makes possible both sequential and random processing of records.

Input file. A file that is opened in the input mode.

Input mode. The state of a file after execution of an OPEN statement, with the INPUT phrase specified for that file and before the execution of a CLOSE statement for that file.

Input-Output file. A file that is opened in the I-O mode.

INPUT-OUTPUT SECTION. The section of the ENVIRONMENT DIVISION that names the files and the external media required by an object program and which provides information required for transmission and handling of data during exectuion of the object program.

Input procedure. A set of statements that is executed each time a record is released to the sort file.

Input unit. Portion of a computer which reads data from an external source into the computing system.

Integer. A numeric literal or a numeric data item that does not include any character positions to the right of the assumed decimal point. Where the term "integer" appears in general formats, integer must not be a numeric data item, and must be neither signed nor zero unless explicitly allowed by the rules of that format.

INSPECT. Verb used to perform manipulation of individual characters in a field.

INSTALLATION. Paragraph in the IDENTIFICATION DIVISION used to show where the program was developed or will be used.

Invalid key condition. A condition caused when a specific value of the key associated with an indexed file is determined to be invalid.

I-O-CONTROL. The name of an ENVIRONMENT DIVISION paragraph in which object program requirements for specific input-output techniques, rerun points, sharing of same areas by several data files, and multiple file storage on a single input-output device are specified.

I-O MODE. The state of a file after execution of an OPEN statement, with the I-O phrase specified, for that file and before the execution of a CLOSE statement for that file.

IRG *(Inter-Record-Gap).* Unused space separating physical records on tape or disk.

Iteration structure. Programming technique which results in the execution of one or more modules repetitively.

Key. A data item which identifies the location of a record, or a set of data items which serve to identify the ordering of data.

Key word. A reserved word whose presence is required when the format in which the word appears is used in a source program.

Label records. Records used by the operating system to identify the data contained on a file.

Level-number. A two-digit number used in the DATA DIVISION to define relationships among data definitions (levels 01 through 49) and to specify special properties of data items (levels 66, 77 and 88).

Library-name. A user defined word that names a COBOL library to be used by the compiler for a given source program compilation.

Library text. A sequence of character-strings and/or separators in a COBOL library.

Literal. A character-string whose value is implied by the ordered set of characters comprising the string.

Logical operator. One of the reserved words AND, OR or NOT. In the formation of a condition, either AND and OR or both can be used as logical connectives. NOT can be used for logical negation.

Low order end. The rightmost character of a string of characters.

Loop structure. See iteration structure.

Margin A, B. Margin A is position 8 of a COBOL source code line; Margin B is position 12.

Mass storage file. A collection of records assigned to a mass storage medium (usually a disk).

Mean. Arithmetic average.

Memory unit. Portion of a computer which stores programs and data.

Merge. The process of combining two files into one.

Mnemonic. An aid to memory.

Mnemonic-Name. A user defined word that is associated in the ENVIRONMENT DIVISION with a specified system-name.

Module. Portion of a program with a single entry point and a single exit. In a COBOL program a module may be a paragraph, group of paragraphs, or a section (see procedure).

MOVE. Verb used to cause the content of a data item to be copied into one or more other data items.

Named condition. A condition which has been assigned a name in an 88 level entry in the DATA DIVISION.

Negated combined condition. The NOT logical operator immediately followed by a parenthesized combined condition.

Negated simple condition. The NOT logical operator immediately followed by a simple condition.

Next executable sentence. The next sentence to which control will be transferred after execution of the current statement is complete.

Next executable statement. The next statement to which control will be transferred after execution of the current statement is complete.

Next record. The record which logically follows the current record of a file.

Nonnumeric item. A data item whose description permits its contents to be composed of any combination of characters taken from the computer's character set. Certain categories of nonnumeric items may be formed from more restricted character sets.

Nonnumeric literal. A character-string bounded by quotation marks. The string of characters may include any character in the computer's character set. To represent a single quotation mark character within a nonnumeric literal, two contiguous quotation marks must be used.

Numeric character. A character that belongs to the following set of digits: 0, 1, 2, 3, 4, 5, 6, 7, 8, 9.

Numeric item. A data item whose description restricts its contents to a value represented by characters chosen from the digits "0" through "9"; if signed, the item may also contain a "+", "−", or other representation of an operational sign.

Numeric literal. A literal composed of one or more numeric characters that also may contain either a decimal point or an algebraic sign, or both. The decimal point must not be the rightmost character. The algebraic sign, if present, must be the leftmost character.

OBJECT-COMPUTER. The name of an ENVIRONMENT DIVISION paragraph in which the computer environment within which the object program is executed is described.

Object program. A program which has been translated into machine language.

OCCURS. Reserved word used in a data description entry to define a table.

ON SIZE ERROR. Clause used with arithmetic verbs to detect overflow and division by zero.

OPEN. Verb used to initiate processing of a file.

Open mode. The state of a file after execution of an OPEN statement for that file and before the execution of a CLOSE statement for that file. The particular open mode is specified in the OPEN statement as either INPUT, OUTPUT, I-O or EXTEND.

Operating system. Software which controls the activities performed by a computing system.

Operational sign. An algebraic sign, associated with a numeric data item or a numeric literal, to indicate whether its value is positive or negative.

Optional word. A reserved word that is included in a specific format only to improve the readability of the language and whose presence is optional to the user when the format in which the word appears is used in a source program.

Output file. A file that is opened in either the output mode or extend mode.

Output mode. The state of a file after execution of an OPEN statement, with the OUTPUT or EXTEND phrase specified, for that file and before the execution of a CLOSE statement for that file.

Output procedure. A set of statements to which control is given during execution of a SORT statement after the sort function is completed.

Output unit. Portion of a computer which writes information onto some external medium.

Packed decimal. Type of data representation in which two decimal digits are represented in each byte.

Paragraph. Subdivision of COBOL program consisting of a paragraph name and one or more sentences.

Paragraph header. A reserved word followed by a period and a space that indicates the beginning of a paragraph in IDENTIFICATION and ENVIRONMENT DIVISIONS. The permissible paragraph headers are:

In the IDENTIFICATION DIVISION:

```
PROGRAM-ID.
AUTHOR.
INSTALLATION.
DATE-WRITTEN.
DATE-COMPILED.
SECURITY.
```

In the ENVIRONMENT DIVISION:

    SOURCE-COMPUTER.

    OBJECT-COMPUTER.

    SPECIAL-NAMES.

    FILE-CONTROL.

    I-O-CONTROL.

Paragraph-name. A user defined word that identifies and begins a paragraph in the PROCEDURE DIVISION.

Phrase. An ordered set of one or more consectuive COBOL character-strings that form a portion of a COBOL procedural statement or of a COBOL clause.

PERFORM. Verb used to initiate execution of a paragraph.

PICTURE. Reserved word used to describe the length, type and other characteristics of a data item.

Procedure. A paragraph or group of logically successive paragraphs, or a section or group of logically successive sections, within the PROCEDURE DIVISION (see module).

PROCEDURE DIVISION. Segment of a COBOL program used to describe the steps required to process data in order to produce desired results.

Procedure-Name. A user defined word which is used to name a paragraph or section in the PROCEDURE DIVISION. It consists of a paragraph-name (which may be qualified), or a section-name.

Program. A sequence of instructions designed to enable a computer to perform some task.

PROGRAM-ID. Paragraph in the IDENTIFICATION DIVISION used to establish a name for the program.

Program-name. A user defined word that identifies a COBOL source program.

Punctuation character. A character that belongs to the following set:

Character	Meaning
,	comma
;	semicolon
"	quotation mark
.	period (decimal point)
(	left parenthesis
)	right parenthesis
	space
=	equal sign

Qualification. Technique used to derive unique names for data items.

Qualified data-name. An identifier that is composed of a data-name followed by one or more sets of either of the connective OR and IN followed by a data-name qualifier.

Qualifier. A data-name which is used in a reference with another data-name at a lower level in the same hierarchy.

Random access. An access mode in which the program specified value of a key data item identifies the logical record that is obtained from, deleted from, or placed into an indexed file.

READ. Verb used to initiate an input operation.

Record. A group of related fields.

Record area. A storage area allocated for the purpose of processing the record described in a record description entry in the file section.

Record description entry. The total set of data description entries associated with a particular record.

Record Key. A key, either the prime record key or an alternate record key, whose contents identify a record within an indexed file.

Record-name. A user defined word that names a record described in a record description entry in the DATA DIVISION.

REDEFINES. Reserved word used in a data description entry to give an alternate description of a data item.

Relation character. A character that belongs to the following set:

Character	Meaning
>	greater than
<	less than
=	equal to

Relation condition. A condition involving a comparison (less than, equal to, greater than, and so forth) of two expressions.

Relational operator. A reserved word, a relation character, a group of consecutive reserved words, or a group of consecutive reserved words and relations characters used in the construction of a relation condition. The permissible operators and their meaning are:

$\begin{Bmatrix} \text{IS [NOT] GREATER THAN} \\ \text{IS [NOT]} > \end{Bmatrix}$ Greater than or not greater than

$\begin{Bmatrix} \text{IS [NOT] LESS THAN} \\ \text{IS [NOT]} < \end{Bmatrix}$ Less than or not less than

$\begin{Bmatrix} \text{IS [NOT] EQUAL TO} \\ \text{IS [NOT]} = \end{Bmatrix}$ Equal to or not equal to

RELEASE. Verb used to output a record onto a sort work-file.

Reserved word. A COBOL word specified in the list of words which may be used in COBOL source programs, but which must not appear in the programs as user defined words or system-names.

RETURN. Verb used to input a record from a sort work-file.

REWRITE. Verb used to write a record onto a file after the record has been read.

SEARCH. Verb used to locate elements having a desired value in a table.

Section. Subdivision of a COBOL program consisting of a section header and one or more paragraphs.

Section Header. A combination of words followed by a period and a space that indicates the beginning of a section in the ENVIRONMENT, DATA and PROCEDURE DIVISION. In the ENVIRONMENT and DATA DIVISIONs, a section header is composed of reserved words followed by a period and a space. The permissible section headers are:

In the ENVIRONMENT DIVISION:

    CONFIGURATION SECTION.
    INPUT-OUTPUT SECTION.

In the DATA DIVISION:

    FILE SECTION.
    WORKING-STORAGE SECTION.
    LINKAGE SECTION.
    COMMUNICATION SECTION.
    REPORT SECTION.

In the PROCEDURE DIVISION, a section header is composed of a section-name, followed by the reserved word SECTION, followed by a segment-number (optional), followed by a period and a space.

Section-name. A user defined word which names a section in the PROCEDURE DIVISION.

SECURITY. Paragraph in the IDENTIFICATION DIVISION which may be used to describe the security clearance required for access to the program.

SELECT. Reserved word used in the sentences of the FILE-CONTROL paragraph of the INPUT-OUTPUT SECTION of the ENVIRONMENT DIVISION to describe each file processed by a program.

Sentence. A sequence of one or more statements, the last of which is terminated by a period followed by a space.

Separator. A punctuation character used to delimit character-strings.

Sequence structure. A programming technique involving the execution of a series of modules one after the other.

Sequential organization. The permanent logical file structure in which a record is identified by a predecessor-successor relationship established when the record is placed into the file.

SET. Verb used to initialize and increment an index variable.

Sign condition. A condition involving the sign (positive or negative) of a data item.

Simple condition. Any single condition chosen from the set:

relation condition
class condition
named condition
sign condition

Software. Programs; often contrasted with hardware.

Sort. To rearrange items into ascending or descending sequence.

Sort work-file. A collection of records to be sorted by a SORT statement. The sort work-file is created and can be used by the sort function only.

Sort work-file description entry. An entry in the file section of the DATA DIVISION that is composed of the level indicator SD, followed by a file-name, and then followed by a set of file clauses as required.

SOURCE-COMPUTER. Paragraph in the CONFIGURATION SECTION of the ENVIRONMENT DIVISION used to specify the computer used to compile the program.

Source program. A program written in a high level language such as COBOL.

Special character. A character that belongs to the following set:

Character	Meaning
+	plus sign
−	minus sign
*	asterisk
/	stroke (virgule, slash)
=	equal sign
$	currency sign
,	comma (decimal point)
;	semicolon
.	period (decimal point)
"	quotation mark
(	left parenthesis
)	right parenthesis
>	greater than symbol
<	less thean symbol

SPECIAL-NAMES. The name of an ENVIRONMENT DIVISION paragraph in which system-names are related to user specified mnemonic-names.

Statement.   A syntactically valid combination of words and symbols written in the PROCEDURE DIVISION beginning with a verb.

Structure diagram.   Schematic representation of the relationships among modules of a program.

Structured programming.   A programming technique which makes use only of the SEQUENCE, IF/THEN/ELSE, and ITERATION structures.

Subscript.   An integer whose value identifies a particular element in a table.

Subscripted data-name.   An identifier composed of a data-name followed by one or more subscripts enclosed in parentheses.

Syntax.   The arrangement of elements required in the construction of a COBOL program.

System-name.   A COBOL word which is used to communicate with the operating environment.

Table.   A set of logically consecutive items of data that are defined in the DATA DIVISION by means of the OCCURS clause.

Table element.   A data item that belongs to the set of repeated items comprising a table.

Tape drive.   Device used for storing data on a continuous strip of magnetic tape.

Track.   One circle used for recording data on a surface of a disk pack; a surface is composed of concentric tracks.

Truth value.   The representation of the result of the evaluation of a condition in terms of one of two values: true or false.

Unary Operator.   A plus (+) or a minus (−) sign, which precedes a variable or a left parenthesis in an arithmetic expression and which has the effect of multiplying the expression of +1 or −1 respectively.

Update.   The process of changing a record (or file) to reflect data being processed.

USAGE.   Reserved word used to define the type of data representation used for a data item.

Utility program.   Program used to perform various routine data processing tasks.

User defined word.   A COBOL word that must be supplied by the user to satisfy the format of a clause or statement.

Variable.   A data item whose value may be changed by execution of the object program. A variable used in an arithmetic expression must be a numeric elementary item.

Verb.   A word that expresses an action to be taken by a COBOL compiler or object program.

Word.   A character-string of not more than thirty characters which forms a user-defined work, a system-name or a reserved word.

WORKING-STORAGE SECTION.   The section of the DATA DIVISION that describes working storage data items, composed either of noncontiguous items or of working storage records or of both.

WRITE.   Verb used to initiate an output operation.

Zoned decimal.   Type of data representation in which each byte contains one decimal digit.

ANSWERS TO SELF TEST EXERCISES

CHAPTER 1

1. 1.u 2.m 3.s 4.q 5.v 6.f 7.h 8.l 9.n 10.e 11.x 12.p 13.i 14.w 15.t 16.k 17.g 18.y 19.b
   20.o 21.a 22.j 23.c 24.r 25.d 26.z
2. 1.e 2.d 3.f 4.c 5.a 6.b

CHAPTER 2

1. 1.j 2.n 3.e 4.s 5.m 6.r 7.y 8.i 9.f 10.g 11.t 12.a 13.x 14.z 15.d 16.p 17.h 18.l 19.w
   20.b 21.q 22.v 23.o 24.v 25.k 26.c
2. IDENTIFICATION DIVISION.
   PROGRAM-ID. SECOND.
   AUTHOR. PAULA.
   INSTALLATION. YOUR COLLEGE.
   DATE-WRITTEN. 1/1/82.
   DATE-COMPILED.
   SECURITY. NONE.

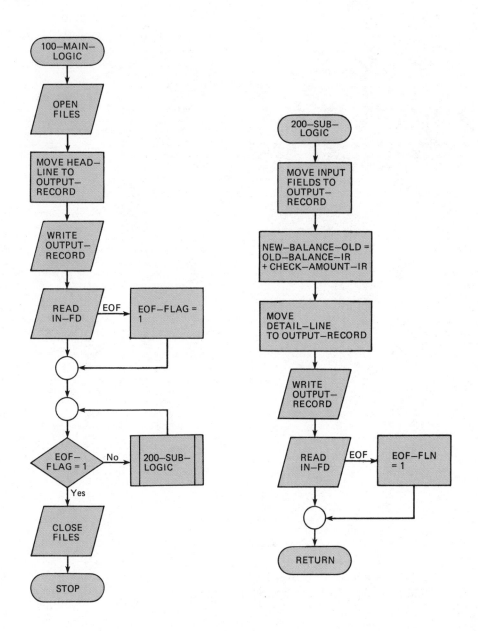

4. Division headers, section headers, paragraph names, FD entries, 01-49 entries.

5. a. valid b. invalid, no alphabetic character c. invalid, embedded space d. invalid, ends with a "-" e. invalid, too long f. invalid, embedded space

6. 1.d 2.a,i 3.i 4.k 5.b,i 6.e 7.c 8.i 9.e 10.f 11.h 12.g,i 13.j 14.j 15.i 16.i 17.c, i

7. 01 NAME-ADDR-REC.
    02 CUSTOMER-NAME-NAR   PIC X(20).
    02 STREET-ADDRESS-NAR   PIC X(20).
    02 CITY-NAR   PIC X(10).
    02 STATE-NAR   PIC XX.
    02 ZIP-NAR   PIC 9(5).
    02 FILLER   PIC X(28).

8.

Type of Item	Where Defined in DATA DIVISION				
	FILE SECTION		WORKING-STORAGE SECTION		
	Used for Input	Used for Output	Used for Input	Used for Control	Used for Output
File	IN-FD	PRINT			
Record	INPUT-RECORD	OUTPUT-RECORD			HEAD-LINE DETAIL-LINE
Field	OLD-BALANCE-IR CHECK-AMOUNT-IR			EOF-FLAG	OLD-BALANCE-DL CHECK-AMOUNT-DL NEW-BALANCE-DL

CHAPTER 3

1.

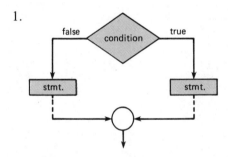

2. Numbers in paragraph names are used to help the reader locate paragraphs. They are required by style but not by the syntax of COBOL.

3. A switch is a variable that can contain one of the two values—1 or 0, ''on'' or ''off.'' Switches are used as communication links among paragraphs of a program.

4. An accumulator is a variable which is used to store a running total. Typically, a sequence of values are added to the accumulator one at a time. Accumulators are used to compute totals.

5.
```
PROCEDURE DIVISION.
100-MAIN-PROCESS.
    PERFORM 200-INITIAL.
    PERFORM 300-SUB-LOGIC UNTIL EOF-FLAG = 1.
    PERFORM 400-TERMINATE.
200-INITIAL.
    OPEN INPUT IN-FD OUTPUT PRINT.
    PERFORM 500-WRITE-HEADINGS.
    PERFORM 600-READ-IN-FD.
300-SUB-LOGIC.
    PERFORM 700-COMPUTE-NEW-BALANCE.
    PERFORM 800-WRITE-DETAIL-LINE.
    PERFORM 600-READ-IN-FD.
400-TERMINATE.
    CLOSE IN-FD, PRINT.
    STOP RUN.
```

```
500-WRITE-HEADINGS.
    MOVE HEAD-LINE TO OUTPUT-RECORD.
    WRITE OUTPUT-RECORD AFTER ADVANCING PAGE.
600-READ-IN-FD.
    READ IN-FD AT END MOVE 1 TO EOF-FLAG.
700-COMPUTE-NEW-BALANCE.
    ADD OLD-BALANCE-IR, CHECK-AMOUNT-IR
        GIVING NEW-BALANCE-DL.
800-WRITE-DETAIL-LINE.
    MOVE DETAIL-LINE TO OUTPUT-RECORD.
    WRITE OUTPUT-RECORD AFTER ADVANCING 1 LINES.
```

Note to Reader: There are many acceptable solutions to this problem. Use the above code only as an example.

Structure Diagram:

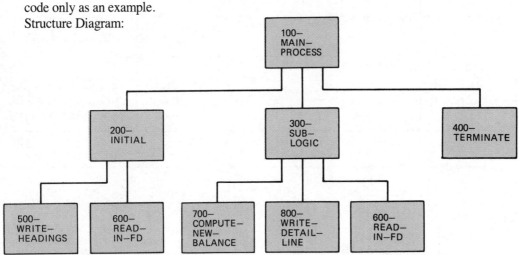

Control Paragraphs:

```
100-MAIN-PROCESS
200-INITIAL
300-SUB-LOGIC
```

Operational Paragraphs:

```
500-WRITE-HEADINGS
600-READ-IN-FD
700-COMPUTE-NEW-BALANCE
800-WRITE-DETAIL-LINE.
```

6. The program will not enter a loop properly because of the omission of PERFORM/UNTIL at line 4. The program will process only one record because of omission of PERFORM 400-READ-INPUT-FILE as the last statement of 300-BUILD-FILE.

CHAPTER 4

1. a. FD   SALES-RECORDS
           DATA RECORD IS SALESMAN.

   b. OPEN INPUT SALES-RECORDS.

   c. READ SALES-RECORDS   AT END MOVE 1 TO EOF-FLAG.

   d. CLOSE SALES-RECORDS.

2. a. ```
   FD   PAYROLL
        DATA RECORD IS NET-PAY.
   ```

   b. OPEN OUTPUT PAYROLL.

   c. WRITE NET-PAY AFTER ADVANCING 2 LINES.

   d. CLOSE PAYROLL.

3. a. | 0 | 0 | 1 | 2 | 3 |

   | 1 | 2 | 3 |

   | 0 | 0 | 0 | 0 | 0 | 1 | 2 | 3 |

   | 1 | 2 | 3 | 4 | 5 | 0 | 0 |

   | 0 | 1 | 2 | 3 | 4 | 5 | 0 |

   b. | | | 1 | 2 | 3 |

   c. | | | $ | 1 | 2 | 3 | . | 4 | 5 |

   | * | 1 | 2 | 3 | . | 4 |

   | 4 | 3 | 2 | 1 |

   | 4 | 3 |

   d. | | | | - | 1 | 2 | . | 3 | 4 |

   | | | | + | 1 | 2 | . | 3 | 4 |

   | | | | | 1 | 2 | . | 3 | 4 | C | R |

   | $ | | | | | 1 | 2 | . | 3 | 4 | | D | B |

   e. | 0 | 0 | 0 | 1 |

   | + | | | | 1 | . | 2 | 3 |

   f. | | | | | 1 | . | 2 | 3 | | |

   | | | | | 1 | . | 2 | 3 | | | |

   g. | $ | 3 | 4 | 5 | 6 | . | 7 | 8 |

   h. | 1 | 2 | 3 | 4 | 5 | 6 | . | 7 | 8 | 0 | 0 |

   | 2 | 3 | . | 4 | 5 | 6 | . | 7 |

   | 0 | 1 | 2 | 3 | 4 |

   | 0 | 1 | 2 | 3 |

4.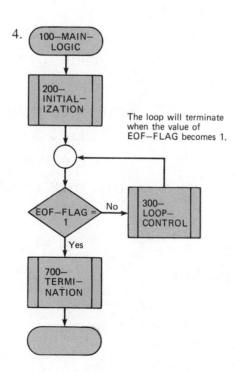

The loop will terminate when the value of EOF–FLAG becomes 1.
   ```

5.   Major heading   6. ⎣3⎦/⎣1⎦⎣1⎦/⎣8⎦⎣2⎦
        column heading
        detail
        total

CHAPTER 5

1. a. ADD A TO B.
     or
     ADD A, B GIVING A.
     or
     COMPUTE A = B + A.

  b. SUBTRACT EXPENSE FROM INCOME GIVING BALANCE.
     or
     COMPUTE BALANCE = INCOME - EXPENSE.

  c. MULTIPLY D BY A.
     or
     MULTIPLY A BY D GIVING A.
     or
     COMPUTE A = A * D.

  d. DIVIDE SALES BY 12 GIVING MONTHLY-AVERAGE.
     or
     DIVIDE 12 INTO SALES GIVING MONTHLY-AVERAGE.
     or
     COMPUTE MONTHLY-AVERAGE = SALES / 12.

  e. COMPUTE VOLUME = 4 / 3 * 3.1459 * R ** 2.
  f. COMPUTE I = P * R * T
  g. MULTIPLY B BY 0.25 GIVING A
     or
     COMPUTE A = B * 0.25

  h. COMPUTE A = P * (1 + R) ** N

2. a. ⎣0⎢7⎦   f.   ⎣0⎢0⎦

    C PIC 99   A PIC V99

                         NOTE: SIZE ERROR because of overflow

  b. ⎣0⎢1⎦   g.   ⎣0⎢0⎢0⎦

    B PIC 99   A PIC 99V9

  c. ⎣1⎢3⎢4̄⎦   NOTE: SIZE ERROR because of division by 0.

    B PIC S999   h.   ⎣3⎢3⎦

  d. ⎣5⎢0⎢0̄⎦   ⎣0⎢0⎦   C PIC 99

    A PIC S99V9   D PIC S99   NOTE: loss of sign on result

                        i. ⎣0⎢2⎢0̄⎦

  e. ⎣0⎢2⎢7̄⎦   B PIC S99V9

    A PIC S999

3.

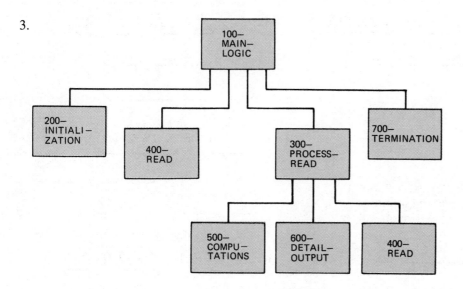

Control paragraphs:	100-MAIN-LOGIC
	300-PROCESS-READ
Operational paragraphs:	200-INITIALIZATION
	400-READ
	500-COMPUTATIONS
	600-DETAIL-OUTPUT
	700-TERMINATION

4. a. The use of group data-items such as 01 COMPUTED-AMOUNTS increases the readability of the program.

   b. The use of the VALUE clause for a numeric data item such as WITH-AMT makes the program easier to debug and maintain.

   c. The placement of a ''−'' in position 7 of a line of code indicates continuation of a COBOL element such as a nonnumeric literal.

   d. The placement of constants such as FICA-FACTOR in WORKING-STORAGE makes the program easier to maintain.

   e. The ROUNDED option will ensure that the employee's pay is rounded to the nearest penny.

5. COMPUTE JULIAN-DATE = (M - 1) * 30 + D

   Note: This formula is only approximate since not all months have 30 days. In some applications the year is also important. The Julian date for the century or decade can be computed by

   $$\text{COMPUTE JULIAN-DATE} = Y * 365 + (M - 1) * 30 + D$$

   where Y represents the year in four-digit or two-digit form.

CHAPTER 6

1. a. X < Y OR Y IS NEGATIVE   b. Z IS ALPHABETIC

c.　X IS NUMERIC AND Z IS NOT ALPHABETIC
　　　　　　　F　　　　　　　　　　　　F
　　　　　　　　　　　　F

d.　NOT Y IS POSITIVE
　　　　　　　T
　　　　　　F

e.　NOT X IS ZERO OR Y IS NOT NEGATIVE
　　　　　F　　　　　　　　T
　　　　　T
　　　　　　　　T

f.　NOT (X > 25 OR Y < 39)
　　　　　　F　　　　T
　　　　　　　T
　　　　　F

g.　X < Y OR X IS ZERO AND Y > 1
　　　F　　　　F　　　　　T
　　　　　　　　F
　　　　F

h.　X < Y AND (Y < 0 OR X > 30)
　　　T　　　　F　　　　F
　　　　　　　　F
　　　　F

2.　IF BALANCE NOT > 20
　　　　MOVE BALANCE TO MINIMUM-PAYMENT
　　ELSE
　　　　IF BALANCE NOT > 100
　　　　　　COMPUTE MINIMUM-PAYMENT =
　　　　　　　　20 + (BALANCE - 20) * 0.1
　　　　ELSE
　　　　　　COMPUTE MINIMUM-PAYMENT =
　　　　　　　　36 + (BALANCE - 100) * 0.2.

3.　a.　IF X > Y
　　　　　　PERFORM OUTPUT
　　　　　　READ FILE-A AT END MOVE 1 TO EOF-A.

　　b.　IF X > Y
　　　　　　PERFORM READ-FILE-A
　　　　　　PERFORM OUTPUT.
　　　　　.
　　　　　.
　　　　　.
　　　READ-FILE-A.
　　　　　READ FILE-A AT END MOVE 1 TO EOF-A.

　　c.　IF ERR-CODE = "NO"
　　　　　　PERFORM COMPUTATIONS.
　　　　　.
　　　　　.
　　　　　.
　　　COMPUTATIONS.
　　　　　ADD A TO B ON SIZE ERROR MOVE 0 TO B.
　　　　　ADD C TO D ON SIZE ERROR MOVE 0 TO D.

```
4. DATA-VALIDATION.
      MOVE "NO" TO VALIDITY-ERROR.
      IF ACCOUNT-NUM-DR NOT NUMERIC
         OR
         ZIP-DR NOT NUMERIC
         OR
         BALANCE-FORWARD-DR NOT NUMERIC
            MOVE "YES" TO VALIDITY-ERROR.
      IF CUSTOMER-NAME-DR = SPACES
         OR
         CUSTOMER-NAME-DR NOT ALPHABETIC
            MOVE "YES" TO VALIDITY-ERROR.
      IF CITY-DR = SPACES
         OR
         CITY-DR NOT ALPHABETIC
            MOVE "YES" TO VALIDITY-ERROR.
      IF STATE-DR = SPACES
         OR
         STATE-DR NOT ALPHABETIC
            MOVE "YES" TO VALIDITY-ERROR.
```

It is not possible to check the field STREET-ADDRESS-DR since it may legitimately contain both alphabetic and numeric characters as well as other characters such as ".", "#", and so on.

5. The PERFORM/UNTIL does not have a clause consisting of one or more statements, so it is not a conditional statement.

6. Modify paragraph 300:

```
300-DECISION.
      IF AGE-PDR > 40 AND AGE-PDR < 65
         PERFORM 400-EMPLOYEE-REPORT.
      READ PERSONNEL-DATA-FILE
         AT END MOVE 1 TO EOF-FLAG.
```

7. Changes/additions to DATA DIVISION:
   1) change content of HEAD-LINE to reflect new content of report
   2) add counters and accumulators:

```
01   COUNTERS.
      03   NUMBER-MALES   PIC 9999 VALUE 0.
      03   NUMBER-FEMALES   PIC 9999 VALUE 0.
01   ACCUMULATORS.
      03   TOTAL-AGE-MALES   PIC 9(9) VALUE 0.
      03   TOTAL-AGE-FEMALES   PIC 9(9) VALUE 0.
```

   3) add final output record:

```
01   SUMMARY-LINE.
      03   NUMBER-MALES-OUT     PIC Z(5).
      03   NUMBER-FEMALES-OUT   PIC Z(5).
      03   AV-AGE-FEM-OUT       PIC Z(4).
      03   AV-AGE-MALE-OUT      PIC Z(4).
```

```
PROCEDURE DIVISION.
100-MAIN-ROUTINE.
      PERFORM 200-INITIALIZATION.
      PERFORM 300-DECISION UNTIL EOF-FLAG = 1.
      PERFORM 700-TERMINATION.
```

(continued)

```
200-INITIALIZATION.
   no change.
300-DECISION.
   IF SEX-PDR = "F"
       PERFORM 400-EMPLOYEE-REPORT
       ADD 1 TO NUMBER-FEMALES
       ADD AGE-PDR TO TOTAL-AGE-FEMALES
   ELSE
       ADD 1 TO NUMBER-MALES
       ADD AGE-PDR TO TOTAL-AGE-MALES.
   READ PERSONNEL-DATA-FILE AT END MOVE 1 TO EOF-FLAG.
400-EMPLOYEE-REPORT.
   no change.
700-TERMINATION.
   COMPUTE AV-AGE-FEM-OUT = TOTAL-AGE-FEMALES / NUMBER-FEMALES
       ON SIZE ERROR MOVE 0 TO AV-AGE-FEM-OUT.
   COMPUTE AV-AGE-MALE-OUT = TOTAL-AGE-MALES / NUMBER-MALES
       ON SIZE ERROR MOVE 0 TO AV-AGE-MALE-OUT.
   MOVE NUMBER-MALES TO NUMBER-MALES-OUT.
   MOVE NUMBER-FEMALES TO NUMBER-FEMALES-OUT.
   WRITE OUTPUT-RECORD FROM SUMMARY-LINE AFTER 2.
   CLOSE PERSONNEL-DATA-FILE.
   CLOSE PRE-1960-EMPLOYEE-REPORT.
   STOP RUN.
```

Note: the file name associated with the printed output file should also be changed.

8. Yes, it is a good idea to define constants such as this in a working storage variable. In this way it will be easier to modify the program to generate reports for any desired year.

9.

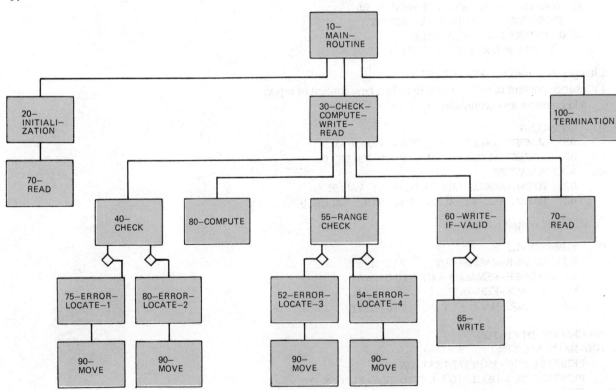

10. The first value printed for usage represents the usage for the previous record since at the time the output was produced, the usage computation for the current record had not been made. The problem can be corrected by writing the value of usage only when there is an error in this amount.

CHAPTER 7

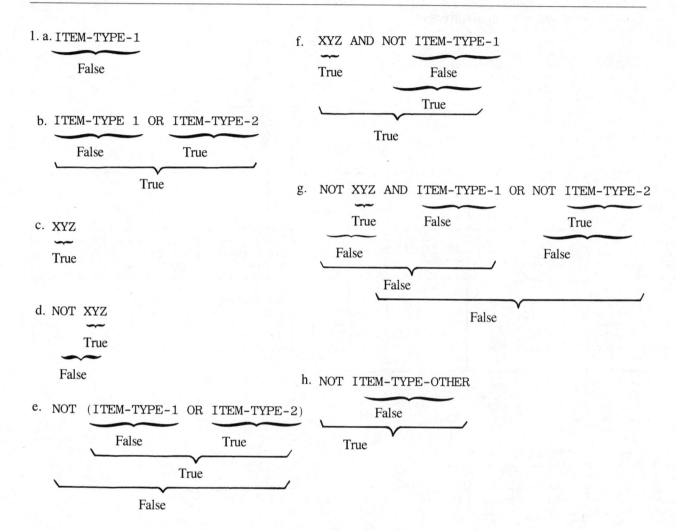

1. a. ITEM-TYPE-1
   False

b. ITEM-TYPE 1 OR ITEM-TYPE-2
   False   True
        True

c. XYZ
   True

d. NOT XYZ
      True
   False

e. NOT (ITEM-TYPE-1 OR ITEM-TYPE-2)
      False   True
           True
      False

f. XYZ AND NOT ITEM-TYPE-1
   True   False
           True
        True

g. NOT XYZ AND ITEM-TYPE-1 OR NOT ITEM-TYPE-2
   True   False   True
   False   False
           False
               False

h. NOT ITEM-TYPE-OTHER
      False
   True

2. In general the method used in Program 7.3 is preferable. The basic disadvantage to the use of a switch is that the initialization test is performed at the same place for all records including the first. Placing the initialization instructions in the initialization paragraph makes the logic simpler and avoids unnecessary tests of a condition which will be true only once during execution of the program.

3. If the last line of the report falls at the last line of a page, page headings will be placed on an otherwise unneeded page. If there were no records in the file, a page containing only page headings and final totals would be produced.

4. If there are no records in the file a page containing only page headings and final totals would be produced. If the last line of the report falls on the last line of a page, the report would terminate. Because of the potential for producing a superfluous page of

output with the method of Programs 7.1 and 7.2, and because no special initialization steps to produce page headings on the first page are needed, the method of Program 7.3 is recommended.

5. The number of lines per page should always be defined as a data item in WORKING-STORAGE to facilitate later revision of the program.

6. The value of HOLD-DEPARTMENT should be written. The value of IR-DEPARTMENT is the new department number; the total being produced is for the old department number contained in HOLD-DEPARTMENT.

CHAPTER 8

1.

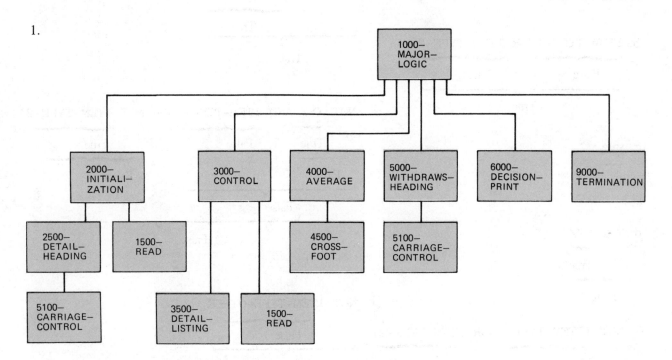

2. a.
```
    PERFORM SEARCH-TABLE
        VARYING INDX FROM 1 BY 1 UNTIL
            PART-NUMBER (INDX) ="9999" OR
            PART-NUMBER (INDX) =KNOWN-PART-NUMBER.
    IF PART-NUMBER (INDX) NOT ="9999"
        MOVE NEW-DESCRIPTION TO PART-DESCRIPTION (INDX).
    .
    .
    .
    SEARCH-TABLE.
        EXIT.
```

b. After a search procedure such as included in part "a" above include:
```
    IF  PART-NUMBER (INDX) NOT = "9999"
        MOVE  DESCRIPTION (INDX) TO DESCRIPTION-OUT
        MOVE  NUMBER-ORDERED TO NUMBER-ORDERED-OUT
        MOVE  KNOWN-PART-NUMBER TO PART-NUMBER-OUT
        MULTIPLY  NUMBER-SOLD BY PART-PRICE (INDX)
            GIVING  INVOICE-AMT-OUT
        WRITE  OUT-LINE-FROM DETAIL-LINE AFTER 1
    ELSE
        PERFORM  ERROR-ROUTINE.
```

3. a.

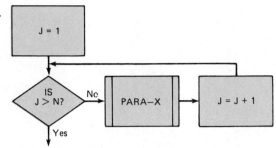

b.

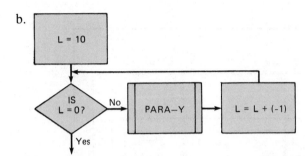

c.

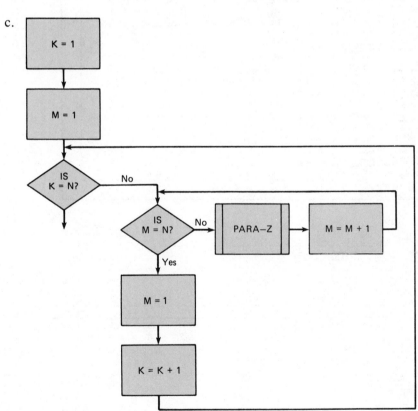

d.

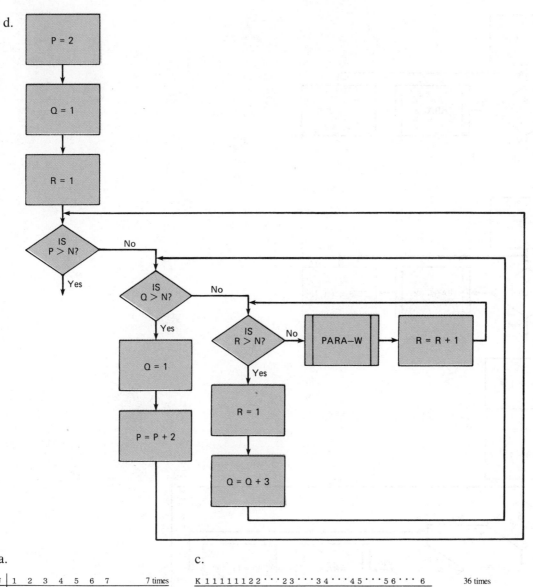

4. a.

```
J │ 1   2   3   4   5   6   7          7 times
  ┼
```

c.

```
K 1 1 1 1 1 1 2 2 ⋯ 2 3 ⋯ 3 4 ⋯ 4 5 ⋯ 5 6 ⋯ 6        36 times
M 1 2 3 4 5 6 1 2 ⋯ 6 1 ⋯ 6 1 ⋯ 6 1 ⋯ 6 1 ⋯ 6
```

b.

```
L │ 10   9   8   7   6   5   4   3   2   1
  ┼
10 times
```

d.

```
P 2 2 ⋯ 2 2 2 ⋯ 2 2 2 ⋯ 2 4 ⋯ 4 4 ⋯ 4 4 ⋯ 4 6 ⋯ 6 6 ⋯ 6 6 ⋯ 6
Q 1 1 ⋯ 7 4 4 ⋯ 4 7 7 ⋯ 7 1 ⋯ 1 4 ⋯ 4 7 ⋯ 7 1 ⋯ 1 4 ⋯ 4 7 ⋯ 7
R   1 2 ⋯ 7 1 2 ⋯ 4 1 2 ⋯ 7 1 ⋯ 7 1 ⋯ 7 1 ⋯ 7 1 ⋯ 7 1 ⋯ 7 1 ⋯ 7
63 times
```

5. a. PRODUCTION-OUTPUT.
      MOVE SPACES TO DAILY-OUTPUT.
      PERFORM DETAIL-OUTPUT
          VARYING D FROM 1 BY 1 UNTIL D > NUM-DAYS.
    DETAIL-OUTPUT.
      PERFORM DATA-MOVE
          VARYING L FROM 1 BY 1 UNTIL L > 5.
      MOVE D TO DAY-DO.
      WRITE OUTPUT-LINE FROM DAILY-OUTPUT AFTER 1.
    DATA-MOVE.
      MOVE PRODUCTION (D) TO
          DAY-PRODUCTION-DO (D).

b. Assume the table AV-PROD is defined as:

```
01   CONSTANTS.
     02   FILLER PIC X(30) VALUE ALL "0".
01   AV-PROD REDEFINES CONSTANTS.
     02   PRODUCTION-BY-LINE OCCURS 5 TIMES PIC 9(6).
```

PRODUCTION DIVISION code required:

```
    PERFORM SUMMATION
        VARYING INDX-1 FROM 1 BY 1 UNTIL INDX-1 > NUM-DAYS
        AFTER INDX-2 FROM 1 BY 1 UNTIL INDX-2 > 5.
    PERFORM COMPUTE-AVERAGES
        VARYING INDX FROM 1 BY 1 UNTIL INDX > 5.
    .
    .
    .

SUMMATION.
    ADD PRODUCTION (INDX-1, INDX-2) TO
        PRODUCTION-BY-LINE (INDX-2).
COMPUTE AVERAGES.
    DIVIDE NUM-DAYS INTO PRODUCTION-BY-LINE (INDX).
```

c. Assume the table DAYS-DOWN is defined as:

```
01   CONSTANTS-2
     02   FILLER PIC X(15) VALUE ALL "0".
01   DAYS-DOWN REDEFINES CONSTANTS-2.
     02   DAYS-DOWN-BY-LINE OCCURS 5 TIMES PIC 999.
```

PROCEDURE DIVISION code required:

```
PERFORM COUNT-ROUTINE
    VARYING INDX-1 FROM 1 BY 1 UNTIL INDX-1 > NUM-DAYS
    AFTER INDX-2 FROM 1 BY 1 UNTIL INDX-2 > 5.
COUNT-ROUTINE.
    IF PRODUCTION (INDX-1, INDX-2) = 0
        ADD 1 TO DAYS-DOWN-BY-LINE (INDX-2).
```

6. MOVE 0 TO SUM-OF-ELEMENTS.
```
PERFORM SUMMATION
    VARYING INDX-1 FROM 1 BY 1 UNTIL INDX-1 > 2
    VARYING INDX-2 FROM 1 BY 1 UNTIL INDX-2 > 5
    VARYING INDX-3 FROM 1 BY 1 UNTIL INDX-3 > 4.
SUMMATION.
    ADD BONUS-AMOUNT (INDX-1, INDX-2, INDX-3) TO
        SUM-OF-ELEMENTS.
```

7. Assume the table AV-BY-TEST-CLASS is defined as

```
01   CONSTANTS-3 PIC X(125) VALUE ALL ZEROS.
01   AV-BY-TEST-CLASS REDEFINES CONSTANTS-3.
     02   CLASS-ENTRY OCCURS 5 TIMES.
          03   TEST-ENTRY OCCURS 5 TIMES.
               04   AVERAGE PIC 9(5).
```

PROCEDURE DIVISION code required would be:

```
    PERFORM SUMMATION
        VARYING INDX-1 FROM 1 BY 1 UNTIL INDX-1 > 5
        AFTER INDX-2 FROM 1 BY 1
```

(continued)

```
              UNTIL INDX-S > NUM-STUDENTS (INDX-1)
           AFTER INDX-3 FROM 1 BY 1 UNTIL INDX-3 > 5.
      .
      .
      .

   SUMMATION.
      ADD GRADE (INDX-1, INDX-2, INDX-3) TO
         AVERAGE (INDX-1, INDX-3).
   COMPUTE-AVERAGES.
      DIVIDE NUM-STUDENTS (INDX-1) INTO
         AVERAGE (INDX-1, INDX-2).
```

8. a.F b.F c.F d.T e.T f.T g.T h.T

CHAPTER 9

1.

	Mode			
	INPUT	OUTPUT	I/O	EXTEND
Valid Input/Output Statements	READ	WRITE	READ REWRITE	WRITE

2. a. IRG—Inter-Record-Gap. An unused space between records on tape or disk.
   b. blocking—Technique used to group several logical records into one physical record on tape or disk.
   c. label records—Records on a tape which precede actual data; label records contain identifying information which is verified when a file is opened in INPUT, I-O or EXTEND mode.
   d. track—one of many concentric circles on a disk surface used for recording data.
   e. rewind—a tape file is repositioned to its beginning.
   f. key field—a field used as the basis for organizing a file.
   g. audit trail—maintenance of complete records to enable an auditor to retrace and verify actions taken by a data processing system.
   h. file status—A two-character field declared in the SELECT entry and updated automatically after each input/output operation related to a file.

3. If a key field can legitimately have a value such as 99999 (for example this value was actually assigned as an account number), the method used in this chapter would have to be modified. It is possible to use other fields each of which is one digit wider than the key field for the file. Each time a record is read, the key field is moved to its corresponding other field. At end-of-file the large value is moved to the other field. Only the other fields are compared when determining action to be taken on a record. In this way an actual key field value such as 99999 will be less than another key field terminal value such as 999999, resulting in appropriate processing for the record. For an alphanumeric key field it will be necessary to use a value such as ALL "Z" to signify end-of-file.

4.
```
   1000-MAIN-PROCESSING.
      PERFORM 2000-INITIALIZATION.
      PERFORM 3000-CONTROL
         UNTIL KEY-A = 99999 AND
         KEY-B = 99999 AND KEY-C = 99999.
      PERFORM 4000-TERMINATION.
   2000-INITIALIZATION.
      OPEN INPUT FILE-A FILE-B FILE-C
         OUTPUT NEW-FILE.
```

```
      PERFORM 2100-READ-FILE-A.
      PERFORM 2200-READ-FILE-B.
      PERFORM 2300-READ-FILE-C.
2100-READ-FILE-A
   READ FILE-A
      AT END
         MOVE 99999 TO KEY-A.
2200-READ-FILE-B
   READ FILE-B
      AT END
         MOVE 99999 TO KEY-B.
2300-READ-FILE-C.
   READ FILE-C
      AT END
         MOVE 99999 TO KEY-C.
3000-CONTROL
   IF KEY-A NOT > KEY-B AND KEY-A NOT > KEY-C
      PERFORM 500-WRITE-FILE-A
   ELSE
      IF KEY-B NOT > KEY-A AND KEY-B NOT > KEY-C
      ELSE
         PERFORM 5200-WRITE-FILE-C.
4000-TERMINATION.
   CLOSE FILE-A, FILE-B, FILE-C, NEW-FILE.
   STOP RUN.
5000-WRITE-FILE-A.
   WRITE NEW-FILE-REC FROM FILE-A-REC.
   PERFORM 2000-READ-FILE-A.
5100-WRITE-FILE-B.
   WRITE NEW-FILE-REC FROM FILE-B-REC.
   PERFORM 2100-READ-FILE-B.
5200-WRITE-FILE-C.
   WRITE NEW-FILE-REC FROM FILE-C-REC.
   PERFORM 2200-READ-FILE-C.
```

5. If the value of AMOUNT-OWED-OMR became negative, the sign would be lost because the field is defined without the S picture code. Correct the problem by defining the field as:

```
02  AMOUNT-OWED-OMR  PIC S9(4)V99.
```

6.
```
7000-ERROR-IN-TRANSACTION.
     MOVE TRANSACTION-RECORD TO ERROR-RECORD.
     IF ACCOUNT-NUMBER-IR = ACCOUNT-NUMBER-OMR
        MOVE "INVALID UPDATE CODE" TO ERROR-MSG.
     IF ACCOUNT-NUMBER-IR < ACCOUNT-NUMBER-OMR
        MOVE "NO RECORD IN MASTER FILE" TO ERROR-MSG.
     WRITE OUTPUT-LINE FROM ERROR-RECORD
     AFTER 1.
     PERFORM 8000-READ-TRANSACTION.
```

7. Transaction records must have the following restriction: For a given key field value, addition must precede changes which must precede deletion. Using the following program it would be possible to add, change and/or delete a record in the same update cycle.

```
PROCEDURE DIVISION
1000-MAIN-LOGIC.
    PERFORM 2000-INITIALIZATION.
    PERFORM 3000-COMPARE UNTIL
        ACCOUNT-NUMBER-TR = 99999 AND
        ACCOUNT-NUMBER-NMR = 99999.
    PERFORM 9000-TERMINATION.
2000-INITIALIZATION.
    OPEN INPUT TRANSACTION-FILE OLD-MASTER-FILE
        OUTPUT NEW-MASTER-FILE.
    READ TRANSACTION-FILE
        AT END
            MOVE 99999 TO ACCOUNT-NUMBER-TR.
    READ OLD-MASTER-FILE
        AT END
            MOVE 99999 TO ACCOUNT-NUMBER-OMR.
    MOVE OLD-MASTER-RECORD TO NEW-MASTER-RECORD.
    MOVE "YES" TO READ-OMR.
3000-COMPARE
    IF ACCOUNT-NUMBER-NMR = ACCOUNT-NUMBER-TR
    AND VALID-UPDATE-TRANSACTION
            PERFORM 4000-UPDATE
    ELSE
        IF ACCOUNT-NUMBER-NMR = ACCOUNT-NUMBER-TR
            AND DELETE-RECORD
                    PERFORM DELETION
        ELSE
            IF ACCOUNT-NUMBER-NMR > ACCOUNT-NUMBER-TR
                AND ADD-RECORD
                        PERFORM 6000-RECORD-ADDITION
        ELSE
            IF ACCOUNT-NUMBER-NMR < ACCOUNT-NUMBER-TR
                PERFORM 7000-WRITE-NEW-MASTER
            ELSE
                PERFORM 8000-ERROR-MESSAGE.
4000-UPDATE.
    IF PAYMENT
        SUBTRACT TRANSACTION-AMOUNT-TR FROM
            AMOUNT-OWED-NMR
        MOVE DATE-OF-LAST-PAYMENT-TR TO
            DATE-OF-LAST-PAYMENT-NMR.
    IF RETURN
        SUBTRACT TRANSACTION-AMOUNT-TR FROM
            AMOUNT-OWED-NMR.
    IF CHANGE-PURCHASE
        ADD TRANSACTION-AMOUNT-TR TO AMOUNT-OWED-NMR.
    IF CHANGE-NAME
        MOVE NAME-TR TO NAME-NMR.
    IF CHANGE-STREET
        MOVE STREET-TR TO STREET-NMR.
    IF CHANGE-CITY
        MOVE CITY-TR TO CITY-NMR.
    IF CHANGE-STATE
        MOVE STATE-TR TO CITY-NMR.
    IF CHANGE-ZIP
        MOVE ZIP-TR TO ZIP-NMR.
    IF CHANGE ADDRESS
        MOVE ADDRESS-TR TO ADDRESS-NMR.
```

```
    IF  CHANGE-AMOUNT-OWED
        MOVE  AMOUNT-OWED-TR  TO  AMOUNT-OWED-NMR.
    IF  CHANGE-CREDIT-MAX
        MOVE  CREDIT-MAXIMUM-TR  TO  CREDIT-MAXIMUM-NMR.
    IF  CHANGE-DATE
        MOVE  DATE-OF-LAST-PAYMENT-TR  TO
              DATE-OF-LAST-PAYMENT-NMR.
    READ  TRANSACTION-FILE
        AT  END
            MOVE  99999  TO  ACCOUNT-NUMBER-TR.
5000-DELETION.
    IF  READ-OMR  =  "YES"
        READ  OLD-MASTER-FILE
            AT  END
                MOVE  99999  TO  ACCOUNT-NUMBER-OMR.
    READ  TRANSACTION-FILE
        AT  END
            MOVE  99999  TO  ACCOUNT-NUMBER-TR.
    MOVE  OLD-MASTER-RECORD  TO  NEW-MASTER-RECORD.
    MOVE  "YES"  TO  READ-OMR.
6000-RECORD-ADDITION
    MOVE  TRANSACTION-RECORD  TO  NEW-MASTER-RECORD.
    MOVE  "NO"  TO  READ-OMR.
7000-WRITE-NEW-MASTER.
    WRITE  NEW-MASTER-RECORD.
    IF  READ-OMR  =  "YES"
        READ  OLD-MASTER-FILE
            AT  END
                MOVE  99999  TO  ACCOUNT-NUMBER-OMR.
    MOVE  OLD-MASTER-RECORD  TO  NEW-MASTER-RECORD.
    MOVE  "YES"  TO  READ-OMR.
8000-ERROR-MESSAGE.
    READ  TRANSACTION-FILE
        AT  END
            MOVE  99999  TO  ACCOUNT-NUMBER-TR.
9000-TERMINATION
    CLOSE  TRANSACTION-FILE
           NEW-MASTER-FILE
           OLD-MASTER-FILE.
    STOP  RUN.
```

8. In order to avoid nested IF statements, it is necessary to delete the input statements from the routines performed by 3000-CONTROL and replace them by the setting of flags indicating what input operation is to be performed by 3000-CONTROL. This is necessary because input operations affect the value of ACCOUNT-NUMBER-IR and/or ACCOUNT-NUMBER-ARR; these values must remain undisturbed until completion of all of the decisions in 3000-CONTROL. The following code could be used with appropriate modifications to 5000-UPDATE, 6000-DELETE and 7000-ERROR-MESSAGE:

```
3000-CONTROL.
    MOVE  "YES"  TO  ERROR-FLAG.
    IF  ACCOUNT-NUMBER-TR  =  ACCOUNT-NUMBER-ARR
        AND  VALID-UPDATE-TRANSACTION
            MOVE  "NO"  TO  ERROR-FLAG.
            MOVE  "YES"  TO  READ-TRANS-FLAG
            MOVE  "NO"  TO  READ-ARF-FLAG
            PERFORM  5000-UPDATE.
```

```
        IF  ACCOUNT-NUMBER-TR  =  ACCOUNT-NUMBER-ARR
             AND  DELETE-RECORD
                   MOVE  "NO"  TO  ERROR-FLAG
                   MOVE  "YES"  TO  READ-TRANS-FLAG
                   MOVE  "YES"  TO  READ-ARF-FLAG
                   PERFORM  6000-DELETE.
        IF  ACCOUNT-NUMBER-TR  >  ACCOUNT-NUMBER-ARR
                   MOVE  "NO"  TO  ERROR-FLAG
                   MOVE  "NO"  TO  READ-TRANS-FLAG
                   MOVE  "YES"  TO  READ-ARF-FLAG
        IF  ERROR-FLAG  =  "YES"
                   MOVE  "YES"  TO  READ-TRANS-FLAG
                   MOVE  "NO"  TO  READ-ARF-FLAG
                   PERFORM  7000-ERROR-MESSAGE.
        IF  READ-ARF-FLAG  =  "YES"
             PERFORM  4000-READ-ACCOUNTS-RECEIVABLE-FILE.
        IF  READ-TRANS-FLAG  =  "YES"
             PERFORM  8000-READ-TRANSACTION-FILE.
```

9. PROCEDURE DIVISION
```
    1000-MAIN-LOGIC.
        PERFORM 2000-INITIALIZATION.
        PERFORM 3000-CONTROL UNTIL
             ACCOUNT-NUMBER-ARR =99999.
        PERFORM 4000-TERMINATION.
    2000-INITIALIZATION.
        OPEN INPUT ACCOUNTS-RECEIVABLE
             OUTPUT NEW-ACCOUNTS-RECEIVABLE-FILE.
        PERFORM 5000-READ-ARF.
    3000-CONTROL.
        WRITE NEW-ACR-REC FROM
             ACCOUNTS-RECEIVABLE-RECORD.
        PERFORM 5000-READ-ARF.
    4000-TERMINATION.
        CLOSE ACCOUNTS-RECEIVABLE-FILE
             NEW-ACCOUNTS-RECEIVABLE-FILE.
        STOP-RUN.
    5000-READ-ARF.
        PERFORM 6000-READ-ARF-REC
             UNTIL
                 ACCOUNT-NUMBER-ARR =9999
                 OR ACTIVE RECORD.
    6000-READ-ARF-REC
        READ ACCOUNTS-RECEIVABLE-FILE
             AT END
                 MOVE 99999 TO ACCOUNT-NUMBER-ARR.
```

CHAPTER 10

1.

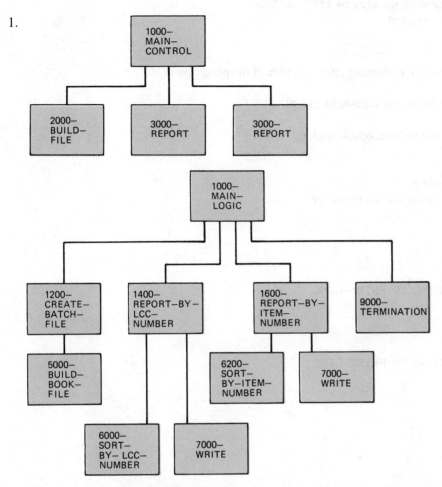

The structure diagram above represents the relationship among program modules (i.e., sections). Each module also can be represented by its own structure diagram. For example, a structure diagram for 2000-BUILD-FILE would be:

Note that the paragraph 2030-BUILD-EXIT is not included as part of the structure diagram; it is included only because COBOL syntax requires its presence, not because it serves an inherently useful function in the design of the program. Remember that a line in a structure diagram means that the lower level module can return control to the upper level module.

2. a. The content of BOOK-FILE is copied onto SORT-FILE.
   b. SORT-FILE is sorted into ascending sequence by CALL-NUMBER.
   c. The content of SORT-FILE is copied onto BOOK-FILE.

3. a. The section 2000-BUILD-FILE is executed.
   b. SORT-FILE is sorted into ascending sequence by CALL-NUMBER.

c. The section 3000-REPORT is executed.

d. The content of BOOK-FILE is copied onto SORT-FILE.

e. SORT-FILE is sorted into ascending sequence by ITEM-NUMBER.

f. The section 3000-REPORT is executed.

4. a. SD entry.

b. Key field.

c. The PERFORM contains provision for returning after execution of the paragraph or section; GO TO does not.

d. Section header which has the form section-name SECTION.

e. Module.

f. Branch to the last paragraph in a multiparagraph section.

g. RETURN

h. RELEASE

i. The only statement in a paragraph.

j. SORT and PERFORM a statement outside the procedure.

k. Branch to its last paragraph.

l. Disk.

5. Modify 1010-MAIN-LOGIC:

```
1010-MAIN-LOGIC.
    MOVE CALL-NUMBER-HEADING TO PRINT-LINE.
    SORT SORT-FILE

         .

         .

         .

    MOVE ITEM-NUMBER-HEADING TO PRINT-LINE.
    SORT SORT-FILE

         .

         .

         .

    STOP RUN.
```

Modify 3020-INITIALIZATION:

```
3020-INITIALIZATION.
    OPEN OUTPUT PRINT.
    WRITE PRINT-LINE AFTER PAGE.
    MOVE 0 TO EOF-FLAG.
    MOVE 1 TO MY-LINE-COUNTER.
    RETURN SORT-FILE AT END MOVE 1 TO EOF-FLAG.
```

6. a.
```
   SORT  SORT-FILE
         ON ASCENDING KEY SS-NUM-SR
         USING DATA-FILE
         GIVING DATA-FILE.
```

b.
```
   SORT  SORT-FILE
         ON ASCENDING KEY ZIP-SR NAME-SR
         USING DATA-FILE
         GIVING DATA-FILE.
```

7.
```
   SORT  SORT-FILE
         ON ASCENDING KEY STATE-SR
         INPUT PROCEDURE IS 2000-BUILD-FILE
         GIVING DATA-FILE.

         .

         .

         .

   2000-BUILD-FILE SECTION.
```

```
      2010-BUILD-FILE-CONTROL.
          MOVE 0 TO EOF-FLAG.
          OPEN INPUT NEW-DATA-FILE.
          READ NEW-DATA-FILE AT END MOVE 1 TO EOF-FLAG.
          PERFORM 2020-RELEASE-READ
              UNTIL EOF-FLAG = 1.
          CLOSE NEW-DATA-FILE.
          GO TO 2030-BUILD-FILE-EXIT.
      2020-RELEASE-READ.
          MOVE SS-NUM-NDR TO SS-NUM-DR.
          MOVE NAME-NDR TO NAME-SR.
          MOVE ST-ADDR-NDR TO ST-ADDR-SR.
          MOVE CITY-NDR TO CITY-SR.
          MOVE STATE-NDR TO STATE-SR.
          MOVE ZIP-NDR TO ZIP-SR.
          RELEASE SORT-RECORD.
          READ NEW-DATA-FILE
              AT END
                  MOVE 1 TO EOF-FLAG.
      2030-BUILD-FILE-EXIT.
          EXIT.

8. SORT   SORT-FILE
          ON DESCENDING KEY ZIP-SR
          INPUT PROCEDURE IS 2000-BUILD-FILE
          GIVING DATA-FILE.

          .

          .

          .

   2000-BUILD-FILE SECTION.
   2010-BUILD-FILE-CONTROL.
      MOVE 0 TO EOF-FLAG.
      OPEN INPUT DATA-FILE.
      READ DATA-FILE
          AT END
              MOVE 1 TO EOF-FLAG.
      PERFORM 2020-COPY-DATA-FILE
          UNTIL
              EOF-FLAG = 1.
      CLOSE DATA-FILE.
      MOVE 0 TO EOF-FLAG.
      OPEN INPUT NEW-DATA-FILE
      READ NEW-DATA-FILE
          AT END
              MOVE 1 TO EOF-FLAG.
      PERFORM 2030-COPY-NEW-DATA-FILE
          UNTIL
              EOF-FLAG = 1.
      CLOSE NEW-DATA-FILE.
      GO TO 2040-BUILD-FILE-EXIT.
   2020-COPY-DATA-FILE
      RELEASE SORT-RECORD FROM DATA-RECORD.
      READ DATA-FILE
          AT END
              MOVE 1 TO EOF-FLAG.
   2030-COPY-NEW-DATA-FILE.
      MOVE SS-NUM-NDR TO SS-NUM-SR
      MOVE NAME-NDR TO NAME-SR.
      MOVE ST-ADDR-NDR TO ST-ADDR-SR.
```

```
          MOVE CITY-NDR TO CITY-SR.
          MOVE STATE-NDR TO STATE-SR.
          MOVE ZIP-NDR TO ZIP-SR.
          RELEASE NEW-DATA-FILE
             AT END
                 MOVE 1 TO EOF-FLAG.
       2040-BUILD-FILE-EXIT.
          EXIT.
```

CHAPTER 11

```
1. FD   DATA-FILE
        DATA RECORDS ARE DATA-REC-A DATA-REC-B.
   01   DATA-REC-A.
        03   BID-NUMBER-DRA  PIC 9(10).
        03   PROJ-DESC-DRA   PIC X(10).
        03   BID-AMT-DRA     PIC 9(8)V99.
        03   REC-ID          PIC X.
   01   DATA-REC-B.
        03   BID-NUMBER-DRB  PIC 9(10).
        03   BID-AMT-DRB     PIC 9(8)V99.
        03   PROJ-DESC-DRB   PIC X(10).
        03   FILLER          PIC X.
```

```
2. READ DATA-FILE AT END MOVE 1 TO EOF-CODE.
       .
       .
       .
   IF REC-ID = "A"
       PERFORM PROCESS-REC-TYPE-A
   ELSE
       IF REC-ID = "B"
           PERFORM PROCESS-REC-TYPE-B
       ELSE
           PERFORM ERROR-IN-REC-ID.
```

```
3.     PERFORM 1000-COMPUTE-SHIFT-DIF THRU
               1040-COMPUTE-SHIFT-DIF-EXIT.
       .
       .
       .
   1000-COMPUTE-SHIFT-DIF.
      GO TO 1010-SHIFT-1
            1020-SHIFT-2
            1030-SHIFT-3
            DEPENDING ON SHIFT-CODE.
   1010-SHIFT-1.
      MOVE 1 TO SHIFT-DIFFERENTIAL.
      GO TO 1040-COMPUTE-SHIFT-DIF-EXIT.
   1020-SHIFT-2.
      MOVE 1.25 TO SHIFT-DIFFERENTIAL.
      GO TO 1040-COMPUTE-SHIFT-DIF-EXIT.
   1030-SHIFT-3.
      MOVE 1.35 TO SHIFT-DIFFERENTIAL.
      GO TO 1040-COMPUTE-SHIFT-DIF-EXIT.
   1040-COMPUTE-SHIFT-DIF-EXIT.
      EXIT.
```

```
4. 01    CONSTANTS-TABLE.
         03    FILLER PIC X(15)  VALUE "000001000000040".
         03    FILLER PIC X(15)  VALUE "010103000400030".
         03    FILLER PIC X(15)  VALUE "030105001000025".
         03    FILLER PIC X(15)  VALUE "050107001500020".
         03    FILLER PIC X(15)  VALUE "070199991900015".
   01    ORDER-TABLE REDEFINES CONSTANTS-TABLE.
         03    ORDER-ENTRY OCCURS 5 TIMES
               ASCENDING KEY IS LOW-ORDER
               INDEXED BY TAB-INDX.
               05    LOW-ORDER   PIC 9999.
               05    HI-ORDER    PIC 9999.
               05    BASE-COST   PIC 99V99.
               05    ITEM-COST   PIC V999.


5. SET TAB-INDX TO 1.
   SEARCH ORDER-ENTRY
       WHEN  (AMOUNT-OF-ORDER > LOW-ORDER (TAB-INDX)
                           OR = LOW-ORDER (TAB-INDX))
       AND  (AMOUNT-OF-ORDER < HI-ORDER (TAB-INDX)
                           OR = HI-ORDER (TAB-INDX))
       COMPUTE ORDER-COST = BASE-COST (TAB-INDX) +
                           (AMOUNT-OF-ORDER - LOW-ORDER (TAB-INDX)
                       * ITEM COST (TAB-INDX)).


6. 01    CONSTANTS-TABLE.
         03    FILLER PIC X(10)  VALUE "100NUTS".
         03    FILLER PIC X(10)  VALUE "125BOLTS".
         03    FILLER PIC X(10)  VALUE "130SCREWS".
         03    FILLER PIC X(10)  VALUE "155WASHERS".
         03    FILLER PIC X(10)  VALUE "460GASKETS".
   01    ITEM-TABLE REDEFINES CONSTANTS-TABLE.
         03    ITEM-ENTRY OCCURS 6 TIMES
               ASCENDING KEY IS ITEM-NUMBER
               INDEXED BY TAB-INDX.
               05    ITEM-NUM   PIC 999.
               05    ITEM-DESC  PIC X(7).


7. SEARCH ALL ITEM-ENTRY
       AT END MOVE "INVALID" TO ITM-DESC-OUT
       WHEN ITEM-NUM = ITEM-NUMBER (TAB-INDX)
           MOVE ITEM-DESC (TAB-INDX) TO
               ITM-DESC-OUT.
```

8. a. A < B AND =C.

   b. A < B OR C AND > D.

   c. Cannot be abbreviated since subject is not the same. Could be rewritten

$$B > A \quad AND \quad B > C$$

and then abbreviated as

$$B > A \quad AND \quad C.$$

   d. A > B OR < D.

   e. A < B AND C.

   f. A NOT > B AND < C AND NOT =C

9. a.
```
| A | B | 1 | 2 | * | 3 | 4 | A |   |   |
```
ITM-R

b.
```
| 1 | 2 | A | A | B |   |   |   |   |   |
```
ITM-R

c.
```
| A | - | 1 | 2 | * | A | B | - | 1 | 2 |
```
ITM-R

d.
```
| A | B | - | C | 1 | 2 | * | 3 | 4 |
```
ITM-R

10. a.
```
| A | B | C | - |
```
FLD-A

```
| D | E | * | 1 | 2 |
```
FLD-B

```
| 3 | - | - | X | Y | * |
```
FLD-C

b.
```
| A | B | C | - |
```
FLD-A

```
| 1 | 2 | 3 | - | - |
```
FLD-B

```
| Z | W |   |   |   |
```
FLD-C

c.
```
| A | B | C |
```
FLD-A

```
| D | E | * | 1 | 2 |
```
FLD-B

```
|   |   |   |   |   |
```
FLD-C

d.
```
| A | B | C |
```
FLD-A

```
| D | E | * | 1 | 2 |
```
FLD-B

```
| X | Y | * | Z | W |
```
FLD-C

e.
```
| A | B | C | - |
```
FLD-A

```
| X | Y | * | Z | W |
```
FLD-B

11.
```
UNSTRING NAME-IN
     DELIMITED BY ALL SPACES
     INTO FIRST-NAME
          MIDDLE-INITIAL
          LAST-NAME.
MOVE SPACES TO NAME-OUT.
STRING LAST-NAME  DELIMITED BY SPACE
       ", "        DELIMITED BY SIZE
       FIRST-NAME DELIMITED BY SPACE
       " "         DELIMITED BY SIZE
       LAST-NAME  DELIMITED BY SPACE
INTO NAME-OUT.
```

12. Assume the following DATA DIVISION entries:

```
01  FIRST   PIC 999.
02  SECOND  PIC 99.
03  THIRD   PIC 9999.
UNSTRING SS-NUM
    INTO FIRST SECOND THIRD.
STRING FIRST, "-", SECOND, "-", THIRD
    DELIMITED BY SIZE
    INTO SS-NUM-OUT.
```

or

Assume the following DATA DIVISION entry:

```
03  SS-NUM-OUT  PIC 999B99B9999
MOVE SS-NUM TO SS-NUM-OUT.
INSPECT SS-NUM-OUT REPLACING
                ALL " " BY "-".
```

13. a. F2F9C8
    b. 013E
    c. 298C
    d. 013E

14. SPECIAL NAMES.
    CURRENCY SIGN IS Q.
    QQQQ,QQQ.99

15. a. | B | B | 1 | A | B | B |

    ITEM-A

    b. | | B | 1 | A | B | A |

    ITEM-A

    c. | A | | 1 | A | B | A |

    ITEM-A

CHAPTER 12

1.

<table>
<tr><td rowspan="2"></td><td rowspan="2"></td><td colspan="3">OPEN MODE</td></tr>
<tr><td>INPUT</td><td>OUTPUT</td><td>I/O</td></tr>
<tr><td rowspan="6">FILE ACCESS METHOD</td><td>SEQUENTIAL</td><td>READ (Format-1)</td><td>WRITE</td><td>READ (Format-1)
REWRITE
START
DELETE</td></tr>
<tr><td>RANDOM</td><td>READ (Format-2)</td><td>WRITE</td><td>READ (Format-1)
WRITE
REWRITE
DELETE</td></tr>
<tr><td>DYNAMIC</td><td>READ (Format-1)
READ (Format-2)
START</td><td>WRITE</td><td>READ (Format-1)
READ (Format-1)
WRITE
REWRITE
START
DELETE</td></tr>
</table>

2. <u>5000-ERROR-IN-TRANS-CODE</u>
       "INVALID TRANSACTION CODE"
   <u>6100-ERROR-IN-ADD</u>
       "RECORD ALREADY PRESENT IN FILE"
   <u>7100-ERROR-IN-DELETE</u>
       "RECORD NOT PRESENT IN FILE"
   <u>8100-ERROR-IN-UPDATE</u>
       "RECORD NOT PRESENT IN FILE"
   <u>9100-ERROR-IN-PROGRAM</u>
       "AN ERROR IN THE INTERNAL LOGIC
       OF THIS PROGRAM HAS OCCURRED"

3. a. SEQUENTIAL/OUTPUT
   b. SEQUENTIAL/INPUT
   c. SEQUENTIAL/I-O
   d. RANDOM/I-O

    e. RANDOM/INPUT
    f. RANDOM/OUTPUT
    g. DYNAMIC/INPUT
    h. DYNAMIC/I-O

4. The WRITE statement is used to add records to a file; the REWRITE statement is used to change an existing record.

5. Format-1 READ generally includes an AT END clause and is used to read records sequentially. Format-2 READ includes an INVALID KEY clause and is used to read records randomly.

6. An indexed file can be created only under the sequential access method. Dynamic access can be used to update a file.

7. START I-S-FILE KEY NOT < 200.

8. The statements in the INVALID KEY clause will be executed since FILE STATUS value ''23'' indicates that no record was found with the specified key field value.

INDEX